Lecture Notes in Artificial Intelligence　13528

Subseries of Lecture Notes in Computer Science

More information about this subseries at https://link.springer.com/bookseries/1244

Gloria Corpas Pastor · Ruslan Mitkov (Eds.)

Computational and Corpus-Based Phraseology

4th International Conference, Europhras 2022
Malaga, Spain, 28–30 September, 2022
Proceedings

Springer

Editors
Gloria Corpas Pastor ⓘD
University of Malaga
Malaga, Spain

Ruslan Mitkov ⓘD
University of Wolverhampton
Wolverhampton, UK

ISSN 0302-9743   ISSN 1611-3349 (electronic)
Lecture Notes in Artificial Intelligence
ISBN 978-3-031-15924-4   ISBN 978-3-031-15925-1 (eBook)
https://doi.org/10.1007/978-3-031-15925-1

LNCS Sublibrary: SL7 – Artificial Intelligence

This Springer imprint is published by the registered company Springer Nature Switzerland AG
The registered company address is: Gewerbestrasse 11, 6330 Cham, Switzerland

Preface

The corpus-based and computational study of phraseology is an important area relevant to the research and practical work of translators, interpreters, terminologists, lexicographers, language instructors, and learners, to mention a few. Computational phraseology has been gaining in prominence in recent years with the computational treatment of multiword expressions essential for a number of natural language processing and translation technology applications. The importance of this field has been evidenced in a number of influential publications including, but not limited to, Constant et al. (2017), Mitkov et al. (2018), Corpas and Colson (2020), and Ramish and Villavicencio (2022).

The Europhras conference series 'Computational and Corpus-based Phraseology' has emerged as one of the leading conferences covering this topic. We were delighted that after two years of restrictions due to COVID-19, we were again able to offer a face-to-face Europhras 2022. The volume you are holding features a selection of regular papers accepted after rigorous reviewing and presented at the latest edition of this popular conference, held during 28–30 September, 2022, in Malaga, Spain.

The conference was jointly organised by the University of Malaga (Research Group in Lexicography and Translation), Spain, the University of Wolverhampton (Research Group in Computational Linguistics), UK, and the Association for Computational Linguistics, Bulgaria, and was sponsored by Sketch Engine the University of Malaga, and Multilingual. Europhras 2022 provided the perfect opportunity for researchers to present their work, fostering interaction and interdisciplinary collaboration. The papers in this volume cover a number of topics including general corpus-based approaches to phraseology, phraseology in translation and cross-linguistic studies, phraseology in interpreting, phraseology in language teaching and learning, phraseology in specialised languages, phraseology in lexicography, cognitive approaches to phraseology, phraseology and figurative language, phraseology in machine translation, and computational treatment of multiword expressions in general. We have deliberately not grouped the contributions around specific topics – as many of them cut across more than one of the above listed topics – but have instead opted to present the papers alphabetically according to the (first) family name of the (first) author.

Every submission to the conference was evaluated by three reviewers. The reviewers were either members of the Programme Committee or additional reviewers. The conference contributions were authored by a total of 75 scholars from 17 different countries: Brazil, Bulgaria, Colombia, Croatia, the Czech Republic, France, Indonesia, Iraq, Italy, Poland, Portugal, Russia, Slovakia, Spain, Sri Lanka, Sweden, and United Kingdom. These figures attest to the truly international nature of Europhras 2022.

We would like to thank all colleagues who made this wonderfully interdisciplinary and international event possible. We would like to start by thanking all colleagues who submitted papers to Europhras 2022 and travelled to Malaga to attend the event. We are grateful to all members of the Programme Committee and the additional reviewers for carefully examining all submissions and providing substantial feedback on all papers, helping the authors of accepted papers to improve and polish the final versions of their papers. A special thanks goes to the invited speakers, namely the keynote speakers of the main conference (Aline Villavicencio, Jean Pierre Colson, Miloš Jakubíček, and María del Carmen Mellado Blanco), the invited speakers of the accompanying workshop on Multiword Units in Machine Translation and Translation Technology (MUMTTT), and the tutorial speakers from Lexical Computing. Words of gratitude go to our sponsors and collaborators: Sketch Engine, Multilingual, the Research Institute of Multilingual Language Technologies of the University of Malaga, the Translation and Interpreting Department of the University of Malaga, and D.O.P Antequera - DCOOP.

Last but not least, we would like to use this paragraph to acknowledge the members of the Organising Committee and the Programme Committee of both the main conference and the MUMTT workshop, who worked very hard during the last 12 months and whose dedication and efforts made the organisation of this event possible. All those who have contributed are listed (in alphabetical order) on the following pages. We would like to single out several colleagues for competently carrying out numerous organisational and reviewing-related tasks and being ready to step in and support the organisation of the conference both on weekdays and during the weekends – in fact, whenever needed. Our big 'thank you' goes out to Rocío Caro Quintana, Javier Alejandro Fernández Sola, Maria Kunilovskaya, and Desiré Martos García.

September 2022   Gloria Corpas Pastor
                                                                       Ruslan Mitkov

References

Constant M., Eryiğit G., Monti J., Van Der Plas L., Ramisch C., Rosner, M. and A. Todirascu. 2017. "Multiword Expression processing: a survey". *Computational Linguistics*, 43(4). 837–892.

Corpas Pastor, G. and J.P. Colson (Eds.). 2020. *Computational Phraseology*. [IVITRA Research in Linguistics and Literature 24]. Amsterdam: John Benjamins.

Mitkov, R., Monti, J., Corpas Pastor, G. and V. Seretan (Eds). 2018. *Multiword Units in Machine Translation and Translation Technology*. [Current Issues in Linguistic Theory 341]. Amsterdam: John Benjamins

Ramish, C. and A. Villavicencio. 2022. "Computational treatment of multiword expressions". In Mitkov R. (Ed) *The Oxford Handbook of Computational Linguistics*. Oxford: Oxford University Press.

Organisation

Europhras 2022 was jointly organised by the University of Malaga (Research Group in Lexicography and Translation), Spain, the University of Wolverhampton (Research Group in Computational Linguistics), UK, and the Association for Computational Linguistics, Bulgaria.

Conference Chairs

Gloria Corpas Pastor	University of Malaga, Spain
Ruslan Mitkov	University of Wolverhampton, UK

Program Committee

Margarita María Alonso Ramos	University of A Coruña, Spain
M. Belén Alvarado Ortega	University of Alicante, Spain
Verginica Barbu Mititelu	Research Institute for Artificial Intelligence, Romanian Academy, Romania
Ignacio Bosque	Complutense University of Madrid, Spain
María Luisa Carrió-Pastor	Polytechnic University of Valencia, Spain
Anna Čermáková	University of Cambridge, UK
Parthena Charalampidou	Aristotle University of Thessaloniki, Greece
Ken Church	Baidu, USA
Jean-Pierre Colson	Université Catholique de Louvain, Belgium
Dmitrij Dobrovolskij	Russian Language Institute, Russia
Peter Ďurčo	University of St. Cyril and Methodius of Trnava, Slovakia
Natalia Filatkina	University of Hamburg, Germany
Elizaveta Goncharova	National Research University Higher School of Economics and Artificial Intelligence Research Institute (AIRI), Russia
María Isabel González Rey	University of Santiago de Compostela, Spain
Stefan Gries	University of California, Santa Barbara, USA
Enrique Gutiérrez Rubio	Palacký University Olomouc, Czech Republic
Kleanthes K. Grohmann	University of Cyprus, Cyprus
Amal Haddad Haddad	University of Granada, Spain
Miloš Jakubíček	Sketch Engine, Czech Republic
Eva Lucía Jiménez-Navarro	University of Cordoba, Spain
Cvetana Krstev	University of Belgrade, Serbia

Natalie Kübler	Université Paris Cité, France
Maria Kunilovskaya	University of Wolverhampton, UK
Ljubica Leone	Lancaster University, UK
Óscar Loureda Lamas	Heidelberg University, Germany
Elvira Manero Richard	University of Murcia, Spain
Ramón Martí Solano	Université de Limoges, France
María del Carmen Mellado Blanco	University of Santiago de Compostela, Spain
Flor Mena Martínez	University of Murcia, Spain
Pedro Mogorrón Huerta	University of Alicante, Spain
Johanna Monti	University of Naples "L'Orientale", Italy
Esteban Tomás Montoro del Arco	University of Granada, Spain
Inés Olza Moreno	University of Navarra, Spain
Adriane Orenha Ottaiano	São Paulo State University, Brazil
Antonio Pamies Bertrán	University of Granada, Spain
Rozane Rebechi	Federal University of Rio Grande do Sul, Brazil
Mª Ángeles Recio Ariza	University of Salamanca, Spain
Ute Römer	Georgia State University, USA
Leonor Ruiz Gurillo	University of Alicante, Spain
Kathrin Steyer	University of Mannheim, Germany
Joanna Szerszunowicz	University of Bialystok, Poland
Yukio Tono	Tokyo University of Foreign Studies, Japan
Agnès Tutin	Université Grenoble Alpes, France
Aline Villavicencio	Federal University of Rio Grande do Sul, Brazil, and University of Sheffield, UK
Tom Wasow	Stanford University, USA
Eric Wehrli	University of Geneva, Switzerland
Michael Zock	Laboratoire d'Informatique Fondamentale de Marseille, France

Additional Reviewers

Dayana Abuin Rios	University of Wolverhampton, UK
Rocío Caro Quintana	University of Wolverhampton, UK
Isabel Durán	University of Malaga, Spain
Richard Evans	University of Wolverhampton, UK
Emma Franklin	University of Wolverhampton, UK
Carlos Manuel Hidalgo-Ternero	University of Malaga, Spain
Nieves Jiménez Carra	University of Malaga, Spain
Alfiya Khabibullina	University of Wolverhampton, UK
Lilit Kharatyan	University of Wolverhampton, UK
Ruslan Mitkov	University of Wolverhampton, UK
Daria Sokova	University of Wolverhampton, UK

Keynote Speakers

Aline Villavicencio	Federal University of Rio Grande do Sul, Brazil, and University of Sheffield, UK
Jean-Pierre Colson	Université Catholique de Louvain, Belgium
María del Carmen Mellado Blanco	University of Santiago de Compostela, Spain
Miloš Jakubíček	Sketch Engine, Czech Republic

MUMTTT 2022 Workshop Chairs

Gloria Corpas Pastor	University of Malaga, Spain
Ruslan Mitkov	University of Wolverhampton, UK
Johanna Monti	University of Naples "L'Orientale", Italy
Maria Pia di Buono	University of Naples "L'Orientale", Italy

MUMTTT 2022 Program Committee

Giuseppe Attardi	University of Pisa, Italy
Verginica Barbu Mititelu	Institute for Artificial Intelligence, Romanian Academy Research, Romania
Jean-Pierre Colson	Université Catholique de Louvain, Belgium
Anna Beatriz Dimas Furtado	University of Wolverhampton, UK
Federico Gaspari	University for Foreigners "Dante Alighieri", Italy
Amal Haddad Haddad	University of Granada, Spain
Philipp Koehn	Johns Hopkins University, USA
Judyta Mężyk	Université Paris-Est Créteil, France, and University of Silesia in Katowice, Poland
Pavel Pecina	Charles University in Prague, Czech Republic
Éric Poirier	Université du Québec à Trois-Rivières, Canada
Carlos Ramisch	Aix-Marseille Université, France
Max Silberztein	Université de Franche-Comté, France
Kathrin Steyer	University of Mannheim, Germany
Beata Trawinski	University of Mannheim, Germany
Agnès Tutin	Université Grenoble Alpes, France

EUROPHRAS 2022 Organizing Committee

University of Malaga (Spain)

María de la Presentación Aguilera Crespillo
Marta Alcaide Martínez
Rosario Bautista Zambrana
Isabel Durán Muñoz

Javier Alejandro Fernández Sola
Mahmoud Gaber
Rut Gutiérrez Florido
Carlos Manuel Hidalgo-Ternero
Hanan Saleh Hussein
Adriana Iglesias Lara
Francisco Javier Lima Florido
Gema Lobillo Mora
Araceli Losey León
Jorge Lucas Pérez
Luis Carlos Marín Navarro
Desiré Martos García
Laura Noriega Santiáñez
Laura Parrilla Gómez
Míriam Pérez Carrasco
Encarnación Postigo Pinazo
María del Pilar Rodríguez Reina
Juan Antonio Sánchez Muñoz
Fernando Sánchez Rodas
Míriam Seghiri Domínguez
Cristina Toledo Báez

University of Wolverhampton (UK)

Dayana Abuin Rios
Isuri Anuradha
Anastasia Bezobrazova
Rocío Caro Quintana
Ana Isabel Cespedosa Vázquez
Amal El Farhmat
Suman Hira
Alfiya Khabibullina
Lilit Kharatian
Maria Kunilovskaya
Gabriela Llull
Kamshat Saduakassova
Kanishka Silva
Daria Sokova

Association for Computational Linguistics (Bulgaria)

Nikolai Nikolov

Europhras 2022 Secretary

Desiré Martos García   University of Malaga, Spain

Webmaster

Javier Alejandro Fernández Sola   University of Malaga, Spain

START Managers

Rocío Caro Quintana   University of Wolverhampton, UK
Maria Kunilovskaya   University of Wolverhampton, UK

Editorial Team

Gabriela Llull   University of Wolverhampton, UK
Dayana Abuin Rios   University of Wolverhampton, UK
Amal El Farhmat   University of Wolverhampton, UK
Daria Sokova   University of Wolverhampton, UK

Student Volunteers (University of Malaga, Spain)

Luis Carlos Marín Navarro (Coordinator)
Ángela Alguacil Suárez
Alba Bandera García
Ana Boza Pardo
Gabriella D'ottavio Simón
Camila Geijo Islas
Patricia Gómez Manzano
Alejandro Gutiérrez Usero
Marta Olivera Moreno
Sandra Raimundo Sánchez
Ana Ranchal Serrano
María de la Cabeza Rodríguez Martínez
Bárbara Ruiz Merino
Rocío Serrano Rey
María Utrera Muñoz

MUMTTT 2022 Organizing Committee

Gennaro Nolano   University of Naples "L'Orientale", Italy
Giulia Speranza   University of Naples "L'Orientale", Italy
Khadija Ait ElFqih   University of Naples "L'Orientale", Italy

Organizing Institutions

LEXYTRAD

Research Group in Computational Linguistics

Bulgarian Association for Computational Linguistics

Partners

University of Malaga

Sponsors

Sketch Engine

Multilingual

Research Institute of Multilingual Language Technologies

Department of Translation and Interpreting, University of Malaga

Antequera

Contents

xvi   Contents

Constructing the Digital Proverbial Thesaurus: Theoretical and Methodological Implications

Melita Aleksa Varga[1] (✉) ⒾⒹ and Kristina Feldvari[2] ⒾⒹ

[1] Department of German Language and Linguistics, Faculty of Humanities and Social Sciences, Josip Juraj Strossmayer University of Osijek, Osijek, Croatia
maleksa@ffos.hr
[2] Department of Information Sciences, Faculty of Humanities and Social Sciences, Josip Juraj Strossmayer University of Osijek, Osijek, Croatia
kfeldvari@ffos.hr

Abstract. The present paper discusses the theoretical and methodical implications which occurred at the beginning of constructing the Croatian paremiological thesaurus. Unlike other languages that already have paremiological dictionaries published, there are no contemporary dictionaries or paremiological collections of Croatian language in known existence. Previous research showed that there is a need to create not only an electronic paremiological dictionary, but a thesaurus as well. The present paper therefore discusses the structure of the Croatian paremiological thesaurus and searching options, as well as the notions of defining the terms, facets and connections between them, exemplified by one of the most popular Croatian proverbs.

Keywords: Croatian proverbs · Paremiological thesaurus · Paremiography

1 Introduction

Croatian paremiography, unlike the paremiography of other nations and languages, who already possess paremiological compilations and dictionaries of proverbs (e.g. American English [1] and Doyle et al. 2012), Bulgarian [2] German [3], Hungarian [4] etc.) either in print or online form, does not incorporate a dictionary of contemporary proverbs. The history of the Croatian paremiological research begins with the 19th century paremiological collections and their analysis by Peter Grzybek in the 1990s, followed by several contemporary attempts in terms of research into the Croatian paremiological minimum and optimum, the most frequently used and known proverbs [5–10], and nowadays with the aim of creating a Croatian proverb database and a Croatian paremiological thesaurus consisting of the Croatian paremiological lore, proverbs, antiproverbs and related items.

There are several contemporary online databases and compilations of the paremiological lore worth mentioning, and these are the Slovenian dictionaries *Slovar slovenskega knjižnega jezika (Standard Slovenian Dictionary, eSSKJ)* and *Slovar pregovorov in sorodnih paremioloških izrazov (Dictionary of Proverbs and Similar Paremiological Units, SPP)* [11], the *Sprichwort–Plattform* [12], and the *Postproverbial Database* [13]. The

G. Corpas Pastor and R. Mitkov (Eds.): EUROPHRAS 2022, LNAI 13528, pp. 1–15, 2022.
https://doi.org/10.1007/978-3-031-15925-1_1

eSSKJ and *SPP* are online dictionaries with a lexicographic presentation of phraseo-logical and paremiological variants based on modern methodological approaches. The precise analysis of different variants using language corpora is combined with special-ized surveys which resulted in the database where proverbs are listed according to their meanings and connected to the explanation of their meaning, variants and examples from Slovenian corpora [14, 15]. *Sprichwort-Plattform* is a multilingual database that lists proverbs from five languages, with exercises for students, which was developed in the course of a project from 2008 until 2010. The proverbs in the database are ordered alphabetically, and each proverb is connected to its equivalent if it exists in the languages covered by the database. The *Postproverbial* is a database containing postproverbials (modified proverbs) found in twelve African languages, where the postproverbials are provided alongside their original versions with the English translations of both original and modified proverbs. None of these paremiological sources is a thesaurus.

The project of constructing a contemporary Croatian paremiological dictionary began in 2011, and since then there have been several empirical studies conducted and published. The analyzed data from the two previous field questionnaire studies from 2014 and 2018 with a representative sample of 1585 informants from all Croa-tian regions (867 and 718, respectively) showed that the Croatian proverbs that were included in the questionnaire have been familiar up to only 27%, and that young people aged 14 and above do not have sufficient knowledge about proverbs and are not familiar with the most common Croatian proverbs [7–10][1]. The analysis of the proverbs from the two questionnaires showed that 73% of the proverbs were actually modifications of the zero-variant (the variant occurring in the Croatian corpora and print collections from the 19th century), meaning that the dictionary and the form of proverbs occurring in the Croatian corpora were not as widespread as we thought they would be, since obviously people were actually using some other variants, be it on the morphological, syntactical, or orthographical level. In some cases, even the anti-proverb was proven to

---

[1] The procedure of getting proverbs into the field questionnaire consisted of several steps. First, there was Grzybek's list containing 134 proverbs from the Croatian dictionaries that have not been considered obsolete, together with other sources, namely Meheš's [16] collection and the authors' own compilation from the internet, resulting in 239 proverbs altogether, which have been correlated with the occurrences in three national corpora, Hrvatski nacionalni korpus (Croatian National Corpus with 216,8 Million token), Hrvatska jezična riznica (Corpus of the Croatian Institute for Languages with more than 100 Million token) und hrWaC (Webcorpus containing a database with all the webpages within the.hr domain, with more than 1.9 billion token). The list was furthermore tested in a pilot study with fellow linguists from all Croat-ian regions. In the end there was a final list of the 105 most common proverbs put together, ranked from the most frequently occurring proverbs in the Croatian corpora to the least fre-quently occurring proverbs in the Croatian corpora. These proverbs have been used in two field researches, with part-text presentation. In 2014 the informants had to fill in the first part of the proverb, in 2018 they had to fill in the second part of the proverb. Both questionnaires were analyzed according the model proposed by Grzybek and Chlosta [17] the results of which have been presented on a conference in Wroczlaw 2021.

be more familiar than the canonical proverb (e.g. the variant *Slika govori tisuću riječi* [The picture speaks thousand words] was used by 48% of the informants, suggesting the variant is more widespread than the original proverb *Slika govori više od riječi* [The picture speaks more than words.]).

Previous research concerning young people showed that they are unfamiliar with Croatian proverbs, and are used to entering free keywords when searching for items in post-coordinated systems like Google. Since there are two possibilities for accessing the topic/subject of the documents (using the natural language or free keyword search) and the controlled vocabulary search [18], there was much greater need to develop a database that would be freely extendable with data from an online-questionnaire in which proverb variants would be collected (similar to the one developed by Matej Meterc for the Slovenian language) [14, 15], and which would have a didactic function as well. Therefore, there was a decision made to build a Croatian proverbial thesaurus with a dictionary database that would give users relevant results regardless of the drawback of searching for proverbs by using free keywords only.

The analysis of Croatian language thesauri returned several results. Croatian thesauri that do not have online databases and are therefore not searchable are the thesauri from the field of monuments and cultural heritage [19] and Croatian literature [20]. Several of the world thesauri that are searchable online are related to individual fields of science such as law (Digital Europa Thesaurus – with a Croatian database [21]; EuroVoc – with a Croatian database [22]), art and architecture (Art & Architecture Thesaurus [23]), and library, information science and technology (Library, Information Science & Technology Abstracts Thesaurus [24]).

As far as current research has shown, there has not been a functioning thesaurus of Croatian multi-word expressions from the field of paremiology. Therefore, the aim of the present paper is to present the theoretical and methodological implications that have arisen during the first stage of the implementation of the current project of constructing a Croatian proverbial thesaurus and to discuss the two issues. The first is the creation of an electronic dictionary of proverbs as an information system that will use its search capabilities (e.g. with the help of Searching Instructions) to provide assistance to the user when searching with free keywords. The second issue is to create a thesaurus as a controlled dictionary that will help the user search for controlled terms (descriptors) by linking free keywords (so-called entry words) to them, and in this way suggest through references the so called "classes of concepts" in which the end user can find terms he may not have known or forgotten to use during the search. This question covers the stages of making facets, broader, narrow and related terms, adding new and linking controlled terms (descriptors) from different facets, adding references "see" (SEE), "use" (USE) and "use for" (UF) to non-descriptors, connecting them in this way to the descriptors

[25]. This way the precision and recall[2] of the search is increased, which is the main aim of every information system.

2   Search Capabilities in the Croatian Paremiological Thesaurus

Since the Croatian paremiological thesaurus will consist of two parts - the electronic dictionary and the thesaurus, it is important to discuss the different search options that have to be implemented at the beginning of the construction of the system in order to get relevant results. The purpose of the search capabilities offered by a particular information system, in our case the paremiological thesaurus, is to establish a link between a user-specific information need and the units in the database that will respond to that need. A search query in which the user describes his information need is the main tool he uses when communicating with the system, and the use of controlled vocabulary or natural language (free keywords) are the two main options for accessing the subject or topic of a document (in our case the subject/topic of proverbs) [25]. The problem with searching and using controlled vocabulary is that when searching for an item or topic, the user needs to find a descriptor (preferred term in the thesaurus) that is used to describe that item or topic. Furthermore, the user must include all relevant word forms (singular/plural, noun/adjective/verb), synonyms, distinguish homonyms to ensure the successful search, or find all the relevant documents he needs [26]. According to the authors Olson and Boll [18], information systems contain various search capabilities that can be divided into four broad categories: free keyword searching, authority control, browsing and other search capabilities.

   In the following parts of the present paper, we will provide a deeper insight in the construction of a thesaurus as a part of an information system that supports the searching of proverbs both with free keywords (searching of the electronic proverb dictionary) and normative control, or searching for proverbs through controlled terms or descriptors (searching of the electronic proverb thesaurus).

2.1   Searching by Using Free Keywords

When the user is implementing searching by using natural language, the best known strategy is the use of operators (for example, Boolean search logic) and truncation, meaning that in a subject search with the help of natural language words, the words are

---

[2] Information Systems can be measured with two metrics: precision and recall. When a user decides to search for information on a topic/theme, the total database and the results to be obtained can be divided into four categories: relevant and retrieved; relevant and not retrieved; non-relevant and retrieved; and non-relevant and not retrieved. Relevant items are those documents that help the user in answering his question. Non-relevant items are items that don't provide actually useful information. Precision is defined as the ratio of the number of relevant and retrieved documents (number of items retrieved that are actually useful to the user and match his search need) to the number of total retrieved documents from the query. Recall is defined as ratio of the number of retrieved and relevant documents (the number of items retrieved that are relevant to the user and match his needs) to the number of possible relevant documents (number of relevant documents in the database) [25].

combined at the time of the search with the help of logical operators. These operators enable a certain degree of solving the problem of synonymy and homonymy in natural language and the problem of different morphological forms of words. They also make it possible to find terms or aspects of terms that do not exist (or are not known to exist) in a controlled dictionary term in a database. The most famous search logic is Boolean search logic where operators are based on set logic. Logical sum (AND), logical product (OR) and logical difference (NOT) operations are used in the search, by placing AND, OR, and NOT between words or groups of words in a query. If more precise results and less recall are desired, the AND operator is used, which finds documents that contain both words from the query. The NOT operator also increases precision and reduces recall, and it is used if a term is to be excluded from the required result set. The OR operator finds all documents that contain any of the elements that the operator links. This operator affects the increase in recall. It is useful for finding synonyms, as well as variants in writing and abbreviations, if the systems do not have automatic solutions for these cases [25]. The problem with searching with Boolean operators is mainly "fake links", i.e. unexpected and irrelevant results that are obtained when the words from the query are in the document, but belong to a different context than the user actually wanted, which can be reduced by using the so-called proximity operators. These operators allow the user to define where in the field or fields the required terms are in relation to each other. The search is most often performed so that the terms appear next to each other or are separated by several words in the same field or in the same subfield. We distinguish several proximity operators: the *ADJ n* operator n finds words that are not more than a certain number of words apart (word ADJn word, where n = 1–99). Similar to this are the operators *WITHIN n* which determines the maximum number of words between the words from query (*n*) and the operator *!n* which in addition to the above determines that the order of words is the same as in the query. The SAME operator finds words that are in the same paragraph (the word SAME the word), and the NEAR operator finds words in the same sentence (the word NEAR the word). The presence of operators in the system can be explicit, i.e. users enter them themselves, or implicit, meaning the system automatically places a specific operator between the words from the query, these commonly being the AND operator, proximity operators, and the OR operator [25]. The placement of implicit operators was introduced into systems because research has shown that users have problems using Boolean operators and that they rarely use them [27]. Borgman [27] states that designing successful Boolean queries requires conceptual knowledge of how search terms can be combined, and the semantic knowledge of how a system processes or executes Boolean queries. The low level of these two types of knowledge is a basic factor leading to unsatisfactory search results. Borgman [27] proposes two solutions to these problems: improving user training methods and improving the system interface that reflects information search behavior. Another possibility that an information system may have is truncation [25]. Abbreviation allows the collection of different morphological forms of the same word, such as singular and plural or nouns, verbs and adjectives. Depending on the system, shortening can be explicit or user-defined, and automatic or implicit, when the system itself shortens a certain number of characters. The suffix is usually abbreviated after a certain character in order to include all forms of words that may have different suffixes. When the abbreviation is explicit, one or more of the following characters are usually used instead of one or more characters: asterisk (*), question mark (?), dollar ($), ladder (#), exclamation mark (!), or percentage (%). Explicit truncation requires the user to recall all possibilities, and implicitly does not take context into account but automatically truncates according to an existing algorithm or existing rules. However, while truncation is one of the possible search aids, using truncation can yield both unexpected and irrelevant words. Thus, the recall increases, but significantly reduces the precision of the search [25]. Although there are lots of advantages of electronic proverb dictionaries with free keywords searching possibilities, especially the ones that are published online and are freely accessible, like the increasing speed of the searching for items or the possibility of having several search options like searching according to alphabet, component, lemma, variant component, variant lemma, and keyword [28], thesauri meet all of the demands of a good electronic dictionary and search options suggested by Hrisztova-Gotthardt [29].

2.2   Searching by Using Thesaurus

The basis of each thesaurus are conceptual signifiers, the so-called descriptors (or pre-ferred terms), which can be defined as approved terms or symbols that unambiguously represent the terms contained in documents and in documentary research. A descriptor can be a single word or it can be made up of several words. It must reflect professional terminology. We can also include inverse forms as non-descriptors in the thesaurus, the so-called co-signifiers (synonyms) of descriptors. Non-descriptors (non-preferred terms) are expressions that represent terms, but they are not accepted as descriptors and we will distinguish them from descriptors by other types of letters or special sym-bols. Non-descriptors are actually "entry terms", or terms end-users tend to write while searching for item. In the thesaurus, the input term or non-descriptor is associated with the descriptor (preferred term) by USE or USE FOR references [30]. For example, if the user searches for the term *car*, he will see a reference that reads car (non-descriptor) USE automobile (descriptor) which instructs him that instead of the non-preferred term car uses the preferred term when searching, which is *automobile*. If the non-descriptor was not connected to the descriptor, the user would receive only documents contain-ing the non-descriptor car when searching with the term *car* (e.g. 1 document in the database), i.e. he would not receive documents mentioning the term *automobile* (e.g. 2 results in the database) and would thus be deprived of two of the three search results. The fundamental difference between thesaurus and the electronic dictionary (i.e. search according to free keywords) is that it is able to list the semantic relationships among the descriptors and show their connections, i.e. to expand the search by allowing the user to see the whole facet (broader, narrower and related terms) and by looking at semantic con-nections between descriptors, expand the query with terms with similar meanings [30]. For example, if the user searches for something about "*the evaluation of the maximum speed of the car*", and enters the following search strategy: *evaluation AND "maximum speed" AND car,* the search engine will return 200 documents that mention these three words. However, if he uses a thesaurus search, it will be possible to see that the free keyword "car" is actually a non-descriptor or a synonym and will be accompanied by the instruction USE "automobile". When he repeats the search with the term "automobile" he will get all documents with term "automobile", but also all documents containing the term "car" (350 documents). Through the thesaurus the entire facet to which the "car" as a synonym belongs to will be visible, e.g. the broader term "motor vehicle". In addition to "automobile" as a narrower term, the user will be able to see other narrower terms from the facet "motor vehicle" such as *truck, motorcycle, van*, etc.

The benefits of this search are twofold - if the user had not remembered that "car" (non-descriptor, non-preferred term) is synonymous with "automobile" (descriptor, preferred term) he would have been deprived of all documents where "automobile" is mentioned. Another advantage is that by looking at the facet, broader term (BT), narrower term (NT), and related (RT), the user will be able to expand their search with new terms from this facet (e.g. truck, motorcycle, van) and in repeated searches use terms that he may not have remembered before. Thus, using the broader term "motor vehicle" instead of just the term "car" the number of documents with the topic *"the evaluation of the maximum speed of the car"*, will be increased to approximately 550 (because now documents will be included where the "maximum speed" of the "car" is mentioned- 200 documents and "maximum speed" of all "motor vehicles" - truck, motorcycle, van– 350 documents).

The THESAURUS TREE in the above mentioned case would be:

BT MOTOR VEHICLE.
   NT AUTOMOBILE -> Car (synonym) USE AUTOMOBILE
   NT TRUCK
   NT MOTORCYCLE
   NT VAN

An example of descriptors usage can be seen on the database ERIC. ERIC is a comprehensive, easy-to-use, searchable, Internet-based bibliographic and full-text database of education research and information. It uses a thesaurus with 4452 descriptors and 7133 synonyms in order to enable the end-user better navigation and better search results [31] (Fig. 1).

One example of a usage of descriptors from the Eric database can be seen in Figs. 1 and 2. In Fig. 2 we can see that the descriptor *Proverb* has related terms *Cultural context* and *Folk culture,* and a synonym *Adages.* The category/facet or the broader term *Humanities*, meaning that the user can search by using this broader term which will result in increasing the search recall.

If we however decide to click on the option *Search collection using this descriptor,* we get search results with the descriptor *Proverbs* placed on top and terms from other categories/facets. This way the user will get 261 results which contain all the synonyms of the term *Proverbs*, which means the results contain the term *Adages* as well. If we were searching the collection only with the synonym *Adages*, we would get only 98 results, which means that without the thesaurus we would be deprived of 163 documents (Fig. 3).

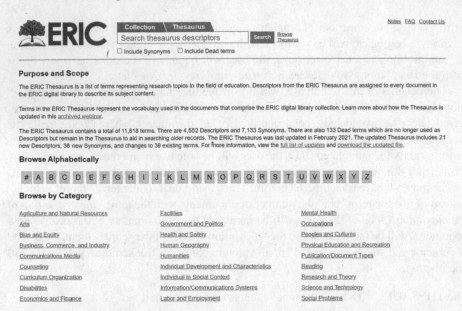

Fig. 1. Excerpt from the descriptors used in the thesaurus of the ERIC database

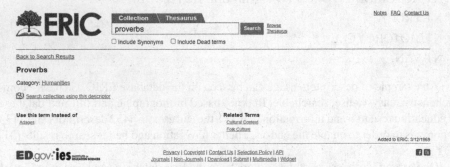

Fig. 2. Thesaurus search results for the descriptor *Proverbs*

Fig. 3. Search results of the database when the descriptor Proverbs is used

If we furthermore accept the suggestion of the thesaurus and want to search the documents on the topic of *Proverbs in Second Language Instruction* (belonging to the broader term *Humanities and Instructions,* category/facet *Language and Speech),* there will be 90 search results covering this topic, and the precision of the search is also enhanced (Fig. 4).

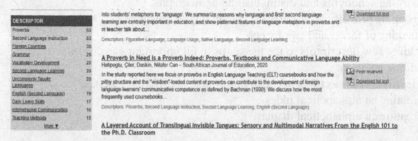

Fig. 4. Search results when the descriptor *proverbs* is used and the suggested term *Second Language Instruction* from another category/facet

On the example of the ERIC thesaurus, we can see that network of the descriptor's relationship (*Proverbs* with other descriptors in the category/facet of *Humanities*) leads to a reduction in ambiguity, and places the descriptor in the targeted semantic environment. This way the end-users who search for information can find their way to the requested items by synonym recognition using related terms of a particular subject area and eventually get the information needed.

3 Croatian Proverb Thesaurus

Unlike general-purpose thesauri, which are based on a single word and are rarely used in information searching, thesauri in today's sense of the word are called *information retrieval thesauri,* IR or structured thesauri. One type of IR thesaurus is the end-user thesaurus as the Croatian proverb thesaurus will be.

End-user thesauri are mostly online post-coordinated systems that include all terms used in the database and clearly distinguish between them. They contain scope notes on usage and meaning of items, and display them upon demand, which makes them much more extensive and user-friendly [30]. This means that upon entering a combination of free keywords into the search bar[3], the thesaurus will automatically suggest proverbs that match the predefined criteria, since it will also have a rich input dictionary focused on user needs. The dictionary will be linked by references to previously approved descriptors established by paremiologists.

---

[3] In the online version of this thesaurus, the user can replace a certain frequent variation of the search term using the automatic shortening technique, if the system allows it as well as Boolean operators and advanced database search capabilities [32].

3.1 The Technical Process of Creating a Thesaurus

The technical process and concrete steps in creating a thesaurus of Croatian proverbs, given by Shearer [33] include:

1. collecting proverbs from literature and other sources,
2. merging synonyms and distinguishing homographs,
3. grouping proverb descriptors into broader facet categories,
4. stacking of facets and sub-facets,
5. adding new descriptors to the thesaurus to fill important gaps,
6. adding notation,
7. identifying connections between descriptors in different facets,
8. creating an alphabetical index,
9. creating an alphabetical display.

Since the first two steps are already done in the course of previous research, and the last steps are going to be conducted in the thesaurus interface, the biggest future challenges for both the paremiologists and information scientists are steps from 2 to 7. The following part of the paper will therefore focus on these concrete steps.

When defining descriptors needed for the thesaurus, the starting point is set to the existing proverbs from the database. One way to start is extracting them and ordering them according to the equivalence to categories, so that equivalent terms refer to only one category, meaning that all synonyms (nondescriptors) will be connected with the referral USE to the descriptor (second step) [33], for instance *falsehood, untruth, misstatement USE lie.* For example, if a user searches for the term *untruth,* he will receive a reference that reads untruth (non-descriptor) USE lie (descriptor) which instructs him to use the preferred term, which is a lie, instead of the non-preferred term *untruth* when searching. If the non-descriptor was not related to the descriptor, the user would only get proverbs that contain the non-descriptor *untruth* (e.g. 1 result in the database - *Bolje neistina koja škodi nego laž koja godi* [Better the untruth that hurts than lie that gives pleasure.], or would not get proverbs where *lie* is mentioned (e.g. 2 results in the database; *U laži su kratke noge* [Lies have short legs], *Tko laže, taj i krade* [He who lies steals]. The third step is grouping proverb descriptors into broader facet categories. The usual way is to group descriptors that denote identical terms, where the same term is identified and named after the group. These categories are called facets and sub-facets. The descriptors in each facet and subface are then further divided. For each subcategory of the group, it is necessary to determine a clear characteristic that is used to distinguish different descriptors. The fourth step involves stacking the resulting facets and sub-facets. An additional structure in the thesaurus is created by grouping facets and sub-facets according to the user's point of view. Descriptors are then subgrouped and organized within groups. There are two types of relations between descriptors: hierarchical and associative relations. There should be the broader (BT) and narrower terms (NT) determined, for instance in the relations of *species – kind* (e.g. *animals* is the BT (broader term) of the term *cats,* but on the other hand *pets* is not a broader term of the term *cats,* since not all cats are pets as well), *entirety – part* (e.g. *head* is the BT of the term *nose,* whereas *forest* is not a BT of the term *tree,* since not all trees belong to a forest). The relations between descriptors can also be associative, based on the coordination (e.g. *rye* and *corn* are *cereal*), genetics (*mother-son*), concurrence (the concurrence of activities, e.g. *education-teaching*), cause and effect, instruments, materials and similarities. The associative relations express the analogy of the meaning, and not equivalence and are marked with the expression RELATED term (e.g. mother RELATED to son). These relations are the hardest to define. In the fifth step of the analysis, but also earlier, it is clear that additional descriptors need to be added to clarify the division of descriptors or their omission. Such descriptors, which fill important gaps in the thesaurus, should be added at this stage, however it is not prudent to add many similar descriptors to any particular part of the thesaurus as this could disrupt the structure of the entire thesaurus and complicate further work. Therefore, this work is usually left for later stages when the structure is fully understood and clear and when it is easy to add descriptors to the appropriate place. In this step it is certainly useful to make notes about the areas that will be expanded later. In step six, the descriptors in the thesaurus are already in a highly structured order, however, thesaurus users need to be able to easily find a specific descriptor. In this regard, it is possible to rearrange the order of the descriptors in alphabetical order, indicating the structure by standard notation (broader term-BT, narrower-NT, related term-RT), which is considered in the ninth step. Classified representation, on the other hand, has its advantages, especially in enabling collocations of related descriptors and displaying a clear thesaurus structure. The mechanization of this order requires the use of working notation. It can be in form of numbers, letters or combinations thereof. It is very important to leave space for the thesaurus to grow both in the existing facets and sub-facets and in the new facets. Notation should therefore leave a multitude of gaps. It is also useful to note the hierarchical level of each descriptor, bearing in mind that too few levels do not provide the necessary clarity when dividing, while too many can cause confusion. A classified organization makes the relationships between terms in the same facet explicitly clear. However, to help the user find other descriptors that are related to the same term, it is necessary to make links to descriptors that are in different facets (seventh step). Such relationships should be enabled reciprocally given that users need to be guided in different ways. The classified approach displays terms in semantic order, however it cannot be accessed without an alphabetical index. The index should be permuted to allow access via any element of the complex descriptor. It is also appropriate to use a set of "stop" words, i.e. to make a "stop" list in order to eliminate unnecessary permutations and to be able to manually exclude them after creating the index. An alphabetical representation of a thesaurus is created based on the use of a hierarchical representation and the association of each descriptor with other descriptors associated with that descriptor [33].

If the user searches for example for proverbs with the topic *krađa (theft)*, the system will return all the proverbs where literally the term *krađa (theft)* appears as a lemma, together with its lexemes (*e.g. krade, kradeš, kradljivica, krao, krao, krasti* etc.).

See proverbs with this keyword: Tko laže taj i **krade** [He who lies steals as well], Od sve **krade** na Božić ni mesa [Out of all the stealing there is no meet for Christmas]

Below is the possibility to view the thesaurus tree, i.e. the categories/facet BT *nemoralne radnje (immoral actions)* and all the narrow terms NT *krađa (theft), laž (lie), osveta (revenge),* and related terms RT *pomoć (iz interesa) (help (through interest)).* In order to ensure better understanding, next to all the Croatian words there are English translations displayed in the parentheses.

1: KRAĐA [THEFT]
See proverbs with this keyword: Tko laže taj i **krade** [He who lies steals as well], Od sve **krađe** na Božić ni mesa [Out of all the stealing there is no meet for Christmas]
See also proverbs: U laži su kratke noge [Lies have short legs], Ruka ruku mije [One hand washes another], Oko za oko, zub za zub [An eye for an eye, a tooth for a tooth]
See thesaurus tree:

BT NEMORALNE RADNJE (IMMORAL ACTIONS)
NT KRAĐA (THEFT)
　　RT POMOĆ (HELP)
NT LAŽ (LIE) *neistina (falsehood, untruth, misstatement) USE laž (lie)*
　　RT POMOĆ (HELP)
NT OSVETA (REVENGE)
　　RT POMOĆ (HELP)

The following are examples if the user enters Croatian search words *laž (lie), osveta (revenge), pomoć (iz interesa) (help (through interest))*

2. LAŽ [LIE] *USE FOR* neistina [untruth, falsehood, misstatement]
See proverbs with this keyword: U **laži** su kratke noge [Lies have short legs], Tko **laže** taj i krade [He who lies, steals too]
See also proverbs: Ruka ruku mije [One hand washes another], Oko za oko, zub za zub [An eye for an eye, a tooth for a tooth] *See thesaurus tree:*

BT NEMORALNE RADNJE (IMMORAL ACTIONS)
NT KRAĐA (THEFT)
　　RT POMOĆ (HELP)
NT LAŽ (LIE) *neistina (falsehood, untruth, misstatement) USE laž (lie)*
　　RT POMOĆ (HELP)
NT OSVETA (REVENGE)
　　RT POMOĆ (HELP)

3. POMOĆ (IZ INTERESA) (HELP (THROUGH INTEREST))
See proverbs: **Pomozi** si sam pa će ti i Bog pomoć
See also proverbs: Ruka ruku mije [One hand washes another], Tko laže taj i krade [He who lies, steals too], U laži su kratke noge [Lies have short legs], Oko za oko, zub za zub [An eye for an eye, a tooth for a tooth] *See thesaurus tree:*

BT NEMORALNE RADNJE (IMMORAL ACTION)
NT KRAĐA (THEFT)
　　RT POMOĆ (IZ INTERESA) (HELP (THROUGH INTEREST))

NT LAŽ (LIE) *neistina (falsehood, untruth, misstatement) USE laž (lie)*
   RT POMOĆ (IZ INTERESA) (HELP (THROUGH INTEREST))
NT REVENGE (OSVETA
   RT POMOĆ (IZ INTERESA) (HELP (THROUGH INTEREST))

We can see from this example that the descriptors that are connected to the proverbs are actually key-words from the proverb itself, which are linked to other keywords and terms that also contain their equivalent proverb. This way the thesaurus fills its didactic function and "teaches" the end-user which proverbs can be used in a certain situation.

4   Conclusion

The proposed example of the construction of a Croatian proverb thesaurus showed the complexity of the process that needs to be done only to fill out the didactic function of the database, namely to give the end-user suggestions which proverbs can be used in a given situation, given the free keywords they have entered. The second step and the second level of the thesaurus is the dictionary database that will display all the information that is necessary to be found in an electronic dictionary, like information of markings, usage, synonymous and antonymous proverbs, anti-proverbs, examples from literature etc. This way the thesaurus will have the possibility to be linked to existing (not only proverb) databases, for example the Croatian linguistic portal where the user will have the possibility to check the meaning of words in certain proverbs. Various examples from practice testify to the irreplaceability and exceptional usefulness of thesauri in searching for information. As an aid to vocabulary control, the thesaurus copes well with resolving language ambiguities and provides security in information retrieval and knowledge sharing. The fundamental value of the thesaurus is to list the semantic relationships among the descriptors and to show their connections. The network of a descriptor's relationship with other terms provides some kind of definition, leads to a reduction in ambiguity, and places the descriptor in its semantic environment. In this way, the future proverb thesaurus will fulfill its basic task which is to provide a semantic map to individual domains of knowledge, including links between domains, facilitate understanding and exchange of information between disciplines and discourse, and provide conceptual information. The user is then facilitated by the analysis and perception of information needs, selection of search terms and forming of search queries, resulting in the presentation of relevant search results of the future proverb database.

References

1. Mieder, W., Kingsbury, S.A., Harder, K.B. (eds.): A Dictionary of American Proverbs. Oxford University Press, New York (1996)
2. [Stojkova] Стойкова, С.: Български пословици и поговорки. София, Издателство Колибри (2007)
3. Wander, K.F.W.: Deutsches Sprichwörter-Lexikon: Ein Hausschatz für das deutsche Volk. 5 Bde. Leipzig, Brockhaus (1867–1880)
4. Litovkina, A. T.: Magyar közmondástár. Tinta Kiadó, Budapest (2005)

5. Aleksa Varga, M., Keglević, A.: Erstellung und Bearbeitung von parömiologischen Umfragen: Eine Fallstudie am Beispiel des Kroatischen. In: Gondek, A., Jurasz, A., Staniewski, P., Szczek, J. (eds.) Deutsche Phraseologie und Parömiologie im Kontakt und im Kontrast, pp. 245–257. Verlag Dr. Kovač, Hamburg (2020)
6. Aleksa Varga, M., Keglević, A.: Hrvatske poslovice u slavenskome okruženju: određivanje hrvatskoga paremiološkog minimuma i optimuma. Slavia centralis **13**(1), 40–51 (2020)
7. Aleksa Varga, M., Keglević, A.: Djelo govori više od riječi. Antiposlovice u jeziku mladih. In: Smajić,D., Krumes, I., Mance, N. (eds.) U jezik uronjeni. Zbornik posvećen Ireni Vodopiji, pp. 66–76. Fakultet za odgojne i obrazovne znanosti, Osijek (2018)
8. Aleksa Varga, M., Keglević, A.: Kroatische und deutsche Antisprichwörter in der Sprache der Jugendlichen. Proverbium **35**, 343–360 (2018)
9. Aleksa Varga, M., Keglević, A.: "Iznimka potvrđuje pravilo" Mladi i poslovice u Hrvatskoj. In: D. Stolac, A. Vlastelić. (eds.) Jezik i njegovi učinci, pp. 23–32. Srednja Europa, Zagreb (2018)
10. Aleksa Varga, M., Keglević, A.: Bekanntheit der häufigsten kroatischen und deutschen Sprichwörter unter Jugendlichen. Linguistische Treffen in Wrocław **14**, 287–297 (2018)
11. Slovar slovenskega knjižnega jezika and Slovar pregovorov in sorodnih paremioloških izrazov. https://fran.si/216/slovar_pregovorov. Accessed 5 July 2022
12. Sprichwort-Plattform. http://www.sprichwort-plattform.org/. Accessed 5 July 2022
13. Postproverbial Database. https://postproverbial.org/. Accessed 5 July 2022
14. Meterc, M.: Aktualna raba in pomenska določljivost 200 pregovorov in sorodnih paremioloških izrazov. Jezikoslovni zapiski. **27**(1), 45–58 (2021). https://doi.org/10.3986/JZ.27.1.03
15. Meterc, M.: Analiza frazeološke variantnosti za slovarski prikaz v eSSKJ-ju in SPP-ju. Jezikoslovni zapiski. **25**(2), 33–45 (2019). https://doi.org/10.3986/JZ.25.2.2
16. Meheš, M.: Hrvatske narodne poslovice. http://os-veliko-trgovisce.skole.hr/upload/os-veliko-trgovisce/images/static3/919/attachment/hrvatske_narodne_poslovice.pdf. Accessed 08 Aug 2018 (2007)
17. Chlosta, C., Grzybek, P.: Zum Teufel mit dem …: Anfang und Ende in der experimentellen Parömiologie. In: Grandl, C., McKenna, K.J. (eds.) Bis dat, qui cito dat. Gegengabe in Paremiology, Folklore, Language, and Literature. Honoring Wolfgang Mieder on His Seventieth Birthday. pp. 109–120. Peter Lang, Frankfurt am Main (2015)
18. Olson, H.A., Boll, J.J.: Subject analysis in online catalogs. 2nd edn. Libraries Unlimited, Englewood (2001)
19. Križaj, L.: Tezaurus spomeničkih vrsta: podatkovni standard u inventarima graditeljske baštine. Ministarstvo kulture RH, Zagreb (2017)
20. Horvat, A.: Tezaurus termina iz književnosti i znanosti o književnosti: (prilog za izradu predmetnog kataloga): magistarski rad. [s.n.], Zagreb (1981)
21. Digital Europa Thesaurus. https://op.europa.eu/hr/web/eu-vocabularies/concept-scheme/-/resource?uri=http://data.europa.eu/uxp/det. Accessed 6 July 2022
22. EuroVoc. https://eur-lex.europa.eu/browse/eurovoc.html?locale=hr. Accessed 6 July 2022
23. Art & Architecture Thesaurus. https://www.getty.edu/vow/AATFullDisplay?find=Graffiti&logic=AND&note=&english=N&prev_page=1&subjectid=300015613. Accessed 6 July 2022
24. Library, Information Science & Technology Abstracts Thesaurus. https://web.s.ebscohost.com/ehost/thesaurus?vid=1&sid=b0536450-ad99-4a16-a580-5ee0083dd4fa%40redis. Accessed 6 July 2022
25. Kowalski, G.J., Maybury, M.T.: Information Storage and Retrieval Systems: Theory and Implementation, 2nd edn. Kluwer Academic Publishers, New York (2005)
26. Wilkes, A., Nelson, A.: Subject searching in two online catalogs: authority control vs. Non-Author. Control. Catalog. Classif. Q. **20**(4), 57–79 (1996)

27. Borgman, C.L.: All users of information retrieval systems are not created equal: an exploration into individual differences. Inf. Process. Manage. **25**(3), 237–251 (1989)
28. Kispál, T.: Paremiography: proverb collections. In: Hrisztova-Gotthardt, H., Aleksa Varga, M. (eds.) Introduction to Paremiology, A Comprehensive Guide to Proverb Studies, pp. 229–242. De Gruyter Open, Warsaw (2015). https://doi.org/10.2478/9783110410167.10
29. Hrisztova-Gotthardt, H.: Vom gedruckten Sprichwörterbuch zur interaktiven Sprichwort-datenbank. Peter Lang Verlag, Bern (2010)
30. Aitchison, J., Gilchrist, A., Bawden, D.: Thesaurus Construction and Use: A Practical Manual, 4th edn. Aslib, London (2000)
31. ERIC. https://eric.ed.gov/. Accessed 18 May 2022
32. Bates, M.J.: Design for a subject search interface and online thesaurus for a very large records management database. In: Proceedings of the 53rd ASIS Annual Meeting, vol. 27, pp. 20–28. Learned Information, Medford, NJ (1990)
33. Shearer, J.R.: A practical exercise in building a thesaurus. In: Roe, S.K., Thomas, A.R. (eds.) The Thesaurus: Review, Renaissance, and Revision, pp. 35–57. The Haworth Information Press, Binghamton (2004)

Lexical Semantic Mind Maps Based on Collocations as a Tool for Teaching Vocabulary: A Case Study

María Auxiliadora Barrios Rodríguez[✉]

Universidad Complutense de Madrid, Madrid, Spain
`auxibarrios@filol.ucm.es`

Abstract. The objective of this study is to propose and evaluate an innovative tool, which we call *lexical-semantic mind maps*, designed to improve learning of vocabulary and collocations. These maps are based on the glosses of the Lexical Function, which forms part of Meaning-Text Theory, and enables a better knowledge of the semantic patterns hidden in the vocabulary. A case study was carried out with a group of seven students. Five different learning strategies were tested: (1) a textbook; (2) a lexical-semantic mind map containing concrete nouns; (3) a lexical-semantic mind map containing abstract nouns; (4) a text created *ad hoc* to learn the semantic patterns that underlie the collocations; (5) a lexical-semantic mind map created *ad hoc*. The core of the analysis consisted of four lexical-semantic relations: *type of*, *useful for*, *hyponym* and the *nuclear semantic features* relation, a relation that emerged during the research analysis.

The findings of this study suggest that students' progress in learning collocations is not necessarily related to an improvement in the semantic knowledge of the words composing these collocations. The textbook based on collocations and two of the lexical-semantic mind maps produced a minimal improvement in the knowledge of the meaning of the words involved in the collocations, whilst the lexical-semantic mind map created *ad hoc* resulted in significant improvements. Thus, lexical-semantic mind maps, the tool proposed in this study, could serve as a model to be further implemented in other research studies under true experimental conditions.

Keywords: Collocations · Acquisition of vocabulary · Second Language Teaching · Meaning-Text Theory · Lexical functions · Lexical-semantic mind maps

1 Introduction

While traditionally learning vocabulary implied memorizing vocabulary lists, nowadays learning words in context and in collocations is recommended (Aitchison 1987; Lewis 1993, 2000; Boers et al. 2006, 2014; Li and Schmitt 2010; López Ferrero and Bataner 2017). The concept of the collocation we are working with is not necessarily attached to frequency of use, but rather to a) prototypical relations (Koike 2001); and b) lexical restrictions (Bosque 2004, 2017; Mel'čuk 1996; Mel'čuk and Wanner 1996; Barrios 2010). We construe a collocation as a set of two or more words, such as *to make someone happy*, selecting the two words by lexical preferences (Barrios 2010).

What do "lexical preferences" mean? If the components of a collocation were selected semantically, the meaning of any collocation could be paraphrased; for instance, *to make someone happy* could be expressed by other synonyms of *make*, such as *do*. But the combination *do someone happy* is not correct. It is only the first verb that is selected and this selection is not strictly speaking semantic: we recognize a sort of lexical restriction and call the verb (*make*) the *collocate* (or value) and the adjective (*happy*) the *base* (or key-word). This lexical selection could be qualified as arbitrary.

However, different scholars have proven that collocations are not as arbitrary as was claimed (Bosque 2004; Apresjan 2000; Sanromán 2003; Higueras 2011; Barrios 2010). A deep examination of the concept of collocation from the Meaning-Text Theory (MTT) proves that there are classes of words that combine with certain bases; that is the case of *to feel* and all the nouns attached to *feelings* (Mel'cuk and Wanner 1996), such as *to feel joy* or *to feel sad*. What we propose in this paper is to apply these semantic paradigms to Second Language Teaching (SLT). We assert that MTT offers a powerful approach to organize the chunks, collocations, and formulas of any language by means of semantic patterns. It has been claimed that MTT has scarcely had an effect on the Second Language Acquisition (SLA) research field (García Salido and Ramos 2018); our work could shed some light on new applications of MTT tools for SLT.

As we propose a new way to apply a theoretical framework to an applied research field, we have found very little previous research: some of the questions we summarize in Sect. 2 were in large part answered in some of our previous papers. Based on experimental work, some years ago we argued that to focus on the semantic analysis of collocations is useful when learning collocations (Barrios 2016). We now inquire as to whether a better knowledge of semantic patterns underlying chunks and collocations may not only boost the correct usage of collocations but also generate a deeper understanding of the meaning of the words which form part of these collocations.

This paper is organized as follows: Sect. 2 presents some preliminary questions related to collocations and the process of learning vocabulary: differences between chunks and collocations (Sect. 2.1), choosing incidental or intentional learning conditions (Sect. 2.2), lexical functions and their relevance when learning collocations (Sect. 2.3), learning collocations in a contrastive situation (Sect. 2.4), and teaching collocations by levels (Sect. 2.5). Section 3 presents our proposal regarding the lexical-semantic mind maps. Section 4 summarizes the methodology applied to evaluate our proposal. Section 5 offers the results and discussion.

2 Literature Review

2.1 Chunks and Collocations

A chunk –*concertar una cita* (make an appointment), *encantado de conocerte* (nice to meet you), *tirar la toalla* (literally to throw a towel, meaning to give up)– is defined as "a sequence of words which native speakers feel is the natural and preferred way of expressing a particular idea or purpose" (Lindstromberg and Boers 2008). The various chunk taxonomies proposed in specialized literature have fuzzy boundaries (Wray 2002), among them collocations, the most frequent type of chunk. Collocations are highly beneficial when learning a foreign language for many reasons, as many researchers have pointed out (Aitchison 1987; Lewis 1993, 2000; Boers et al. 2006, 2014; Li and Schmitt 2010), and the concept of collocation has been systematically analysed, among others, in the MTT approach, as we will see in the next paragraphs.

The MTT (Mel'čuk 1996, 2014; Polguère and Mel'čuk 2006) has been implemented in English and French (Polguère 2000) and Russian (Apresjan 2000), among others languages. The MTT "includes a theory of lexical functions (LFs), in which a number of abstract and limited semantic notions apply to bases or keywords, giving collocates or values as results" (Bosque 2017). Outside that model Bosque's dictionaries (2004, 2006) offer semantic classes that are useful for learners of Spanish as a foreign language, such as change verbs, influence verbs and feeling verbs (Bosque 2017).

We construe a collocation as a set of two or more words, selected together by lexical preferences such as *ejercicio suave* (light exercise) or *viento ligero* (soft wind). Consider that in these collocations the meaning of *light* and *soft* share a similar sense ('not big'). However, while we can say *light or gentle exercise*, we cannot say **soft exercise*. Our data claims that semantic motivation seems to be the key issue in assisting learners in the process of learning vocabulary in context (which means, learning chunks, collocations, etc.) For instance, the verb *dar* (to give) is combined with most nouns expressing love, such as *beso* (kiss) *and abrazo* (hug), but not *caricia* (caress), which combines with *hacer* (to do). The verb *tener* (to have) combines with most nouns of illness, such as *diabetes, cardiopatía* (heart disease) and *cancer,* but not *alcoholismo* (alcoholism) and *locura* (madness). And the verb *hacer* (to do) combines with some nouns of individual sports, such as *natación* (swimming), *esquí* (skiing) and *pilates*, whilst *jugar al* (to play) combines with nouns of collective sports, such as *fútbol* (football), *baloncesto* (basketball), *tenis* (tennis), etc. (examples taken from Barrios 2015).

2.2 Incidental or Intentional Learning Conditions When Learning Collocations?

The work mentioned above also suggests that the teacher's role is crucial because problematic collocations need to be highlighted for each group (Barrios 2016). This author compared one hundred twenty-six Spanish light verb collocations with their equivalent English collocations and concluded that only fifty-two could cause problems from a contrastive point of view. Her study demonstrates that having advanced students (B2-C1 levels) explicitly learn these kinds of collocations is almost 40% more efficient than just relying on incidental acquisition. Barrios (2016) proposed focusing on different collocations from a contrastive point of view, giving priority to light verb collocations and adjective-noun collocations.

2.3 Are Lexical Functions Useful When Learning Collocations?

Studies developed within the MTT framework have shown that paying attention to the meaning of collocations is very useful when learning collocations, particularly through Lexical Functions. The concept of lexical function (LF) was developed by Mel'čuk (1996) and Apresjan (2000), among others, and corresponds to a formalization of a lexical relation. It is useful for understanding the meaning of the expressions involved (Sanromán and Alonso Ramos 2007). The meaning of an LF can be translated into one or several expressions, which are called paraphrases or glosses (Polguère 2000). For instance, the LF called CausFunc$_0$ can be paraphrased by 'to cause something to exist', and corresponds to *create, produce, make* or *invent*. These productive and basic verbs are called glosses, and can form part of different collocations, such as *to build a house, to create a danger, to unleash a war, to put forward an idea, to spread a rumor*, etc.

The MTT presupposition is that verbs like *to have, to take, to receive, to do, to make* and *to give*, usually called *light verbs*, lose their meaning and allow the noun to produce most of the meaning of the collocation (in fact, *to have a shower* means *to shower*). The lexical relation between the light verb and the noun is also an LF. For this collocation, the LF is Oper, which means 'to do'. As Boguslavsky et al. (2006) claims, formalization of these collocations should be done as in (1):

(1) Oper$_1$(ducha) = darse, Oper$_1$(shower) = to have, Oper$_1$(douche) = prendre, Oper$_1$(doccia) = fare, Oper$_1$(душ) = принимать

Light verb collocations are usually construed as collocations formed by verbs without meaning. However, light verbs conserve some features of meaning. Consequently, meaning in collocations can be analysed even in light verb collocations. In fact, Barrios (2015) presents some paradigms of collocations attached to the most productive Spanish light verbs: *dar* (to give), *hacer* (to make) and *tener* (to have). To quote just one example, the author shows some nouns of movement, such as *salto* (jump), *bote* (bounce), *brinco* (leap), *giro* (turn), *vuelta* (turn), *paso* (step) and *paseo* (walk), all of which combine with the verb *dar* (to give).

Consequently, LFs are useful as a taxonomy for learning collocations, because they make hidden semantic patterns explicit, including collocations of light verbs. In another online resource called PATTY the semantic patterns are grouped into one taxonomy. Both LF and PATTY taxonomies are semantically meaningful, although PATTY is a larger resource, created automatically and based on the data of knowledge. LFs, in turn, are based on linguistic items, and demand manual tasks. A few examples of maps are presented below (see Sect. 3.2) to illustrate an example of types of tools that can be created with the taxonomy of LFs.

2.4 Should Collocations Be Learnt in a Contrastive Situation?

Leonardi (2010) claims that learning lexis in a contrastive situation is positive. In particular, the author points out that translation is a productive activity in SLA because it is a process which involves reading, writing, speaking and listening, the four skills that define language competence. Regarding the acquisition of collocations and the influence of the mother tongue, in her empirical study with English-speakers learning Spanish, Barrios (2016) demonstrated that students learn collocations more easily with equivalents in their native language.

This empirical work proves that it is not necessary to pay attention to the form when teaching full verb collocations, such as *ponerse la ropa* (to put on clothes), *llevar puesta la ropa* (to wear clothes) or *quitarse la ropa* (take off your clothes) because this type of collocation can usually be translated word by word. Neither does it make sense, for the author, to teach learners (focus on learning collocations) light verb collocations that are similar in L1 and L2, because they are learned unconsciously; for instance, *dar una clase* (give a lecture), *dar un beso* (give a kiss), *tener una herida* (have an injury), and *tener vergüenza* (have shame, be ashamed). We conclude that at advanced levels, we should focus on teaching collocations with differences in both languages, most of them involving light verbs, such as *tener alergia* (literally "to have allergy") and its equivalent *to be allergic*.

2.5   Is It Useful to Teach Collocations by Levels?

García and Alonso (2018) proposed a method to classify collocations according to levels (A to C, according to the *Common European Framework of Reference*, 2001), and based on frequency criteria. We decided to select the level for each collocation taking into account semantic criteria. Usually, the glosses (*causar, provocar*) should be taught at A levels, while most collocations should be taught at B and C levels.

Higueras (2011) suggested that collocations should be taught starting at the very first levels. This is particularly relevant when collocations are productive, such as collocations attached to the meaning 'big', which corresponds to the LF called Magn. For instance, *big mistake* is a collocation expressing this meaning that is adequate for level A, while *serious mistake* and *huge mistake* express the same meaning for levels B and C, respectively. Bosque's lexicographic work (2004, 2006) offers an excellent corpus of Spanish collocations based on the semantic criteria: for instance, for the entry *mistake* there are twenty-four different synonymic word combinations for the meaning 'big mistake' (Bosque 2006). Working with such dictionaries, teachers can create conceptualizations for many sets of semantically motivated collocates and adapt the difficulty of learning to students' level.

A very interesting point is that first level learners do not need to focus on collocations intentionally because collocations for them are related to a process of acquisition of vocabulary (Higueras 2011). Thus, instead of drawing the students' attention to the collocation *per se*, this type of collocations can be used as a tool to learn vocabulary in a context for beginners: think of words such as *clothes, put on, wear, take off, lecture, kiss, injury, shame*, etc., involved in the collocations mentioned in Sect. 2.4.

3   Proposal: Applying Glosses of LFs to Lexical-Semantic Mind Maps

3.1   Research Question

As claimed in Sect. 2, previous work has only focused on collocations as a tool for learning vocabulary. The core problem of hidden semantic patterns appears to be ill-defined. Barrios' study (2019) proved that the application of semantic patterns to lexical-semantic mind maps by means of glosses of LFs is extremely motivating for students. However, a challenging question remains unanswered: we will try to provide insight to whether this tool is effective for SLT, particularly for the meaning of words.

The paraphrase 'it is useful for' is a feature of meaning which is present in all the nouns that name objects, such as artefacts; it is attached to the LFs Real and Fact. We could exploit these LFs as systematic semantic patterns within the lexical fields of home, transport, etc. When learning the vocabulary of artefacts, the sense 'it is useful for' is present in collocations such as *to write with the pencil, to drive a car, to wear boots*. We could also work with lexical relations attached to the sense 'type of' (*boot/footwear*). Both 'it is useful for' and 'type of' are paraphrases of very productive LFs.

We could also work with hypernyms. First of all, hypernyms allow the students to gain a deep understanding of the organization of the lexicon which portrays the cognitive process of categorization (*joy* and *sadness* are 'feelings'; *hot* and *cold* are 'physical sensations', etc.) Secondly, hypernyms also allow the students to work with collocations in an inverse manner: they understand that we express *sentir* (to feel) combined with words for all types of emotions (such as *alegría*, joy, or *tristeza*, sad). Thirdly, we could invite the students to predict other uses of the collocate associated to the hyperyms: for instance, we could ask them if the verb *sentir* (*to feel*) combines with nouns other than emotions, testing if they are able to consider something different, such as physical sensations (*sentir frío*, to feel cold; *sentir calor*, to feel hot, etc.). Finally, we should test the students in respect to discovering exceptions to generalizations; for instance, some nouns of feelings, such as *celos* (jealous) combines not only with *sentir* (to feel) but also with *tener* (to have) (*tengo celos*, I'm jealous).

As explained in the Introduction, our hypothesis is that if the students discover some of the semantic patterns that underlie the collocations analysed, they may have a better knowledge not only of the collocations but also of the meaning of the words involved in these collocations. Going back to the example of the verb *to feel*, after working in the manner we propose, the students should not only know the collocations of the lexical field of emotions and physical sensations better, but should also be able to answer with greater precision what the words *emotion* and *sensation* (physical feeling) mean, which implies understanding their differences.

In summary, the question that we would like to answer in this paper is the following: could glosses of LFs help not only learn vocabulary but also achieve a better understanding of the vocabulary learned? In other words, after working with glosses, could the students improve their learning because their knowledge of the meaning of the words combined in each collocation is deeper?

3.2   Lexical-Semantic Mind Maps

In 2016 we began to apply the glosses of LFs to a particular tool that we call *lexical-semantic mind maps*. As we teach future Spanish teachers, we explain how to create this particular type of mind map oriented to SLT. Different students published their tools for six years, working within a type of collaborative project (see some of the results in https://masespanol.es/). Students learned how to discover semantic and lexical relations working with phraseological dictionaries and corpora. As explained before, the basis of the conceptualization of lexical-semantic mind maps consists of semantic patterns based on glosses of Lexical Functions. After the training, the students try to present all this rich linguistic information in a pedagogical manner.

Figure 1 shows some pages of the map created by one of the students (Adrian Muela), who put forward several explicit lexical relations associated with different glosses of LFs: the first picture reflects the gloss "type of" for the word *paint*: *water-based paint, tempera, acrylic nail polish,* etc.; the second one reflects "it is useful for" relations, such as *sandpaper for sanding, putty to cover the walls, masking tape to protect skirting boards,* etc.:

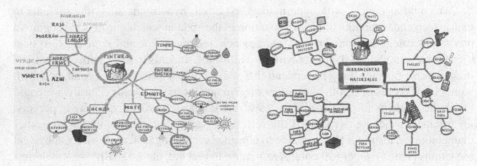

Fig. 1. Mind maps of "Pintor" (Painter): "type of" and "it is useful for" relations

We tested the students' evaluation of the tool and were able to confirm that these types of maps are highly motivating (Barrios 2019). However, until now we were not able to verify if this tool necessarily resulted in a better and deeper knowledge of vocabulary than others, such as books, texts and exercises.

During the last year we used a lexical-semantic mind map created *ad hoc* for learning the vocabulary related to *temperament, character* and *personality*. These three concepts are complex. In our previous experience with Spanish students, we confirmed that some books working with these concepts create more confusion than accurate knowledge. To prepare a clear lexical-semantic mind map, we investigated the meaning of the three words in books written by experts. Then we collected collocations containing these words. Later, we distributed the collocations by means of glosses of LFs. Finally, we distributed the content of our material in a lexical-semantic mind map created *ad hoc* by levels.

Figure 2 shows the first map containing the three words and the key-words attached to each one. The Spanish word *temperamento* (temperament) is related to the set of psychological features inherited biologically (a person's disposition when they are a baby). *Carácter* (character) is the set of psychological features developed during child-hood through education and cultural environment. And *personalidad* (personality) is the result of the experience and the decisions of each person throughout life.

The second map of Fig. 2 shows some of the collocations selected by the first level (A) students: *tener/no tener temperamento* (to have temperament or not), *tener/no tener carácter* (to have character or not) y *tener/no tener personalidad* (to have personality or not). The first two Spanish expressions are synonyms, and they are sometimes attached to negative connotations (such as the behaviour of a choleric person). The last Spanish expression means to be and behave as a unique and self-confident person. As the examples prove, collocations are not necessarily attached to the real meaning of the three words. For this reason, this map (see Fig. 2) was particularly interesting in respect to our research:

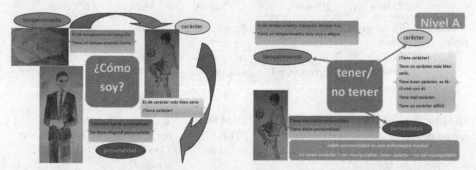

Fig. 2. Two excerpts from the mind map "¿Como soy?" (How am I?)

The principal difference between the first excerpt from the mind map and the second one (both in the Fig. 2) lies in the meaning: both are focused on collocations by means of glosses of Lexical Functions, but the first one only contains some examples of the use of the map's three keywords (*temperament, character* and *personality*), while the second one was developed taking into account a deep knowledge of the meaning and collocations of the three words from the gloss of the LF Oper (*tener*, to have), as well as the SLL level (in this case level A).

4 Evaluation of Our Proposal

4.1 The Design of the Test

We follow the case study methodology (Stake 2010) because we are not interested in students as variables but rather as persons (Maxwell 2012), particularly as persons involved in a process of training as future Spanish language teachers. Our objective is to understand these processes deeply, but not to replicate our research within a quantitative methodology. Consequently, we construe reliability as the security of checking the data and the procedures (Flick 2012). Seven students of the Master's Degree in Spanish as a Second Language at the Complutense University (non-native speakers of Spanish from Asian countries, level C, 21–22 years old) participated in the study. The study was carried out during regular lessons by means of tasks that were part of the subject matter.

In order to answer our research questions, we designed five tests, which will be explained in the next sub-sections. The tests focused on the lexical and semantic relations presented in the previous sections. In all five cases, the test was a simple questionnaire with five or six words to be defined by the students. The same test was used as pre-test and post-test to measure the efficacy of teaching, as shown in the following paragraphs.

We worked with the scheduled assignments listed in Table 1 (bear in mind that we worked with vocabulary in Spanish, but have translated the content of the Table into English for practical reasons):

Table 1. The five assignments with their corresponding vocabulary

Schedule	Assignment 1, 1st week	Assignment 2, 2nd week	Assignment 3, 3th week	Assignment 4, 4th week	Assignment 5, 5th week
Words to define	*sick, surgeon, patient, alcohol, thermometer, vaccine*	*medicine, pulmonologist, bathroom scale, injection, pill*	*happy, euphoric, melancholic, sad, choleric*	*football, calisthenics, enrage, frustrated, physical exercise, track*	*temperament, character, personality, mood, humour*
Didactic material	Vocabulary book, 1st subject: "In the hospital"	Mind Map: "I'm sick"	Mind Map: "The emotions"	Text created *ad hoc*: "Am I an athlete?"	Mind Map created *ad hoc*: "How am I?"

The objective of rewriting the definitions of assignment 1 was to verify if there was any difference between the definitions before and after learning the vocabulary in class. Students wrote the second definitions a week after the class because we wanted to measure the effects of the different learning activities on long term memory. In conclusion, we worked with an identical pre-test and post-test for each activity. In order to keep the students from guessing our procedure, in the midst of these tasks we introduced some exercises not related to our study.

Why did we use definitions in the test? First of all, because definition represents a viable method to know meaning. Secondly, because most of the semantic and lexical relations present in the glosses of LFs we are interested in (hypernym, *type of* and *useful for*) are usually explicit in the definitions. Consequently, definitions allow us to know if there is any difference before and after the class with respect to the knowledge of each word. The richer the definition is in lexical-semantic relations including collocations, the more complete the knowledge of the meaning is. We consider that changes in the same definitions from one week to another would prove (or not) our hypothesis.

Why did we select this vocabulary? The vocabulary of the two first assignments was selected because it includes three interesting lexical-semantic relations: hypernyms, *type of* and *useful for*. In addition, on several previous occasions we used the book (Baralo et al. 2017) and the lexical semantic mind-map with concrete nouns (see Fig. 3) with students of Spanish, confirming that they improve their vocabulary with both methodologies. The lexicon of emotions was selected because it contains types of abstract and complex nouns, and the sports vocabulary because this type of lexicon is half way between concrete vocabulary and abstract vocabulary. Finally, personality vocabulary, as mentioned before, was selected because we had worked on it without success using the texts and definitions of a Vocabulary book (Prada et al. 2012). Understanding this small set of words constitutes a challenge, even for native Spanish speakers. Consequently, this vocabulary could be considered as one of the most difficult sets of words we could teach.

Lastly, the final question that arises is: Why maps and texts? We selected three maps and two texts in order to measure differences between a traditional tool (text and exercises), and our tool (lexical-semantic mind maps). We used one text created *ad hoc* (assignment 4) because we wanted to compare the results with those of the text from the book (assignment 1). We used a mind map created *ad hoc* (assignment 5) because we wanted to compare the results with the ones from the students' maps (assignment 2 and 3).

4.2   Description of the Concrete Texts and Lexical-Semantic Mind Maps Used

Regarding the concrete tasks, the first week we used a text and exercises from Baralo et al. (2017), which is a learning vocabulary book (level B2). This book focuses on vocabulary and collocations more than on grammar. The text and all the exercises of the subject selected were about going to the hospital. The second week we used the lexical semantic map "I'm sick" (by Paula Hernandez, https://masespanol.es/proyecto-innova cion-2017-18-mapas-mentales-lexico-colocaciones-y-locuciones/), a map comprising, in turn, six maps.

Figure 3 shows the first one, which summarizes all the content of the following maps: if I'm sick, I go to the pharmacy; if I do not recover, I go to the outpatient clinic; if the doctor thinks that it is necessary, I go to the hospital. The second illustration shows the fifth map, which reflects the lexical-semantic relations *part of the body-specialist*:

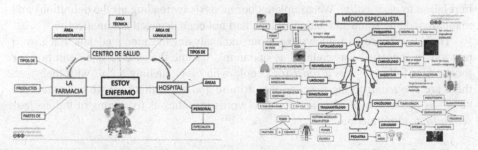

Fig. 3. Two excerpts from the mind map "Estoy enfermo" (I am sick)

The third week we used a map developed by two students (Montserrat Plata and Laura Labrada, see the previous link). Focusing on lexical and semantic relations of emotions The fourth week we used a text created *ad hoc* with some collocations about to be (or not to be) very athletic, such as *to practice sports*, *to go to the mountains*, *to play basketball*, etc. And the last week we used the lexical-semantic mind map created *ad hoc* about personality (see Sect. 3).

4.3   Applying Qualitative Techniques

After collecting the definitions written by the students, we manually copied all the contents in a word document and analysed the results with the Atlas-Ti program. We were interested in three lexical-semantic relations, hypernym, *type of, useful for*; and one semantic relation which we call *nuclear semantic features*. The last one is directly related to the meaning of words and describes semantic features we consider relevant to the understanding of this meaning. We discarded the relation *part of* because it is not usual in the selected lexical fields.

The Atlas-Ti program allows annotation of the texts. For each test, we created one text containing the first and second definitions of the seven students. We annotated the five texts by means of semantic labels combining the automatic annotation of the Atlas-Ti program with semi-automatic and manual annotations. We used automatic annotations for some formulas clearly attached to lexical-semantic relations, such as "is a type of" (for *type of* relations) or "it is useful for" (for *useful for* relations). We used a semi-automatic annotation (we manually deleted the false results) for the expression "is a" (for the relation of hypernymy).

The *nuclear semantic features* relation was annotated automatically and some values were added manually. For instance, we defined *health* as a *nuclear semantic feature* for the words *sick* and *patient*. We automatically obtained the definitions containing the word *health* and maintained the results for those two words, deleting other results, such as *alcohol*. The same was done with the words *emotion*, *positive* and *negative*, present in the definitions of the lexical field of emotions. The words *sport*, *team*, *ball*, *goal*, *foot* were also labelled as *nuclear semantic feature* within the definition of the word *football*, as were the other words of this lexical field. For the last test we considered the words *genetics* and *birth* as nuclear in the definition of the word *temperament*; the words *education*, *childhood* and *culture* in the definition of *character*; and *experience* in relation to *personality*. We completed our analysis by reading all the definitions and manually adding some annotations which had not been detected automatically.

The Atlas-Ti program allows exporting and analysing the annotated data. Each word previously annotated was counted as one item. Assume the case of one definition for *football*, as follows: "it is a *sport* for people who play touching a *ball* with their *feet*, there are two *teams* trying to score one or more *goals*". In this case we had annotated "is a" as one *hyponym* item, and the five words in italics as five items of the *nuclear semantic feature* relation.

5 Results and Discussion

Figure 1 summarizes the results by tests. Each chart shows one of the four lexical-semantic relations analysed. The columns reflect the number of items counted; the base of each column reflects the test by means of a correlative number: 1_1 is the first part of the first test, 1_2 the second part of the first test, and so on and so forth (consider that some tests do not yield any data pertaining to some of the relations in which we are interested).

The data indicates that the richest lexical-semantic relation in terms of number of items is *nuclear semantic features*, while the poorest is *useful for*. From our point of view, this is a consequence of the selection of the lexical fields, because as mentioned in Sect. 3, the relation *useful for* is very productive for artefacts, a type of noun only present in test 1 and 2. On the other hand, as mentioned in Sect. 4.2, *nuclear semantic features* were particularly abundant in test 4 (see Sect. 4). In this sense, this first datum is not relevant for our research question.

The relation *type of* increases lightly after the first and second assignment, whilst slightly decreasing after the fourth assignment. The principal difference between these assignments (regarding their design) is that the first two assignments are focused on vocabulary (both contain collocations only to facilitate the vocabulary learning process), while assignment 4 is focused directly on collocations as a subject of learning. The book and the map present their vocabulary content hierarchized or structured, including the relation *type of*; the text of assignment 4 about *to be or not athletic* does not contain structured vocabulary in any sense, which may explain the results.

The *useful for* relation does not yield significant differences. However, minimal differences are conversive: whilst the text of the book about the hospital causes a minimal decrease of the *useful for* relation, the mind map "I'm sick" causes a minimal increase in this relation. This could be related to the fact that the *useful for* relation is only explored within the MTT framework, which explains why the mind-maps contain this relation in an explicit way (see Fig. 2, the ophthalmologist *is useful for* the eyes, etc.), whilst the book does not.

Results related to the hypernym relation are not relevant for tests 3, 4 and 5 (which show similar or slightly higher number of items after their respective assignments). The first two assignments, however, are cause for reflection regarding the results. In fact, the post-test of the first assignment shows the highest results (25 items) followed by the pre-test of this assignment (22 items); the following position is the one of the pre-test of the map of the assignment 2 (16 items) and its post-test (11 items). That could be related to the fact that the book about the hospital collects the vocabulary in a traditional way (for which hypernym is the first and principal manner of categorization). In this sense it is valid to think that the assignment with this book consolidates (and even helps improve) the students' previous hierarchized knowledge. On the other hand, the map "I'm sick" is based on a wider range of lexical-semantic relations (by means of the glosses of the LFs), among others the phases of the process of being sick given (from the pharmacy to the family doctor, and then to the specialist, etc.) In addition, the information is distributed visually as a mind map, which does not follow the hierarchy related to the hyponym, which could explain the results summarized in Fig. 4.

The analysis of the data of the *nuclear semantic features* relation points out that the text of the book based on vocabulary and collocations (assignment 1) and the map (assignment 2) are related to a minor increment in the *nuclear semantic features* (5 items plus for the first test and 6 items plus for the second one), whilst the mind map of emotions (assignment 3) is related to a loss of items reflecting this relation (11 items lost). In this respect, we interpret that the book about the hospital and the map "I'm sick", which contains concrete nouns, had a minimal positive influence on students regarding knowledge of the meaning of words (with no significant differences between both assignments). However, the mind map for emotions (focused on abstract nouns), had a negative influence.

The comparison of the results of the pre-test and post-test for assignments 4 and 5 is relevant for our research question. Assignment 4 suggests a strong loss of *nuclear semantic features* (35 items are lost) and assignment 5 causes a relevant advantage (21 items are gained). Why is there such a large difference between both assignments? As mentioned when reflecting on the results of *type of*, assignment 4 focused on learning collocations related to sports, but did not necessarily imply any relevant result regarding the meaning of these words, which is the issue measured by the *nuclear semantic features* relation.

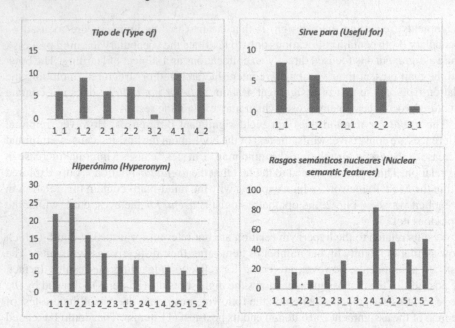

Fig. 4. Comparative charts by tests for the four lexical-semantic relations analysed

The mind map about personality, however, was created *ad hoc* showing the collocations in order to better know the meaning of the words involved in these collocations. As a result, the students understood better the meaning of the words *temperament, character* and *personality*. In any case, both assignments were useful for learning collocations.

In summary, the analysis of the results shows that the text of the book based on collocations was helpful to learn hypernyms and *type of* relations. The lexical-semantic map containing concrete nouns was helpful to learn *type of*, *useful for* and some other specific lexical-semantic relations, albeit the map containing abstract nouns did not prove to be efficient. Furthermore, the text created *ad hoc* to learn the patterns that underlie the collocations of the lexical field of sports was not effective to learn any of the lexical-semantic relations measured, although they were useful to learn collocations. And finally, the lexical-semantic map created *ad hoc*, based on collocations by means of glosses of LFs, led to a significant improvement in the knowledge of the meaning of the words. Consequently, our data suggest that lexical-semantic mind maps created by means of glosses of LFs, the tool proposed in this study, could be exploited in order to teach the meaning of words in SLT. This study could serve as a model to be further implemented in other research studies and evaluated under true experimental conditions.

Acknowledgments. This work was carried out within the framework of project DiRetEs (II) and was supported by the Ministry of Science and Innovation of Spain (PID2021-122894-NB-I00) and the FEDER Program (European Union).

References

Aitchison, J.: Words in the Mind: an Introduction to the Mental Lexicon. Basil Blackwell, Oxford (1987)

Apresjan, J.: Systematic Lexicography. Oxford University Press, Oxford (2000)

Baralo, M., Genís, M., Santana, M.E.: Vocabulario B2. Anaya, Madrid (2017)

Barrios, M.A.: El dominio de las Funciones Léxicas en el marco de la Teoría Sentido-Texto. Estudios de Lingüística del español (30) (2010). http://elies.rediris.es/elies.html

Barrios, M.A.: Las colocaciones del español. Arco/Libros, Madrid (2015)

Barrios, M.A.: Propuesta metodológica para la enseñanza de las colocaciones de verbo soporte a estudiantes anglófonos: un estudio empírico. MarcoELE **23**, 1−13 (2016). http://marcoele. com/colocaciones-verbales/

Barrios, M.A.: Mapas conceptuales y mentales: una experiencia de aprendizaje colaborativo. In: Gázquez Linares, J.J., et al. (eds.) Innovación docente e investigación en Arte y Humanidades, pp. 881–893. Dykinson, Madrid (2019)

Boguslavsky, I., Barrios, M.A., Diachenko, P.: CALLEX-ESP: a software system for learning Spanish lexicon and collocations. In: Méndez, A., Solano, A., Mesa, J.A., Mesa, J. (eds.) Current Development in Technology-Assisted Education, pp. 22−26. Formatex, Badajoz (2006)

Boers, F., Eyckmans, J., Cappel, J., Stengers, H., Demecheleer, M.: Formulaic sequences and perceived oral proficiency: putting a Lexical Approach to the test. Lang. Teach. Res. **10**(3), 245–261 (2006)

Boers, F., Demecheleer, M., Coxhead, C., Webb, S.: Gauging the effects of exercises on verb-noun collocations. Lang. Teach. Res. **18**(1), 54–74 (2014)

Bosque, I.: Redes. Diccionario Combinatorio del Español Contemporáneo. S.M., Madrid (2004)

Bosque, I.: Diccionario Combinatorio Práctico del Español Contemporáneo. S.M., Madrid (2006)

Bosque, I.: On the conceptual bases of collocation: restricted adverbs and lexical selection. In: Torner, S., Bernal, E. (eds.) Collocations and Other Lexical Combinations in Spanish, pp. 9–20. Routledge, Abingdon (2017)

Flick, U.: Introducción a la investigación cualitativa. Trad. Tomás del Amo. Ediciones Morata, Madrid (2012)

García Salido, M., Alonso Ramos, M.: Asignación de niveles de aprendizaje a las colocaciones del Diccionario de Colocaciones del español. Signos **51**(97), 153–174 (2018)

Higueras García, M.: Lexical collocations and the learning of Spanish as a foreign language: state of the art and future projects. In: Cifuentes Honrubia, J.L., Rodríguez, S. (eds.) Spanish Word Formation and Lexical Creation, pp. 439–463. John Benjamins, Amsterdam (2011)

Koike, K.: Colocaciones léxicas en el español actual. Universidad de Alcalá de Henares, Alcalá de Henares (2001)

Leonardi, V.: The Role of Pedagogical Translation in Second Language Acquisition. Peter Lang, Bern (2010)

Lewis, M.: The Lexical Approach. Language Teaching Publications, London (1993)

Lewis, M.: Teaching Collocation. Further Developments in the Lexical Approach. Language Teaching Publications, London (2000)

Li, J., Schmitt, N.: The development of collocation use in academic texts by advanced L2 learners: a multiple case study approach. In: Wood, D. (ed.) Perspectives on Formulaic Language: Acquisition and Communication, pp. 22–46. Continuum, New York (2010)

Lindstromberg, S., Boers, F.: Teaching Chunks of Language. From Noticing to Remembering. Helbling Languages, Rum (2008)

López Ferrero, C., Battaner, P.: Learning Spanish L1 vocabulary in context. In: Torner, S., Bernal, E. (eds.) Collocations and Other Lexical Combinations in Spanish. Theoretical, Lexicographical and Applied Perspectives, pp. 267–286. Routledge, Abingdon (2017)

Maxwell, J.A.: Qualitative Research Design. An Interactive Approach. Sage Publications, Thousand Oaks (2012)

Mel'čuk, I.: Lexical functions: a tool for the description of lexical relations in a lexicon. In: Wanner, L. (ed.) Lexical Functions in Lexicography and Natural Language Processing, pp. 37–102. John Benjamins, Amsterdam (1996)

Mel'čuk, I.: Semantics: From Meaning to Text, vol. III (Studies in Language Companion Series 129). John Benjamins, Amsterdam & Philadelphia (2014)

Mel'čuk, I., Wanner, L.: Lexical functions and lexical inheritance for emotion lexemes in German. In: Wanner, L. (ed.) Lexical Functions in Lexicography and Natural Language Processing, pp. 37–102, 209–278. John Benjamins, Amsterdam (1996)

Polguère, A.: Towards a theoretically-motivated general public dictionary of semantic derivations and collocations for French. In: Heid, U., et al. (eds.) Proceedings of the Ninth EURALEX International Congress, pp. 517–527. Euralex, Stuggart (2000)

Polguère, A., Mel'čuk, I.: Dérivations sémantiques et collocations dans le DiCo/LAF. In: Blumenthal, P., Hausmann, F.J. (eds.) Langue française, 150. Collocations, corpus, dictionnaires, pp. 66–83. Larouse, Paris (2006)

de Prada, M., Salazar, D., Molero, C.M.: Uso interactivo del vocabulario y sus combinaciones más frecuentes (B2–C2). Edelsa, Madrid (2012)

Sanromán Vila, B.: Semántica, sintaxis y combinatoria léxica de los nombres de emoción en español. Universidad de Helsinki, Helsinki (2003)

Sanromán Vila, B., Alonso Ramos, M.: Collocation dictionary as an elaborate pedagogical tool for Spanish as a foreign language. In: Nenonen, M., Niemi, S. (eds.) Collocations and Idioms 1: Papers From the First Nordic Conference On Syntactic Freezes, pp. 282–296. Joensuun Yliopisto, Joensuu (2007)

Stake, R.E.: Investigación con estudio de casos. Fillella, R. (trad). Morata, Madrid (2010)

Wray, A.: Formulaic Language and the Lexicon. C. University Press, Cambridge (2002)

Teaching and Learning French Formulas

Elena Berthemet[(⊠)]

Centre de Linguistique en Sorbonne, Paris, France
elenaberthemet@gmail.com

Abstract. The appropriate use of formulas in discourse involves the ability to manage a complex interplay of linguistic, paralinguistic, and pragmatic properties. Given this complexity, we will try to answer the following question: what type of information about formulas do learners need to develop their own pragmatic competence? The problem is addressed from both theoretical and applied points of view. Although the present study is based on analysis of French formulas, it seems that a similar method can be applicable to other foreign languages. The article is structured as follows. Section 1 presents an overview of the previous work on phraseology and the research questions for this study. Section 2 discusses the nature of formulas. Once their main characteristics have thus been identified, Sects. 3 and 4 consider semantic, prosodic, gestural, and pragmatic challenges learners face in learning formulas. Section 5 focuses on the treatment of formulas in dictionaries. A model for describing formulas is illustrated in Sect. 6. Some conclusions are drawn at the end.

Keywords: Interactive communication · Dictionaries · Phraseology · Pragmatics · Prosody · Semantics

1 Previous Research on Phraseology

The study of phraseology in the broad sense is now approached in a multitude of different ways. Most theoretical and descriptive approaches to phraseological units focus on their structural, semantic, pragmatic, discourse, cognitive, psycholinguistic, cultural and corpus linguistic aspects. There is a rich body of theoretical work:

- International studies [34, 8, 13–16, 18, 19, 30, 32, 36, 40];
- French studies [6, 7, 10, 20, 21, 25];
- Russian studies [1–3, 33, 35, 40].

There is a substantial amount of work on second language learning and teaching of phraseological units and development of phraseological competence [8, 9, 11, 14, 17, 19, 22, 39, 40] and on phraseography [2, 8, 14, 27].

Evidence from a variety of studies suggests that phraseological units help users to be more fluent. In fact, "It is now widely accepted that [...] phraseological competence is an important part of native-like, fluent, and idiomatic language use. [...] The use of phraseological units such as collocations [...] and idioms may impact positively or

G. Corpas Pastor and R. Mitkov (Eds.): EUROPHRAS 2022, LNAI 13528, pp. 31–46, 2022.
https://doi.org/10.1007/978-3-031-15925-1_3

negatively on the three dimensions of language proficiency – complexity, accuracy, and fluency" [31]. Moreover, phraseological units provide "a platform for more fluent and accurate output that Dechert called "islands of reliability" [12]. In fact, as it will be pointed in the next sections, using formulas allows non-natives" to interact with others and to become integrated into the new society.

Although there is a wealth of studies about phraseological units, not much attention has been given to teaching formulas. Due to their properties, discussed in Sects. 2–4, formulas pose considerable difficulties, even for advanced students. For learners, formulas are problematic both from decoding and encoding perspectives. For instance, non-natives may not recognize the communicative function of these signals, or may use them in an inappropriate situation, or with the wrong intonation. The present study sets out to examine the following inter-related questions: (1) What information do learners need when learning formulas? (2) How do prosody and gestures interact with the meanings of formulas? (3) What information is significant? (4) How can this information be presented lexicographically? Each formula is written in *italics* and followed by an English translation in single quotation marks: *Tu parles!* 'You speak'.

Let us start with a definition of a formula.

2 What is a Formula

In this work the umbrella term *formula* is used instead of the words *actes de langage stéréotypés* (Kauffer), *conversational routines* (Coulmas, Kesckes), *conventional expressions* (Bardovi-Harlig), *formulas* (Bardovi-Harlig, Kerbrat-Orecchioni, Pamies), *politeness formulas* (Ferguson, Pagliaro), *pragmatic routines* (Bardovi-Harlig), *pragmatèmes* (Melcuk, Polguère), *pragmatèmes polylexicaux* (Blanco Escoda, Mejri), *routine formulae, formules routinières, Routineformeln* (Cowie, Gläser, Gonzalez Rey), *situationbound utterances* (Kecskes), *social lubrificators* (Binon, Verlinde) and *speech formulae* (Granger, Paquot) for purely economic reasons.

Formulas are phraseological units which function in human communication and are reactions to the context, i.e., to what is said, seen or to any other verbal or non-verbal type of information. They share a great amount of features with other idioms: multi-words, property of reproduction, non-compositional semantics, and, usually, the difficulty to translate them literally. Formulas do not describe the reality but rather perform speech acts, and/or convey emotions and sentiments. They differ from idioms in that they are: independent clauses most of the time, context-dependent, semantically more transparent than idioms (their meaning is weakly compositional) and found in conversational (interactive) direct speech.

Since formulas engage both the speaker and the listener, knowledge of formulas is crucial for interactive communication. Pragmatic competence, defined as "the ability to communicate and interpret meaning in social interactions" [38] is vital for successful communication. Pragmatic competence involves an interplay of linguistic, para- and extralinguistic knowledge. How to teach pragmatic competence? How to teach formulas? Answering these questions is no easy task, and relies on the function of formulas in speech considered in the next sections.

It should be mentioned that since a great number of formulas are found in informal dialogic speech and express the speaker's emotions and sentiments, some of them include impolite or indecent words and are perceived as subnormal (colloquial, rude, or vulgar). Therefore, the question about the place of formulas like *T'es con* 'You are fool' and *Mon cul* 'My ass' in the teaching vocabulary can arise. We think that, even though they contain words deviating from the norm, these 'impolite' formulas can be taught and described in learners' dictionaries. First, they are part of everyday conversations, and if a non-native misunderstands a formula, it can result in communication failure. For instance, s/he could understand *T'es con* 'You are fool' in the literal sense and interpret it as an offence, whereas the speaker used it with the meaning "Your joke makes me laugh". Second, low-register formulas are also part of the phraseological system and cannot be excluded from it merely because they contain words that are not socially acceptable. For example, the neutral formula *Mon œil* 'My eye' and its rude equivalent *Mon cul* 'My ass' both mean "I don't believe you". The majority of formulas do not appertain to academic vocabulary. However, identification and awareness of such formulas may help students to better integrate into the new society. In fact, the corresponding register should be indicated to help students not to use them in an inappropriate context. Unfortunately, this article is too short to explore the question of stylistic labels in phraseology, so we will move straight on to the meaning of formulas.

3 Understanding Formulas

A general consensus in pragmatics is that meaning, that is the meaning-in-use, is dynamic. Some aspects of meaning can be found in language, others in usage and users. Thus, the function of formulas results from the interaction between linguistic, paralinguistic, and pragmatic properties. In this section, the following characteristics of formulas will be considered: interactivity (Subsect. 3.1), context dependency (Subsect. 3.2), multimodality (Subsect. 3.3 and 3.4) and pragmatics (Sect. 4).

3.1 Interactivity

The meanings of formulas are intersubjective, constructed and negotiated through conversations. They can be viewed as a result of *co-construction* [28] or *intercompréhension* 'interunderstanding' [23] emerging from an interactional conversation. That means that it is not sufficient for the speaker to use an appropriate formula: the hearer also takes part in the construction of the meaning. In fact, "meaning is the result of interplay between the speaker's private context and the hearer's private context in the actual situational context as understood by the interlocutors" [22]. Meanings are intersubjective because they emerge "from the memories, emotions, perceptions, experiences, and the life worlds of those who participate in the communication" [28]. It is interesting to notice the use of the prefixes "inter" and "co" in the words *co-construction*, *interunderstanding*, *interactional*, and *interplay*, insisting on the involvement of both the message producer and the interpreter. In other words, when the speaker takes part in a conversation, he speaks, listens, acts and interacts, i.e., speaking equals changing.

Conversations are structured and governed by rules, determined by the sociolinguistic settings of the linguo-cultural community. These rules differ according to cultures: each participant has to use an appropriate register, to speak in turn, to respect speaking time, and to consider relations between interlocutors. As Kathleen Bardovi-Harlig points out, "the study of formulas within the framework of pragmatics emphasizes the degree to which use of a formula is part of a social contract. Using formulas for pragmatic functions not only follows tacit social agreements, but it also signals the membership of participants in particular speech communities" [4]. In this sense, formulas can be considered as linguo-cultural markers of communication.

Depending on the formula, contexts can require an answer (another prefabricated unit or a freely compositional phrase) or not. Because students don't have this common sociolinguistic ground on which the understanding is built, the "situations requiring a pragmatic routine in one language but an ad hoc formulation in the other; [and] situations requiring a pragmatic routine in one language but no remark in the other" [5] are not easy to acquire.

The next formulas comment and/or analyse a situation, and therefore do not require an answer (Table 1):

Table 1. Comment and analyse formulas

Formula	Paraphrase
Tu parles! 'You speak'	Yes, of course! or Of course not!
Tu veux ma photo? 'Do you want my picture?'	Why are you staring at me?
Simple comme bonjour 'Easy like hello'	It is easy to do
Tu n'as (plus) que tes yeux pour pleurer 'You have (only) your eyes for crying'	It is too late to repair the damage
C'est cuit 'It is cooked'	It is too late
C'est du gâteau 'It is a piece of cake'	It is easy to do
T'es con 'You are fool'	Your joke makes me laugh

For example, it is inappropriate to respond by saying *Oui* 'Yes' or *Non* 'Non' to *Tu parles!* 'You speak'. The same stands for *Tu veux ma photo?* 'Do you want my picture?' unless the hearer wants to provoke the hearer.

3.2 Context Dependency

Formulas are context-dependent. For instance, the formula *Ça va?* 'How are you?' has different meanings depending on:

• The place where it is said

  o In a store, it means 'what do you think about it?';
  o To a doctor, its meaning is 'do you have health problems?';
  o Between friends, in response to a proposal to have a drink, it stands for 'no thanks'.

- The geographical location

  o   In France, one of its functions is a refusal for a proposal 'no, thanks';
  o   In Belgium, it will be used to ask if the hearer has understood the speaker's words.
      For example, *Le palais des congrès se trouve à 800 mètres, ça va ?*.

The next point that deserves to be described in the article concerns prosodic properties of formulas.

3.3   Prosodic Properties of Formulas

We think that prosodic information should be included in linguistic meanings. In fact, to understand a formula, learners have to understand not only the words but also how these words are said. However, prosodic information is difficult to formalise.

The examples in this chapter are taken from a corpus of pronunciation of fifteen formulas by twenty students in first year of Master's degree in French as a Foreign Language, who are native speakers of French. They were recorded in 2021 and 2022. Each formula is polysemic and has at least two meanings, a literal and an idiomatic one. First, participants were asked to imagine the extralinguistic situation and to read aloud scripted sentences assigned with a particular meaning. The work was made at home, using the program https://vocaroo.com/. The corpus consists of 80 audio recordings, with an average of three versions of each meaning. Participants were told that the aim of study was to analyse the link between pronunciation and meaning. Second, all good quality records were listened to by all the students during the class. They were asked to choose the meaning they heard and to check it on the paper. Then, the results were gathered, and the records were analysed in two ways: by listening, and by software (http://www.praat.org/).

Several observations can be made based on this analysis. The first concerns possible criticisms of the methodology: formulas were used out of context; pronounced with a pedagogical goal; some of the recordings sound unnatural, and some of them are of poor quality. The second is that human ears are possibly not the best analysers of the prosody. The third is about the number of occurrences which is not sufficient to draw any substantial conclusions. Finally, the occurrences of the same formula can display a range of prosodic variants. It is not easy to decide if that variation is individual, i.e., speaker-dependent or formulaic, i.e., meaning-dependent.

The analysis yielded four different groups:

1) Formulas with prosody superior to a verbal utterance,
2) Weakly context-dependent formulas,
3) Highly contextual formulas,
4) Context-ambiguous formula.

Some examples are analysed below. In this work, prosody is considered from a semantic perspective rather than a phonological one. This restriction is imposed merely for practical reasons. Our aim is to give the student an idea of the most important notions: pitch, pauses, and prosodic stress. Non-linguistic words such as 'sounding happy, sad or excited' were used as well. Conventions for the transcription are the following: the up arrow ↑ means the rise in pitch, the down arrow ↓ indicates the fall in pitch, the symbol # marks a short pause. The main prosodic stress is in SMALL CAPITALS. English translations are in 'single quotation marks'.

In the first column the reader will find the French formula and its English translation, in the second column its pronunciation, and in the third one its meaning. In this last column, the sign '~' replaces the formula, the letter 'A' is used for the speaker, the letter 'B' for the hearer. Each definition is conceived on the same model: 'A says ~ to B for what purpose(s): *Paraphrase*'. The paraphrase is a free compositional phrase which may replace the formula.

In two following formulas prosody is superior to a verbal utterance (Table 2):

Table 2. Formulas with prosody superior to a verbal utterance

Formula	Pronunciation	Meaning
Ah ça! 'Ah, this'	Ah↑ ça↑	1) (litt.) A dit ~ à B pour parler du sujet évoqué auparavant, mais oublié par A: *Ah, oui, je n'y pensais plus.* '(lit.) A says ~ to B to speak about a topic discussed earlier, but forgotten by A: *Ah, yes, I had forgotten this*'
	Ah↓ ça↓	2) A dit ~ à B pour lui exprimer son accord: *Je suis complétement d'accord avec ça.* 'A says ~ to B to express his/her agreement: *I completely agree with you*'
Il (ne) fallait pas! 'You should not have'	Il (ne) FAllait↑ pas↑	1) (litt.) A dit ~ à B pour lui exprimer sa désapprobation: *Tu n'aurais pas dû le faire.* '(lit.) A says ~ to B to express his/her disapproval: *You should not have done this*'
	Il (ne) FAllait↑ pAs↓	2) A dit ~ à B pour le remercier d'un cadeau: *C'est très gentil de ta part.* 'A says ~ to B to thank B for a gift: *It is so kind of you*'

As for the *Ah ça!* 'Ah, this' formula, the "agreement" meaning is usually spoken with a descending intonation: Ah↓ ça↓, while the literal meaning is spoken with a rising intonation: Ah↑ ça↑. The "disapproval" meaning of *Il (ne) fallait pas* 'You should not have' is spoken with a rise in pitch, while its second meaning is marked by a tonic accent on pAs↓ and the fall in pitch. Given that these two formulas were recognised by all participants, we may assume that the intonation here plays an important role.

The next two formulas were not recognised by one or two students (Table 3).

Table 3. Weakly context-dependent formulas

Formula	Pronunciation	Meaning
Je te jure! 'I swear to you!'	Je te JUre↑ !	1) (litt.) A dit ~ à B pour faire un serment: *Tu peux me croire, je te dis la vérité.* '(lit.) A says ~ to B to swear an oath: *You can believe me, I am telling the truth*'
	Je te JUre↓ !	2) A dit ~ à B pour exprimer son mécontentement: *Ça m'énerve.* 'A says ~ to B to express his discontent: *It makes me angry*'
Tu m'étonnes! 'You astonish me!'	Tu m'étonnes↑	1) (litt.) A dit ~ à B parce que B l'a surpris: *Je suis surpris par ce que je viens d'entendre/voir.* '(lit.) A says ~ to B because A is surprised by B: *I am surprised by what I have heard/seen*'
	Tu m'étonnes↓	2) A dit ~ à B pour exprimer son accord avec ce que B a dit: *Je suis d'accord avec toi ! Bien sûr que oui!* 'A says ~ to B to express his agreement with what B has just said: *I agree with you! Yes, of course!*'

As can be seen, using a rising tone of voice indicates that *Je te jure* 'I swear to you!' has the 'oath' meaning, while a descending intonation conveys the 'discontent' meaning. However, these changes are subtle. As for the two meanings of *Tu m'étonnes!* 'You astonish me!', they are clearly distinguished by a rising intonation for the 'surprise', and a fall in pitch for the 'agreement' and a tonic accent on 'm'Étonnes'. It must be said that extralinguistic situation could play a role in disambiguating the meaning of these two formulas.

Students were not unanimous in recognising the meaning of the next two formulas (Table 4):

The formula *C'est terrible!* 'It is terrible' is used both for the "fear" and the "wonder". None of the recorded pronunciations plays a role in disambiguating of the meaning. The formula *C'est pas vrai!* 'It's not true' is highly polysemic. It can be used for "disbelief, astonishment, disapproval, and admiration". Only the first meaning, the literal one, is characterized by a slightly different intonation because it is not marked by a tonic accent on 'vrai', while the three other meanings are marked by a tonic accent on 'vrAI'. For this formula, it was difficult to identify the underlying meaning. The only distinctive property could be the context. In fact, the communicative situation, be it extralinguistic situation, sad or happy voice, and mimics, may help the hearer to understand what the speaker meant.

Table 4. Highly contextual formulas

Formula	Pronunciation	Meaning
C'est terrible! 'It is terrible'	C'est # TErrible↑	A dit ~ à B pour partager son angoisse: *C'est horrible !* 'A says ~ to B to convey his/her fear: *It is horrible!*'
	C'est # TErrible↑	A dit ~ à B pour partager son émerveillement: *C'est extraordinaire !* 'A says ~ to B to convey his/her wonder: *It is extraordinary!*'
C'est pas vrai ! 'It's not true'	C'est pAs vrai ↑	(litt.) A dit ~ à B pour exprimer son l'incrédulité: *Ce que j'entends/vois est faux.* '(lit.) A says ~ to B to express his/her disbelief: *What I hear/see is false.*'
	C'est pAs vrAI ↑	A dit ~ à B pour exprimer sa surprise, son étonnement: *Je ne m'attendais pas du tout à ça.* 'A says ~ to B to express his/her surprise, astonishment: *I was not expecting this at all.*'
	C'est pAs vrAI ↑	A dit ~ à B pour exprimer sa désapprobation: *Je suis choqué par ce que je viens d'apprendre.* 'A says ~ to B to express his/her disapproval: *I am shocked by what I have just found out.*'
	C'est pAs vrAI ↑	A dit ~ à B pour exprimer son admiration: *Ce que je vois, j'entends me plait beaucoup.* 'A says ~ to B to express his/her admiration: *I like what I see, what I hear.*'

However, sometimes, even the context doesn't help the hearer to identify the meaning of the formula. For instance, the formula *Tu parles!* 'You speak' is highly ambiguous. As it is shown in Table 5, its function is to agree or not agree with the speaker.

Table 5. Context-ambiguous formula

Formula	Pronunciation	Meaning
Tu parles! 'You speak'	Tu parles↓	1) A dit ~ à B parce qu'il n'est pas d'accord avec ce que B a dit: *Bien sûr que non !* 'A says ~ to B because A doesn't agree with B: *Of course not!*'
	Tu parles↓	2) A dit ~ à B parce qu'il est d'accord avec ce que B a dit: *Bien sûr que oui !* 'A says ~ to B because A completely agrees with B: *Yes, of course!*'

What can be concluded from this brief analysis? Although the prosody does help disambiguate the meaning of formulas, as in *Ah ça!* 'Ah, this' and *Il (ne) fallait pas* 'You should not have', it is not clear to what extent it contributes to the meaning. Can the meaning of a formula be deduced by taking into consideration only the prosody? The answer is probably no. In light of the above discussion, we think that prosody can be considered as a contribution to meaning: in some instances, it is involved with the message a speaker conveys, in other instances, it is not decisive.

3.4 Gestural Properties of Formulas

As explained below in Table 6, gestures also contribute to the meanings of formulas. Let us consider the two meanings of the formula *Ah la barbe!* 'Ah, the beard':

Table 6. Gestures in formulas

Formula	Pronunciation	Meaning
Ah la barbe! 'Ah, the beard'	Ah # la barbe↑	1) (litt.) A dit ~ à B parce qu'il vient de voir une barbe qui l'a impressionné: *Je suis surpris par sa barbe.* '(lit.) A says ~ to B because he/she has just seen a huge beard: *I am astonished by his beard.*'
	Ah la barbe↓	2) A dit ~ à B pour exprimer son mécontentement: *Ça m'énerve ! J'en ai marre!* 'A says ~ to B to express his/her discontent: *That's so annoying! I am fed up!*'

As can be seen, the second meaning of the formula *Ah la barbe!* 'Ah, the beard' is vocally marked by a descending intonation and visually by rolling eyes, sighing, rubbing the cheek with phalanges, making a hand movement like sweeping something away, swinging arms ahead, or moving a hand above the head. Taking up the idea of Langacker, gestures can be considered "an optional component of a demonstrative's linguistic form" [24].

4 Pragmatic Properties of Formulas

4.1 Speech Acts

The final question concerns the pragmatic properties of formulas. Learning formulas means learning their functions. Following Baranov and Dobrovol'kiĭ [2], formulas are illocutionary acts. Used in a conversation, they are addressed to the hearer, and are intended to act on him or to interact with him. As one can see below, formulas may fulfil a variety of different functions such as *agreement, disagreement, disapproval, disbelief, encouragement, order, permission, prevention,* etc. (Table 7):

As can be seen, functions can overlap: a single formula often performs more than one function. Another purpose closely related to speech acts is to express the speaker's emotions and sentiments.

Table 7. Functions of formulas

Functions (speech acts and affects)	Formula	Paraphrase
Agreement	*Ah ça!* 'Ah that'	I completely agree with that
	Tu m'étonnes! 'You astonish me'	I completely agree with you
	Tu parles 'You speak'	Yes, of course!
Disagreement	*Ben voyons* 'What's going on?'	Oh, please!
	Tu parles 'You speak'	Of course not!
Disbelief	*Je demande à voir* 'I ask to see'	I need evidence to believe you
	Mon cul 'My ass'	I don't believe you
	Mon œil 'My eye'	I don't believe you
Encouragement	*Si ce n'est pas trop demander* 'If it is not too much to ask'	If you please?
	C'est quand tu veux! 'It is when do you want!'	You can do it right now!
Prevention	*Ça sent le cramé [roussi]* 'It smells burnt'	I think it can go wrong
	Fais gaffe 'Take care'	Look out
Order to stop + disapproval	*Tu la boucles !* 'You close it'	Shut up!
	Arrête ton numéro! 'Stop your performance!'	Stop faking!
Agreement + permission + order to stop + irritation	*C'est bon!* 'It is good!'	I agree with you! It is possible to do it! Please stop! You are getting on my nerves!
Oath + discontent	*Je te jure!* 'I swear to you!'	It makes me angry
Order to leave + irritation	*Du balai!* 'With the broom!'	Go away!
	Du vent! 'With the wind!'	Go away!

4.2 Affect

Some formulas convey the emotions and sentiments of the speaker. The primary function of affect formulas is to convey speakers' feelings about the world. Thus, the formula *Ça par exemple!* 'This for example' is used to express 'surprise', while the formula *C'est énorme!* 'It is enormous' is employed to communicate 'astonishment'. It is not possible to determine if affect formulas are false or true. For example, when someone says *C'est pas possible!* 'It's not possible', which expresses 'exasperation', one could not answer *Oui, c'est vrai* 'Yes, it is true' (Table 8).

Table 8. Affect in formulas

Affect	Formula	Paraphrase
Astonishment	*C'est énorme!* 'It is enormous'	It is huge
Discontent	*Ah la barbe!* 'Ah, the beard !'	Ça m'énerve ! J'en ai marre !
Exasperation	*C'est pas possible!* 'It's not possible'	I can't believe it
Surprise	*Ça par exemple!* 'This for example'	What a surprise!

It is worth noting that speech acts are often also affective, but affects do not always entail speech acts.

5 Formulas in Dictionaries

Despite the general consensus on the importance of formulas in conversation, there is little agreement on how to present formulas in dictionaries. As mentioned earlier, the meaning of formulas is weakly compositional. However, it doesn't mean that a Russian or Chinese learner who knows all the words in *Vous êtes mademoiselle?* 'You are miss?' will understand that it means 'can you tell your name, please?'. In fact, a literal understanding, i.e., word-by-word translation, can result in communication failure. Thus, it is not possible to answer this formula by *Oui* 'Yes', because the speaker is in fact asking the hearer for her name.

How can learners understand the meaning of a formula? They can consult a bilingual dictionary, then a monolingual dictionary and the Internet. Let us try to see what information an English student would find for the formula *Tu parles!* 'You speak!'. The meaning of this frequently used formula is complex. Broadly speaking, it can be paraphrased by *Bien sûr que oui* 'Yes, of course', or by *Bien sûr que non* 'Of course not'. The tricky issue is to know which one it is being used, because, as we will discuss below, neither the prosody, nor the situation play a major role in disambiguation of this formula.

Let us take the bilingual *French-English Collins online free dictionary* (https://www.collinsdictionary.com/dictionary/french-english/tu-parles). As can be seen in Fig. 1, one equivalent, *You must be joking!* is offered:

tu parles!

you must be joking!

Fig. 1. *Tu parles!* 'You speak' in bilingual *French-English Collins dictionary*

The problem is that this English equivalent corresponds only to one of two French meanings. In fact, the second meaning, that of agreement, is not included. Therefore, the English student may end up conveying the opposite meaning to the original French phrase.

The bilingual *Larousse* (https://www.larousse.fr/dictionnaires/francais-anglais/par ler/57899) gives both meanings, and two equivalents *You bet!* and *You must be joking!* (Fig. 2):

◁)) ça t'a plu ? — tu parles !
    a. [bien sûr] ◁)) did you like it? — you bet!
    b. [pas du tout] ◁)) did you like it? — you must be joking!

Fig. 2. *Tu parles!* 'You speak' in bilingual *Larousse* dictionary

This introduction of the formula in a mini dialogue allows the user to see one of the linguistic contexts of use. Thus, the learner observes that this formula is used as an answer, and not as introductory reply in a dialogue.

Most of the time, learners, especially those studying languages for specific purposes, only use bilingual dictionaries. It is worth noting that sometimes a given situation may not be lexicalized in one of the languages. For example, French formulas *Cache ta joie* 'Hide your joy!', *Comme un lundi* 'As on Mondays', *Merci mon chien!* 'Thank you, my dog!', and *Plutôt deux fois qu'une* 'Rather two times than one' are difficult to explain to a Russian student because not only does the equivalent not exist, but in addition situations in which these formulas are used are difficult to explain. In this sense, monolingual dictionaries could compensate for this asymmetry.

Le *Trésor de la Langue Française informatisée* (http://atilf.atilf.fr/) is one of the richest sources for the French language. However, as indicated on the main page, editing was completed in 1994 and it has not been updated since then. In spite of this fact, this resource is frequently referenced in French linguistic research. A search query for the formula *Tu parles!* 'You speak' yields the following result (Fig. 3):

Absol. [Marque l'incrédulité, le désaccord, la réprobation du locuteur] *Pour Heredia, je suis un paresseux. (Tu parles!)* (VALÉRY, *Corresp.* [avec Gide], 1899, p.366). *Goethe eut le sentiment qu'il avait encore bien des choses à apprendre. «De ce jour, clama-t-il, magnifiquement, selon les habitudes de son génie, commence une époque nouvelle! » Tu parles! par la suite, comme le système était excellent, on se mit à fabriquer des héros en série, et qui coûtèrent de moins en moins cher, à cause du perfectionnement du système* (CÉLINE, *op.cit.*, p.88). [Marque l'approbation du locuteur, le fait qu'il renchérit sur ce qui vient d'être dit] —*Dans les premiers temps, c'était franc, mon vieux. Y en avait, j'l'ai vu, qui collaient leurs musettes et même leur armoire dans une voiture de gosse qu'i's poussaient sur la route. —Ah! tu parles! c'était l'bon temps d'la guerre! Mais on a changé tout ça* (BARBUSSE,*Feu*, 1916, p.198).

Fig. 3. *Tu parles* 'You speak' in TLFi

This definition provides the user with three examples dated 1899, 1916, and 1932, and two functions: (1) marque l'incrédulité, le désaccord, la réprobation du locuteur 'indicates hearer's disbelief, disagreement, disapproval', and (2) marque l'approbation du locuteur, le fait qu'il renchérit sur ce qui vient d'être dit 'indicates hearer's approval, confirming what has just been said'. The two functions broadly correspond to the entry in the bilingual *Larousse*, namely *Bien sûr que oui* 'Yes, of course' and *Bien sûr que non* 'Of course not'. As for the examples, it should be added that the words, as well as the described situation do not help learners to understand the meaning of this situation-bound formula. For instance, the last example *Dans les premiers temps, c'était franc, mon vieux. Y en avait, j'l'ai vu, qui collaient leurs musettes et même leur armoire dans une voiture de gosse qu'i's poussaient sur la route ! – Ah ! tu parles ! c'était l'bon temps d'la guerre ! Mais on a changé tout ça* deserves a few criticisms. First, learners probably do not know words like *musette* 'French bagpipes', which is obsolete, and *gosse* 'Kid', appertaining to the colloquial style register. Second, the context suggests that the war is good: *c'était l'bon temps d'la guerre!* 'in good times of the war'. Even a French native may have hard time understanding what the example really means. Therefore, such ambiguous examples might make it more difficult for learners to understand the meaning of a formula such as this.

6   Proposal for a Description Model

It is probably impossible to develop a universal model describing formulas. The description model proposed in this section has been structured according to users' needs and the peculiarities of formulas as discussed above. A detailed explanation of each point would, unfortunately, exceed the scope of this paper.

The definition is an explanation of the actual meaning of the formula. We would like to stress that in the case of formulas, prosody, gestures, and functions are an integral part of the meaning rather than a secondary or an extra meaning. Therefore, the description includes, beyond strictly semantic features, pragmatic elements, as well as prosodic and gestural properties.

The entry *Tu parles!* 'You speak' could take the following form (Fig. 4):

Tu parles! (invar., fam.)
Fonctions : accord, désaccord

(1)   ◁)) A dit ~ à B parce qu'il n'est pas d'accord avec ce que B a dit : *Bien sûr que non.*
Ex. : Il a réussi son examen ? – Tu parles ! Il a passé toutes ses vacances à la plage.
Syn. : Ben, voyons ! Ben, non ! Hors de question ! Laisse-moi rire ! Mon cul ! Mon œil ! Penses-tu !
Langage du corps : On peut lever les yeux au ciel ou froncer les sourcils.

(2)   ◁)) A dit ~ à B parce qu'il est d'accord avec ce que B a dit : *Bien sûr que oui.*
Ex. : Il a encore loupé son examen ? – Tu parles !
Syn. : Ben, oui ! Et comment ! Pas qu'un peu ! Sans doute ! Tout à fait !
Langage du corps : On peut lever les yeux au ciel ou acquiescer de la tête.

Profil combinatoire : Employé comme une composante d'une phrase (*tu parles beaucoup, lentement, ...*) l'idiome perd son sens phraséologique et doit être compris au sens littéral. Suivi de la préposition *que/si + syntagme verbal* (ex. : Alexandre, je vais faire du vélo, tu viens ? Tu parles que/si je viens.), l'idiome a le sens 'bien sûr que ...'. Suivi de la préposition *de + substantif* (ex. : Tu as vu ce que les cousins ont offert pour les 80 ans de papa ? Un sachet de pruneaux, tu parles d'un cadeau !), l'idiome désigne 'c'est choquant/décevant/surprenant comme ...'.

Fig. 4. Proposal for a description model

First, the user is informed of the invariability of *Tu parles!* 'You speak' and its familiar register. The second field is devoted to functions: depending on the context, this formula performs an act of agreement or disagreement. The third field, definition, is conceived on the model: 'A says ~ to B for what purpose(s): *Paraphrase*' (see Subsect. 3.3). Thus, this formula has two definitions: (1) 'A says ~ to B because A doesn't agree with B: *Of course not!*'; and (2) 'A says ~ to B because A completely agrees with B: *Yes, of course!*'. These definitions are written in simple, easy-to-understand and unambiguous language. Each definition is followed by: (1) pedagogical examples, (2) links to functionally similar formulas, and (3) body language. The final field is a commentary field, containing the combinatorial properties of the formula. As it can be seen, when inserted in a clause, and depending on its combinatorics, *tu parles!* 'you speak' can acquire two additional meanings to its literal meaning: 'of course' and 'it is disappointing'.

This description model seems to be complete because the user is provided with semantic features, as well as pragmatic, prosodic and body language elements.

7   Conclusion

The main question of this paper was: What type of information about formulas do learners need to develop their own pragmatic competence? As we have shown, teaching and learning formulas addresses a wide range of elements: forms, prosody, gestures, functions, contexts, linguo-cultural conventions, and social relationships. Each of these points is important because they all contribute to meaning. Therefore, the description in dictionaries should incorporate these elements to give learners the whole picture of formulas. It is a matter of theoretical as well as practical interest to find out to what extent prosody and gestures contribute to meaning, and how this information can be lexicographically presented.

Acknowledgments. I am grateful to Pascale Chamerois and Rebecca Clayton, my students, and anonymous reviewers for helpful comments on the drafts of this article.

References

1. Arhangel'skiĭ, V.: Ustoĭčivye frazy v sovremennom russkom âzyke. Izdatel'stvo Rostovskogo Universiteta, Rostov-Na-Donu (1964)
2. Baranov, A., Dobrovol'kiĭ, D.: Aspekty teorii frazeologii. Znak, Moskva (2008)
3. Baranov, A., Dobrovol'skiĭ, D.: Osnovy frazeologii. Flinta, Nauka, Moskva (2013)
4. Bardovi-Harlig, K.: Formulas, routines, and conventional expressions in pragmatics research. Ann. Rev. Appl. Linguist. **32**, 223 (2012)
5. Barron, A.: Acquisition in Interlanguage Pragmatics: Learning How to Do Things with Words in a Study Abroad Context, p. 186. John Benjamins, Amsterdam (2003)
6. Blanco Escoda, X., Mejri, S.: Les pragmatèmes. Classiques Garnier, Paris (2018)
7. Blumenthal, P., Mejri, S.: Les séquences figées: entre langue et discours. Steiner, Stuttgart (2008)
8. Burger, H., Dobrovol'skij, D., Kühn, P., Norrick, N.R.: Phraseologie: ein internationales Handbuch zeitgenössischer Forschung. Phraseology: An International Handbook of Contemporary Research. Walter de Gruyter, Berlin, New York (2007)

9. Cacciari, C., Tabossi, P.: Idioms: Processing, Structure, and Interpretation. Erlbaum, Hillsdale (1993)
10. Cahiers de lexicologie 2019, n° 114 – 1, Les phrases préfabriquées: Sens, fonctions, usages (2019)
11. Carter, R.: Vocabulary: Applied Linguistic Perspectives. Routledge, London, New York (1998)
12. Conklin, K., Schmitt, N.: The processing of formulaic language. Ann. Rev. Appl. Linguist. **32**, 47 (2012)
13. Corpas Pastor, G., Mitkov, R.: Computerised and Corpus-Based Approaches to Phraseology. Monolingual and Multilingual Perspectives. Springer, Cham (2019).https://doi.org/10.1007/978-3-030-30135-4
14. Cowie, A.P.: Phraseology: Theory, Analysis, and Applications. Oxford University Press, Clarendon Press, Oxford, New York (1998)
15. Dobrovol'skij, D., Piirainen, E.: Figurative Language: Cross-Cultural and Cross-Linguistic Perspectives. Elsevier, Amsterdam, Boston, London (2005)
16. Everaert, M., Linden, E.-J., Schenk, A.: Idioms: Structural and Psychological Perspectives. Erlbaum Associates, Hillsdale (1995)
17. González Rey, I.: La didactique du français idiomatique. EME, Fernelmont (2007)
18. Granger, S., Meunier, F.: Phraseology: An Interdisciplinary Perspective. John Benjamins, Amsterdam, Philadelphia (2008)
19. Granger, S., Meunier, F.: Phraseology in Foreign Language and Teaching. John Benjamins Publishing Company, Amsterdam, Philadelphia (2008)
20. Gréciano, G.: Signification et dénotation en allemand: la sémantique des expressions idiomatiques. Université de Metz, Metz (1983)
21. Gross, G.: Les expressions figées en français: noms composés et autres locutions. Ophrys, Gap, Paris (1996)
22. Kecskés, I.: Intercultural Pragmatics, p. 139. Oxford University Press, Oxford, New York, Auckland (2014)
23. Kerbrat-Orecchioni, C.: Heurs et malheurs du partage du sens. In: Cislaru, G., Nyckees, V. (dir.) Le partage du sens. Approches linguistiques du sens commun, p. 199. ISTE editions, London (2019)
24. Langacker, R.W.: Metaphoric gesture and cognitive linguistics. In: Cienki, A., Müller, C. (eds.) Metaphors and Gesture, p. 250. John Benjamins, Amsterdam (2008)
25. Langages 2013/1, n° 189, Vers une extension du domaine de la phraséologie (2013)
26. Liddicoat, A.J., Scarino, A.: Intercultural Language Teaching and Learning, pp. 1–2. Wiley-Blackwell, Oxford (2013)
27. Melerovič, A., Mokienko, V.: Frazeologizmy v russkoǐ reči. Russkie slovari, Astrel', Moskva (2001)
28. Moeschler, J.: Complexité et dynamique du sens. Interrélations entre pragmatique cognitive et pragmatique interculturelle. Langages 2021/2, n° 222, pp. 43–58 (2021)
29. Moon, R.: Fixed Expressions and Idioms in English: A Corpus-Based Approach. Clarendon Press, Oxford (1998)
30. Pamies, A., Balsas, I., Magdalena, A. (eds.): Lenguaje figurado y competencia interlingüística Granada Aspectos teóricos. Editorial Comares, Granada (2018)
31. Paquot, M., Granger, S.: Formulaic language in learner corpora. Ann. Rev. Appl. Linguist. **32**, 130 (2012)
32. Phraseologie und parömiologie. Homepage. https://paedagogik.de/phraseologie-und-paroem iologie/. Accessed 26 Apr 2022
33. Popov, R.: Frazeologizmy sovremennogo russkogo âzyka s arhaičnymi značeniâ-mi i formami slov. Vysšaâ škola, Moskva (1976)

34. Polio, C.: Annual Review of Applied Linguistics. Formulaic Language, vol. 32 (2012)
35. Rahilina, E.: Lingvistika konstrukciĭ. Azbukovnik, Moskva (2010)
36. Sailer, M., Markantonatou, S.: Multiword Expressions: Insights from a Multi-Lingual Perspective. Language Science Press, Berlin (2018)
37. Soloduho, È.: Problemy internacionalizacii frazeologii. Izdatel'stvo Ka-zanskogo Universiteta, Kazan' (1982)
38. Taguchi, N.: Teaching pragmatics: trends and issues. Ann. Rev. Appl. Linguist. **31**, 298 (2011)
39. Wood, D.: Perspectives on Formulaic Language: Acquisition and Communication. Continuum, London, New York (2010)
40. Wray, A.: Formulaic Language: Pushing the Boundaries. Oxford University Press, Oxford (2008)

Multi-word Term Translation:
A Student-Centered Pilot Study

Sandra Bullón (iD) and Pilar León-Araúz(✉) (iD)

Department of Translation and Interpreting, University of Granada, Granada, Spain
pleon@ugr.es

Abstract. The translation of multi-word terms (MWTs) poses several challenges for translators, namely due to their frequent lack of transparency, semantic ambiguity and overall cognitive complexity. MWTs have long been a question of interest in Natural Language Processing and Terminology. However, few researchers have explored this phenomenon in the translation classroom. This paper aims to narrow this gap by analyzing the translation of MWTs through the lens of translation students at the University of Granada. More specifically, we (1) explore the perceptions of translation students regarding MWTs, and (2) perform a contrastive analysis of the performance of undergraduate and postgraduate students of translation when faced with MWTs.

Keywords: Multi-word term · Translation · Student-centered pilot study

1 Introduction

Multi-word terms (MWTs) are terms in which a nominal head is complemented by one or several modifiers, e.g., *long-range transboundary air pollution*. They are found in both general and specialized discourse, but are especially widespread in the latter [1]. The translation of MWTs poses several challenges for translators and terminologists alike, namely due to their frequent lack of transparency, semantic ambiguity and overall cognitive complexity. These properties, together with their unsystematic treatment in terminological resources, make it indispensable for translators to be able to handle them correctly—from identifying and understanding them in the source language (SL) to rendering them in the target language (TL), which often requires knowledge of corpus querying [2].

MWTs have long been a question of great interest in Natural Language Processing (NLP) [3, 4] and Terminology [5–7]. However, despite the vital role they play in scientific translation, there is an unmistakable lack of robust research on the didactics of these units in specialized translation training. This paper aims to narrow this gap by analyzing the translation of MWTs through the lens of translation students at the University of Granada. More specifically, we (1) explore the perceptions of translation students regarding MWTs, and (2) perform a contrastive analysis of the performance of undergraduate (UG) and postgraduate (PG) students of translation when faced with MWTs. The results are part of an unpublished student-centered pilot study conducted in 2021 [8].

© The Author(s), under exclusive license to Springer Nature Switzerland AG 2022
G. Corpas Pastor and R. Mitkov (Eds.): EUROPHRAS 2022, LNAI 13528, pp. 47–61, 2022.
https://doi.org/10.1007/978-3-031-15925-1_4

2 Multi-word Terms, Terminology and Translation

In scientific and technical communication, MWTs are the most frequent type of lexical unit [9] and one of the most productive term formation mechanisms, thanks to their multiple combinatorial possibilities [10]. They are also referred to in the literature as complex nominals, noun compounds or nominal compounds, due to the fact that they usually have a nominal head. Complex nominals are defined as a "syntactic construction dominated by a N node and composed (in its simplest form) of a head noun preceded by a modifier which is either another noun or a nominal adjective" [11]. The semantic opacity of these units, together with the syntactic ambiguity they exhibit in combinations of more than 3 words make the interpretation of MWTs a challenge for translators.

MWTs take various shapes across different languages. For instance, English MWTs are most commonly the result of pre-modification [11], i.e., noun heads are modified by other nouns or adjectives, whereas post-modification is the preferred terminogenesic process in Spanish [12]. Two main lines of research have been pursued on the translation of MWTs: (1) bilingual terminological extraction [13], and (2) contrastive analysis in two or more languages [10, 14], to which our study seeks to contribute.

The first step in the translation of MWTs is the correct identification of these in the source text. This is not always an easy task given that these units are sometimes made up of over five components, e.g., *polyurethane foam disk passive air sampler*. Furthermore, they could be made up of general language words that may not be considered part of the term by translators who are not acquainted with the terminological value of seemingly general words [15], e.g., *fine* in *fine particulate matter*. Once an MWT is identified as such, translators must determine the internal dependencies underlying the constituents, both on a structural and a semantic level. From 3 components onwards, the interpretation of MWTs poses a new challenge: the disambiguation of their structural dependencies. This, often known as bracketing [16], involves the grouping of the dependent constituents so that the MWT is "reduced to its basic form of modifier + head" [10], e.g., *[mineral dust] aerosol*. Bracketing paves the way for the semantic analysis of MWTs. By way of example, if *biomass burning aerosol* is bracketed as **biomass [burning aerosol]* instead of *[biomass burning] aerosol*, the concept could be understood as an aerosol which *is* burning and *made up* of biomass, instead of one *resulting from* the burning of biomass. The correct interpretation of the semantic relations codified in MWTs plays a vital role in the translation of MWTs from languages with a high degree of noun-packing, like English, into heavily inflected ones, such as Spanish. More precisely, awareness of the internal dependencies allows the translator to produce TL-oriented equivalents, for instance, making conceptual information explicit (e.g., *acid rain pollution* > *contaminación derivada de la lluvia ácida*) or making structural shifts by modulation (e.g., *photochemical smog* > *smog fotoquímico, niebla tóxica estival*).

Another obstacle faced by translators when dealing with MWTs is the discrimination between a myriad of term variants. MWTs are especially prone to term variation, given that they are, by definition, composed of two or more elements (e.g., *air/airborne/airborne/atmospheric pollution*). Their cognitive and structural complexity, together with their unsystematic treatment in terminological resources, result in a wide variety of translation solutions, including (a) omissions, (b) structural shifts, (c) transpositions, (d) expansions and (5) inaccuracies [17]. This can hinder the search for interlinguistic equivalents. Consequently, faced with several translation variants for the same ST, translators need to make a decision based on context, considering the potential causes which may have led to them.

Corpora constitute invaluable sources for the comprehension and translation of MWTs [10]. For example, a quantitative analysis of specialized translation corpora annotated by error types revealed a significant decrease in errors in students using corpora [18]. The key errors identified pointed to the "need to place additional focus on the difficulties of comprehending, analyzing and transferring" the meaning of terms, MWTs (referred to as *complex noun groups*), and collocations. Nevertheless, not all translators have good command of corpus querying, which often results in reluctance to use them [19, 20]. For translators to start using corpora, they need to first realize that corpora have the potential to help them find answers to questions for which there are often no clear answers in dictionaries, glossaries, Google searches and other resources they are accustomed to using [21]. However, first of all, trainers need to know how they usually approach the translation of MWTs.

3   Materials and Methods

As previously mentioned, the purpose of this study was to unveil the ins and outs of the performance of translation students regarding MWTs throughout the whole translation process. This section describes the instruments, research design, study participants and the assessment procedure employed.

3.1   Research Design and Instruments

In order to measure the performance of translation students when facing MWTs, we designed a survey covering different obstacles (i.e. MWT definition, MWT identification, semantic and structural decoding of the MWT, term variation). Our previous research [9] indicated several variables which reportedly altered translation quality, including (1) term length, (2) syntactic structure, and (3) semantic relations within the MWT. These three, together with (4) level of studies, were the variables considered in our explorative study to assess a series of research questions: (1) students' definition of MWT and the associated challenges; (2) the extent to which students are able to identify MWTs in scientific and technical texts; (3) their performance when asked to translate scientific and technical MWTs from scratch; (4) the criteria students adopt to discriminate between MWT variants; (5) the extent to which students are able to disambiguate the semantic dependencies in MWTs.

We developed a question bank which contained multiple choice questions (both single- and multiple-answer ones), rating scales, and open-ended questions. The survey consisted of 38 questions organized in the sections contained in Table 1, although only the results of 32 questions will be covered in this paper.

Table 1. Sections in the survey.

Section	Action requested
1. Introduction and demographic data	Level of studies, native language and prior knowledge about MWTs
2. Defining MWTs	Participants provide a definition of MWT in their own words as well as examples
3. Identifying MWTs	Participants identify MWTs within a close-ended list, with no other context, and within the title of a scientific paper
4. Translating English MWTs into Spanish from scratch	Participants translate into Spanish a series of MWTs
5. Decoding semantic relations within MWTs	Participants are requested to decide which of the semantic relations outlined in the options were accurate for 3-word MWTs showing different syntactic structures (A+N+N, N+N+N, N+A+N)
6. Choosing the best translation equivalent for MWTs without context	Participants choose the best equivalent among three given MWTs

The MWTs selected are 3-word MWTs and MWTs of more than 4 words. They were extracted from an *ad hoc* 1.5-million-word English corpus on air pollution and air quality treatment by looking for the most frequent nouns pre-modified by adjectives, nouns, adverbs and participles. Our goal was to study not only the performance of trainees but also to look into a potential correlation between the number of constituents and translation quality (see Sect. 3.3). In Sect. 5 different options are provided with a view to analyzing potential differences in the output quality when they are presented with choices versus when they are not, as well as examining the criteria they base their translation decisions on.

3.2 Participants

Eligibility criteria required individuals (1) to be native speakers of Spanish, and (2) to be enrolled in one of the Terminology modules offered in the University of Granada. By the end of the survey period, a total of 10 Spanish Translation students at the University of Granada completed and returned the questionnaire. More specifically, the sample population was composed of (a) 5 third-year UG students (Bachelor's Degree) in Translation and Interpreting, currently enrolled in the Terminology module, and (b) 5 PG students (Master's Degree in Professional Translation) enrolled in the Terminology Management and Language Engineering module.

3.3 Procedure

A crucial step within the research design was the operationalization of translation quality. Different initiatives have been undertaken in recent years to design translation quality metrics, namely the Multidimensional Quality Metrics (MQM) framework [23], and the Dynamic Quality Framework (DQF) [24]. Although both provide a comprehensive catalog of error types, these were envisioned to evaluate quality on sentence and/or text level. We thus adapted them for term-oriented metrics retaining two clear-cut parameters, (1) accuracy and (2) fluency, as defined in Table 2.

Table 2. Variable operationalization.

Variable	Definition	Scope of assessment
Accuracy	"Extent to which the informational content conveyed by a target text matches that of the source text" [23]	Comparing the content of source and target texts
Fluency	"Fluency includes those issues about the linguistic 'well formedness' of the text that can be assessed without regard to whether the text is a translation or not" [23]	Linguistic and textual features of the target text

A 0-1 scoring system was designed, where 0 meant the translation did not meet minimum requirements regarding both accuracy and fluency; 0.5 points, where the output was accurate but could be improved in terms of fluency; and 1 point when the equivalent met the domain's expectations in terms of both accuracy and fluency.

4 Results and Discussion

For space reasons, quantitative results (frequencies and scores) are only presented to illustrate one or two of the MWTs in each section.

4.1 Background Knowledge of MWTs

The first section of the questionnaire required respondents to give information on whether they had received specific training on MWTs before. 70% of them claimed to have learned about them in an academic context, either during their undergraduate or postgraduate studies. Only 1 out of 5 PG participants indicated that they received training during their postgraduate studies. In response to the follow-up question: 'If you have [learned about the translation of MWTs during your studies], which course/module was it? Please summarize what you have learned briefly', most of them reported that they had covered this topic in their undergraduate Terminology module (3) and/or their undergraduate Scientific and Technical Translation module (3). Other responses to this question included undergraduate Documentation (1) and Legal Translation (1) modules, and Fundamentals of Translation (PG) and Translation Theory (UG) ones (2). However, they all agreed that this was a "broad" or "basic" coverage, a claim further supported by the results in the following sections.

4.2 MWTs: Definition and Challenges

Participants were initially asked to provide a definition of MWT in their own words. 3 out of 5 UG participants believed MWTs to be strictly composed of two words. Most of them considered the number of components to be the only feature which defines these units and differentiates them from other terms/words. Respondents were also asked to indicate one or more examples of MWTs. The overall response was positive, as individuals provided examples of scientific MWTs such as *heart valve* or *autism spectrum disorder*. However, examples also included general language idioms such as *bite the bullet*.

As opposed to UG respondents, many PG individuals alluded to the notion of 'collective meaning', commenting on how each 'element' has its own meaning but together with the rest of them make up a different one. None of the PG students surveyed restricted the length of MWTs to only 2 components—instead, the majority of them suggested that these are composed of several (two or more) words. The examples provided once again included general language phraseological units (*it's raining cats and dogs*) and compounds (*easy-going, non-refundable*) together with specialized terms such as *complex instruction set computing*.

These findings have several implications for the treatment of MWTs. While the translator is, by definition, a problem-solver, it can be argued that one can hardly deal with a problem they do not anticipate or understand in the first place. These findings suggest that 60% of the UG population believes an MWT can only be composed of up to two constituents. It may be the case therefore that they could fail to identify 3-, 4- and 5-word combinations altogether, which naturally has direct consequences on target term (TT) production: to begin with, they would be looking up the wrong ST in their documentation sources, and whether they found an entry for it or not, the resulting translation could never be an accurate one, as it is inevitably missing part of the conceptual load.

The final part of this section was concerned with students' perception of the challenges of MWTs. Six broad challenges emerged from the analysis of open-ended answers: (1) unclear understanding of the MWT, largely due to the opacity of the semantic relations implicit in these; (2) lack of established translation equivalents, sometimes as a result of neology in the SL; (3) lack of MWT representation in their go-to translation resources; (4) need for subject knowledge of the domain where the term is used; (5) major call for accuracy and meeting the high expectations of expert-to-expert communication; (6) difficulty to discriminate between term variants.

Taken together, the answers provided essential insights into the difficulties of MWT translation. Unfortunately, besides the discernible lack of representation of these units in terminological resources, none of the commented issues was brought up by more than one respondent at a time. Moreover, some answers were vague and intuition-based. For instance, in claiming that MWTs cannot be translated word for word, one of the respondents is merely stating what translation trainees are taught to do in most (if not all) situations throughout their studies. However, this does not necessarily imply that students are aware of the structural disambiguation or bracketing process which should precede TT production, or the proliferation of term variants in Spanish as a result of terminology dependency, for example.

4.3 Identifying MWTs

Participants were asked to (1) indicate which of the strings of words given (*general voltage, wind power, original discrete wavelet transform, adaptive chaos particle optimization algorithm*) were considered MWTs; and then (2) identify the MWTs in the title of a scientific paper (i.e. *Matrix-Assisted Laser Desorption/Ionization Time-of-Flight Mass Spectrometry with a Matrix of Carbon Nanotubes for the Analysis of Low-Mass Compounds in Environmental Samples*). Table 3 shows the results for (1).

Table 3. Structures identified as MWT by study participants.

Multi-word term	Freq. UG	Freq. PG
General voltage	2	3
Wind power	3	5
*Original discrete wavelet transform	2	4
Adaptive chaos particle optimization algorithm	3	2

The single most striking observation in (1) is that the majority of respondents in both samples accurately pointed *wind power* out as an MWT. Several factors could explain this result: term length and prior knowledge. We did not consider *original discrete wavelet transform* to be an MWT, in view of the fact that the actual MWT spans only from *discrete* to *transform*, as suggested by the acronym *DWT*. Notably, most PG respondents reported *original discrete wavelet transform* to be an MWT, while only 2/5 UG individuals felt it qualified as one. This finding, together with the results reporting over half of PG respondents to have accurately identified *general voltage* as an MWT, suggests that the PG population may have a less restricted definition of MWTs than their UG counterparts. While this was already observed in Sect. 4.2, we now observe that, unlike most UG individuals, PG individuals are seemingly aware that general language words such as "general" or "original" could potentially be part of MWTs.

Contrary to expectations, 3 out of 5 UG respondents accurately selected *adaptive chaos particle optimization algorithm* as an MWT, despite it not meeting the definition proposed by 3 out of 5 of them in the previous section. This discrepancy could be attributed to frequency being the main lighting guide of this sample, given that a simple search of this term on Google retrieves many papers containing a variant or hyponym of it in the title.

Overall, 40% of PG respondents accurately pinpointed the MWTs in the list, while all of the UG individuals failed to do so. This indicates that translation students, especially UG ones, may not have an accurate pre-defined concept of MWT and therefore struggle to identify them.

Table 4 shows the results of (2): the identification of MWTs in the title of a paper.

According to the definition of MWT we adhere to in this research, the headline above contains four MWTs. Nonetheless, these can vary slightly depending on whether general words such as "analysis of" or "matrix of" are considered part of the MWT.

Table 4. MWTs identified as such by study participants in the headline by frequency.

Multi-word term	Freq. UG	Freq. PG	Total (%)
Matrix-assisted laser desorption/ionization time-of-flight mass spectrometry	1	4	50%
*Matrix of carbon nanotubes	2	2	40%
Carbon nanotubes	2	3	50%
*Analysis of low-mass compounds	2	0	20%
Low-mass compounds	3	5	80%
Environmental samples	3	4	70%

We deemed both options to be correct in our analysis. Over half of the PG respondents accurately identified the MWTs in the headline. In contrast, the UG sample exhibited a poorer performance regarding the identification of these units, especially those with more than two constituents. Further analysis showed that only 1 out of 5 UG respondents identified *matrix-assisted laser desorption/ionization time-of-flight mass spectrometry* as one MWT, whereas 4 out of 5 PG respondents accurately did. This unit exhibits a high degree of semantic density in a critically condensed structure, omitting all non-essential elements (e.g., prepositions). These features, together with the use of a slash, makes the term completely obscure for non-experts in the field, but does not make the text any less likely to be commissioned for a translation into Spanish. PG respondents, once again, rose up to the challenge more effectively than their UG counterparts. Hence, it could conceivably be hypothesized that there is a positive correlation between level of translation training and MWT identification performance.

Surprisingly, though, each of the 10 respondents identified a different collection of MWTs. It can therefore be assumed that there is a lack of consistency in the criteria on what makes an MWT on the part of participants. The forthcoming results, as well as the ones discussed thus far, present evidence that translators can benefit from receiving specific training on the treatment of these units in their specialized translation and terminology modules.

4.4   Translating MWTs

The next section of the survey was concerned with the translation of 5 isolated MWTs from scratch (*urban air pollution, particulate matter pollution, point source pollution, aggregate anthropogenic carbon dioxide equivalent emissions* and *surface albedo radiative effect*). For example, *urban air pollution* elicited four different translation equivalents (Table 5). All four were found to meet minimum standards of accuracy (0.5 points, e.g., *contaminación de aire urbano*), with some being suitable both in terms of accuracy and fluency (1 point), e.g., *contaminación atmosférica urbana*. Two of the proposed equivalents, *contaminación del aire urbano* and *contaminación de aire urbano*, were more on the literal side, lacking the expected fluency. In line with Spanish word formation rules and conventions, there is a preference for the relational adjective, *contaminación atmosférica*. Moreover, the latter of these is missing the article *el*, an omission which further makes the resulting translation sloppier in terms of fluency.

Table 5. Score and frequency of translation equivalents for *urban air pollution*.

Urban air pollution	Score	Freq. UG	Freq. PG	Total (%)
Contaminación atmosférica urbana	1	2	4	60%
Contaminación del aire urbano	0.5	1	1	20%
Contaminación de aire urbano	0.5	1	1	10%
Contaminación urbana atmosférica	1	1	1	10%

It is interesting to note that these variants are the product of two different bracketing structures: *[urban air] pollution* and *urban [air pollution]*. Although we maintain *urban air pollution* is a specification of the hypernym *air pollution*, if the translator skips the analysis of the internal dependencies within the MWT, they are left with two variants which seem equally viable *contaminación atmosférica urbana* and *contaminación urbana atmosférica* and do not especially alter the meaning of the ST (both *pollution* and *air* are found in an *urban* context). In truth, other language phenomena such as metonymy often arise in the translation process, fueling the intrinsic ambiguity of these units. This further stresses the need for translators to have well-founded background knowledge on the treatment of MWTs as part of a strong terminological competence, which they would reasonably expect to forge in higher education.

Furthermore, these language devices (metonymy, transposition, structural shifts) are one of the most productive term variation mechanisms [17]. If the translator is aware of the proneness of these units to term and translation variation, they can use it to their advantage: from discursive variants to enhance the readability of the target text, to cognitive ones which highlight different dimensions of the same concept. Instead of being the passive recipient of an overload of translation possibilities, the translator can become an active agent of the process, making informed decisions about the existing variants or choosing to create new ones to meet the domain's expectations.

Turning now to the 4+-word MWTs, when asked to provide a translation for *aggregate anthropogenic carbon dioxide equivalent emissions*, individuals submitted five different candidates (Table 6). Only two of these (40%) received the maximum score: *emisiones antropogénicas agregadas, expresadas en dióxido de carbono equivalente*, and its comma-less orthotypographic variant. Nevertheless, an outstanding performance can be seen in the PG group, as all 5 of them proposed one of the two. The rest of equivalents (60%), once again, were lacking some semantic aspects of the ST, or overtly missed the semantic relations coded between the formants, e.g. *emisiones equivalentes de dióxido de carbono antropogénico agregado*. The latter is an example of the myriad of inaccuracies which can arise should the analysis of the structural and semantic dependencies within the MWT be skipped. This applies to both *ad hoc* translations and choosing from pre-existing equivalents documented in the literature. Even when the translation reads fine, as is the case, the translator should always be on the lookout for potential inaccuracies or translation errors within. It should also be noted that one of the participants failed to provide a translation for this MWT altogether.

Table 6. Score and frequency of translation equivalents for *aggregate anthropogenic carbon dioxide equivalent emissions.*

Aggregate anthropogenic carbon dioxide equivalent emissions	Score	Freq. UG	Freq. PG	Total (%)
Emisiones antropogénicas agregadas, expresadas en dióxido de carbono equivalente	1	1	3	40%
Emisiones antropogénicas agregadas expresadas en dióxido de carbono equivalente	1	0	2	20%
Emisiones de dióxido de carbono equivalente	0	1	0	10%
Emisiones equivalentes de dióxido de carbono antropogénico agregado	0	1	0	10%
Dióxido de carbono equivalente	0	1	0	10%

Overall, PG respondents obtained much higher scores than their UG counterparts (83% as opposed to 38%), suggesting a positive correlation between level of studies and MWT translation quality (Fig. 1). Upon filling out of the survey, PG participants had completed an advanced specialization course on Terminology Management and Language Engineering, which highlights a valorization of postgraduate training in translation. Nevertheless, the errors found at this and later stages also support the need to implement the treatment of MWTs into the curriculum in order to prepare future professionals for the reality of the scientific and technical translation market.

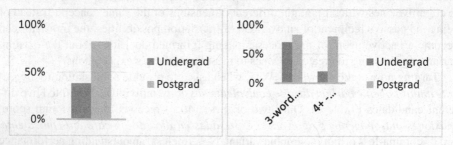

Fig. 1. Performance of UG and PG participants in MWT translation from scratch; Performance of study participants in MWT translation from scratch by term length

It is also interesting to break down the results according to the variables (Fig. 1). The performance of PG respondents was relatively high for both 3 and 4+-word MWTs, but it was still mildly influenced by the number of constituents. The negative correlation between number of constituents and translation quality was especially prominent in UG respondents, with a 50% drop (from 70% to 20%).

4.5   Decoding the Semantic Relations in Multi-word Terms

To avoid question bias and the so-called assimilation effect, we called individuals' attention to this aspect only after they were asked to (1) define, (2) identify, and (3) translate these freely. They were confronted with 4 3-word MWTs (*passive air sampler, soil dust aerosol, ozone mixing ratio, biomass burning aerosol*) and were provided with three possible choices.

Passive air sampler (Table 7) exhibits an Adj+N+N syntactic structure. A total of 2 out of 5 PG respondents correctly chose *air sampler HAS ATTRIBUTE passive* as the right option, and only 1 out 5 UG respondents did. The bracketing grouping (*passive [air sampler]*) complies with several of the indicators advanced in [6], e.g., *air sampler* appears as an independent term, is found combined with other elements (*microbial air sampler*), and has an antonym (*active air sampler*). Analyzing the internal dependencies has cognitive implications, as it is the basis for an accurate semantic analysis of the MWT and its subsequent application: translation [6]. These disappointing results, however, point at participants lacking background knowledge of these and other bracketing indicators, or even the need to carry out these disambiguation tasks altogether.

Table 7. Semantic relations encoded in *passive air sampler*

Passive air sampler	Freq. UG	Freq. PG	Total (%)
Air sampler HAS ATTRIBUTE passive	1	2	30%
*Sampler MEASURES passive air	1	2	30%
*Sampler MADE OF passive air	3	1	40%

Participants were then requested to decode an MWT strictly made up of nouns (N + N + N): *soil dust aerosol*. Once again, only 1 out of 5 UG respondents successfully decoded the underlying semantic relation. Nevertheless, PG respondents showed a significantly superior performance here, with 4 out of 5 accurately pointing at *aerosol MADE OF soil dust* as the right option (Table 8).

Table 8. Semantic relations encoded in *soil dust aerosol*

Soil dust aerosol	Freq. UG	Freq. PG	Total (%)
*Dust aerosol LOCATED_IN soil	1	1	20%
*Dust aerosol CAUSED_BY soil	3	0	30%
Aerosol MADE_OF soil dust	1	4	50%

By definition, this syntactic structure does not hint at any specific bracketing grouping. However, the translator can find clues to the structure (and ultimate translation) of this MWT by looking for knowledge-rich contexts such as the following:

Soil dust aerosols are created by the wind erosion of dry soil.

Among the natural aerosol sources, soil dust is a major contributor to global aerosol mass load and optical thickness.

The first context serves to discard *dust aerosol CAUSED_BY soil*, as erosion, and not soil, is identified as the cause. The second one hints at the *aerosol MADE_OF soil dust* as one of the correct semantic relations encoded by the constituents in the term.

In general terms, PG respondents were found to be more efficient at decoding the semantic relations between the constituents in MWTs than their UG counterparts. This can be seen in Fig. 2, with a remarkable difference of 40 percent points.

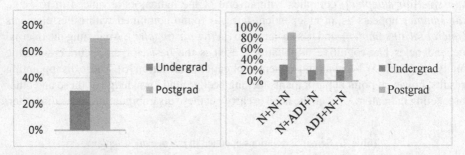

Fig. 2. Performance of study participants' in pinpointing the semantic relations in MWTs; Performance of UG and PG participants in pinpointing the semantic relations in MWTs by syntactic structure

If we look at each of the independent variables (Fig. 2), we can see that PG respondents still exhibited a significantly better performance than their UG counterparts. Terms with a N + N + N structure were found to be the least prone to errors in the decoding process, in both samples. This is especially notable in PG respondents, whose scores were in the 40% range for all structures except for this one, where it jumped to 90%. Conversely, when an adjective was placed in the middle or the forefront of the MWT, both groups appeared to struggle to decode what the relation was. These preliminary results suggest there is a correlation between syntactic structure and translation quality in MWTs. However, further data collection is required to determine exactly how this variable affects translation quality.

4.6 Choosing the Best Translation

By means of single-answer multiple choice questions, survey respondents were next asked to choose the best translation (out of the three proposed) for the given MWT (*environmentally hazardous substance, acid rain pollution, ozone depletion potential*). For *environmentally hazardous substance*, it should be noted that while all three options were found in the literature, these included one that was lacking either in terms of accuracy or fluency: use of *-mente* adverb in (1), inaccuracy in the use of the preposition (*con* instead of *por*) in (2), and omission of the article *el* in (3), respectively.

As shown in Table 9, the results obtained for UG respondents mirrored those for PG respondents. This pattern is found consistently in all three MWTs and constitutes an

Table 9. Best translation equivalents for *environmentally hazardous substance*

Environmentally hazardous substance	Freq. UG	Freq. PG	Total (%)
Sustancia ambientalmente peligrosa	1	1	20%
Producto nocivo para el medio ambiente	2	2	40%
Material dañino para el medio ambiente	2	2	40%

important finding in the understanding of the research problem. So far, the results discussed provided evidence that the UG population encounters more difficulties throughout the whole translation process of MWTs than the PG population. Nevertheless, when the roadblocks prior to term production (identification, structural and semantic disambiguation) are 'seemingly' out of the way, both populations appear to make the same translation decisions. More specifically, the scores for both groups were 80% in the first question and an unparalleled 100% in the second and third ones. Given that all respondents have (1) a translation background and (2) Spanish as a native language, the emerged results hint that translation students have sufficient knowledge to see for themselves what makes a good translation for MWTs. Unfortunately, given the unsystematic representation of these units in terminological resources, having to choose the best out of several translations is hardly ever the case. Put another way, when presented with overall adequate term possibilities, translation students would in fact be able to put their language and translation competence to use to make sure the end-product meets certain standards of quality. An implication of this is the fact that the errors found in previous sections may not be related with gaps in their general translation knowledge, but rather with a lack of training on what MWTs are and how the rendering of these phraseological units into Spanish should be approached.

5 Conclusions

In this paper we analyzed the perceptions and background knowledge of students regarding MWTs and assessed the extent to which the level of studies has an effect on translation quality. We also gained knowledge about the relationship between certain variables (term length, syntactic structure, semantic opacity) and MWT translation quality in terms of two metrics: accuracy and fluency.

Our research findings confirm the assumption that MWTs constitute a stumbling block for specialized translation students. We gained a better understanding of the difficulties posed by MWTs for future translation professionals: term identification, structural and semantic disambiguation, discrimination between term variants, and term production at the lack of established equivalents. It can be concluded that completing postgraduate translation courses has a positive impact on the translation of MWTs in scientific and technical texts. Nonetheless, preliminary results suggest there is much room in for improvement in regard to MWT training, as quality across both the UG and the PG group failed to meet the domain's expectations.

Performance in the earliest phases of the treatment of MWTs was consistent throughout the rest of the process (e.g., most UG participants failed to identify MWTs correctly at the start, and later struggled to provide translations which met the standards in terms of accuracy and fluency). This hints that translation errors for MWTs could be the result of a domino effect. Lack of awareness of the properties of MWTs could lead to translators failing to identify them as such; if MWTs are overlooked, translators may not see any reason to carry out an analysis of their internal dependencies, which would result in them using any (however inaccurate) equivalent they can find, regardless of the role term variation, neology and secondary term formation play in the English-Spanish language pair. Or, what is worse: they could find themselves providing a literal, word-for-word translation for it which, albeit formally adequate, does not convey the same meaning.

Returning briefly to the notion of the translator as a problem-solver, it is unrealistic to expect translators to deal with a problem, albeit ever-present in scientific texts, which they do not anticipate or understand the peculiarities of. Therefore, we defend the view that translators need a solid foundation on MWTs they can base their translation decisions on. Translation studies would benefit from actively including MWTs in the specialized translation curriculum.

This research was conceived as a pilot study. The generalizability of these findings is thus subject to certain limitations. These preliminary findings will serve as a base for future studies with a larger study sample. We also plan to take this study a step forward and design a new survey to be conducted after training students in both the challenges of MWTs and the use of corpora for their translation.

Acknowledgments. This research was carried out as part of the projects PID2020-118369GB-I00 and A-HUM-600-UGR20, funded by the Spanish Ministry of Science and Innovation and the Regional Government of Andalusia.

References

1. Bowker, L.: Terminology and translation. In: Handbook of Terminology, pp. 304–323. John Benjamins, Amsterdam/Philadelphia (2015)
2. Cabezas-García, M., León-Araúz, P.: Procedimiento para la traducción de términos poliléxicos con la ayuda de corpus. In: Sistemas fraseológicos en contraste: enfoques computacionales y de corpus, pp. 203–229. Comares, Granada (2021)
3. Girju, R., Moldovan, D., Tatu, M., Antohe, D.: On the semantics of noun compounds. Comput. Speech Lang. **19**(4), 479–496 (2005)
4. Nakov, P.: On the interpretation of noun compounds: syntax, semantics, and entailment. Nat. Lang. Eng. **19**, 291–330 (2013)
5. Cabezas-García, M., Faber, P.: Exploring the semantics of multi-word terms by means of paraphrases. In: Temas actuales de terminología y estudios sobre el léxico, pp. 193–217. Comares, Granada (2017)
6. Cabezas-García, M., León-Araúz, P.: On the structural disambiguation of multi-word terms. In: Corpas Pastor, G., Mitkov, R. (eds.) EUROPHRAS 2019. LNCS (LNAI), vol. 11755, pp. 46–60. Springer, Cham (2019). https://doi.org/10.1007/978-3-030-30135-4_4
7. Sanz-Vicente, L.: Approaching secondary term formation through the analysis of multiword units: an English-Spanish contrastive study. Terminology **18**(1), 105–127 (2012)
8. Bullón, S.: The tanslation of multi-word terms: a student-centered analysis. Unpublished master's dissertation, Universidad de Granada (2021)

9. Meyer, I., Macintosh, K.: Refining the terminographer's concept-analysis methods: how can phraseology help? Terminology **3**(1), 1–26 (1996)

10. Cabezas-García, M.: Los compuestos nominales en terminología: formación, traducción y representación, PhD Thesis. Universidad de Granada, Granada (2019)

11. Levi, J.: The Syntax and Semantics of Complex Nominals. Academic Press, New York (1978)

12. Fernández-Domínguez, J.: Compounds and multi-word expressions in Spanish. In: Complex Lexical Units: Compounds and Multi-Word Expressions, pp. 189–219. De Gruyter, Berlin/Boston (2019)

13. Daille, B., Dufour-Kowalski, S., Morin, E.: French-English multi-word term alignment based on lexical context analysis. In: Proceedings of LREC 2004. Lisbon (2004)

14. Fernández-Silva, S., Kerremans, K.: Terminological variation in source texts and translations: a pilot study. Meta **56**(2), 318–335 (2011)

15. Cabré, M.T.: La terminología: representación y comunicación. Institut Universitari de Lingüística Aplicada, Barcelona (1999)

16. Marsh, E.: A computational analysis of complex noun phrases in navy messages. In Proceedings of the 10th International Conference on Computational Linguistics. Stanford (1984)

17. León-Araúz, P., Cabezas-García, M.: Term and translation variation of multi-word terms. MonTI. Monografías de Traducción e Interpretación, pp. 210–247 (2020)

18. Kübler, N., Mestivier, A., Pecman, M.: Teaching specialised translation through corpus linguistics: translation quality assessment and methodology evaluation and enhancement by experimental approach. Meta **63**(3), 807–825 (2019)

19. Bowker, L.: Corpus resources for translators: academic luxury or professional necessity. Tradterm **10**, 213 (2004). https://doi.org/10.11606/issn.2317-9511.tradterm.2004.47178

20. Gallego-Hernández, D.: The use of corporoa as translation resources: a study based on a survey of Spanish professional translators. Perspectives **23**(3), 375–391 (2015)

21. Frankenberg-García, A.: Are translations longer than source texts? A corpus-based study of explicitation. In: Corpus Use and Translating, pp. 47–58. John Benjamins, Amsterdam/Philadelphia (2009)

22. Bullón, S.: The translation of compound nominals in the field of air quality treatment. Unpublished bachelor's degree dissertation. Universidad de Granada, Granada (2020)

23. Lommel, A., Uszkoreit, H., Burchardt, A.: Multidimensional quality metrics (MQM): a framework for declaring and describing translation quality metrics. Revista tradumàtica: traducció y tecnologies de la informació i la comunicació **12**, 455–463 (2014)

24. Görög, A.: Quality evaluation today: the dynamic quality framework. In: Proceedings of Translating and the Computer, Geneva (2014)

Interpreting Tomorrow? How to Build a Computer-Assisted Glossary of Phraseological Units in (Almost) No Time

Gloria Corpas Pastor[1,2](✉) (iD)

[1] IUITLM, University of Malaga, Malaga, Spain
gcorpas@uma.es
[2] RIILP, University of Wolverhampton, Wolverhampton, UK

Abstract. Preparation is widely considered as one of the most important phases of an interpreting assignment, especially if the subject is highly specialised, pertains to a developing domain, or involves under-resourced languages. This preliminary phase usually involves gathering information about a given domain, including key concepts, terminology, and associated phraseology. Interpreters tend to carry out these documentary searches mainly manually, which turns to be a rather time-consuming process. This paper presents a novel documentation procedure for the automatic compilation of domain-specific phraseological glossaries in English, French, and Spanish. After a brief overview of the underlying CAI system (VIP), we will describe our computer-assisted protocol for automatic corpus compilation, phraseology extraction and translation of candidates. Our ultimate goal is to offer interpreters tools and resources tailored to their needs that could enhance their performance and reduce the time spent in the preliminary preparation phase.

Keywords: Computer-assisted interpreting · Glossary building · Phraseology

1 Introduction

Preparation is widely considered as one of the most important phases of an interpreting assignment, especially if the subject is highly specialised, pertains to a developing domain, or involves under-resourced languages (cf. Gile 1995; Fantinuoli 2017; Xu 2018; Gaber et al. 2020). Although terminology work is an essential part of any interpreting assignment, very often interpreters are faced with a highly specialised topic, almost no reference materials and very little time (if any) to prepare and practice its domain-specific terminology and specialised phraseology. While specialised terminology may be hard to capture in just a few hours, grasping adequate knowledge of domain-specific phraseological units usually turns into 'mission impossible'. This is particularly problematic since mastering the specific phraseology of the specific subject matter of the assignment is one of the main stumbling blocks that interpreters face in their daily work (Cattaneo 2004; Markič 2012; Crezee and Grant 2013; Aston 2015; Corpas and Gaber 2021, etc.).

Within Gile's Gravitational Model of language availability (Gile 2009), advance preparation activates and increases the frequency or familiarity of relevant source and

G. Corpas Pastor and R. Mitkov (Eds.): EUROPHRAS 2022, LNAI 13528, pp. 62–77, 2022.
https://doi.org/10.1007/978-3-031-15925-1_5

target language information in the long-term memory. In the case of terms, they remain available for prompt access and retrieval during interpretation. In this context, preparation should be understood as a continuous and constantly developing process, that usually begins some time before the interpreting assignment and lasts until the very moments before the assignment begins (Moser-Mercer 1992). Mastering the relevant concepts of a given domain and using the appropriate terminology and phraseology throughout the event in which the interpreter is to participate are key aspects that determine the quality of a given interpretation.

There is a general consensus that pre-interpreting preparation has a positive influence on the interpreting output (Gile 1995/2009; Fantinouli 2017; Chang et al. 2018; Pérez-Pérez 2018; Corpas Pastor and Gaber 2021; etc.). Previous studies have highlighted the impact of advance preparation for terminology accuracy. For instance, Díaz Galaz (2011) reported that pre-interpreting preparation supports the simultaneous interpreting process, resulting in shorter ear-voice span and greater accuracy, even in difficult segments with specialised terminology, complex syntactic structure, and non-redundant information. Similar results with corpus-driven terminology preparation were obtained by Pérez-Pérez (2018) and Xu (2018). In the same vein, Song and Tang (2020) established a relatively large impact on the accuracy of terminology and the logical coherence of the target-language speech, while exerting a minimal impact on the voice quality factor.

Phraseology is also another well-known determinant of the quality of an interpretation. It can be measured by the interpreter's understanding of phraseology and the interpreter's expertise in dealing with such units (Crezee and Grant 2013; Aston 2015). Thus, in the preparation phase, the interpreter also needs to acquire (and automate) the specialised and commonly used phraseology specific to a given domain. In this sense, various authors have advanced phraseology-driven corpus-based preparation (textual and audiovisual materials) in order to develop the phraseological competence of practitioners and trainee interpreters on a specific topic (Aston 2015; Corpas Pastor and Gaber 2021). This kind of pre-interpretation preparation not only facilitates the immediate retrieval of a given phraseological unit, but it also helps interpreters to reduce their cognitive load and focus on other aspects of processing that also require their attention (Nolan 2005; Tolosa-Igualada and Mezcua 2010; Markič 2012; Crezee and Grant 2013).

In a professional setting the client is expected to provide the interpreter with all relevant documents available (background papers, texts of speeches to be delivered, slides and any other reference material) well in advance (cf. Pérez Pérez 2018). Regrettably, this tends not to be always the case. Most interpreters receive incomplete information (if any at all) at very short notice, which usually covers little more than the topic, the program or agenda, and the schedule. Too often interpreters find themselves with very limited time to prepare new topics. The scenario gets even more complicated when the interpreting assignment is related to a highly specialised field of knowledge. In this case, in-depth knowledge of the specific domain, both at the conceptual and linguistic level (specialised terminology, phraseological units, etc.), is absolutely essential for high-quality professional interpreting.

No wonder, interpreters usually draw up their own ad-hoc glossaries when preparing for an interpretation. According to Jiang (2005), all interpreters have created some kind of glossary at some stage in their careers. This is usually done by identifying reliable sources of information (e-resources, digital documents, dictionaries, other reference materials, etc.), extracting key concepts, terms, phraseology, lexical bundles, etc. from them and compiling a glossary with all the relevant information.

Glossary building can be considered an essential part of any interpretation job, that also requires considerable time and effort on the part of practitioners. In general, interpreters still resort to manual procedures and traditional formats (spreadsheets, tables in .doc or .pdf formats), with very little automation beyond a handful of terminology management systems currently available (e.g., InterpretBank, Interpreters' Help, Glossary Assistant, etc.). In this paper we present a novel documentation procedure for the automatic compilation of domain-specific phraseological glossaries in English, Spanish and French. After this short introduction, Sect. 2 will briefly outline the VIP system as a convenient background for our documentation protocol. Then, Sect. 3 will cover automatic corpus compilation and glossary building through various substeps. Our automated procedure provides guidance and support from beginning to end of a given interpreting assignment, including practicing multiword terms and phraseology. The ultimate goal is to offer interpreters tools and resources tailored to their phraseological needs that could enhance their performance and reduce the time spent in the preliminary preparation phase.

2   Voice-Text Integrated System for InterPreters (VIP)

The VIP[1] system has been designed and implemented as a computer-assisted system for interpreters (practitioners and trainees). It is the first free, open-source platform specially designed to cater for the needs of interpreters. VIP[2] is composed of an open, interactive catalogue of interpreting-related tools and resources (Component A) and a suite of platform-integrated functionalities to assist interpretation at all phases: preparation, delivery, training, and life-long learning (Component B).[3]

Component A is a relational database management system (RDBMS) that uses Structured Query Language (SQL) to access the catalogue database. The VIP catalogue includes computer-assisted interpreting (CAI) tools and resources: terminology management tools (e.g., InterpretBank), note-taking devices (e.g., Evernote), automatic speech recognition (ASR) systems (e.g., Otter AI); remote interpreting (RI) systems

---

[1] http://www.lexytrad.es/VIP/index_en.php (Last accessed: 09–07-2022).

[2] So far there have been three versions of the system (v. 1.0, v. 1.1, v. 1.2). VIP v.1.2 is the current, on-going version of the system (see Sect. 2.2). It fuses characteristics and functionalities present in the seed project (*VIP - Voice-text Integrated system for interPreters*, ref. no. FFI2016-75831-P, 2016–2020), as well as some of the improvements and new features envisaged in other four continuation projects: *Voice-text integrated system for InterPreters: Proof of Concept* (ref. no. E3/04/21, 2021–2022), *Optimisation and multilingual adaptation of the corpus module for the integration of French into the VIP system* (ref. no. 03/2021, 2021–2022); *Voice-text integrated system for InterPreters: Proof of Concept* (ref. no. PDC2021-121220-I00, 2021–2023), and *VIP II - Multi-lingual and Multi-domain Adaptation for the Optimisation of the VIP system* (ref. no. PID2020-112818GB-I00, 2021–2025).

[3] For a detailed description of the VIP system, the reader is referred to Corpas Pastor (2020, 2021a and 2021b).

(e.g., Interprefy); (iii) machine interpretation (MI) systems (e.g., Ambassador); training materials (e.g., ORCIT) and virtual platforms (e.g., IVY); as well as other resources that can also aid the interpreting process with special focus on corpus tools.

The catalogue allows users to suggest new tools, report any issues and perform advanced searches. Figure 1 illustrates an advanced query (search and comparison) of terminology systems for interpreters according to selected features (multiple glossary management, remote glossary exchange, etc.), OS (Windows) and languages supported (English, French and Spanish).

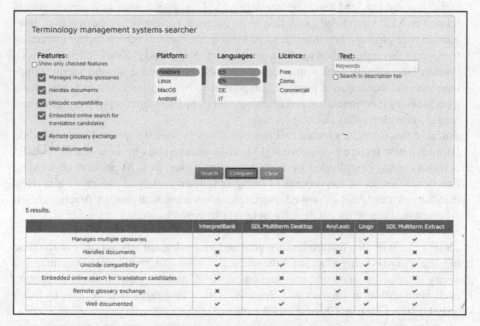

Fig. 1. Terminology management systems compared (VIP catalogue screenshot)

Component B was initially divided in three modules (v. 1.0) to be used to prepare for an interpretation (Module I), when delivering the service (Module II) and for training (Module III). For better usability, v. 1.1 and v. 1.2 contain a new distribution into "families" or sets of functionalities:

– *Corpus functionalities* include former Module I (automatic corpus compilation, corpus uploading, comparable and parallel corpus management, corpus query, term and pattern extraction) and some other new functionalities, such as corpus renaming, merging and splitting; oral and multimodal corpus compilation and management; manual import of resources for corpus compilation through URL pasting; automatic deduplication and non-text filtering; export of results in .xl format; semi-automatic alignment of parallel corpora; direct access to CQP; and enlarged number of document formats supported.

- *Glossary functionalities* integrate some features formerly in Modules II and II (glossary management and query), as well as novel functionalities: management and query of synonyms; merging, splitting, and sharing of glossaries; collaborative glossary creation; customisation of glossary directionality and languages; increase of search options per selected languages; and optimisation of MT candidate translation equivalents; integration of comparable corpus and parallel corpus functionalities with MT output, etc.
- *Complementary functionalities* also comprise functionalities formerly in Module I (named entity recognition, NER) and Module II (automatic text summarisation, automatic note-taking, and machine translation, MT), together with new developments related to NER (improved extraction from corpora, pattern-filtered extraction, integration with glossary functionalities) and automatic summarisation (better extraction techniques through synthesis and integration with corpus and glossary functionalities). Further functionalities and improvements are also envisaged in the short term (mindmap generation, increases browser compatibility, ASR optimisation and integration with glossary functionalities, and improvement of MT through corpus integration and neural network training, among others).
- *Training functionalities* include all functionalities previously grouped under Module III, plus a new feature to improve sight-translation exercises by selecting the parallel corpora created or uploaded by users to generate exercises. At present, all training functionalities are in the process of being optimised (enlarged choice of exercises, difficulty scales, ASR-improved exercises, integration with corpus functionalities, AI-improved image recognition for note-taking symbols, etc.).

VIP v. 1.2 will also feature multilingual and multi-domain adaptation. For the time being, the system is being adapted for the medical domain (automatic corpus compilation, glossary generation, automatic summarisation, NER, and MT), and it already supports French (in addition to English and Spanish). Other languages will be also included shortly (Italian, German, Chinese and Arabic).

3   Creating a Glossary of Phraseology from Scratch

Specialised discourse is particularly characterised by specific multiword units, whether they are classed as multiword terms (e.g., *tidal energy*) or as phraseological units (e.g., *generate electric power*). In this paper we will adopt a broad approach to specialised phraseology that includes examples like the ones above, irrespective of their linguistic functions and/or syntactic patterns.[4] After all, interpreters are not concerned with such distinctions when building their glossaries.

This section presents an automated procedure for the automatic creation of a trilingual corpus-based glossary of phraseological terms (English, French and Spanish) using VIP (v. 1.2). Our protocolised methodology will make use of all VIP functionalities (see Sect. 2). It comprises two phases: (I) automatic corpus compilation and (II) automatic

---

[4] Contrary to Gouadec (1994) and Gläser (2007), we believe there is no clear-cut boundary between terminology and phraseology, in the sense that multiword terms possess a purely naming function and specialised phraseology simply describes relations between terms.

glossary creation. Phases I–II involve various substeps (i.e., elements that break each step into a series of separate actions or tasks), as described below.

In order to illustrate our methodology, we have simulated a preparatory phase (advanced preparation) for a cheval interpretation, i.e., a type of interpretation where the interpreter has a sufficient command of a second language to work in two booths in the same event (cf. Pinenaar and Cornelius 2018, p. 12). If preparing for an interpretation in two languages may seem time-consuming and even stressful, things can get *slightly* more complicated when three languages are at play. As context of the simulation, we have chosen an international conference on renewable energy. This seems to be an extremely hot topic nowadays. For instance, according to the Conference Index, there are 179 international conferences scheduled just for August 2022.[5]

3.1 Automatic Corpus Compilation

When pressed for time (as most interpreters are when preparing for a job assignment), being able to compile a corpus automatically can be an excellent asset. VIP (v.1.2) provides interpreters with corpus functionalities that allow for (semi-)automatic corpus creation on any domain. Within *Monolingual corpus management*, users can select *Semi-automatic corpus compilation*, choose the language (Spanish or English, French or Spanish) and then enter a simple or a Boolean query sequence. The seed words used will retrieve a set of related webpages that can be selected automatically, limited in number, or, else, inspected individually and then selected manually. In this paper we will opt for the fastest way: compiling corpora automatically.

VIP also allows a granular approach to corpus compilation. For instance, automatic corpus compilation can be done in one go (all documents are added at a time in a single loop) or, else, the search can be refined through various loops (for instance, a small pilot corpus is compiled in order to filter relevant multiword units and terms as seed words for extended corpus compilation). In this paper we will adopt the second approach: compiling corpora in a multi-loop fashion. Six comparable corpora (i.e., corpus of non-translated texts) will be crawled in English, French and Spanish.

The three loops identified correspond to the various substeps needed to create more focused and enlarged corpora: (i) pilot corpus compilation, (ii) summarisation and seed words extraction; (iii) extended corpus compilation through refined sets of seeds.

Pilot Corpus Compilation. Three small comparable corpora on renewable energies have been compiled as pilots in a linear fashion: Energ1_EN, Energ1_ES, and Energ1_FR. VIP allows users to import the corpus to be queried straightaway or, else, import the corpus and download the files in .txt or .vrt (our choice in this case study). Users can also create3 one file with all the information (i.e., all .txt files together) or else create one file per website (our choice in this case study). We have used the main conference topic as seed word (EN *renewable energy*, ES *energía removable*, FR *énergie renouvelable*). Figure 2 illustrates the automatic compilation of the pilot French corpus. Comparability of the pilot corpora is ensured by their similar size regarding the number

---

[5] https://conferenceindex.org/ (Accessed 15 June 2022). In this website an average of 150 renewable energy conferences are advertised per month until September 2023.

of documents, tokens (running words) and types, their similar lexical density (type/token ratio, TTR), and their similar list of frequent terms. Table 1 shows the number of documents, running words (tokens), types and lexical density (token/type ratio, TTR) of the three pilot corpora.

Table 1. Size and lexical density of pilot corpora

	docs.	tokens	types	TTR
Energ1_EN	11	17,244	3,861	4.46
Energ1_ES	14	16,504	3,778	4.36
Energ1_FR	210	16,626	3,135	5.30

Comparability also shines through the coverage of terms. For instance, the 10 most frequent terms in the three corpora are as follows: *energy, power*[6], *wind, electricity, source, biomass, water, renewables, heat, fuel* (EN); *energía, fuente, emisión, electricidad, renovables, desarrollo, producción, gas, combustible, eólica* (ES); *energiè, électricitè, production, eau, biomasse, gaz, développement, source, hydrogène, éolienne* (FR). Most equivalents of these top occurring terms in one language are to be found in the other two languages (60%), usually within the same frequency rank (or the immediately lower rank). There is a higher coincidence when only two languages are compared: 80% (ES-EN) and 90% (EN-FR, ES-FR).

Summarisation and Seed Words Extraction. Once the three pilot corpora have been compiled, a domain survey can be generated through extractive automatic summarisation.[7] This is a faster way to acquire domain knowledge in general. Timewise, there is a substantial difference if the interpreter makes use of this functionality to prepare for an interpretation. By default, documents are reduced 80%. Advanced summarisation provides text reduction on demand (by specific word count or reduction rate established by the user). Figure 3 illustrates advanced summarisation of file no. 3 of the Spanish pilot corpus (318 words, 20% of the original document). Thus, instead of reading 16,504 words in Spanish about the conference topic, the interpreter would only need to read 3,300 words of Spanish summaries in order to learn specialised knowledge, terminology, and phraseology. A similar situation would be found with regards to the English and French summaries.

The resulting summaries can be inspected manually or downloaded (and uploaded to the system) as subcorpora of summaries: EN_Summary, ES_Summary and FR_Summary. This substep facilitates (and speeds up) the process of locating refined seed words, as summaries are term-rich documents, with higher lexical density (i.e., lower TTR). For instance, the summary file no. 3 (TTR 2.05; 318 tokens/155 types) contains simple and multiword terms, including types of renewable energies (*biomasa,*

[6] *Energy* and *power* are synonyms in the English top frequency rank.

[7] This step could be omitted though, as users can extract refined seed words through direct pattern query from the pilot corpora. However, it should be noted that this is a more time-consuming option.

Fig. 2. Automatic compilation of Energ1_FR

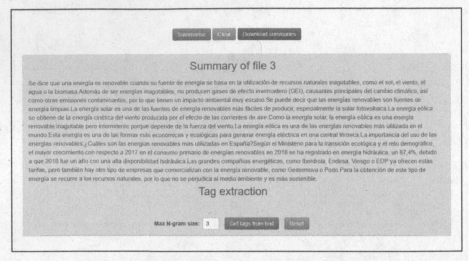

Fig. 3. Automatic summarisation of Energ1_ES documents

gases de efecto invernadero, energía limpia, energía solar, energía eólica…), acronyms (*GEI*), collocations (*impacto ambiental, producir energía, perjudicar el medio ambiente, causante principal…*), and even encyclopaedic information: "Se dice que una energía es renovable cuando su fuente de energía se basa en la utilización de recursos naturales inagotables como el sol, el viento, el agua o la biomasa"[8] (Fig. 3).

An enlarged set of multiword seeds have been extracted from summary subcorpora. Query searches have been filtered through term building patterns (N + N, N + A, A + N, N + prep + N). Multiword seeds seem to increase refinement and comparability of web-crawled corpora (cf. Corpas Pastor 2021b). The extended comparable corpora have been compiled by means of the following 10 multiword seeds (translation equivalents extracted from both pilot corpora and summary subcorpora):

– EN: *renewable energy, wind power, solar power, geothermal energy, climate change, solid biomass, energy efficiency, fossil fuel, carbon emissions, greenhouse gas.*
– ES: *energía renovable, energía eólica, energía solar, energía geotérmica, cambio climático, biomasa sólida, eficiencia energética, combustible fósil, emisiones de carbono, gas de efecto invernadero.*
– FR: *énergie renouvelable, énergie éolien, énergie solaire, énergie géothermique, changement climatique, biomasse solide, efficacité énergétique, combustible fossile, émissions de carbone, gaz à effet de serre.*

Extended Corpus Compilation. The trilingual set of refined seeds is used recursively to create the following extended comparable corpora: Energ2_EN, Energ2_ES, and

---

[8] 'Energy is said to be renewable when it is sourced from renewable resources such as the sun, wind, water, or biomass.' (Our translation).

Energ2_FR. Comparability has been secured by (i) using a trilingual set of multi-word seeds (translation equivalents), and (ii) webcrawling corpora with similar sizes (types/tokens) and lexical density (TTR),[9] as shown in Table 2.

Table 2. Size and lexical density of extended corpora

	docs.	tokens	types	TTR
Energ2_EN	65	284,428	22,716	12.52
Energ2_ES	61	283,549	19,893	14.25
Energ2_FR	62	283,033	25,609	11.05

A further indicator of comparability is the percentage of coincidence among the 10 most frequent single-noun terms in the three extended corpora: 80% for EN-EN-FR; 90% for EN-ES (see Table 3). The remaining 20% (EN-EN-FR) and 10% equivalent terms (EN-ES) are also found within the top 20 most frequent terms.

Table 3. The ten most frequent terms in the extended corpora

	Energ2_EN	Energ2_ES	Energ2_FR
1.	energy	energía	énergie
2.	power	gas	électricité
3.	electricity	combustible	eau
4.	wind	emisión	vent
5.	fuel	electricidad	gaz
6.	gas	biomasa	chaleur
7.	oil	calor	émission
8.	carbon	carbono	éolienne
9.	heat	biogás	marée
10.	biomass	viento	co2

3.2 Automatic Glossary Creation

The VIP system enables the creation of monolingual and multilingual glossaries. They can be built from corpora or manually compiled. Several functionalities allow users to create, download, upload and delete glossaries, perform external searches in order to locate translation equivalents or, else, translate terms automatically through machine translation (and post-editing, if needed). In this paper we will show how to create a

---

[9] In order to ensure a similar number of running words in the three corpora, we have downloaded them, adjusted the number of tokens (by adding or removing files), and uploaded them to the system, if needed. Since the size of individual documents tend to vary, a future version of VIP (v. 1.4) will also feature automatic corpus compilation by number of tokens.

glossary of phraseology terms automatically. This is performed in a two-phase fashion: (i) corpus-based extraction of phraseology and glossary population, and (ii) postediting and validation of the corpus-based glossary. Both substeps (and related tasks) are performed (semi-)automatically.

Phraseology Extraction and Glossary Population. In this preliminary task, the three extended corpora (Energ2_EN, Energ2_ES and Energ2_FR) are queried through (customisable) patterns and n-grams. Results are displayed in a query page as items that can be selected by users and added to a glossary. Glossaries can be created beforehand or, else, on the spot. In this case, we have already set up a trilingual glossary named EnergGlos (see Fig. 4).

Some examples of phraseology and multiword-term building pattern extraction are shown below:

(1) N + N: *fossil fuel, energy source, power plant, climate change, wind turbine* (EN); *efecto invernadero, medio ambiente, gas invernadero efecto pantalla, combustible biodiesel* (ES); *empreinte carbone, état membre, kilowatt heure, puissance crête* (FR).

(2) A + N/N + A: *natural gas, clean energy, nuclear power, solar panel, global warming* (EN); *combustible fósil, energía geotérmica, radiación solar, impacto ambiental, agua salobre* (ES); *certificat vert, changement climatique, énergie cinétique, densité énergétique, marée haute* (FR).

(3) N + prep + N: *source of energy, cost per megawatt, flow of water, supply of electricity, barrel of oil* (EN); *combustible de biomasa, dióxido de carbono, emisión de CO2, gasificación de lejía, astilla de madera* (ES); *effet de serre, dioxyde de carbone, vitesse du vent, pompè à chaleur, gaz d' enfouiss* (FR).

(4) V + N/V + * + N: *produce heat, provide energy, pump water, cut emissions, address climate change* (EN); *liberar etanol, accionar un motor, generar electricidad, transformar en energía, calentar un fluido* (ES); *réduire le emission, brûler un combustible, transformer en energie, baisser le thermostat, installer un éolienne* (FR).

Patterns and n-grams can be also extracted for a specific word form or lemma (see some instances of cognates below):

(5) A + N/N + A term-patterns: *renewable electricity, solar electricity, green electricity, domestic electricity, CO_2-neutral electricity* (EN); *electricidad fotovoltáica, electricidad renovable, electricidad solar, electricidad excedentaria, electricidad barata* (ES); *électricité verte, électricité consommé, électricité renouvelable, électricité ólienne, osmotique* (FR).

(6) 5-grams: *general electricity transmisión and distribution, global electricity power generation capacity, electricity from renewable enerygy sources, rapid expansion of renewable electricity* (EN); *sistemas de distribución de electricidad, electricidad mediante turbinas de vapor, colectores solares para generar electricidad, electricidad fotovoltaica y termoeléctrica producida* (ES); *capacité de production d' électricité, le coût de l' électricité, MWh d' électricité verte produite, produire son électricité grâce à, électricité issue de la biomasse* (FR).

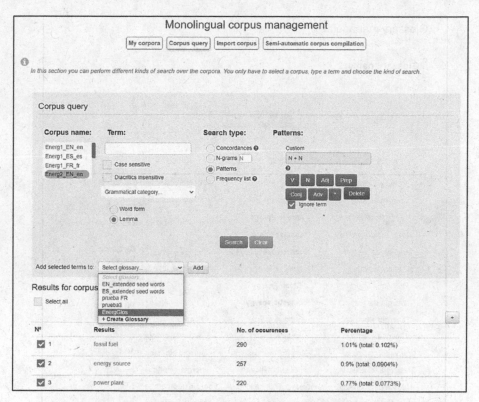

Fig. 4. N + N pattern extraction from Energ2_EN to be added to EnergGlos

Postediting and Validation. Lemma selection for the phraseology glossary (EnergG-los) can be done automatically on the fly by just clicking on the multiword units selected by the user from their pattern queries on the three corpora. Thus, interpreters can build their own trilingual glossary by adding as many entries as needed. The glossary being created is stored under *Glossary management* and it provides automatic translation candidates through neural machine translation (NMT), as illustrated in Fig. 5.

Columns (EN, ES, FR) can be ordered by users according to their preferences, entries can be alphabetically sorted, postedited or removed, external searches can be performed to find or check translation equivalents (NMT systems, on-line translation memories and e-dictionaries), etc. In addition, new entries can be added manually if needed (for instance, novel or relevant multiword units found through direct corpus concordance searches). Glossaries can be also imported in the system, added to existing glossaries, merged, shared, downloaded, queried on-line, etc. Figure 6 shows an excerpt of EnergGlos in.xls format. In order to guide the user to build glossaries automatically, entries which have been directly selected from corpora are highlighted in bold. This indicates that the marked multiword units are considered to be "correct", a fact that can be used to delete entries or validate translation equivalents.

By way of illustration, in the process of building the EnergGlos glossary the interpreter will find ES **energía mareotriz** (also **energía oceánica**) machined translated as

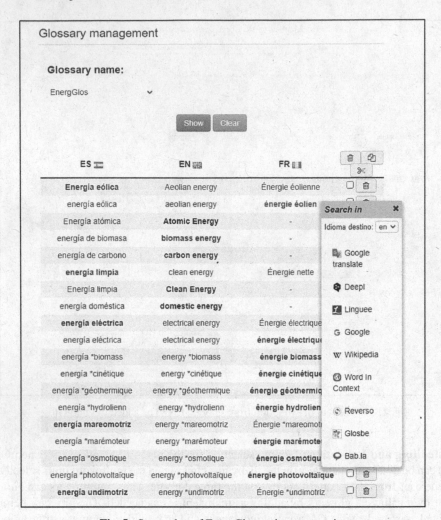

Fig. 5. Screenshot of EnergGlos under construction

EN *energy *mareomotriz* and FR *énergie *mareomotríz*, (i.e., with the adjectival part left untranslated, as indicated by a wildcat). But just a line below, the user will get the "correct" equivalent in French (extracted from Energ2_FR) and also highlighted in bold: **energie marèmoteur**, as well as other less frequent synonyms *énergie marine* and *énergie océanique*. The English equivalent can be found through external searches (for instance, in Linguee or DeepL), and the correspondences found (*tidal energy, tidal power* and the less frequent *ocean energy*) can be checked against the "correct" corpus-based terms found in our trilingual glossary (**tidal energy**, **marine energy**, **ocean energy**) or through direct corpus query (**tidal power**). Then, depending on their needs, the interpreter may decide to keep all synonymous phraseological terms in the three languages, the most frequent multiword unit for each language, or all synonyms in the source language (e.g., EN) and only the most frequent translation equivalent for French and Spanish.[10]

	A	B	C	D	E
1	EN	ES	FR		
2	biomass energy	energía de la biomasa	énergie de la biomasse		
3	carbon dioxide concentrations	concentraciones de dióxido de carbono	concentrations de dioxyde de carbone		
4	clean energy	energía limpia	énergie propre		
5	co2-neutral electricity	electricidad neutra en carbono	électricité neutre en carbone		
6	electricity generation capacity	capacidad de producción eléctrica	capacité de production d'électricité		
7	energy efficiency	eficiencia energética	efficacité énergétique		
8	fossil energy	energía fósil	énergie fossile		
9	geothermal energy	energía geotérmica	énergie géothermique		
10	GHG	GEI	GES		
11	greenhouse effect gas	gas de efecto invernadero	gaz d'effet serre		
12	heat a fluid	calentar un fluido	chauffer un fluide		
13	hydraulic energy	energía hidráulica	énergie hydraulique		
14	kinetic energy	energía cinética	énergie cinétique		
15	low-carbon energy	energía baja en carbono	énergie bas carbone		
16	ocean energy	energía oceánica	énergie océanique		
17	offshore wind energy	energía eólica marina	énergie éolienne offshore		
18	photovoltaic-thermoelectric energy	electricidad fotovoltaica y termoeléctrica	énergie photovoltaïque-thermoélectrique		
19	release ethanol	liberar etanol	libérer l'éthanol		
20	renewable energy	energía renovable	énergie renouvelable		
21	salty water	agua salobre	eau saumâtre		
22	sustainable energy	energía sostenible	énergie durable		
23	systems of distribution of electricity	sistemas de distribución de electricidad	systèmes de distribution d'électricité		
24	the cost of the electricity	el coste de la electricidad	le coût de l'électricité		
25	tidal energy	energía mareomotriz	énergie marémoteur		
26	wind energy	energía eólica	énergie éolien		

Fig. 6. EnergGlos in excel

4 Conclusion

Interpreters are constantly faced with strenuous and arduous tasks, not only during delivery of the service but also when preparing for a given specific interpreting job. Conference interpreting involves a particularly heavy cognitive load, especially when the interpreter has to perform in two different booths.

Main stumbling blocks of advance preparation are terminology and phraseology. In this paper we have adopted a broad approach to specialised phraseology that includes both multiword terms and phraseological units for two main reasons: (a) there is no clear-cut boundary between them and (b) interpreters do not seem to bothered by these fine linguistic categorisations in their daily work.

This paper presents a novel protocol for advance preparation using the VIP system that automates the whole process (from corpus compilation to glossary building), in order to save time and (cognitive) effort and facilitate interpreters' work. To the best of our knowledge, this is the first study that presents a methodology to automatically create a domain-specific trilingual glossary designed for cheval interpretation.

---

[10] In VIP 1.2 synonyms can only be entered as separate entries. In the next version synonyms will be linked to single entries.

References

Aston, G.: Learning phraseology from speech corpora. In: Leńko-Szymańska, A., Boulton, A. (eds.) Multiple Affordances of Language Corpora for Data-Driven Learning, Studies in Corpus Linguistics, vol. 69, pp. 65–84. John Benjamins, Amsterdam, Philadelphia (2015)

Cattaneo, E.: Idiomatic expressions in conference interpreting. Universita Degli Studi di Bologna, Sede di Forlì, SSLMIT, Forlì, Italy. Graduation thesis (2004)

Corpas Pastor, G.: Technology solutions for interpreters: the VIP system. Hermēneus. Revista de Traducción e Interpretación **23**, 91–123 (2021a)

Corpas Pastor, G.: Interpreting and technology: is the sky really the limit. In: Mitkov, R., Sosoni, V., Giguère, J.C., Murgolo, E., Deysel, E. (eds.) TRanslation and Interpreting Technology Online. Proceedings of the Conference, pp. 15–24 (2021b)

Corpas Pastor, G., Gaber, M.: Extracción de fraseología para intérpretes a partir de corpus comparables compilados mediante reconocimiento automático del habla. In: Corpas Pastor, G., Bautista Zambrana, M.R., Hidalgo Ternero, C.M. (eds.) Sistemas fraseológicos en contraste: enfoques computacionales y de corpus, pp. 271–291. Granada, Comares (2021)

Crezee, I., Grant, L.: Missing the plot? Idiomatic language in interpreter education. Int. J. Interpret. Educ. **5**(1), 17–33 (2013)

Chang, C., Wu, M.M., Kuo, T.G.: Conference interpreting and knowledge acquisition: how professional interpreters tackle unfamiliar topics". Interpreting **20**(2), 204–231 (2018)

Fantinuoli, C.: Computer-assisted preparation in conference interpreting. Transl. Interpret. **9**(2), 24–37 (2017)

Díaz Galaz, S.: The effect of previous preparation in simultaneous interpreting: preliminary results. Across Lang. Cult. **12**(2), 173–191 (2011)

Gaber, M., Corpas Pastor, G., Omer, A.: Speech-to-Text technology as a documentation tool for interpreters: a new approach to compiling an ad hoc corpus and extracting terminology from video-recorded speeches. TRANS: Revista de Traductología, **24**, pp. 1–18 (2020)

Gile, D.: Basic Concepts and Models for Interpreter and Translator Training. John Benjamins, Amsterdam, Philadelphia (1995[2009])

Gouadec, D.: Nature et traitement des entités phraséologiques. In: Terminologie et phraséologie: acteurs et amenageurs; actes de la deuxième Université d'Automne en Terminologie, Rennes 2, Septembre 1993, pp. 167–193 (1994)

Gläser, R.: Fachphraseologie. In: Handbücher zur Sprach- und Kommunikationswissenschaft/Handbooks of Linguistics and Communication Science (HSK), vol. 1, pp. 482–505. Walter de Gruyter (2007)

Moser-Mercer, B.: Terminology documentation in conference interpretation. Terminology et Traduction **2**(3), 285–303 (1992)

Jiang, H.: A survey of glossary practice of conference interpreters (2005). aiic.net. https://aiic.net/p/7151

Markič, J.: Acerca de la (in) traducibilidad de las unidades fraseológicas en la interpretación de conferencias. Phraseologie im Wörterbuch und Korpus Phraseology in Dictionaries and Corpora, pp. 193–203 (2012)

Nolan, J.: Interpretation: Techniques and Exercises. Multilingual Matters, Clevedon, UK (2005)

Pinenaar, M., Cornelius, E.: Interpreting Terminology | Terminologie van het tolken | Tolkerterminologie | Mareo a botoloki | Amatemu okutolika. African Sun Media (2018)

Pérez-Pérez, P.: The use of a corpus management tool for the preparation of interpreting assignments: a case study. Int. J. Transl. Interpret. Res. **10**(1), 137–151 (2018)

Song, X., Tang, M.: An empirical study on the impact of pre-interpreting preparation on business interpreting under Gile's efforts model. Theory Pract. Lang. Stud. **10**, 1640–1650 (2020)

Tolosa-Igualada, M., Mezcua, A.R.: La opacidad de las unidades fraseológicas y su tratamiento por intérpretes en formación. In: Opacidad, idiomaticidad, traducción, pp. 365–383. Servicio de Publicaciones (2010)

Xu, R.: Corpus-based terminological preparation for simultaneous interpreting. Interpret. Res **20**(1), 29–58 (2018)

Readability and Communication in Machine Translation of Arabic Phraseologisms into Spanish

Mohamed El-Madkouri[1] and Beatriz Soto Aranda[2]([✉])

[1] Universidad Autónoma de Madrid, Campus de Cantoblanco,
C. Francisco Tomás y Valiente, 1, 28049 Madrid, Spain
`el-madkouri@uam.es`
[2] Universidad Rey Juan Carlos, Calle Infantas, 55,
28300 Aranjuez, Madrid, Spain
`beatriz.soto@urjc.es`

Abstract. Even though translation from Arabic into Spanish is far from the accuracy level achieved for other language pairs such as English/Spanish, considerable progress has been made in machine translation from Arabic into other languages [1, 2, 4, 45]. From this perspective, this research aims to assess how Arabic proverbs are translated into Spanish by three machine translation tools - Google Translate, Reverso Context, and Tradukka – in order to determine the translation's quality, and measure their accuracy, as well as the tools' ability to recognize said proverbs as independent semantic linguistic units. To this end, we have used twenty Fusha Arabic proverbs: three that have no Spanish equivalent; six that also exist in Spanish; three that bear certain resemblance to existing Spanish proverbs; and eight that possess functional equivalents in Spanish. The study concludes that the machine translation tools tested present a low accuracy level, requiring post-editing by a human translator. They make errors rendering Arabic proverbs that it is possible to translate verbatim as they also exist in Spanish and do not recognize proverbs as independent phraseological units when translating proverbs in context, with few exceptions in the case of Reverso Context.

Keywords: Proverbs · Arabic · Spanish · Machine translation

1 Introduction

Significant studies have analyzed the issue of proverbs from didactic, critical, typological, and theoretical perspectives in the last decades [3, 12, 17, 18, 28, 34, 36], even though none has refuted Baker's statement concerning the two main problems in translating idioms and fixed expressions, including proverbs. Said problems include, on the one hand, the ability to recognize and interpret them correctly, and on the other hand, the difficulties involved in rendering the various aspects of meaning that they convey into the target language [6].

From this point of view, phraseological units present two key issues for natural translation, mainly if translators have not developed a deep diachronic and synchronic

G. Corpas Pastor and R. Mitkov (Eds.): EUROPHRAS 2022, LNAI 13528, pp. 78–89, 2022.
https://doi.org/10.1007/978-3-031-15925-1_6

linguistic knowledge during their training. From a diachronic perspective, phraseology is no exception to the movements of History and change over time. Like any linguistic phenomenon, phraseologies can fall into disuse and then reappear as relics in linguistic productions of later ages, not to mention classical texts translated decades after they were written, when the sociohistorical conditions that prompted their production had completely changed. In short, the discursive production conditions are different from those of reception in both temporal and spatial dimensions.

From a synchronic point of view, phraseology can be found in all texts, regardless of their typology - whether in literary, media, or scientific discourses. However, as one of the primary functions of language is communication, the same goes for translating. Thus, we can potentially translate any text into another language if it aims to communicate something and do it naturally or automatically by using machine translators.

Nonetheless, the research on proverbs in the machine translation domain is still limited, especially for Arabic [25–27, 33, 37]. Despite this, Translation undergraduate students often use tools such as Google Translator or Reverso Context when translating proverbs, due to their increased dependence on computer software and Internet applications, along with the lack of Arabic-Spanish phraseological dictionaries, even though specific literature on this topic is available [7–9, 17, 19, 20, 30–32, 35, 39, 41, 44]. Along with the difficulty of recognizing a proverb - given their level of linguistic competence-, students must also deal with other challenges such as the semantic connotations that proverbs may acquire in a specific discursive context or the semantic transferences between Fusha Arabic and the various oral Arabic dialects [42, 43].

2   Proverbs in the Field of Phraseology and Their Translation

The Royal Spanish Academy's Spanish dictionary defines a proverb as a sharp and sententious saying in widespread use. On his part, [10] Casares presents a more precise definition of a proverb, specifying that it must fulfill the following characteristics: a) it must be a complete and independent phrase; b) it must possess an allegorical or direct meaning; c) it must use a sententious and elliptical formula to express a thought in the form of a judgment. According to [16], we can add various technical features: it presents a bi-member structure, it is anonymous, and it is transmitted orally. Finally, [13, pp. 148–150] defines proverbs as phraseological statements that are highly used and fulfil the following characteristics:

– Basic distinguishing features include lexicalization, syntactic and textual autonomy, general truth value, and anonymity.
– Additional distinguishing features include metaphorical meaning, phonic peculiarities, syntactic anomalies, or syntactic structures in which their elements preserve specific relationships, a conventional nature, and a didactic or dogmatic purpose.

From a translation perspective, it is worth mentioning that proverbs exist across natural languages, so they can be defined as linguistic universals, even though many of them are culturally shaped. For example, the Spanish proverb *salir de Málaga para entrar en Malagón*, also known as *salir de Guatemala para ir a Guatepeor*, includes a Spanish geographical location. Its verbatim translation is "leave Malaga to enter

Malagon" but it means "getting out of a bad situation and into one worse than the previous one," and its functional equivalent in English is "jumping out of the frying pan into the fire." In the case of the Spanish one *a cada cerdo le llega su San Martín*, it refers to the name of an animal that is forbidden to eat in Islam, which is the reason why it is not used in Arabic. The aforementioned Spanish proverb means "you always get your comeuppance in the end" and has an English functional equivalent: every dog has its day.

In order to translate phraseological units, Corpas Pastor [11 p. 281] distinguishes four main steps: 1) identification of the phraseological unit; 2. interpretation of said unit; 3. search of correspondences at the lexical level; and 4. establishment of equivalents at the textual level. Thus, from a translation perspective, Corpas Pastor [11] suggests two main translation techniques:

1. Translating the proverb by resorting to another existing fixed expression in the target language (LM) which maintains full equivalence. This technique is known as substitution technique. In this line of thought, [35] speaks of replacing the image of the source culture with another image in the target culture with the same function and communicative effect, although it differs denotatively.
2. Paraphrasing when translating an image without functional equivalence in the target language, agreeing with [35]. In this case, Sevilla Muñoz [40] recommends using a hypernym, a more generic term.

In the case of translation from Arabic into Spanish, previous works have analyzed the translation of proverbs from a theoretical-comparative perspective, studying the usefulness of the translating techniques [19, 43]. Likewise, some empirical-oriented studies have analyzed the translation methods to render proverbs in specific literary corpora [31, 38], and the Koran [24]. However, no empirical studies on machine translation have been founded.

In this respect, two issues are to be kept in mind when translating from Arabic into Spanish: on the one hand, even though Arabic and Spanish are not closely related languages with different cultural backgrounds, there are sayings of universal value; and on the other hand, the seven-century-long periods of Muslim presence in the Iberian Peninsula made its mark on the Spanish language. Scholars talk about two thousand Spanish words coming from Arabic, including names, verbs, adverbs, interjections, adverbial locutions, and fewer adjectives of manner [21], but also phraseological units and, within them, proverbs [14]. Therefore, authors such as [22] have supported the hypothesis of finding dynamic functional equivalents between proverbs used in both languages.

3   Objectives and Methodology

The purpose of this research is to observe whether the machine translation tools Google Translate (hereinafter GT) and Reverso Context (hereinafter RC) recognize Arabic proverbs as independent linguistic-semantic units or, on the contrary, they render its translation as if its constituents were isolated linguistic units. We have chosen

Tradukka (hereinafter T) as a *tertium comparationis*. We will try to answer the following questions:

a Which of the machine translation tools evaluated identifies the proverb?
b What are the strategies used to translate them?
c Are the rendered target translations meaningful in Spanish?
d Are they useful for translators?

For this purpose, we have compiled 20 Arabic proverbs classified into three groups: 1. three Arabic proverbs that have no Spanish equivalent (see Table 1); 2. six Arabic proverbs that also exist in Spanish (see Table 2); 3. three Arabic proverbs that bear certain resemblance to existing Spanish proverbs, with lexical variations (see Table 3); and 4. eight Arabic proverbs that possess functional equivalents in Spanish (see Table 4).

From the methodological point of view, we have used three criteria for selecting the corpora of the present research: use, frequency, and relevance, in order to use proverbs belonging to a not very specialized, everyday language that aims to reach the average reader. For this purpose, we conducted an internet search, looking at Arabic newspaper pages, blogs, Facebook, and other communication platforms. These proverbs are in use and can appear in written texts, as well as in conversations, because Arabic speakers use code-switching (dialectal Arabic - Fusha Arabic) and use high-level expressions to change the register or in order to focus their attention on specific words.

4 Results and Discussion

To analyze the results, we have divided the corpus into four tables following the distribution mentioned on the previous section. Each table contains the Arabic proverb and the translations rendered by the machine translation tools tested. Below each table, we have included an explanation of the results, the verbatim translation of the Arabic proverb into Spanish and English, its Spanish and English functional equivalent, if any, and, finally, a translatological commentary.

Table 1. Proverbs with no equivalent in Spanish

Arabic proverb	GT translation	RC translation	T translation
اجود من حاتم	Mejor que Hatim	Mejor/Hatim	Mejor que Hatim
إنَّ البغاث بأرضنا يستنسر	La pestilencia de nuestra tierra es agradable	El alivio en nuestra tierra está furioso	El alivio en nuestra tierra está furioso
لا ناقة لي فيها ولا جمل	No tengo camello ni camello en ella	No tengo elegancia ni frases	No tengo nada que ver con esto

The verbatim translation of the proverb (اجود من حاتم) into Spanish is *más generoso que Hatim* [More generous than Hatim.] As there is no functional equivalent in Spanish, it is necessary to paraphrase or neutralize the translation. GT, RC, and T have recognized the word "Hatim" as a personal name. However, they have translated the adjective (أجود) as "better" rather than "more generous." The word used in the target text could be interpreted as a hypernym of the source word, but as the proverb refers to Hatim, a legendary figure in Arab culture known for his extraordinary generosity, the target translation is not accurate.

The verbatim translation of the proverb (إنّ البغاث بأرضنا يستنسر) into Spanish is *el bugat en nuestra tierra se hace águila* [The bugat in our land becomes an eagle.] The word "bugat" refers to a wimpy little bird and it is more symbolic than real. There is no equivalent in Spanish. Its meaning is "among us, the weak is emboldened."

Notice that none of the three machine translation tools provide an accurate translation of the Arabic proverb, not even a verbatim translation. They do not recognize the word (البُغاث) which, according to the Al-Maany Dictionary, can be translated as *milano* [kite] or *gorriones* [sparrows] nor the verb (إستنسر).

The verbatim translation of the proverb (لا ناقة لي فيها ولا جمل) into Spanish is *en ello no tengo ni camella ni camello* [I have neither a camel nor a camel in it] and its pragmatic meaning is "this is not my problem". There is no functional equivalent in Spanish. RC translation is wrong. GT offers a literal translation, with the following errors: it assigns masculine gender to the word (ناقة), when it is feminine, and having no other linguistic context, it assigns feminine value to the affix (ها), when it should be translated as 'it'. Finally, T presents a pragmatic translation.

Table 2. Arabic proverbs for which there are identical Spanish proverbs.

Arabic proverb	GT translation	RC translation	T translation
إذا كان الكلام من فضة يكون الصمت من ذهب	Si el habla es plata, el silencio es oro	Si el discurso de la plata es silencio de oro	Si las palabras son de plata, el silencio es de oro
ما مضي فات	¿Qué es demasiado tarde?/Lo que se fue es pasado	Eso quedó en el pasado /lo hecho/hecho está	Pasado
ليس كل ما يلمع ذهبا	No todo lo que reluce es oro	No es oro todo lo que brilla/no todo lo que brilla es oro	No todo lo que brilla es oro
العقل السليم في الجسم السليم	la mente está sana en el cuerpo sano	la mente está sana en el cuerpo sano	Mente sana en un cuerpo sano
الوقاية خير من العلاج	Es mejor prevenir que curar	Es mejor prevenir que curar	Es mejor prevenir que curar
الوحدة خير من جليس السوء	La unidad es mejor que un mal Gillies	La unidad es mejor que mala	La soledad es mejor que una mala niñera

The verbatim translation of (إذا كان الكلام من فضة يكون الصمت من ذهب) into Spanish is *si la palabra es plata, el silencio es oro* [If words are silver, silence is gold] although nowadays the proverb *en boca cerrada no entran moscas* [it is better to remain silent and be thought a fool than to speak and remove all doubt] is more widely used. According to the Multilingual Proverbs Book of the Cervantes Institute, there is an equivalent in Spanish: *si hablar fuera de plata, el silencio sería de oro*. Each engine offers a different target text. In the case of Tradukka, it proposes a verbatim translation, retaining the grammatical category of (الكلام) and (الصمت.) GT resorts to a nominal sentence. The target text proposed by RC does not make sense in Spanish: *si el discurso de la plata es silencio de oro*.

The verbatim translation of the proverb (ما مضي فات) is *lo pasado, pasado está*. This Arabic proverb exists in Spanish. It is also common to use *a lo hecho, pecho* [What's done is done.] Tradukka does not recognize the phrase and is only able to translate it as 'past'. In the case of GT, it offers two target texts. In the first one "What is too late?" a confusion with (ما) is observed by interpreting it as an interrogative mark and not as a negation one. The rest of the target text does not correspond to the meaning of the source text. In contrast, RC offers two translations that could be acceptable: one as a paraphrase *eso se quedó en el pasado* and another as a functional equivalent *lo hecho, hecho está*.

The proverb (ليس كل ما يلمع ذهبا) exists in Spanish. The three machine translation tools render similar target texts, although GT is closer to the equivalent expression in Spanish. In the case of RC, it offers a paraphrase in a contextualized example. Thus, it translates the phrase (لكن ثانيةً ليس كل ما يلمع ذهباً) as *aunque las cosas no son siempre lo que parecen*.

The proverb (العقل السليم في الجسم السليم) exists in Spanish with two variants, the Latin source text *mens sana in corpore sano* and its Spanish translation *mente sana en cuerpo sano*. The translations of the three tools are close to the Spanish proverb with minor differences.

The proverb (الوقاية خير من العلاج) exists in Spanish with the expression *más vale prevenir que curar* [Better safe than sorry.] The three tools translate (الوقاية) successfully and (العلاج) by infinitives, using the technique of transposition (change of grammatical category), although the target text is a literal translation that reproduces the syntactic structure of the source text. However, Reverso Context offers the Spanish proverb in its coined form in a contextualized example: (الوقاية خير من العلاجوقد أظهرت التجربة الأوروبية الأوروبية بالفعل أن) with the meaning of *De hecho, la experiencia europea ha puesto de manifiesto que más vale prevenir que curar*.

The verbatim translation of the proverb (الوحدة خير من جليس السوء) is *mejor soledad que mala compañía* [better solitude than bad company]. This Arabic proverb exists in Spanish; *mejor solo que mal acompañado* [Better to be alone than in bad company]. The three tools offer different translations. Tradukka makes a mistake by translating (جليس) as "nanny" instead of "company", GT's translation does not make sense because it has read (جليس) as if it were a proper name 'Gilles', RC's translation does not make sense either, because it has not identified and translated the word (جليس). Nonetheless, when translating a contextualized example, it uses the Spanish equivalent correctly: (دائما الوحدة خير من جليس السوءكمايقولون) *como suele decirse: mejor solo que mal acompañado* [Like they generally say: better off alone than in bad company.]

Table 3. Arabic proverbs that exist in Spanish with variations.

Arabic proverb	GT translation	RC translation	T translation
أصاب عصفورين بحجرواحد	Golpea dos pájaros de un tiro.	Golpea dos pájaros con una piedra	Golpea dos pájaros de un tiro.
اعمل خير وارميه بحرا	Haz el bien y tíralo al mar.	Haz el bien y tira el mar.	Haz el bien y tíralo al mar.
عصفور في اليد ولا عشرة على الشجرة.	Pájaro en mano y no diez volando	Pájaro en mano y diez volando	Un pájaro en la mano y no diez volando

The verbatim translation of the proverb (أصاب عصفورين بحجرواحد) is *mató dos pájaros con una sola piedra* [She/he killed two birds with one stone.] This Arabic proverb exists in Spanish with a small variation *mató dos pájaros de un tiro*, using the word "shot" instead of "stone". GT and T have translated (بحجرواحد) by "with one shot" and not "with only a stone", approximating the Spanish proverb, although they keep the verb "to hit" instead of "to kill". Although the original text is isolated, both tools translate the verb in present tense instead of past tense. RC also uses past tense instead of the present tense and gives a verbatim translation of the proverb.

The verbatim translation of (اعمل خيرا وارميه بحرا) is *haz el bien y échalo al mar* [do good and throw it into the sea] and its functional equivalent is *haz el bien y no mires con quién* [do good and do not look to whom/Do what is right, no matter what happens.] All three tools give a verbatim translation of the proverb. GT and T offer identical translations. RC made a mistake by not recognizing the pronoun attached to the verb.

The verbatim translation of (عصفور في اليد ولا عشرة على الشجرة) is *un pájaro en la mano y no diez en el árbol* [one bird in the hand and not ten in the tree.] In Spanish it is equivalent to the proverb *más vale pájaro en mano que dos/cien volando* [a bird in the hand is better than two/a hundred in the air/a bird in hand is worth two in the bush.] It should also be noted that none of the machine translation tools tested have rendered a verbatim translation of the second part of the proverb in Spanish but have resorted to the image used in the equivalent Spanish proverb.

The verbatim translation of (إن هذا الشبل من ذلك الأسد) is *este cachorro es de ese león* [this cup belongs to that lion] and has a functional equivalent in Spanish *de tal palo, tal astilla* [like father, like son.] All three tools render the propositional content of the Arabic proverb. However, RC uses the functional equivalent in Spanish in the translation of a contextualized example. Thus, it translates the sentence (هذا الشبل من ذاك الأسدالآن علمت من أين أتوا بعبارة"") as *ahí supe de dónde sacaron la expresión "de tal palo, tal astilla"* [That's how I knew where they got the expression 'Like father, like son'.]

The Arabic proverb (لقد أعذر من أنذر) is in past tense and its verbatim translation in Spanish is *se perdonó a quien advirtió* [The one who warned was spared]. The functional equivalent is *El que avisa no es traidor* [He who warns is not a betrayer/forewarned is forearmed]. None of the three machine translation tools render a proper translation, not even a literal version. However, RC uses the equivalent Spanish proverb when it appears in a sentence. Thus, it translates (وإن لم ينصلح فلقد أعذر من أنذر) as

Table 4. Arabic proverbs with functional equivalents in Spanish

Arabic proverb	GT translation	RC translation	T translation
إن هذا الشبل من ذلك الأسد.	Este cachorro es de ese león.	Este cachorro es de ese león.	Este cachorro es de ese león.
لقد أعذر من أنذر	Perdoné a los que me advirtieron	Él me ha excusado.	Lo siento, lo advierto
إذا كنت في قوم فاحلب في إنائهم.	Si estás en un pueblo, ordeña en su vasija	Si estás en un pueblo te gusta construirlo	Si estás en un pueblo, ordeña a su manera.
إذا وقع الجمل كثرت السكاكين.	Si el camello cae, los cuchillos se multiplican	Si las frases caen, los cuchillos abundan	Si el camello cae, hay· demasiados cuchillos
أحبّك يا نافعي ولو كنت ادوّي.	Te amo, Nafei, incluso si tomo medicamentos.	Te quiero, mis beneficiaries	Te amo Nafii, aunque fuera un niño
إن مع العسر يسرا.	Algunas dificultades son fáciles	Con las dificultades es fácil.	La facilidad con la dificultad
لمصيبة اذا عمت خفت و اذا خصت هالت	La calamidad, si se esparce, asusta, y si se la señala, quedará marcada.	Si tienes miedo, si cuentas a Halt.	M El dinero si se acaba, me asusto y si tengo esto
إن اللبيب من الإشارة يفهم.	El corazón del signo entiende	El labio de la señal entiende	El núcleo de la señal entiende

pero si no, quien avisa no es traidor [But! If not: forwarned.], *pero si no, más vale prevenir que lamentar* [But if not, better to be safe than sorry.].

(إذا كنت في قوم فاحلب في إنائهم.) is an Arabic proverb that means *si estás en un pueblo, ordeña en su vasija* [If you are in a community, milk in their pot.]. Its Spanish functional equivalent is *allá donde fueres, haz lo que vieres* [when in Rome, do as the Romans do.] GT provides a literal translation of the proverb. T does as well, although it paraphrases the second part, which is wrong.

The Arabic proverb (إذا وقع الجمل كثرت السكاكين.) means *cuando el camello cae, las navajas abundan* [when the camel falls, knives abound.] It has a functional equivalent *a perro flaco, todos son pulgas* [when it rains, it pours.] All three tools render a verbatim translation of the Arabic proverb. The Arabic verb (كثر) refers to the sense of 'to increase, to multiply, to become great'. RC renders the word (الجمل) as "phrases" by mistranslating its vocalization.

The verbatim translation of (أحبّك يا نافعي ولو كنت عدوّي.) is *te quiero porque me eres útil, aunque seas mi enemigo* [I love you because you are useful to me, even if you are my enemy.] Its Spanish functional equivalent is *por el interés, te quiero Andrés* [it is like where there's muck there's brass.] The three tools render wrong translations since they recognize only part of the proverb: "I love you". The active participle (نافعي) is confused with a personal name.

The Arabic proverb (إن مع العسر يسرا.) means in Spanish *después de la dificultad, viene la facilidad*. In Spanish there are several functional equivalents, among them, *tras la tempestad viene la calma* [after storm comes a calm.] The tools tested render incorrect translations, although RC's translation is closer to the source text. It is worth mentioning that RC does provide a more accurate translation by paraphrasing, by translating the proverb in context:

(ووســـط الافـــاق الملبـــدة بالغيوم خلال الحـــــرب البـــاردة كان وجود امم المتحدة يبشرنا بأنه مع العسر يسرا.)

'Las Naciones Unidas han seguido siendo una fuente de esperanza en el horizonte oscuro de la guerra fría'. [The UN has remained a source of hope on the dark horizon of the cold war].

It is interesting to note that the proverb constitutes a koranic verse (94: 5.) and was rendered into Spanish as *luego de toda dificultad viene la facilidad* [After every difficulty comes ease] [23, 604], *y, ciertamente, con cada dificultad, viene la facilidad* [And, certainly, with every difficulty comes ease] [5, p. 947] and *¡la adversidad y la felicidad van a una!* [Adversity and happiness go together] [15, p. 275].

The verbatim translation of (المصيبة اذا عمت خفت و اذا خصت هالت) is *la calamidad, si se extiende, asusta, y si se limita, aterra* [Calamity, if widespread, is frightening, and if limited, terrifying.] Its functional equivalent in Spanish is *mal de muchos, consuelo de tontos* [who in distress make sorrow less.] The translations provided by the tools are wrong, although GT's translation is partially more accurate to the verbatim translation.

The Arabic proverb (إن اللبيب من الإشارة يفهم.) means *el sagaz entiende con una insinuación* [The shrewd understands with a hint.] Its functional equivalent is *a buen entendedor, pocas palabras bastan* [Word to the wise is sufficient.] The three tools translate the Arabic proverb in diverse ways, all of which are wrong. By reproducing the syntactic order of the source text, in which the verb appears in the last position, the target text converts the verbal complement (من الإشارة) into a noun complement of the subject. As for the word (اللبيب), according to the Al Maany dictionary, it means "reasonable, sensible, insightful." T has chosen a technical meaning, which is not valid for this phraseological unit. RC has used the word "lip," which is a lexical mistake, while GT has translated it as "heart," as a metaphorical synonym for "core."

5   Conclusion

The analysis of these twenty samples of Arabic proverbs has shown that the machine translation tools assessed (Google Translate, Reverso Context, and Tradukka) are unreliable so far for the translation of Arabic proverbs into Spanish, so it is, therefore, necessary to compile a corpus of Arabic proverbs sufficiently representative and to assess their translation to validate these results. Nevertheless, Reverso Context provides a more accurate translation for contextualized examples, so further research replicating the study of each proverb within excerpt fragments is necessary to support the findings of this study.

It is striking that the machine translation tools assessed not only fail to identify proverbs as independent phraseological units but also render translations with a plethora of syntactic and lexical mistakes affecting the quality of translation and causing the meaning of the translations to be unintelligible. It happens with proverbs that do not exist in Spanish but also with those proverbs shared by source and target cultures and languages. In this respect, it would be helpful to analyze the role of english as a pivot language for bridging low-resource language pairs such as Arabic and Spanish.

Therefore, translation aspires to be communication. however, in this state of the art, the machine translation tools still need to be further implemented to support Arabic translators, and in particular, students who have not yet acquired full translation competence as well as not very experienced translators. as trainers, it is important to make our students aware not only of the current unreliability of these tools and, therefore, the need to strengthen their ability to search for information in other sources such as dictionaries, as well as to improve their cultural competence in Arabic but also that a field of work and research, that of machine translation, with great possibilities is opening before them. Finally, more research on this topic is needed, and improvements in the computational field from engineers, linguists, and translators.

References

1. Alqudsi, A., Omar, N., Shaker, K.: A hybrid rules and statistical method for arabic to english machine translation. In: 2019 2nd International Conference on Computer Applications and Information Security (ICCAIS), pp. 1–7 (2019). https://doi.org/10.1109/CAIS.2019.8769545
2. Alqudsi, A., Omar, N., Shaker, K.: Arabic machine translation: a survey. Artif. Intell. Rev. **42**(4), 549–572 (2012). https://doi.org/10.1007/s10462-012-9351-1
3. Amigo Extremera, J.J.: ¿Cultuqué? El concepto de cultura en los Estudios de Traducción. Transl. Interpreting **7**(1), 26–46 (2015)
4. Anizi, M., Dichy, J., Hassoun, M.: Improving information retrieval in arabic through a multi-agent approach and a rich lexical resource. In: 4th International Conference on Information Systems & Economic Intelligence, pp. 67–73, Marrakech, Morocco (2011). https://hal.archives-ouvertes.fr/hal-00679582. Accessed 10 Jul 2022
5. Assad, M.: El Mensaje del Qur'an. Traducción y comentarios. Junta Islámica, Almodovar del Río (2001). https://www.oozebap.org/biblio/pdf/Coran.pdf. Accessed 10 Jul 2022
6. Baker, M.: In Other Words (A Coursebook on Translation). Routledge, London (1992)
7. Boughaba, M.: Consideraciones terminológicas sobre la fraseología y la lexicología árabes. Paremia **31**, 239–247 (2021). https://cvc.cervantes.es/lengua/paremia/pdf/031/020_boughaba.pdf. Accessed 10 Jul 2022
8. Boughaba, M.: La equivalencia fraseológica en la traducción español-árabe: el caso de las locuciones, LinRed (2017). https://linred.web.uah.es/articulos_pdf/LR-articulo-24042017.pdf. Accessed 10 Jul 2022
9. Boughaba, M.: Las unidades fraseológicas y la traducción de culturemas entre el español y el árabe. Paremia **23**, 209–216 (2014). https://cvc.cervantes.es/Lengua/paremia/pdf/023/019_boughaba.pdf. Accessed 10 Jul 2022
10. Casares, J.: Introducción a la lexicografía moderna. Consejo Superior de Investigaciones Científicas, Madrid (1992 [1950])
11. Corpas Pastor, G. (ed.): Diez años de investigación en fraseología: análisis sintáctico-semánticos, contrastivos y traductológicos. Frankfurt am Main/Madrid: Vervuert/Ibero americana (2003)
12. Corpas Pastor, G. (ed.): Las lenguas de Europa: Estudios de fraseología, fraseografía y traducción. Comares, Granada (2000)

13. Corpas Pastor, G.: Manual de fraseología española. Madrid: Gredos: Madrid (1996). http://www.jzb.com.es/resources/el_sagrado_coran.pdf. Accessed 10 Jul 2022
14. Corriente, F.: La investigación de los arabismos del castellano en registros normales, folklóricos y bajos. Real Academia de la Lengua, Madrid (2018). https://www.rae.es/sites/default/files/Discurso_ingreso_Federico_Corriente.pdf. Accessed 10 Jul 2022
15. Cortés, J.: Versión castellana de El Corán. Biblioteca Islámica "Fatima Zahra", San Salvador (2005)
16. Cousillas, M.: Literatura popular en la Costa de la Muerte (Enfoque semiótico). Ventoprint, La Coruña (1998)
17. Dobrovol'skij, D.: Idioms in contrast: a functional view. In: Corpas, G. (ed.) Las Lenguas de Europa. Estudios de Fraseología, Fraseografía y Traducción. Granada: Editorial Comares, pp. 367–388 (2000)
18. Dobrovol'skij, D., Piirainen, E.: Figurative Language. Cross-Cultural and Cross-Linguistic Perspectives. Amsterdam, Elsevier (2005)
19. El-Madkouri Maataoui, M.: La traducibilidad del refranero entre el árabe el español. Tonos Digital: Revista de estudios filológicos 20 (2010). http://www.tonosdigital.com/ojs/index.php/tonos/article/view/585/443. Accessed 10 Jul 2022
20. Elshazly, A.: Unidades fraseológicas y traducibilidad. Análisis contrastivo de equivalencias interlingüísticas en un corpus paralelo árabe-español, español-árabe. PH Thesis, Universidad Autónoma de Madrid (2017)
21. El-Shboul, A.I.H.: Los arabismos en la historia lingüística del español: una estrategia para el aprendizaje del español y el árabe como lenguas extranjeras. Paremias **44**, 2 (2018). https://doi.org/10.15517/RFL.V44I2.34696
22. Forneas Besteiro, J.M.: Ocho refranes árabes y otros tantos españoles ¿paralelismos o algo más? Paremias **8**, 183–193 (1999)
23. García, I.: Traducción comentada de El Corán. Islam House, Bogotá (2013). https://noblecoran.com/images/libros/coran-traduccion-isa-garcia.pdf. Accessed 10 Jul 2022
24. Gogazeh, Z.M., Al-Afif, A.H.: Los proverbios árabes extraídos del Corán: recopilación, traducción y estudio. Paremia **17**, 129–138 (2007). https://cvc.cervantes.es/lengua/paremia/pdf/016/012_gogazeh-alafif.pdf. Accessed 10 Jul 2022
25. Hidalgo Ternero, C., Corpas Pastor, G.: Estrategias heurísticas con corpus para la enseñanza de la fraseología orientada a la traducción. In: Seghiri, M. (ed.) La Lingüística de Corpus Aplicada al Desarrollo de la Competencia Tecnológica en los Estudios de Traducción e Interpretación y la Enseñanza de Segundas Lenguas, pp. 183–206. Peterlang, Berlin (2020)
26. Hidalgo Ternero, C., Corpas Pastor, G.: Herramientas y recursos electrónicos para la traducción de la manipulación fraseológica: un estudio de caso centrado en el estudiante. CLINA: Interdisc. J. Trans. Interpreting Intercult. Commun. **6**(2), 71–94 (2020)
27. Hidalgo Ternero, C., Corpas Pastor, G.: La variación fraseológica: análisis del rendimiento de los corpus monolingües como recursos de traducción. Etudes Romanes de Brno **1**, 359–379 (2021)
28. Nadal, L.L: Iñesta, E.A. Pamies. Fraseología y Metáfora. Aspectos Tipológicos y Cognitivos, vol. 12, p. 203. Método, Granada (2002)
29. Martín de León, C., Marcelo Wirnitzer, G., et al.: En más de un sentido: Multimodalidad y construcción de significados en traducción e interpretación. ULPGC, Las Palmas (2021)
30. Mohamed Ould Baba, A.: Los proverbios árabes clásicos más usados. Anaquel de Estudios Árabes **23**, 131–144 (2012). https://doi.org/10.5209/rev_ANQE.2012.v23.39700
31. Mohamed Ould Baba, A.: Los proverbios y expresiones contenidas en la obra Al-Bayān wa-t-tabyīn de Al-Gáḥiẓ (776–869). Paremia **12**, 137–149 (2003). https://cvc.cervantes.es/lengua/paremia/pdf/012/013_ould.pdf. Accessed 10 Jul 2022

32. Mohamed Ould Baba, M.: Introducción a la paremiología árabe. Memorabilia, **14**, 77–98 (2012). https://ojs.uv.es/index.php/memorabilia/article/view/2082/1591. Accessed Jul 10 2022

33. Mouna A., Dichy, J.: Assessing word-form based search for information in arabic: towards a new type of lexical resource. In: Second International Conference on Arabic Language Resources and Tools, Le Caire, Egypt (2009). http://www.elda.org/medar-conference/pdf/75.pdf. Accessed 10 Jul 2022

34. Negro Alousque, I.: La traducción de las expresiones idiomáticas marcadas culturalmente. Revista de Lingüística y Lenguas Aplicadas **5**, 133–140 (2010)

35. Newmark, P.A.: Textbook of Translation. Phoenix, New York (1995)

36. Olmedo Ruiz, M.: Los tipos de traducción automática y su evaluación mediante perífrasis verbales y expresiones idiomáticas (alemán-español). PH Thesis, Universidad Autónoma de Barcelona (2018)

37. Rayyan, M.: Fraseología y lingüística informatizada: elaboración de una base de datos electrónica contrastiva árabe – español / español – árabe de fraseologismos basados en partes del cuerpo. Universidad de Granada, PH Tesis (2014)

38. Sadiq Feidi, F.: La sabiduría árabe antigua reflejada en los proverbios de Al-Maydani: traducción y análisis paremiológico de un corpus seleccionado. PH Thesis, Universidad Complutense de Madrid (2016)

39. Sagban, M.K.: La fraseología comprada del español y del árabe de Irak y su aplicación a la enseñanza de las unidades fraseológicas en el aula de E/LE. PH Thesis, Universidad de Granada (2010)

40. Sevilla Muñoz, M.: The process of phraseological translation. Paremia **29**, 149–158 (2019)

41. Shaban Mohammad Salem, T.: La fraseología en español y en árabe estudio, comparación, traducción y propuesta de un diccionario. PH Tesis: Universidad Complutense de Madrid (2013)

42. Soto Aranda, B.: De los estudios gramaticales al paradigma comunicativo: nuevos horizontes para la enseñanza del árabe marroquí en España como lengua para fines específicos (LFE). Tonos digital: Revista de estudios filológicos, 12 (2006) https://www.um.es/tonosdigital/znum12/secciones/Estudios%20W-Arabemarroquiensenanza.htm. Accessed 10 Jul 2022

43. Soto Aranda, B.: The change of meaning in the translation from Arabic to Spanish. In: El-Madkouri Maataoui, M., Penas Ibáñez, A., Österberg, R. (eds.): Léxico y semántica: nuevas aportaciones teóricas y prácticas. Stockholm University Press, Stockholm (in press)

44. Taleb Mohamed, M.L.: Estudio contrastivo y traductológico del refrán en árabe y español: la traducción de refranes hasaníes al español. Universidad de Granada, PH Tesis (2015)

45. Zakraoui, J., Moutaz, S., Al-Ma'adeed, S., Aljaam, J.: Evaluation of Arabic to English Machine Translation Systems. 185–190 (2020). https://doi.org/10.1109/ICICS49469.2020.239518. Accessed 10 Jul 2022

Detecting Bajan Phraseology:
A Metalexicographic Analysis

Cristiano Furiassi[(✉)] [iD]

University of Turin, 10124 Turin, Italy
cristiano.furiassi@unito.it

Abstract. Within the broad spectrum of phraseology, this article focuses on the phrasemes typically used in Bajan, the English-based creole spoken in Barbados, and attempts to show how they work as harbingers of culture by highlighting the uniqueness of Bajan identity within (but also outside) the Anglophone Caribbean. By relying on the amateur lexicographic works on Bajan (and Barbadian English) produced over the past seven decades and on their comparison with the professional reference tools compiled by Richard Allsopp, namely the *Dictionary of Caribbean English Usage* and the *New Register of Caribbean English Usage*, Bajan-proper phraseological items are quantified and commented on. In greater detail, this study aims at depicting the distinct worldview of Bajan speakers by looking at the images conveyed through specific idioms which employ local toponyms; although the colonial history of Barbados is hitherto evident in the Bajanisms selected, the jocular connotations attached to them convert such idioms into emblems of the Barbadian character. A further intent of this analysis is to confirm the hypothesis that, for linguists and laypeople alike, Bajan and Barbadian English, the variety of English spoken simultaneously on the island, are separated by a fine line, especially if lexical and phraseological parameters are set.

Keywords: Bajan · Idioms · Lexicography · Phraseology · Proverbs · Toponyms

1 Introduction

Phraseology is perhaps the most striking hallmark of Caribbean English and English-based Caribbean creoles. Indeed, the rendering of regional peculiarities by means of semantically rich formulae seems to be a prototypical linguistic trait of Anglophone speakers descending, for the largest part, from the West Africans who were forcibly transplanted to the Caribbean by British colonizers during the transatlantic slave trade.

After acknowledging the distinction between Bajan and Barbadian English, clarifying the difference between amateur and professional lexicography, providing an operational definition of phraseology and describing the lexicographic sources investigated, the analysis develops along both quantitative and qualitative lines: as for the former, Bajan lexis and phraseology are isolated and weighted; as for the latter, Bajan "toponymic idioms" (Szerszunowicz 2009: 172) are analyzed.

The first aim of this piece of research is to detect Bajan-only entries through a metalexicographic analysis which consists in comparing professional Caribbean English

© The Author(s), under exclusive license to Springer Nature Switzerland AG 2022
G. Corpas Pastor and R. Mitkov (Eds.): EUROPHRAS 2022, LNAI 13528, pp. 90–104, 2022.
https://doi.org/10.1007/978-3-031-15925-1_7

dictionaries and amateur glossaries of Bajan and Barbadian English, hence highlighting the fundamental role played by amateur lexicographers in tracing instances of both lexical and phraseological items typical of Bajan. Secondly, another goal of this article is to determine the number of words and phraseological units, among those included in the glossaries examined, that can be considered representative of Bajan as opposed to those instead peculiar to Barbadian English, so as to verify whether, at least as far as vocabulary is concerned, Bajan and Barbadian English are in this respect quite close or somewhat distant. Finally, among the typically-Bajan phrasemes detected through the metalexicographic analysis hinted at above, the focus is shifted to the idioms that include references to place names indicating geographical locations on the island of Barbados, thus emphasizing the extent to which they function as a "cultural agent" (Allsopp and Furiassi 2020: 107).

2 What is Bajan

Bajan, the respelled medial clipping of *Barbadian*, is originally an ethnonym referring to the natives of Barbados, namely Barbadians (see Rickford 1992: 195). In everyday usage, however, the adjective *Bajan* can be associated to other concepts, such as, for example, the phrase *Bajan dollar*, the domestic currency officially known as *Barbadian dollar*. The creole spoken island-wide in Barbados is also referred to as *Bajan* or, less appropriately, *Bajan dialect*. In fact, Bajan is not a dialect *per se*, namely a mutually intelligible geographical variety of English (see Campbell 2020: 229 and Wolfram and Schilling 2016: 2), but it should be regarded as a separate and independently evolved English-based creole.

Even though the official language of Barbados is English or, more precisely, Barbadian English, most residents also speak Bajan, a creole influenced by various West African languages. In ordinary conversations taking place in Barbados, bilingualism is apparent: while Barbadian English is used in writing and formal settings, Bajan, the mother tongue of a considerable section of the population, is often only spoken and relegated to informal contexts (see Fenigsen 1999: 66; 2011: 112). As of today, Bajan and Barbadian English, "continue to be locked in a diglossic hierarchy of dichotomizing discourses and values informed by over three centuries of British colonialism" (Fenigsen 2003: 461).

Regardless of its complex historical origins, here overlooked for the sake of space, at present Bajan is the closest creole to English within the Anglophone Caribbean. Notwithstanding this resemblance, native or proficient English speakers would normally struggle to understand it. Indeed, Bajan is the offspring of West African captives who, once displaced to plantations in Barbados and enslaved, were forced to speak English by the British colonizers, both landowners and indentured servants – the latter mostly of Irish origin. Over time, Bajan became a means of communication among slaves, almost completely opaque to slaveholders' ears.

The line between Bajan and Barbadian English is seldom easy to draw. The *status quo* is partly justified by the fact that Bajan has been defined as an "intermediate" creole (Winford 2000: 215; 2003: 313) because of its proximity to English, its superstratum or lexifier. According to Fenigsen (2011: 111), "nearly the entire lexicon was drawn from the regional Englishes spoken by the resident British colonizers". However, though based on English, Bajan is in fact a new language creation.

3 Professional vs Amateur Lexicography

According to Jeannette Allsopp (2020: 298), "[a]mong all the agents of language standardisation, dictionaries have remained at the forefront of this process, [...] they have become one of the most important instruments whereby the status of particular languages or language varieties has been determined". If it is true that scholarly dictionaries produced by professional lexicographers "confer legitimacy upon a language" (Dolezal 2020: 726), it might not always be the case with the outcomes of amateur lexicography.

Despite the existence of several Caribbean territory-specific English dictionaries, no academic dictionary of either Bajan or Barbadian English has been compiled yet.[1] Therefore, in order to take stock of the lexical and phraseological inventory of Bajan and Barbadian English, the only realistic option is to resort to the entries included in the few and nonetheless rare amateur glossaries published to date. The necessity of turning to "works by Caribbean folklorists" (Williams 2019), both printed and online, is justified by their being repositories of oral tradition and unwritten usage.

The dichotomy between the labels *professional* and *amateur* – the latter expressing no particular value judgement – is clarified by Lambert (2020: 411), who places them along a continuum: "[p]rofessional lexicography is involved in compiling both traditional and scholarly historical dictionaries [...] and generally tends to employ a higher standard of lexicographic rigor [...]. In contrast, amateur lexicographers usually produce short works [...] aimed at the popular market. [...] While not scholarly in approach, these are nevertheless generally reliable sources [...] and they certainly should not be dismissed out of hand".

The main issue with glossaries compiled by language enthusiasts is that the labels they apply to the types of items they include seldom correspond to the terminology adopted in products that are the offspring of professional lexicography and do not always conform with the definitions widespread in linguistic literature. Especially the term *dialect* – as appears in the titles of the glossaries analyzed (see Sect. 5) – is particularly misleading: as explained earlier (see Sect. 2), Bajan is not a dialect *sensu stricto*, but an English-derived creole largely incomprehensible to native speakers' ears.

On a final note, it must be emphasized that, especially as far as printed editions are concerned, most of the amateur glossaries examined are extremely difficult to retrieve both within and outside Barbados. This may be due to the fact that, whereas scholarly dictionaries tend to benefit from the resources made available by institutions and publishers, amateur glossaries are usually self-published and, consequently, are not supported by the distributional means at the disposal of (major) publishing houses.

---

[1] Various regional dictionaries have been compiled – by professional and non-professional lexicographers alike – on the Englishes and English-based creoles of the Anglophone Caribbean, such as Bahamian, Belizean, Bermudan, Dominican, Jamaican, Saban, Saint Lucian, Trinidadian and Tobagonian (see Allsopp 2003: xix–xx; Winer 2006: 204–205; Allsopp 2009: 354–376; Allsopp 2020: 300–305; Furiassi 2014: 92–94; Myrick 2019: 144–145 and Lambert 2020: 420–421 for a comprehensive overview).

4 Phraseology as a Sign of Bajan Identity

Barbadians tend to display "a strong sense of national identity" (Blake 2017: 190), which can be experienced in various aspects of both Bajan and Barbadian English, such as "accent, idiom, structure and word" (Roberts 2008: 1). As far as Barbadian identity is concerned, this may be perceived predominantly through the use of Bajan-specific vocabulary and phraseology. However, when compared with single lexical items, phraseological ones prove to be culturally weightier (see Dobrovol'skij and Piirainen 2005: 34), a fact which enhances their ability to characterize particular notions, situations and behaviors, thus reflecting "the identity of the people from which they spring" (Allsopp 2012: 86). On the whole, Bajan phraseology manages to convey a patently non-European worldview by distancing itself from the English superstrate, at least to a certain extent.

Notwithstanding the wide-ranging definition of phraseology attested in the literature,[2] as regards this article, the workable framework adopted is based on the notion of "set phrase" or "phraseme" devised by Mel'čuk (1995: 179; 2012: 32), that is a multi-word expression formed by at least two syntactically linked lexemes. Accordingly (and more accurately), two main types of phrasemes are targeted (see Sect. 7): idioms, that is semantically non-compositional lexical phrasemes (see Mel'čuk 1995: 167; 2012: 42) which, within a text, act as words (see Klein and Lamiroy 2016: 16), and proverbs, "a central type of phrasemes" (Piirainen 2008: 214) which, due to their quotational nature, are used in texts as sentence-like units (see Klein and Lamiroy 2016: 17–19). Finally, the qualitative part of the analysis is centered on idioms precisely inspired by toponyms (see Sects. 7.1 to 7.5).

As an intrinsic part of the folklore of their creators, idioms and proverbs often consist of succinct formulae intended to offer practical guidance. Deemed to express beliefs generally considered to be axiomatic, both idioms and proverbs bear meanings that go beyond the literal. However, it is not until such meanings are applied to a wider set of circumstances that the true essence of these types of phrasemes is captured.

5 Lexicographic Sources

The sources considered for analysis, listed in chronological order according to their latest edition, are described below (see Sects. 5.1 to 5.8). As for professional lexicography, the dictionaries inspected are Allsopp's *Dictionary of Caribbean English Usage* (2003) and *New Register of Caribbean English Usage* (2010) – the former only available in print, the latter also accessible in digital format. As far as amateur lexicography is concerned, the following printed glossaries were examined: Collymore's *Barbadian Dialect* (2005), Hoyte's *How to Be a Bajan* (2007), Ward's *Bajan Slang Dictionary* (2012), Davis's *From Bajan to Standard English* (2014) and *Understanding Bajan Dialect* (2009). In addition, the online amateur glossaries analyzed are *How to Speak like a Bajan* (2018), Callaghan's *Dialect of Barbados* (2020), *Dictionary of Bajan Dialect Words* (2022) and *Dictionary of Bajan Dialect Phrases* (2022).

---

[2] On the overarching notion of phraseology, see, *inter alia*, Mel'čuk (1995: 167–232; 2012: 36–42), Cowie (1998: 1–20), Dobrovol'skij and Piirainen (2005 : 29–43) and Klein and Lamiroy (2016: 15–19).

5.1 Allsopp's *Dictionary of Caribbean English Usage* (2003) and *New Register of Caribbean English Usage* (2010)

The most recent and authoritative lexicographic contributions to Caribbean English are the *Dictionary of Caribbean English Usage* (*DCEU*) and the *New Register of Caribbean English Usage* (*NRCEU*), which were conceived to provide a record of current English spoken in the Caribbean archipelago, Guyana and Belize, ignored by virtually all the most renowned publishers of English dictionaries (see Allsopp 2003: xix, xxii).[3] The former, the *DCEU*, listing over 20,000 entries, was originally published in 1996 by Oxford University Press and reprinted in 2003 by the University of the West Indies Press, with 1992 being the cut-off point in data-editing; the latter, the *NRCEU*, was published in 2010 and consists of a supplement of about 700 entries – data collection was however suspended in 2007.

The *DCEU* and the *NRCEU* can be defined as both "descriptive" and "prescriptive" (Allsopp 2003: xxv, xxvi), hence setting a shared norm for Caribbean English and, at the same time, recognizing its inner regional variation. Both dictionaries are a representation of "lexical entries and idioms associated primarily with 'acrolectal' and 'mesolectal' varieties", which, as a consequence, "excludes entries associated with 'deeper' creole forms" (Aceto 1996: 412). Therefore, the *DCEU* and the *NRCEU* are supposed to include only entries belonging to varieties of English spoken throughout the Anglophone Caribbean – Barbadian English among them – and disregard those which pertain to Bajan.

The key to the normative purpose of both dictionaries can be assumed by respectively reading the front matter of the *DCEU* and the *NRCEU*, where Richard Allsopp (2003: lvii–lvii; 2010: xviii) recognizes various "levels of formalness" or "levels of usage", namely "Formal [F]", "Informal [IF]", "Anti-formal [AF]" – sub-categorized into "Creole [AF-Cr]", "Jocular [AF-Joc]", "Derogatory [AF-Derog]", "Vulgar [AF-Vul]" and "Erroneous or Disapproved [X]". Among the above-listed microstructural features, the most salient in light of the present investigation (see Sect. 6) is the employment of the label *AF-Cr*, which identifies entries deemed to be "[a]nti-formal", i.e. "[d]eliberately rejecting [f]ormalness", and, at the same time, "[a] Creole or Creolized form or structure" (Allsopp 2003: lvii).

5.2 Collymore's *Barbadian Dialect* (2005)

Barbadian Dialect, a short book first published in 1955, is one of the major endowments to the study of Barbadian English and Bajan words and phrases. This avant-garde and inspirational glossary, "a little treasure trove of Bajan heritage" (Baugh 1992), became so popular that seven editions have been published to date, mostly posthumously: the latest one, dated 2005, contains a total of 1,250 entries. Frank Appleton Collymore, widely recognized as a pillar of Caribbean literature, art and culture, was the editor of the literary journal *Bim* from 1942 until 1974 and is the author of this volume, which, as he himself concedes, was carried out "in an amateurish sort of way" (Collymore 2005).

---

[3] The existence of this *lacuna* is corroborated by the surprisingly late addition of the entry *Barbadian English* – defined as "[t]he English language as spoken or written in Barbados or by Barbadians" – to the *Oxford English Dictionary Online*, which can only be found starting from the September 2021 update (see Salazar 2021).

On the one hand, in the preface to the fifth edition, Wickham (1976) indeed claims that "the collection is not to be regarded as a work of scholarship or erudition but simply the expression of an amateur's interest in the richness of the Barbadian vocabulary"; on the other hand, in the foreword to the sixth edition, Baugh (1992) highlights "[t]he glossary's unpretentious and admittedly, winsomely amateur character".

5.3 Hoyte's *How to Be a Bajan* (2007)

Harold Hoyte's *How to Be a Bajan*, which counts 242 entries overall, was published in 2007. The author was a journalist and the founder of the quality newspaper *The Nation*. Since Hoyte's (2005) "souvenir handbook" touches upon several aspects of Barbadian lifestyle, as appears clear from the introduction, where the volume is defined as "informative" and "witty" and presented as "[a] quick read" and "an easy reference" (Hoyte 2005: 1), only *Chapter 3: Bajan Words and Bajan Names* (pp. 24–33) and *Chapter 3: Bajan Sayings* (pp. 34–41) are considered for analysis. In addition to 79 words and 82 sayings or proverbs, Hoyte's lexical inventory also includes 68 nicknames or pseudonyms and 13 names of children's games. As far as the latter chapter is concerned, it must be noticed that the "sayings" present therein, not always transparent, e.g. *You think I am Moojun cow?*, are listed without any paraphrase or explanation.

5.4 Ward's *Bajan Slang Dictionary* (2012)

The self-published, pocket-size paperback *Bajan Slang Dictionary* is, as admitted by its author, Nicholas Ward – singer, songwriter, web designer and social media manager – "to be taken in the lighthearted and tongue-in-cheek fashion that it was written and intended" and supposed to be "entertaining, enjoyable, enlightening and even possibly educational" (Ward 2012). This booklet, comprising 82 entries, each accompanied by an illustration by the author himself, was published in 2012 and described as "a perfect gift for anyone from overseas" (Ward 2012).

5.5 Davis's *From Bajan to Standard English* (2014) and *Understanding Bajan Dialect* (2009)

E. Jerome Davis, former high school teacher and later consul and chief liaison officer at the Consulate General of Barbados in Canada from 1996 to 2005, is the author of two self-published pamphlets on Bajan: *From Bajan to Standard English*, appearing for the first time in 2007 and followed by two editions, respectively in 2008 and 2014, and *Understanding Bajan Dialect*, published in 2009 and adapted from the first edition of *From Bajan to Standard English*. Davis's *Understanding Bajan Dialect* was conceived as a souvenir and addressed to tourists and visitors: as it is wider in scope, only the 95 entries included in *Section Two: Bajan Words and Phrases* (pp. 8–11) are taken into consideration. If compared to *Understanding Bajan Dialect*, *From Bajan to Standard English*, "specifically designed to be used by individuals and schools", adopts a rather prescriptive stance, as Davis (2014: 1) himself explains: "[t]his book should serve to assist those who find themselves under pressure when making the transition from dialect to Standard English".

As far as *From Bajan to Standard English* is concerned, only *Chapter Eight: Bajan Words/Expressions and their English Equivalents* (pp. 36–42), comprising 68 entries, and *Chapter Eleven: Bajan Words and Expressions (Part 2)* (pp. 58–64), including 54 entries, are taken into account for this analysis, hence totaling 122 entries. However, it is worth noting that none of the 19 "expressions" included in *Chapter Eleven* (p. 59) are actually instances of phraseology; in fact, they are merely examples created by the author in order to clarify usage and are consequently excluded *in toto* from the overall entry count, which is reduced to 103. All in all, if the two glossaries are compared, out of a total of the 103 entries present in *From Bajan to Standard English*, only 8 are not to be found in *Understanding Bajan Dialect*, while the remaining ones are repeated in both glossaries. As a consequence, the quantitative analysis conducted below (see Sect. 6) is based exclusively on *From Bajan to Standard English*.

5.6 *How to Speak like a Bajan* (2018)

How to Speak like a Bajan is an online glossary available since 2018 on the *Royal Westmoreland Barbados Blog*, run by Royal Westmoreland Barbados, a golf and beach resort; it includes 40 "words, phrases, and expressions" and 5 "proverbs", for a total of 45 entries.

5.7 Callaghan's *Dialect of Barbados* (2020)

Dialect of Barbados is a succinct online resource compiled by Brett Callaghan, founder and managing director of the travel and tourism destination website *Totally Barbados*, on which the 24-entry glossary has been available since 2020.

5.8 *Dictionary of Bajan Dialect Words* (2022) and *Dictionary of Bajan Dialect Phrases* (2022)

The two glossaries, *Dictionary of Bajan Dialect Words*, including 420 entries, and *Dictionary of Bajan Dialect Phrases*, incorporating 41 entries, are provided by the Sun Group Inc., a family-run business chaired by Bernard Weatherhead and consisting in an amalgamation of companies which provide tourist services. They both appear as part of the *Barbados Pocket Guide* and are therefore clearly aimed at a tourist audience. Although it is not possible to trace the year in which these glossaries were made available for the first time, they were retrieved in 2022. It must be noted that only 26 of the 41 "phrases" included in the *Dictionary of Bajan Dialect Phrases* are true phrasemes; the remaining 15 are in fact examples made up by the author. For this reason, the entries therein included and considered for analysis amount to 446.

6 Methodology and Quantitative Data

The aim of the methodological approach described in this section is twofold: on the one hand, since this analysis focuses on the English-based creole spoken in Barbados, it was necessary to first discriminate, among the entries included in the above-mentioned glossaries, those that exclusively pertain to Bajan from those that are representative of Barbadian English; on the other hand, once Bajan-only entries were ascertained, the phraseological units belonging to Bajan were extracted. In order to detect phrasemes, also lexemes, that is single lexical entries, must be considered for analysis: as a matter of fact, whereas in professional lexicography idioms – as a non-exhaustive example – tend to have their proper dictionary articles (see Mel'čuk 2012: 43–44), in amateur glossaries the situation if far more complex as no established practice is followed.

As the entries present in the various amateur glossaries surveyed are never clearly signaled as pertaining to either Bajan or Barbadian English, it was necessary to compare each one of them with the *DCEU* and the *NRCEU*, the two professionally compiled reference dictionaries of Caribbean English. Therefore, each of the 2,192 entries found in the seven amateur glossaries taken into account was manually cross-checked against the about 20,700 entries listed in both the *DCEU* and the *NRCEU*:[4] if an entry was in fact included in the *DCEU* or the *NRCEU*, it was then considered as belonging to Barbadian English; if an entry was excluded from the *DCEU* and the *NRCEU* or, in spite of being included therein, was marked by the usage label *AF-Cr*, it was considered as belonging to Bajan (see Sect. 5.1). The quantitative data gathered from this comparison are summarized in Table 1 below.

Before proceeding with the quantitative analysis, it is worth mentioning that it was decided *a priori* to consider as 'included' not only the words and phraseological units that are identical in Bajan and Barbadian English, e.g. *cuh-dear*, meaning 'Dear me!', but also those that, preserving the same meaning, present differences exclusively in spelling, e.g. Bajan *peenie* vs Barbadian English *peeny*, meaning 'tiny'. On the contrary, entries with major differences in spelling, which may lead to unintelligibility, were marked as 'excluded', e.g. Bajan *grig* vs Barbadian English *grain*, meaning 'peas or beans' or 'a fish-spear or harpoon'. Notice that Bajan spelling is unstandardized, a feature common to virtually all English-based Caribbean creoles. Consequently, in order to represent the distance between the creole and the superstrate, words and phraseological units, though retaining the orthographic system of English, tend to be spelled according to their pronunciation. Even so, phonemic spelling may be subject to a great deal of idiosyncratic variation (see Hellinger 1986: 58, 62).

Table 1 is divided into five columns: the first column lists the amateur glossaries considered, either by mentioning the compiler or by citing the title in abbreviated form; the second column indicates the figures corresponding to the entries present in each glossary and included in *DCEU* or the *NRCEU*, hence belonging to Barbadian English; the third column records the entries included in the *DCEU* or the *NRCEU* but marked as *AF-Cr*, thus belonging to Bajan; the fourth column displays the entries excluded from the *DCEU* or the *NRCEU*, equally belonging to Bajan; the fifth and final column illustrates the total number of entries appearing in each glossary. Quantitative findings are represented both as raw and normalized data, i.e. percentages. The final line at the bottom of the table shows the overall number of entries scrutinized, i.e. 2,192.

---

[4] Thanks are due to Giorgia Avino, a BA graduate at the University of Turin, Italy, for her precious contribution to the quantitative part of the analysis.

Table 1. A comparison between Bajan/Barbadian English glossaries and the *DCEU/NRCEU*

Glossaries	Entries incl. in *DCEU/NRCEU*		Entries incl. in *DCEU/NRCEU* but marked as *AF-Cr*		Entries excl. from *DCEU/NRCEU*		Overall entries
	Barbadian Eng.		Bajan		Bajan		
	Raw	Pct.	Raw	Pct.	Raw	Pct.	Raw
Collymore (2005)	727	58%	11	1%	512	41%	1,250
Hoyte (2007)	81	34%	1	-	160	66%	242
Ward (2012)	48	58%	4	5%	30	37%	82
Davis (2014)	35	34%	26	25%	42	41%	103
How to Speak like a Bajan (2018)	22	49%	-	-	23	51%	45
Callaghan (2020)	16	67%	3	12%	5	21%	24
Dictionary of Bajan Dialect (2022)	220	49%	20	5%	206	46%	446
	1,149	52%	65	3%	978	45%	2,192

By analyzing the percentages listed in the second, third and fourth column of Table 1, it is apparent that, in most glossaries, the entries belonging to Barbadian English, displayed in the second column, balance the entries belonging to Bajan, displayed in the third and fourth column. On the one hand, three glossaries display a higher inclusion rate by covering more words belonging to Barbadian English than to Bajan: Callaghan (2020), i.e. 67%, Ward (2012), i.e. 58%, and Collymore (2005), i.e. 58%. On the other hand, four glossaries show a lower inclusion rate by incorporating more words belonging to Bajan than to Barbadian English: *Dictionary of Bajan Dialect* (2022), i.e. 49%, *How to Speak like a Bajan* (2018), i.e. 49%, Davis (2014), i.e. 34%, and Hoyte (2007), i.e. 34%. Moreover, if particular attention is paid to the bottom line of Table 1, out of 2,192 entries examined, 1,149, i.e. 52%, belong to Barbadian English, whereas 1,043, i.e. 48% belong to Bajan,[5] almost achieving a perfect fifty-fifty ratio. The important assumption proved by these findings is that, regardless of whether each single glossary is considered or a more general bird's eye view is held, the difference between Barbadian English and Bajan at the lexical and phraseological level is definitely blurred.

The final step to be taken before proceeding to the qualitative analysis of data is to merge the figures indicated in the fifth column of Table 1, i.e. 2,192, by counting

---

[5] This percentage is obtained by adding the 65 entries, i.e. 3%, included in the *DCEU* or the *NRCEU* but marked as *AF-Cr*, to the 978 entries, i.e. 45%, excluded from the *DCEU* or the *NRCEU*.

only once the entries that appear in more than one source glossary, thus eliminating duplicates: this manually conducted operation led to the identification of 905 entries peculiar to Bajan.

7 Qualitative Findings: Bajan Toponymic Idioms

The final list of 905 Bajanisms, which does not differentiate between lexical and phrase-ological items, required further manual scanning, so as to isolate only those entries that represent instances of phraseology. In particular, 87 Bajan idioms and proverbs were singled out – mostly linked to the following semantic fields:

- local flora and fauna, e.g. *If crab don't walk, crab don't get fat*, meaning 'little is achieved by staying at home';
- maritime life, e.g. *The sea en' got nuh back door*, meaning 'the sea is dangerous and, if in trouble, there is no guarantee of a way out';
- personal relationships, e.g. *The same mout' that court you, don't marry you*, meaning 'the same person encouraging someone to undertake a certain activity might not be around in times of need';
- household items, e.g. *Don't rush the brush and throw 'way de paint*, meaning "haste usually causes problems and wastes precious resources'.

Among this fairly large list of Bajan phrasemes, it was decided to focus attention and comment on the five idioms based on Barbadian toponyms, which stand out as prototypically cultural since they cannot be encountered elsewhere: *as hot as Mapp's mill-yard*, *lazaretto dog dead in St. Philip*, *sleeping in Pollard' cellar*, *Speightstown compliment* and *to be living at Easy Hall*. Curiously, all the idioms characterized by Barbadian place names are found only in Collymore's *Barbadian Dialect*, a fact which confirms Lambert's (2020: 420) assessment of Collymore's thoroughly researched work, which, regardless of its amateur nature, is defined as "academic in style".

7.1 *As Hot as Mapp's Mill-Yard*

The typically Bajan simile *as hot as Mapp's mill-yard* is found under the entry *Mapp's mill-yard* (Collymore 2005: 66). Quite surprisingly, Collymore naively confesses that he has "not been able to discover its origin". However, a clarification is provided by Forde (1987: 37–38), who includes the variant *Dis place hot as Mapp's millyard* and the alternative *Dis place hot as Bayley's millyard*, both meaning 'extremely hot'. The genesis of this idiom may be ascertained by referring to Bussa's rebellion, which took place between April 14th and April 16th 1816, and originated at Bayley's Plantation, next to Mapp's Plantation, both located in the parish of St Philip.[6] The insurgents, led by an African-born slave called Bussa, set the plantations and the adjacent buildings on fire, hence the allusion to hotness (see Beckles 2006: 108–116). Bayley's Plantation was established between 1719 and 1738; by 1765 it was in the possession of Joseph Bayley (see Hughes 1978).

---

[6] Barbadian parishes are administrative subdivisions which approximately correspond to shires in the UK and counties in the USA.

7.2 Lazaretto Dog Dead in St. Philip

The entry *lazaretto dog dead in St. Philip*, recorded in Collymore (2005: 60), "implies that some philandering husband has met his death while visiting his lady love far from home". A similar idiom, *De Lazaretto dog dead at Ragged Point Lighthouse*,[7] which refers to a more specific Barbadian landmark located within the same parish of St Philip and would therefore explain the association with Collymore's entry, is cited in Forde (1987: 2), who provides a more precise but somewhat different definition: "[d]o not expect people to put geographical limits on their movements (Also used in reference to gallivanting men.)". These figurative meanings both derive from the geographical location of the two places: the Lazaretto, which used to be a leprosarium in the 1850s, is situated near Batts Rock beach, about three miles north of the city of Bridgetown, in the parish of St Michael; Ragged Point, where the third oldest of Barbados' four lighthouses was erected in 1875, is the easternmost tip of the island. It is indeed the fifteen-mile distance between the two locations – quite considerable, at least as far as island standards are concerned – that explains the idiom.

7.3 Sleeping in Pollard' Cellar

The idiom *sleeping in Pollard' cellar*, included in Collymore (2005: 81) under the entry *Pollard' cellar*, "implies that the person referred to has no settled place of abode but that [...] he sleeps *wherever night catch him*". According to Collymore, "[t]his reference may be to the 'large hurricane-shelter cellar' at Pollard's Plantation in the parish of St. Philip". Pollard's Plantation was once a sugar estate in the 1700s, yet no evidence confirming the existence of a hurricane shelter was found. However, Mulcahy (2004: 659) mentions that "Walter Pollard, the son of a prominent Barbadian planter, [...] found Barbados "exhausted" [...] most of all from the hurricane of 1780".

7.4 Speightstown Compliment

The entry *Speightstown compliment*, defined as "[a] left-handed compliment", that is an insincere praise, is present in Collymore (2005: 100). The origin of this idiom might be traced to the fact that "in former days, Speightstonians were supposed to be less urbane in their manners than dwellers in the metropolis". Even though no evidence relating to these alleged attitudes of Speightstonians was discovered, the parochialism traditionally characterizing two neighboring towns, namely Speightstown and Bridgetown, the capital, might have given rise to the idiom. Located on the west coast of Barbados in the northern parish of St Peter, twelve miles away from Bridgetown, Speightstown, popularly known as Little Bristol, is the second largest city on the island. Formally settled around 1630, two years after Bridgetown was established, it used to be Barbados' busiest port in the early days of British colonization.

---

[7] The variant *De Lazaretto dog die at de lighthouse* appears in Blackman (1985: 2).

7.5 *To Be Living at Easy Hall*

The idiomatic phrase *to be living at Easy Hall*, retrieved from Collymore (2005: 35–36), under the entry *Easy Hall*, means "living a life of idleness – doing no work, and being supported by someone else". However, a more detailed meaning is attributed to this idiom by Griffin (2009) and Culpepper and Griffin (2015), who, in a similar fashion, respectively specify that *living at Easy Hall* refers to "someone who doesn't have a job and is supported by his female relatives" or "one who does not work but is sustained by his relations, usually female". These allusions to wealthy female relatives may be closely connected with Elizabeth, wife of Abel Alleyne Culpeper, almost certainly a woman of wealth who was associated with Easy Hall and whose tomb reports an inscription attesting to her virtues (see Culpepper and Griffin 2015). Owned by the Culpeper family since the early 1800s, Easy Hall Plantation is located on Barbados' east coast, across the parishes of St Joseph and St John, at the top of Hackleton's Cliff. Additionally, it must be noticed the close similarity between this idiom and the originally American English phrase *easy street*, equally idiomatic, which identifies "a situation marked by financial independence" (*Merriam-Webster Unabridged Online*) or "comfortable circumstances, affluence" (*Oxford English Dictionary Online*).

8 Conclusion

The conclusions that can be drawn from the present analysis are manifold and range from observations on the extraction of lexical and phraseological entries from amateur lexicographic tools and the part they play in contributing to the linguistic identity of Barbadians, through considerations on the creole status of Bajan in relation to Barbadian English, to reflections on the cultural specificities of Bajan phrasemes.

The detection of Bajan vocabulary and the foregrounding of Bajan phraseology was made possible by relying on a metalexicographic analysis based on works compiled by amateur Barbadian lexicographers, who managed to reveal a considerable amount of raw phraseological and lexical material, thus providing a sound basis on which prospective professionals can elaborate. The publications surveyed in this article highlighted the key position occupied by amateur lexicographers. Regardless of their being unsophisticated if compared to professional standards, these "celebrations of localized lexis, native inventiveness, and unique local culture" (Lambert 2020: 412) undoubtedly represent a pioneering effort in their various passionate attempts at chronicling the linguistic idiosyncrasies of Bajan. Although the majority of the amateur glossaries surveyed appear in a pamphlet-sized format and are produced for the local and tourist markets, they are in fact the most genuine voices of Bajan society.

As far as the standing of Bajan is concerned, the data gathered attest to the fact that the border between Bajan and Barbadian English is indeed fuzzy. Therefore, it can be affirmed (and confirmed) with fair certainty that Bajan and Barbadian English are not too dissimilar as far as vocabulary is concerned, hence justifying the positioning of Bajan among intermediate creoles.

Finally, the phrasemes detected contribute to testifying to the unique nature of Bajan, at least in quantitative terms. In this respect, the typically-Bajan idioms commented on confirm how culture is mostly mirrored in phraseology, especially in those instances involving the names of places spread throughout the island of Barbados. All in all, it seems that the colonial past is particularly persistent: the slavery period is indeed still evident in the use of idioms which exploit toponyms related to former plantations and refer to events which occurred there. However, even though such retentions might remain firmly fixed, they have been completely reshaped and endowed with a humorous effect. As a consequence, this paradox is converted into an unmistakable trademark of Bajan linguistic identity and an act of resilience of Barbadians.

References

Aceto, M.: Review of Dictionary of Caribbean English Usage. Ed. by Richard Allsopp. (French and Spanish supplement edited by J. E. Allsopp.) Oxford: Oxford University Press, 1996. Pp. lxxviii, 697. Language **74**(2), 412–413 (1998)

Allsopp, J.: Dictionaries of Caribbean English. In: Cowie, A.P. (ed.) The Oxford History of English Lexicography, vol. 1, pp. 353–377. Oxford University Press, Oxford (2009)

Allsopp, J.: Caribbean lexicography: a chronicle of the linguistic and cultural identity of one people. In: Allsopp, J., Rickford, J.R. (eds.) Language, Culture and Caribbean Identity, pp. 81–90. Canoe Press, Mona (2012)

Allsopp, J.: Dictionaries of Caribbean English: agents of standardisation. In: Ogilvie, S. (ed.) The Cambridge Companion to English Dictionaries, Part III, pp. 298–305. Cambridge University Press, Cambridge (2020)

Allsopp, J., Furiassi, C.: Caribbean English phraseology in the Dictionary of Caribbean English Usage: reflections of an African worldview. TEXTUS: English Stud. Italy **XXXIII**(1), 107–125 (2020)

Allsopp, R. (ed.): Dictionary of Caribbean English Usage. Oxford University Press, Oxford (1996)

Allsopp, R. (ed.): Dictionary of Caribbean English Usage. University of the West Indies Press, Mona (2003)

Allsopp, R. (ed.): New Register of Caribbean English Usage. University of the West Indies Press, Mona (2010)

Baugh, E.: Foreword. In: Collymore, F.A. (ed.) Barbadian Dialect: Notes for a Glossary of Words and Phrases of Barbadian Dialect, 6th edn. The Barbados National Trust, Wildey (1992)

Beckles, H. McD.: A History of Barbados, 2nd edn. Cambridge University Press, Cambridge (2006)

Blackman, M.: Bajan Proverbs. 2nd edn. M. Blackman, Montreal (1985)

Blake, R.: Historical separations: race, class and language in Barbados. In: Cutler, C., Vrzić, Z., Angermeyer, P. (eds.) Language Contact in Africa and the African Diaspora in the Americas: In Honor of John V. Singler, pp. 177–199. John Benjamins, Amsterdam (2017)

Callaghan, B.: Dialect of Barbados: What is Bajan Dialect? Totally Barbados, February 18th, 2020. https://www.totallybarbados.com/articles/culture/dialect. Accessed 15 May 2022

Campbell, L.: Historical Linguistics: An Introduction, 4th edn. MIT Press, Cambridge, MA (2020)

Collymore, F.A.: Barbadian Dialect: Notes for a Glossary of Words and Phrases of Barbadian Dialect, 7th edn. Cave Shepherd & Co., Bridgetown (2005)

Cowie, A.P.: Introduction. In: Cowie, A.P. (ed.) Phraseology: Theory, Analysis, and Applications, pp. 1–20. Clarendon Press, Oxford (1998)

Culpepper, W.L., Griffin, Jr., L.W.: Culpeper Island. Culpepper Connections! The Culpepper Family History Site, January 2nd, 2015. https://www.culpepperconnections.com/archives/bd/island.htm. Accessed 15 May 2022

Davis, E.J.: Understanding Bajan Dialect for Tourists and Visitors to Barbados. E. J. Davis, Bridgetown (2009)

Davis, E.J.: From Bajan to Standard English, 3rd edn. E. J. Davis, Bridgetown (2014)

Dictionary of Bajan Dialect Phrases. Sun Group Inc., St George (2022). https://www.barbad ospocketguide.com/our-island-barbados/about-barbados/bajan-dialect.html#Bjan%20phrases. Accessed 15 May 2022

Dictionary of Bajan Dialect Words. Sun Group Inc., St George (2022). https://www.barbadospock etguide.com/our-island-barbados/about-barbados/bajan-dialect.html#Dictionary. Accessed 15 May 2022

Dobrovol'skij, D., Piirainen, E.: Figurative Language: Cross-Cultural and Cross-linguistic Perspectives. Elsevier, Amsterdam (2005)

Dolezal, F.T.: World Englishes and Lexicography. In: Nelson, C.L., Proshina, Z.G., Davis, D.R. (eds.) The Handbook of World Englishes, 2nd edn, pp. 725–740. Wiley-Blackwell, Malden, MA (2020)

Fenigsen, J.: "A broke-up mirror": representing Bajan in print. Cult. Anthropol. 14(1), 61–87 (1999)

Fenigsen, J.: Language Ideologies in Barbados: processes and paradigms. Pragmatics 13(4), 457–482 (2003)

Fenigsen, J.: "Flying at Half-Mast"? Voices, genres, and orthographies in Barbadian Creole. In: Hinrichs, L., Farquharson, J.T. (eds.) Variation in the Caribbean: From Creole Continua to Individual Agency, pp. 107–132. John Benjamins, Amsterdam (2011)

Forde, G.A.: De Mortar-Pestle: A Collection of Barbadian Proverbs. The National Cultural Foundation, St James (1987)

Furiassi, C.: Caribbean English vocabulary: setting a norm through lexicographic practice. In: Molino, A., Zanotti, S. (eds.) Observing Norm, Observing Usage: Lexis in Dictionaries and in the Media, pp. 89–107. Peter Lang, Bern (2014)

Griffin, D.: A Short Explanation of the Origin of Apartment Names. Maresol Barbados Apartments, 1 February 2009. https://www.maresolbarbadosapartments.com/apartment-names/. Accessed 15 May 2022

Hellinger, M.: On writing English-related creoles in the Caribbean. In: Görlach, M., Holm, J.A. (eds.) Focus on the Caribbean, pp. 53–70. John Benjamins, Amsterdam (1986)

How to Speak like a Bajan–The Ultimate Guide. Royal Westmoreland Barbados Blog, January 22nd, 2018. https://www.royalwestmoreland.com/blog/uncategorised/how-to-speak-like-a-bajan-the-ultimate-guide. Accessed 15 May

Hoyte, H.: How to Be a Bajan: A Souvenir Handbook for Those Who Want to Learn the Bajan Way of Life. HH Investments, St George (2007)

Hughes, R.G.: Barbadian Sugar Plantations, 1640 to 1846. University of the West Indies, Cave Hill (1978). https://www.bajanthings.com/ronnie-hughes-barbados-plantation-index-1630-1846/. Accessed 15 May 2022

Klein, J.R., Lamiroy, B.: Le figement: Unité et diversité. Collocations, expressions figées, phrases situationnelles, proverbs. L'Information grammaticale 148, 15–20 (2016)

Lambert, J.: Lexicography and world English. In: Schreier, D., Hundt, M., Schneider, E.W. (eds.) The Cambridge Handbook of World Englishes, Part III, pp. 408–435. Cambridge University Press, Cambridge (2020)

Mel'čuk, I.: Phrasemes in language and phraseology in linguistics. In: Everaert, M., van der Linden, E.-J., Schenk, A., Schreuder, R. (eds.) Idioms: Structural and Psychological Perspectives, pp. 167–232. Lawrence Erlbaum Associates, Mahwah, NJ (1995)

Mel'čuk, I.: Phraseology in the language, in the dictionary, and in the computer. Yearbook Phraseol. 3, 31–56 (2012)

Merriam-Webster Unabridged Online. Merriam-Webster, Springfield, MA. http://unabridged.mer riam-webster.com. Accessed 15 May 2022

Mulcahy, M.: Weathering the storms: hurricanes and risk in the British Greater Caribbean. Bus. Hist. Rev. 78(4), 635–663 (2004)

Myrick, C.: The value of local dictionaries in the Caribbean: the example of Saba. Dictionaries: J. Dict. Soc. North Am. **40**(1), 139–164 (2019)

Oxford English Dictionary Online. Oxford: Oxford University Press. http://www.oed.com. Accessed 15 May 2020

Piirainen, E.: Figurative phraseology and culture. In: Granger, S., Meunier, F. (eds.) Phraseology: An Interdisciplinary Perspective, pp. 207–228. John Benjamins, Amsterdam (2008)

Rickford, J.R.: The Creole Residue in Barbados. In: Doane, N., Hall, J., Ringler, D. (eds.) Old English and New: Essays in Language and Linguistics in Honor of Frederic G. Cassidy, pp. 183–201. Garland, New York (1992)

Roberts, P.A.: The Roots of Caribbean Identity: Language. Race and Ecology. Cambridge University Press, Cambridge (2008)

Salazar, D.: A carnival of words: Caribbean English in the OED September 2021 Update. OED Blog, 6th September 2021. https://public.oed.com/blog/a-carnival-of-words-caribbean-english/. Accessed 15 May 2022

Szerszunowicz, J.: Some remarks on the evaluative connotations of toponymic idioms in a contrastive perspective. In: Corrigan, R., Moravcsik, E.A., Ouali, H., Wheatley, K. (eds.) Formulaic Language, vol. 1, pp. 171–184. John Benjamins, Amsterdam (2009)

Ward, N.: Bajan Slang Dictionary: An Incomplete A-Z of Select Barbadian Dialect. N. Ward, Bridgetown (2012)

Wickham, J.: Preface. In: Collymore, F.A. Barbadian Dialect: Notes for a Glossary of Words and Phrases of Barbadian Dialect, 5th edn. The Barbados National Trust, Wildey (1976)

Williams, D.-A.: When regional English Got their words. OED Blog, October 10th, 2019. https://public.oed.com/blog/when-regional-englishes-got-their-words/. Accessed 15 May 2022

Winer, L.: Caribbean lexicography. In: Brown, K. (ed.) Encyclopedia of Language & Linguistics, vol. 2, 2nd edn., pp. 204–205. Elsevier, Amsterdam (2006)

Winford, D.: "Intermediate" creoles and degrees of change in creole formation: the case of Bajan. In: Neumann-Holzschuh, I., Schneider, E.W. (eds.) Degrees of Restructuring in Creole Languages, pp. 215–246. John Benjamins, Amsterdam (2000)

Winford, D.: An Introduction to Contact Linguistics. Blackwell, Oxford (2003)

Wolfram, W., Schilling, N.: American English: Dialects and Variation, 3rd edn. John Wiley & Sons, Chichester (2016)

Image Schemas and Image Schematic Complexes: Enhancing Neural Machine Translation Networks

Amal Haddad Haddad(✉) ⓘ

Universidad de Granada, 18071 Granada, Spain
amalhaddad@ugr.es

Abstract. Machine Translation (MT) is a Natural Language Processing (NLP) application which has taken off and reported considerable progress in recent years. Most recent applications of MT employ neural networks imitating the principles of human understanding and creation of meaning at conceptual and cognitive levels (Nerlich and Clarke 2000: 141). They are based on techniques which try to simulate the mechanisms of learning in biological organisms carried out through the neurons (Aggarwal 2018: 1; Theordoris 2020: 903). However, human intelligence and the cognitive models which humans use through language should be subject to more examination in order to have the capacity to unveil more basic cognitive features. For this reason, a more holistic understanding of certain aspects of human intelligence based on cognitive models is still required in order to take machine learning a step further (Goertzel et al. 2012: 124). Image schemas and image schematic complexes are among the cognitive issues which would benefit from further studies as its basic structure is fundamental in natural language processing and conceptualisation (Hedblom et al. 2019). They are common in all languages and all cultures but their use is not always universal. This variation influences the quality of MT, as in some cases, this variance is not taken into consideration while feeding the neural networks of MT. This preliminary study has the objective of studying the novel idea of image schemas and image schematic complexes and proposing an applied methodology to use them in MT.

Keywords: Image schemas · Cognitive models · Machine translation

1 Introduction

Machine learning employs artificial neural networks and generally refers to "any type of algorithms and methods that perform tasks that traditionally required human intelligence" (Theordoris 2020: 2). Artificial neural networks of machine learning are based on techniques that simulate the mechanisms of learning in biological organisms carried out through the neurons (Aggarwal 2018: 1; Theordoris 2020: 903). Deep neural networks, are artificial neural networks that use sophisticated mathematical modelling to process data. The main achievements of those deep neural networks are their high rate of accuracy in predicting data in comparison with other applications (Theordoris 2020: 3).

G. Corpas Pastor and R. Mitkov (Eds.): EUROPHRAS 2022, LNAI 13528, pp. 105–115, 2022.
https://doi.org/10.1007/978-3-031-15925-1_8

All data adaptive applications are considered examples of the practical applications of machine learning, such as statistical learning, pattern recognition, adaptive signal processing, system identification, image analysis, and speech recognition, etc. having in common that they process data and are able to make predictions that can lead to decisions (Theordoris 2020: 2); hence its stretch relation with Artificial Intelligence (AI).

Machine Learning techniques are extensively used in language processing and machine translation (Aggarwal 2018: 45; Theordoris 2020: 976). In these types of applications, the input data is a sequence of words, which are encoded as numbers, correlated at the same time to dictionaries and contexts of use, leading to an output of a sequence of predicted words (Theordoris 2020: 982), i.e. machine translation also referred to as automatic translation.

Neural Machine Translation (NMT), as a Natural Language Processing (NLP) application (Mitkov 2022), is a field which aims at processing, analysing and synthesising natural language with the help of computer based analysis (Theordoris 2020: 1017). This type of study is possible thanks to the fact that languages are usually sequential in nature and very often, the meaning of a word depends on its part of speech or where it is located in a sentence as well as its context of use (Theordoris 2020: 1017). This NLP application is growing fast and is used extensively everywhere.

According to Chowdhary (2020: 604), NLP requires high-level symbolic capabilities such as: a) access and acquisition of lexical, semantic; and episodic characteristics; b) creation and propagation of dynamic bindings; c) manipulation of constituent recursive structures; d) coordination of many processing and learning modules; e) identification of basic language constructs (e.g., objects and actions); and f) presentation of abstract concepts. In this paper, we propose the study of a linguistic model to enhance the last requisite, i.e. a model to give more insights towards the presentation of abstract concepts which enables obtaining more precise cognitive structural information of how the human brain works in one language and how it may differ in other languages, with the objective of obtaining more precise machine translations both in general and specialised languages as it is based on predictive models based on conscious use of language (Behnke et al. 2022: 1475).

The model we propose is inspired by recent cognitive models and more specifically, it is based on the conceptual complexes analysis introduced by Ruiz de Mendoza (2017). This approach suggests the detailed examination of language by means of attesting the usage of linguistic patterns in context in order to obtain more reliable information (Ruiz de Mendoza 2017: 300). We argue that studying these models and combining their understanding with AI technologies would improve the accuracy of some prepositional aspects of MT. This proposal is in line with the model fit imperative approach discussed in Cassimatis (2012: 17). This approach impinges on the importance of carrying out research in the field of cognitive modelling orientated towards AI technologies related to machine learning, capable of giving more hints on human-level intelligence. Cassimatis (2012) claims that more cognitive model research orientated towards machine learning is still necessary to comprehend and simulate human intelligence.

This paper is organised as follows: in Sect. 2 we provide an introduction to the cognitive models and their relevance to machine learning technologies. In Sect. 3 we describe the conceptual complexes approach suggested by Ruiz de Mendoza (2017), considered as one of the relevant cognitive models to be further studied to provide results orientated towards MT technologies. In Sect. 3.1 we focus on the image schemas and image schematic complexes and their utility in building cognitive architecture diagrams that may be implemented to enhance some aspects of machine learning techniques. In Sect. 4 we detail the basis of the hypothetical methodology to be used, based on the results of automated extraction of image schemas suggested in Hedblom (2020: 167) and Morras Cortés (2019). In Sect. 5 we detail the suggested approach towards the automatic extraction and annotation of image schemas and image schematic complexes in a parallel corpus. Finally, in Sect. 6 we highlight the main conclusions and suggest future work.

2 Cognitive Models

The study of cognitive models is one of the foundations to comprehend the conceptual principles of human understanding and creation of meaning (Nerlich and Clarke 2000: 141). It seeks, among other things, to show how analogical processes are ubiquitous in human cognition (Gentner and Smith 2013: 668) as they are indeed originated firstly in the human thoughts then manifested in language (Kövecses 2005: 8). In this context, a cognitive operation is defined as:

> [...] any mental mechanism whose purpose is to contribute to the inferential processes that are necessary to derive a full semantic representation out of a linguistic expression or any other symbolic device (e.g., a drawing) in order to make it fully meaningful in the context in which it is to be interpreted (Ruiz de Mendoza 2011: 103).

In relation to the study of cognitive models orientated towards machine learning, authors including Goertzel et al. (2012: 124) claim that it is necessary to carry out studies which may offer holistic understanding of certain aspects related to human intelligence, whose logic may be applied to machine learning. These authors suggest studying cognitive models in a way that may help in building cognitive architecture diagrams for human intelligence, defined as "diagrams systematically laying out all the pieces needed to generate human intelligence and how they interact with each other". Cognitive synergy, or the study of cognitive modelling in consonance with AI objectives is one of the main ways to build further steps in the long road of machine learning (Goertzel et al. 2012: 125).

One of the main characteristics which distinguishes the competent language users is their cognitive ability to access the conceptual level of meaning realised in a particular lexical form, and in the case of translators, this ability goes beyond comprehension and enable them to generate multiple potential target-text solutions in order to reach a given target audience (Massey 2021: 52). Further comprehending those basic conceptual abilities at cognitive levels is in our opinion, key to improve AI data inputs.

Many cognitive models were studied based on linguistic evidence, such as the Conceptual Metaphor Theory (Lakoff and Johnson 2003), Conceptual Metonymy Theory (Lakoff and Johnson 2003; Kövecses and Radden 1998), Frame Semantics (Fillmore

1986), Image Schemas (Johnson 1987), Cognitive Domains (Langacker 1987), Idealised Cognitive Models (Lakoff 1987), Mental Spaces (Fauconnier 1985) and Conceptual Complexes (Ruiz de Mendoza 2017). The advantage of those models is that they provide realistic data as their results are obtained from the precise observation of the use of language in discourse, and not only of what we theoretically suppose we know about language (Briones et al. 2019: 224). In this study, we focus on a very small parcel categorised under the conceptual complexes field, called image schema and image schematic complexes. We believe that the study of this aspect would unveil some of the basic notions on which human intelligence is based and which would need an in depth empirical study in the future.

3   Conceptual Complexes

Conceptual complexes are "combinations of cognitive models whose existence can be detected from a careful examination of the meaning effects of some linguistic expressions" (Ruiz de Mendoza 2017: 300); in other words, concepts can be integrated into one another and this integration is visible in language through our linguistic choices. This theory is based on the Idealised Cognitive Model (Lakoff 1987), the Conceptual Integration Model (Fauconnier and Turner 2002) as well as the Mental Spaces (Fauconnier 1985). These models are combined through the identification of possible patterns of interaction (Ruiz de Mendoza 2018: 14) in a way that they can be integrated within each other, resulting in more complex conceptual structures (Ruiz de Mendoza 2017: 306). The advantage is that their study "endows the linguistic account with a greater ability to predict the meaning effects of linguistic expressions" (Ruiz de Mendoza 2017: 300). Ruiz de Mendoza (2017) focuses on frame complexes, image schematic complexes, metonymic complexes, and metaphor complexes. However, in the scope of this study, we will only focus on image schemas and image schematic complexes.

3.1   Image Schemas and Image Schematic Complexes

Ruiz de Mendoza (2017: 3011–3014) defines image schemas as schematisations or abstractions of spatial experience or a schematisation of topological structure:

> They capture spatial orientations (e.g. up/down and front/back), space regions, and positions (e.g. in/out, on/off, at/away from), part-whole structure, and forward/backward motion (along a path). They hold for the various topological properties of physical reality (Ruiz de Mendoza 2017: 301).

This shows for instance how in some cultures death is perceived as a path of which we depart or pass away (Ruiz de Mendoza 1998: 261) or how bodies are envisaged as a container in which objects come in and out (Díaz 2008: 55).

Image schemas play a vital role in fitting language to experience (Dodge and Lakoff 2005: 60) as they are acquired on the basis of our earliest bodily experiences (Barcelona 2003: 6), and they "engender meaningful structures through interaction and manipulation of objects in moving through space" (Nielsen and Havbro Faber 2021: 13).

They are characterised by a number of structural elements and express abstract logic propositionally (Díez 2002: 48). Their spatial abstraction implies a materialisation of conceptual structures, which helps in the re-description of spatial experience by means of a perceptual analysis process of meaning, in which the spatial structure is expressed in terms of a conceptual structure (Mandler 1992: 591), and hence, its importance for children's acquisition of concepts. In other words, they are considered basic patterns of conceptualisation of language, and that is why in our opinion, they are key elements in building cognitive architecture diagrams for machine intelligence, simulating human intelligence.

Image schemas are also considered a milestone in comprehending abstract phenomena both in general and specialised language as they help in the construction of conceptual metaphor and metonymy and the conceptual complexes which surround them (Barcelona 2003: 6; Ruiz de Mendoza and Galera 2012; Barbosa de Oliveira and Ferrareto 2019). Johnson (1987: 126) elaborated a list of the most common image schemas in English language which helped in locating metaphor and metonym in specialised discourse: CONTAINER, COUNTERFORCE, MASS/COUNT, CYCLE, MERGING SUPERIMPOSITION, SURFACE, BLOCKAGE, PART/WHOLE, BALANCE, RESTRAINT, REMOVAL, PATH, NEAR/FAR, SPLITTING, ITERATION, OBJECT, ATTRACTION, MATCHING, COMPULSION, ENABLEMENT, LINK, SCALE, FULL/EMPTY, CONTACT, COLLECTION, CENTRE/PERIPHERY and PROCESS. By way of example, thanks to the image schemas, we are able to understand and conceptualise phenomena such as global warming and greenhouse effects through the container image schema. Figure 1 shows for instance how the Earth is visualised as a container through our understanding of the global warming phenomenon, as suggested in Niebert and Gropengiesser (2012: 6).

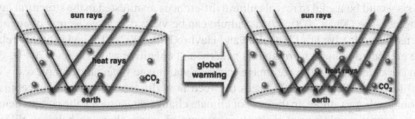

Fig. 1. Image schema representation of the Earth as a container visualised through the comprehension of global warming phenomenon (Niebert and Gropengiesser 2012: 6)

Even more, they can also enhance and extend metaphoric use to cover cases where no visual information is present (Liebert et al. 1997: 180). These authors expose a very interesting and illustrative example on how image schemas provide a structure to comprehend the term 'information skyway' by stablishing resemblance between cyberspace and street highways (Liebert et al. 1997: 189).

Image schemas may be enriched by combining them with metaphor or metonymy or by integrating into them frame-like constructs with an image-schematic basis (Ruiz de Mendoza 2017: 304). These combinations give as a result image schematic complexes. As an example, this author uses the sentence 'The bird flew into the cave' and 'The ship sailed off its course into the rocks', which is on the one hand an image schema based on the notion of 'motion-along-a-path', which contains a moving object, a path of motion, and a destination of motion, and at the same time, it is enriched with the image schema of a container. In those examples, the container image is represented through the words 'cave' and 'rocks' consecutively thanks to the use of the preposition 'into'.

The main catachrestic which makes image schemas suitable for machine learning studies and AI architecture, is that on the one hand, they are prepositional, in the sense that they depend on prepositional articulation in discourse in order to mould our perception; and on the other hand, unlike other cognitive models, they remain schematic, i.e., their structure does not change topologically, as our perception of motion, space, position, etc. does not change.

At a cross-linguistic level, Dodge and Lakoff (2005: 57–58) showed that languages vary widely in the meanings of their spatial-relations terms, but despite this variation, the cross-linguistic differences can be categorised under universal schemas, such as paths, bounded regions, contact, forces, etc. The reason behind that is due to the fact that in spite of the complex and diverse systems yielding each language to structure and express its spatial relations, they are based on simple universal primitives in one language, but combine differently in other languages. Linguistic analysis and corpus based analysis help in showing how different languages may use and combine image schemas. For instance, Talmy (1983) and Langacker (1987) highlighted the diversity in the ways languages describe space and location. This same idea is further explained in Dodge and Lakoff (2005: 67). That is how some languages like English uses propositions like 'above' while other languages like Mixtec uses expressions like 'ahead' to explain position (Dodge and Lakoff 2005: 64). The cross linguistic study of the topological features of languages is necessary to understand the schematic images and the image schematic complexes (Dodge and Lakoff 2005: 61). This cross linguistic conceptual analysis would be useful to reveal cultural differences manifested in the structural layers of language use (Khan 2020: 79), as culture can be viewed as a "collection of cognitive patterns at a collective level" (Nielsen and Havbro Faber 2021: 15) and is highly related to the embodied cultural learning in a generic and cognitive way (Kimmel 2013).

In our opinion, the study of image schemas and image schematic complexes is very useful to comprehend the differences between how different languages conceptualise phenomena. For example, in the case of climate change phenomena, the comprehension of such aspect would reveal if there were gaps of comprehension between different cultures. Studies like Nielsen and Havbro Faber (2021), through studying the image schemas in the discourse of risk, resilience and sustainability in the domain of climate change, show how different languages perceive the risk factor differently through the conceptualisation of their image schemas and image schematic complexes.

4   Background Methodology

In this section, we put forward our methodological framework which we base on the hypothesis and approach proposed by Hedblom (2020: 167). Our objective is to perform automated extraction of image schema in English specialised discourse through the use of corpus analysis and the identification of asymmetries between different languages. To this end, first of all, the preparation of a representative parallel corpus in a specific domain of study is required. This corpus will be necessary for the extraction of image schemas and image schematic complexes. Secondly, the program would extract the image schemas according to the hypothesis established by Hedblom (2020: 168):

- Hypothesis I (H1): Image schemas are conceptual building blocks that capture the essence of concepts, including abstract ones.
- Hypothesis II (H2): Following from H1, image schemas are consistent over languages as a concept's meaning is consistent over languages.

Hedblom developed her methodology on the SOURCE- PATH- GOAL image schemas and to this end, her method would be applied to detect those types of images schemas. The method will be applied focusing on the differences between prepositions used to build image schemas. Afterwards, the automatic procedure will be complemented by manual analysis in order to obtain more accurate results based on human evaluation of results, and detect the image schematic complexes and the possible asymmetries across languages. In this stage, previous corpus annotation would facilitate the automatic extraction and reduce the percentage of errors.

Finally, the results will be used to enrich the neural networks of machine translation in order to obtain better automated translations of domains, both in general and specialised languages.

For the implementation of the study, we take as a case study and a basis, the results on prepositions used in the creation of image schemas and image schematic complexes presented in Morras Cortés (2019), above all, we use the comparative sets of prepositions in English and Spanish and how they vary in relation to the image schemas they convey.

5   Towards Automatic Extraction and Annotation of Image Schemas for Neural Machine Translation

Based on comparable corpus-based analysis, using the British National Corpus (BNC) in English and the Spanish Web 2011 (esTenTen11), and orientated by the conceptual parameters, defined as "a highly schematic bundle of conceptual information that is phenomenologically based" (Morras Cortés 2019: 4), Morras Cortés (2019) compares between the prepositions *between, among, amid, to* and *for* and its parallel equivalents in Spanish; i.e. he compares between the preposition *entre* in Spanish as equivalent to the prepositions *between, among* and *amid*; the preposition *a* as equivalent to *to* and the preposition *para* as equivalent to *for*, used in the construction of image schemas in context. His results showed that there are differences in the perception of time and space between Spanish and English and in the schematic images constructed according to them.

For instance, in English, there is a distinction between the prepositional-landmark elements of *between, among*, and *amid* while in Spanish it does not follow the same criteria. The structure is simpler in Spanish as it relies on the preposition *entre a*s equivalent of all the mentioned prepositions in English: "it does not discriminate the conceptual nature of the elements that elaborate it" and makes the preposition *entre* inclusive of all the conceptual parameters that can be found in the four aforementioned English prepositions (Morras Cortés 2019: 131).

In the case of the propositions *to* in English and *a* in Spanish, they present less semantic overlap, than the previous set of prepositions, however, the preposition *to* is generally conceptualised as a primary goal while the preposition *a* in Spanish does not necessarily need to be considered as primary goal and has a more polysemous character which sometimes may include the meaning of prepositions like *at, for, on,* and *by* (Morras Cortés 2019: 186). In relation to the English preposition *for* and the Spanish preposition *para,* the preposition *for* is distinguished for the obliqueness characteristic and is mainly related to lexical concepts concerning reasons, purposes, and intentions, as well as its association with temporal cognition and temporal conceptualisation. On the other hand, the Spanish preposition *para,* contains characteristics of both the preposition *to* and *for* in English, as it involves both purpose and obliqueness.

As shown in the study of Morras Cortés (2019), there is a difference in use between the prepositions in English and their hypothetic equivalents in Spanish and the image schema and image schematic complexes underlying the structures they yield.

Taking this fact into consideration, the idea would be to extract the information of schematic images and image schematic complexes from a parallel *ad hoc* corpus in a certain domain of study. Automated extraction will be carried out according to the method suggested in Hedblom (2020) and further complemented by post-editing to extract the image schematic complexes.

A detailed comparison between the meaning embodied in both English and Spanish based on the use of those prepositions and the image schematic complexes they reproduce is to be annotated making a distinction between the images associated to each preposition. As a result of this analysis and annotation, an inventory of possible translations will be created to feed the neural networks in machine translation.

6   Conclusions

This study seeks to explore a possible application of a cognitive model aspect rooted in the basic layers of human intelligence, which is image schema and image schematic complexes (Cassimatis 2012: 17). More specifically, we propose a new approach to machine translation from a cognitive linguistic point of view.

In line with Ruiz de Mendoza (2017: 306), we extend the study of conceptual complexes in order to formulate scientific generalisations capable of accounting for more data by means of a smaller set of rules and principles. In our opinion, those smaller sets of cognitive rules may be key in obtaining more precise results if inserted in neural machine translation models.

More specifically, our study focuses basically on the image schema and image schematic complexes, taking advantage of their prepositional and schematic conditions which facilitates its systematic study. Orientational image schemas are based on both physical and cultural background experience, but they are not arbitrarily determined, and at the same time not universal, as they are embedded in a socio-cultural context (Nielsen and Havbro Faber 2021: 14–17), that is why the controlled analysis of its use among languages may be a clue to enhancing the quality of machine translation.

We argue that the study of this aspect may give a wider perspective of how to offer better solutions to conceptually decipher aspects like metaphor and metonymy in specialised discourse and its corresponding automated translation in different languages.

As highlighted in Morras Cortés (2019), there are more prepositions in English used in different contexts to visualise and represent the different image schemas and images schematic complexes in discourse, while Spanish is usually more limited and uses the same preposition to express a big set of image schemas and image schematic complexes. In other words, Spanish uses only one preposition to express what in English is expressed by more than one preposition. For this reason, and depending on the directionality of MT, it is useful to associate each preposition with all the possible image schemas and image schematic complexes it represents in a specified domain and feed the neural networks with all of them, so that the automated machine translation can offer a more realistic translation based on real context of use and based on empirical testing and refined examination. It also permits taking the cultural differences of conceptualisation into account as it allows for the detection of non-universal image schemas of conceptualisation of phenomenon in a determined domain of study, which means that it can be applied in general language as well as in specialised language domains.

As for the evaluation of the results, future studies envisage the involvement of NLP experts with a view to automating the extraction of image schemas and evaluating performance. While future studies will be more focused on NMT and NLP issues, we believe that the approach we propose will add an insightful layer to machine translation research from the perspective of cognitive modelling, as suggested in studies like Schäffner and Shuttleworth (2013), Hedblom et al (2019) and Massey (2021).

Acknowledgments. This research was carried out as part of the project PID2020-118369GB-I00, Transversal integration of culture into an environmental terminological knowledge base (TRANSCULTURE), funded by the Spanish Ministry of Science and Innovation. Funding was also provided by an FPU grant (FPU18/05327) given by the Spanish Ministry of Education.

References

Aggarwal, C.C.: Neural Networks and Deep Learning. Springer, Cham (2018)

Barbosa de Oliveira Baptista, A.E., Rosana Ferrareto, L.R.: Mechanism for developing scientific concepts. In: 11th International Proceedings on Proceedings of Conference on Education and New Learning Technologies (EDULEARN19), pp. 10424–10431. Palma, Spain (2019)

Barcelona, A.: Metaphor and Metonymy at the Crossroads : A Cognitive Perspective. De Gruyter Mouton, Berlin (2003)

Beate, H. (ed.): From Perception to Meaning: Image Schemas in Cognitive Linguistics. Mouton de Gruyter, Berlin (2005)

Behnke, H., Fomicheva, M., Specia. L.: Bias mitigation in machine translation quality estimation. In: 60th International Proceedings on Proceedings of the Annual Meeting of the Association for Computational Linguistics, vol. 1, pp. 1475–1487, Association for Computational Linguistics: Dublin, Ireland (2022)

Benczes, R., Barcelona, A., Ruiz de Mendoza, F.J. (eds.): Defining Metonymy in Cognitive Linguistics: Towards a Consensus View. John Benjamins: Amsterdam/ Philadelphia (2011)

BNC Consortium: The British National Corpus, XML Edition. Oxford Text Archive (2007)

Briones, S., Carlsen, E., Saster, M.S.: Conocimiento y lenguaje: las metáforas de la salud. Cuadernos de Humanidades 20/21, pp. 231–240 (2019)

Cassimatis, N.L.: Artificial intelligence and cognitive modelling have the same problem. In: Wan, P., Goertzel, B. (eds.) Theoretical Foundations of Artificial General Intelligence. Atlantis Thinking Machinespp, vol. 4, pp. 11–24. Atlantis Press, Paris (2012). https://doi.org/10.2991/978-94-91216-62-6_2

Bibel, W., Jorrand, P. (eds.): Fundamentals of Artificial Intelligence an Advanced Course. LNCS, vol. 232. Springer, Heidelberg (1986). https://doi.org/10.1007/BFb0022678

Daniel, R. (ed.): The Oxford Handbook of Cognitive Psychology. Oxford University Press, Oxford (2013)

Di Stefano, M. (ed.): Metáforas en uso. Editorial Biblos, Argentina (2008)

Díaz, H.: El enfoque cognitivista. In Di Stefano Mariana (ed.), pp. 41–62 (2008)

Díez Velasco, O.I.: Metaphor, metonymy and image-schemas: an analysis of conceptual interaction pattern. J. English Stud. 3, 47–63 (2002)

Dodge, E., Lakoff, G.: Image schemas: from linguistic analysis to neural grounding. In: Beate, H. (ed.), From Perception to Meaning, pp. 57–92 (2005)

Fauconnier, G.: Mental Spaces. Cambridge University Press, Cambridge (1985)

Fauconnier, G.: Turner, M.: The Way We Think: Conceptual Blending and the Mind's Hidden Complexities. Basic Books, New York (2002)

Fillmore, C.J.: Pragmatically controlled zero anaphora. In: 12th International Proceedings on Proceedings of Annual Meeting of the Berkeley Linguistics Society, pp. 95–107 (1986)

Gentner, D., Smith, L.A.: Analogical learning and reasoning. In: Reisberg, D. (ed.) The Oxford Handbook of Cognitive Psychology, pp. 668–681 (2013)

Goertzel, B., Iklé, M., Wigmore, J.: The architecture of human-like general intelligence. In: Wang, P., Goertzel, B. (eds.), Theoretical Foundations of Artificial General Intelligence. Atlantis Thinking Machines, vol. 4, pp. 123–144. Atlantis Press, Paris (2012)

Hedblom, M.: Image Schemas And Concept Invention: Cognitive, Logical, and Linguistic Investigations. Springer, Cham (2020)

Hedblom, M.M., Kutz, O., Peñaloza, R., Guizzardi, J.: Image schema combinations and complex events. KI - Künstliche Intelligenz 33, 279–291 (2019)

Herbert, P., Acredolo, L. (eds.): Spatial Orientation: Theory, Research, and Application. Plenum Press, New York (1983)

Johnson, M.: The Body in the Mind. University of Chicago Press, Chicago (1987)

Khan, H.M.: A cross-linguistic analysis of conceptual complexes in the domain of economics. RAEL Rev. Electr. Linguist. Aplicada 19, 78–96 (2020)

Kilgarriff, A., Renau, I.: esTenTen, a vast web corpus of Peninsular and American Spanish. Procedia Soc. Behav. Sci. 95, 12–19 (2013)

Kimmel, M.: The arc from the body to culture: How affect, proprioception, kinesthesia, and perceptual imagery shape cultural knowledge (and vice versa). Integral Rev. 9(2), (2013)

Kövecses, Z.: Metaphor in Culture: Universality and Variation. Cambridge University Press, Cambridge (2005)

Kövecses, Z., Radden, G.: Metonymy: developing a cognitive linguistic view. Cogn. Linguist. 9, 37–77 (1998)

Lakoff, G.: Women, Fire and Dangerous Things: What Categories Reveal About the Mind. The University of Chicago Press, Chicago (1987)

Lakoff, G., Johnson. M.: Metaphors We Live by. The University of Chicago Press, Chicago (2003)

Langacker, R.W.: Foundations of Cognitive Grammar, vol. I. Theoretical prerequisites. Stanford University Press, Stanford (1987)

Liebert, W.A., Redeker, G. Waugh. L.R.: Discourse and Perspective in Cognitive Linguistics. John Benjamins Publishing Company, Amsterdam (1997)

Mandler, J.M.: How to build a baby II conceptual primitives. Psychol. Rev. **99**, 587–604 (1992)

Massey, G.: Re-framing conceptual metaphor translation research in the age of neural machine translation: investigating translators' added value with products and processes. Train. Lang. Cult. **5**(1), 37–56 (2021)

Mitkov, R.: The Oxford Handbook of Computational Linguistics. Oxford University Press, Oxford (2022)

Morras Cortés, J.A.: A contrastive study of the semantics of English and Spanish prepositions: a cognitive linguistic perspective. Ph.D. thesis. Universidad de Córdoba, Córdoba (2019)

Nerlich, B., Clarke, D.D.: Semantic fields and frames: historical explorations of the interface between language, action, and cognition. J. Pragmat. **32,** 125–150 (2000)

Niebert, K., Gropengiesser, H.: Understanding and communicating climate change in metaphors. Environ. Educ. Res. **19**(3), 1–21 (2012)

Nielsen, L., Havbro Faber, M.: Toward an information theoreticontology of risk, resilience and sustainability and a blueprint for education - Part II. Sustain. Resilient Infrastruct. (2021)

Preisler, B., Fabricius, A.H., Haberland, H., Kjærbeck, S., Risager, K. (eds.): The Consequences of Mobility: Linguistic and Sociocultural Contact Zones. Roskilde University, Roskilde (2005)

Ruiz de Mendoza Ibáñez, F J.: Complejos conceptuales en la construcción de significado. In: 9th International Proceedings on Proceedings of XI Congreso Internacional de la Asociación Española de Lingüística Cognitiva (AELCO), pp. 1–41 (2018)

Ruiz de Mendoza Ibáñez, F.J.: Conceptual complexes in cognitive modelling. Revista Española de Lingüística Aplicada **30** (1), 297–322 (2017)

Ruiz de Mendoza Ibáñez, F.J.: Metonymy and cognitive operations. In: Benczes, R., Barcelona, A., Ruiz de Mendoza, F.J. (eds.) Defining Metonymy in Cognitive Linguistics, pp. 103–124 (2011)

Ruiz de Mendoza Ibáñez, F.J.: On the nature of blending as a cognitive phenomenon. J. Pragmat. **30**, 259–274 (1998)

Ruiz de Mendoza Ibáñez, F.J., Galera Masegosa, A.: Modelos cognitivos, operaciones cognitivas y usos figurados del lenguaje. Forma y Función **25,** 11–38 (2012)

Schäffner, C., Shuttleworth, M.: Metaphor in translation: possibilities for process research. Target Int. J. Transl. Stud. **25**(1), 93–106 (2013)

Talmy, L.: How language structures space. In: Pick, H.L., Acredolo, L.P. (eds.) Spatial Orientation, pp. 225–282. Springer, Boston. https://doi.org/10.1007/978-1-4615-9325-6_11

Theordoris, S.: Machine Learning: A Bayesian and Optimization Perspective. Science Direct, London (2020)

Wan, P., Goertzel, B. (eds.): Theoretical Foundation of Artificial General Intelligence. Atlantis Press, Amsterdam (2012)

Reassessing *gApp*: Does MWE Discontinuity Always Pose a Challenge to Neural Machine Translation?

Carlos Manuel Hidalgo-Ternero[1] and Xiaoqing Zhou-Lian[2(✉)]

[1] University of Malaga, Avda. Cervantes, 2., 29071 Málaga, Spain
cmhidalgo@uma.es
[2] Universidad Rey Juan Carlos, Paseo de los Artilleros s/n., 28032 Madrid, Spain
xiaoqing.zhou@urjc.es

Abstract. In this paper we present research results with *gApp*, a text-preprocessing system designed for automatically detecting and converting discontinuous multiword expressions (MWEs) into their continuous forms so as to improve the performance of current neural machine translation systems (NMT) (see Hidalgo-Ternero 2021; Hidalgo-Ternero and Corpas Pastor 2020, 2022a, 2022b and 2022c, among others). To test its effectiveness, an experiment with the NMT systems of Google Translate and DeepL has been carried out in the ES>EN/ZH directionalities for the translation of somatisms, i. e., MWEs containing lexemes referring to human or animal body parts (Mellado Blanco 2004). More specifically, we have analysed "Verb Noun Idiomatic Constructions" (VNICs), such as *tocar los cojones*, *tocar los huevos*, *tocar las narices*, and *tocar las pelotas*. In this regard, some of the unexpected results yielded by the study of these multiword expressions will question the widely accepted conception of phraseological discontinuity as an unequivocal synonym of worse NMT performance.

Keywords: Neural Machine Translation (NMT) · Multiword expressions (MWEs) · Text preprocessing system *gApp*

1 Introduction

The recent emergence of neural networks in natural language processing has represented a real breakthrough in the field of machine translation, bringing forth Neural Machine Translation (NMT), which has resulted in a considerable qualitative leap compared to the previous ruled-based and statistical models (Bentivogli et al. 2018; Junczys-Dowmunt et al. 2016; Shterionov et al. 2018; Wang et al. 2022). The paradigm shift that NMT has prompted can be easily observed in the latest European Language Industry Surveys: for the first time in 2018 more than half of all language service companies (LSC) in Europe state that they employ machine translation (ELIS 2018) and 78% of the interviewed LSCs are planning to incorporate or augment the use of MT and post-editing (ELIS 2020). In this line, all sectors concerned (training institutes, buyers, and language developers

G. Corpas Pastor and R. Mitkov (Eds.): EUROPHRAS 2022, LNAI 13528, pp. 116–132, 2022.
https://doi.org/10.1007/978-3-031-15925-1_9

as well as independent professionals) also recognise MT and post-editing by far as the most prominent trend in the industry (ELIS 2021).

Despite these advances, NMT systems still have an important Achilles' heel: multi-word expressions (MWEs). As well as their quintessential problematic features such as syntactic anomaly, non-compositionality, diasystematic variation and ambiguity, among others, a further challenge arises for NMT: MWEs do not always consist of adjacent tokens (e.g., *I took his words to heart.*), which seriously hinders their automatic detection and translation (Constant et al. 2017; Corpas Pastor 2013; Foufi et al. 2019; Monti et al. 2018; Ramisch and Villavicencio 2018; Rohanian et al. 2019). To overcome the challenges that discontinuous MWEs still pose for even the most robust NMT systems (cf. Colson 2019; Zaninello and Birch 2020), we have designed *gApp*,[1] a text-preprocessing system for the automatic identification and conversion of discontinuous MWEs into their continuous form in order to improve NMT performance. In this regard, several experiments, summarised in Table 1, have previously been carried out so as to prove *gApp*'s effectiveness.

Table 1. Results of previous experiments with *gApp*

	Language directio-nalities	NMTs analysed	NMTs' accuracy before *gApp*	NMTs' accuracy after *gApp*	Improvement after *gApp*	Manual conversion
1	ES>EN	DeepL	80.7%	90.7%	10%	+3.2%
		Google Translate	60.7%	75.4%	14.6%	+2.1%
2	ES>EN	DeepL	49%	62.5%	13.5%	+0.5%
	ES>DE		43.5%	52.5%	9%	+0.5%
3	FR>EN	DeepL	40%	58%	18%	=
	FR>ES		41.5%	58%	16.5%	=
4	ES>EN	ModernMT	50%	60%	10%	=
	ES>DE		23.3%	33.3%	10%	=
	ES>FR		49.3%	60%	10.7%	=
	ES>IT		56.7%	60.7%	4%	=
	ES>PT		56%	58.7%	2.7%	=
	ES>EN	DeepL	70.7%	81.3%	10.7%	+0.7%
	ES>DE		59.3%	66.7%	7.3%	+0.7%
	ES>FR		69.3%	74%	4.7%	+0.7%
	ES>IT		76%	80%	4%	+0.7%

(continued)

[1] *gApp* is available through the following link: http://lexytrad.es/gapp/app.php. This application is registered in Safecreative: https://www.safecreative.org/work/2011165898461-gapp.

Table 1. (*continued*)

	Language directio-nalities	NMTs analysed	NMTs' accuracy before *gApp*	NMTs' accuracy after *gApp*	Improvement after *gApp*	Manual conversion
	ES>PT		68%	74%	6%	+0.7%
	ES>EN	Google Translate	66%	75.3%	9.3%	=
	ES>DE		35.3%	43.3%	8%	=
	ES>FR		65.3%	73.3%	8%	=
	ES>IT		78.7%	79.3%	0.7%	=
	ES>PT		72.7%	79.3%	6.7%	=
5	ES>EN	VIP	45.5%	67%	21.5%	−0.5%
	ES>EN	DeepL	77%	85.5%	8.5%	=
	ES>EN	Google Translate	64%	77.5%	13.5%	−1%
6	IT>EN	ModernMT	25.5%	42%	16.5%	+1%
	IT>DE		28%	37%	9%	=
	IT>EN	Google Translate	64.5%	82.5%	18%	+0.5%
	IT>DE		50.5%	61%	10.5%	−1%
	IT>EN	DeepL	75%	75%	0%	−0.5%
	IT>DE		62%	67.5%	5.5%	=
Total (experiments 1–6)			58.3%	70.9%	12.5%	+0.6%

In this context, the current study analyses, for the first time, the neural machine translation of MWEs in the ES>EN/ZH directionalities after *gApp*'s automatic conversion. To this end, the performance of the NMT systems Google Translate and DeepL will be examined against 400 cases: 200 with the discontinuous and 200 with the continuous form of MWEs, contrasting *gApp*'s conversion and the manual conversion; the latter will hence constitute our gold standard. The MWEs under study include the following ones: *tocar los cojones*, *tocar los huevos*, *tocar las narices*, and *tocar las pelotas*, which will be thoroughly analysed in the next section.

The remainder of the paper is structured as follows. Section 2 introduces the MWEs under study, and Sect. 3 illustrates the research methodology. In Sect. 4, the system's precision and recall will be tested, in order to assess to what extent *gApp* can enhance the performance of Google Translate and DeepL under the challenge of MWE discontinuity in the Spanish-into-English and the Spanish-into-Chinese directionalities. A discussion of the results will follow (Sect. 5). Section 6 provides concluding remarks on how to optimise *gApp* following this study's findings.

2 The MWEs Under Study

In order to test *gApp*'s effectiveness in the ES>EN/ZH directionalities, for the present study we have selected the following four Spanish MWEs:

· *tocar los cojones, tocar los huevos, tocar las narices,* and *tocar las pelotas*: (vulg.) 'molestar o fastidiar' ('to bother') (DFDEA 2017, pp. 183, 413, 552 and 638):

      o Primary correspondence(s) in English: *to get on someone's nerves*
      o Primary correspondence(s) in Chinese: 惹恼 *rěnǎo*
    (1) Me estás tocando mucho los cojones/los huevos/las narices/las pelotas.
        EN: lit. 'You are touching a lot my bollocks/eggs/noses/balls.'
           You're really getting on my nerves.
        ZH: lit. '你正在使劲地摸我的睾丸 / 蛋 / 鼻子/ 球。'
           Nǐ zhèngzài shǐjìn de mō wǒ de gāowán/ dàn/ bízi/ qiú.
           你正在惹恼我。
           Nǐ zhèngzài rěnǎo wǒ.

Following Ramisch's (2015) taxonomy, the four MWEs chosen for this study class as idiomatic expressions, since they have a non-compositional meaning (which is why they are also defined as semantically non-decomposable idioms or SNDIs (Bargman and Sailer 2018)). Concerning their fixedness, following Parra et al.'s (2018) taxonomy for MWEs in Spanish, they can be classified as flexible, since other elements can appear embedded within the constituents of the MWEs. With regards to their morphosyntactic structure, they belong to the category of verb-noun idiomatic constructions (VNICs) (Fazly et al. 2009) as they all consist of a verb and a noun in its direct object position. Finally, considering the nature of their constituents, they are somatisms, i.e., idioms containing terms that refer to human or animal body parts. In this regard, we have decided to analyse specifically idiomatic expressions because their non-compositional meaning makes them become potentially easier to detect and translate by NMT systems when all the constituents are contiguous, as we proved in experiments 1–6 (Table 1).

Regarding the relation between the MWEs under study, they are *variants through paradigmatic relation* (Koike 2007), in a relation of co-hyponymy, with a permanent verb "tocar" and an interchangeable noun phrase "los cojones/los huevos/las narices/las pelotas…". The concordances retrieved from the analysed corpora[2] allowed us to observe that all these four variants can be diaphasically marked as informal and, more specifically, *tocar los cojones, tocar los huevos* and *tocar las pelotas* can be classified as *vulgar*, as they contain somatonyms explicitly referring to the *balls* as body parts.

With regards to the frequency of appearance of the different MWEs in the corpus esTenTen18, in Table 2 we summarise their raw frequency (Row 1), their normalised frequency per million tokens (Row 2) and the percentages (Row 3) representing these MWEs' appearances in their continuous (C.) or discontinuous (D.) forms in relation to their total occurrences (T.).

---

[2] All the corpora employed in the present study are described in Sect. 3 ("Methodology").

Table 2. Frequency of appearance of the different MWEs in the corpus esTenTen18

tocar los cojones			tocar los huevos			tocar las narices			tocar las pelotas		
C.	D.	T.	C.	D.	T.	C.	D.	T.	C.	D.	T.
4083	572	4655	3288	419	3707	5169	1006	6175	1766	277	2043
0.21	0.03	0.24	0.17	0.02	0.19	0.26	0.05	0.31	0.09	0.01	0.1
87.7%	12.3%		88.7%	11.3%		83.7%	16.3%		86.4%	13.6%	

The four MWEs mainly appear throughout the corpus in their continuous forms with analogous scores (87.7% for *tocar los cojones*, 88.7% for *tocar los huevos*, 95% for *tocar las narices*, and 94.7% for *tocar las pelotas*). Continuous occurrences are hence around 6 times more frequent than discontinuous ones. In this context, along the study we will intend to test our main hypothesis: that *gApp* can improve NMT performance by converting MWEs into their canonical state, i.e., their continuous form.

3 Methodology

This section presents the research methodology employed in order to assess to what extent *gApp* can optimise the performance of the NMT systems Google Translate and DeepL in the ES>EN and ES>ZH directionalities. Analogously to Hidalgo-Ternero (2020), the concordances containing the discontinuous somatisms under study have been retrieved from two giga-token web-crawled corpora of Spanish (esTenTen18 and Times-tamped JSI web corpus 2014–2021 Spanish), both available through Sketch Engine. While the esTenTen18 corpus comprises over 17 billion words of general Spanish (European and American varieties), the Timestamped JSI web corpus 2014–2021 Spanish contains over 16.4 billion words of news articles obtained from their RSS feeds (Kilgarriff et al. 2004).

In order to analyse the different translation outcomes offered by Google Translate and DeepL in English and Chinese for the source-text somatisms, we have used the Sketch Engine corpora enTenTen20 (38.1 billion words) and Timestamped JSI web corpus 2014–2021 English (60.4 billion) for English, as well as zhTenTen17 Simplified (13.5 billion) for Chinese.

Despite the challenges that user-generated content's (UGC[3]) ubiquitous source-text error, noise and out-of-vocabulary tokens still pose to even the most robust NMT systems (Belinkov and Bisk 2018; Lohar et al. 2019), a heterogeneous sample in terms of language varieties, text sources and types (including UGC) was selected for the analysis so as to alleviate sampling bias, which could otherwise originate from uniquely examining NMT canonical training data for the somatisms under study. In this way, a total of 400 cases was analysed, comprising 200 discontinuous and 200 continuous forms (i.e., after the conversion) of the somatisms *tocar los cojones, tocar los huevos, tocar las narices*, and

[3] By *user-generated content*, we mean 'content published on an online platform by users. The term social media comprises platforms that contain user-generated content. Users do not need programming skills to publish content on a social media platform.' (Wyrwoll 2014).

tocar las pelotas, split by different unigrams, bigrams or trigrams. Besides these relevant results, for each somatism 50 irrelevant results were compiled, in order to calculate, at a first stage, both the precision and recall of this system, considering all the constituents of the MWE. In this regard, let us illustrate some instances of irrelevant results for the MWEs *tocar los cojones* and *tocar las narices*.

(2) Yeray: ¡que coño ha sido ese disparo! Julio: el gilipollas este de cristian que se cree el rey aquí dando órdenes. Cristian: Y tú **tocando la guitarra de los cojones** cuando deberïas estar vigilando: Julio: […] pero quien coño te crees aquí coño!
Yeray: What the fuck was that shot! Julio: That asshole Cristian who thinks he's the king here giving orders. Cristian: And you **playing your fucking guitar** when you should be on guard: Julio: […] but who the fuck do you think you are here, you cunt!

(3) Sinceramente creo que CoD 4 fue un salto de un tema que ya esta demasiado **tocado (hasta las narices** de las Thompson o MP40-44).
I sincerely believe that CoD 4 was a leap from a subject that is already greatly **overspoken (sick to death** of the Thompson or MP40-44).

Examples 2 and 3 illustrate instances of the pattern "tocar (1–3 tokens) los cojones" and "tocar (1–3 tokens) narices", which however do not correspond to the discontinuous forms of the MWEs *tocar los cojones* and *tocar las narices*, respectively, since all the constituents of those sequences have there a literal meaning. In example 2, *de las narices* is a MWE employed to mark derogatorily the noun phrase *la guitarra* ('the guitar'), which is the object of the main verb *tocar* ('to play [an instrument]'). Analogously, in Example 3, the prepositional phrase *hasta las narices* constitutes a different MWE with the meaning of "en situación de hartura o hartazgo total" ('being completely fed up') (DFDEA 2017, p. 550). In this context, both the verb *tocar* ('to touch'), in the form of a participial adjective, and *hasta las narices* belong to different clauses, with "hasta las narices de las Thompson o MP40-44" conforming a parenthetical remark within the main clause. That is the reason why these constitute irrelevant results which must hence be filtered out (i.e., not converted) by *gApp*.

Once both parameters were quantified, at a second stage, the results concerning Google Translate and DeepL's performance for the different concordances were classified within three main categories: before *gApp*, after the automatic conversion with *gApp*, and after the manual conversion, which hence constituted our gold standard. The same study was conducted for both language directionalities: ES>EN and ES>ZH. The NMTs' outputs for these different scenarios were then manually assessed following an instance-based MT evaluation (Zaninello and Birch 2020) with several possible target-text candidates for each of the somatisms in both their continuous and discontinuous forms. To this end, morphological, syntactic, and/or orthotypographic divergences or source-text/translation imprecisions affecting other elements in the sentences were not considered *per se* as errors if they were unrelated to the phenomenon of MWE discontinuity for the somatisms under study.

4   Results

In this section, the results will be examined and showed at those two stages: first, *gApp*'s precision and recall for each of the MWEs under study will be presented so as to then evaluate to what extent *gApp* can enhance the performance of Google Translate and DeepL under the challenge of MWE discontinuity in the ES>EN and ES>ZH directionalities.

Regarding *gApp*'s precision and recall, in the case of *tocar los cojones*, the system automatically converted 51 forms, 50 of which were true positives and 1 was a false positive. In this way, *gApp*'s precision came to 98% (50/51 cases) and its recall to 100% (50/50 cases). With regard to *tocar los huevos*, *gApp* carried out 52 conversions, 50 of which were true positives and 2 were false positives. Therefore, this system's precision amounted to 96.2% (50/52 cases) and its recall to 100% (50/50). With regard to the idiom *tocar las narices*, *gApp* converted 53 forms in total (50 true positives and 3 false positives), which resulted in a precision of 94.3% (50/53) and recall of 100% (50/50). Finally, in the case of *tocar las pelotas*, *gApp* performed 53 conversions, 49 of which were true positives and 4 were false positives, therefore, its precision came to 92.5% (49/53) and its recall to 98% (49/50). A summary of *gApp*'s precision and recall is presented in Table 3.

Table 3. *gApp*'s precision and recall

	gApp's precision	*gApp*'s recall
tocar los cojones	98%	100%
tocar los huevos	96.2%	100%
tocar las narices	94.3%	100%
tocar las pelotas	92.5%	98%
Average	95.3%	99.5%

Regarding Google Translate's improvement before and after *gApp*, in Fig. 1 we can observe distinctly different results for the MWEs under study.

For these MWEs *gApp* could equal the manual conversion. In the case of *tocar los cojones*, the ES>ZH directionality has a slightly better performance than the ES>EN directionality in the continuous scenario. In relation to the latter one, this conversion into the continuous form of the somatism meant a 10% improvement (5 case-difference) compared to the discontinuous scenario, while, in regard to ES>ZH directionality, the improvement amounted to 12% (6 case-difference). An illustration of the conversion from the discontinuous to the continuous form of *tocar los cojones* with *gApp* is presented in Table 4 and Google Translate's performance before and after this conversion through *gApp* is shown in Table 5 (the whole sequence is in bold, the MWE is underlined).

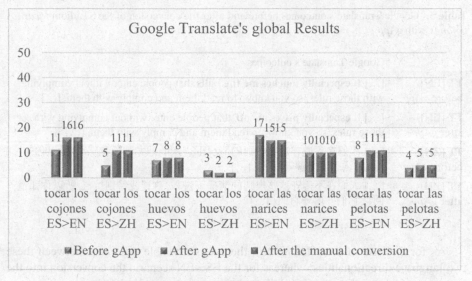

Fig. 1. Google Translate's results for the MWEs under study

Table 4. Source-text KWIC extracts with tocar los cojones before and after gApp

	KWIC extracts
ST [ES] Discontinuous form (original version, before *gApp*)	[…]ª **Me toca especialmente <u>los cojones</u>** que la gente entre sin cumplir esas normas, así que ya sabéis: a leerlas y cumplirlas. […]
ST [ES] Continuous form (after *gApp*)	[…] **Me toca los cojones especialmente** que la gente entre sin cumplir esas normas, así que ya sabéis: a leerlas y cumplirlas. […]

ªThe source texts were originally longer, however, due to space constraints, the different texts here presented only show the KWIC extracts with the translation of the somatisms both in their continuous and discontinuous forms.

The instances in Table 6 show distinctly different results before and after the automatic conversion of the source-text somatism for both ES>EN and ES>ZH directionalities. In the discontinuous scenario, *tocar los cojones* has been translated into *to touch someone's balls* in English and 球让我感动 (Qiú ràng wǒ gǎndòng) in Chinese which means *the ball(s) touch(es) my heart*. *Balls* in English can refer to *testicles* (vulgar, slang), and *cojones* is a vulgar way of saying *testicles* in Spanish, so the translation into English presents a literal meaning. The Chinese translation seems to have pivoted through English: the literal meaning of *ball* is 球 *qiú*, an object in the shape of a sphere. This is why they cannot be considered appropriate equivalents for the somatism *tocar los cojones*. It was only after the conversion with *gApp* that Google Translate could properly detect and offer an adequate equivalent in English and Chinese for the ST somatism.

Table 5. Google Translate's outcomes before and after the conversion of the ST idiom *tocar los cojones* with *gApp*

	Google Translate's outcomes
TT [EN] before *gApp*	[...] It **especially touches me the balls** that people enter without complying with those rules, so you know: to read them and comply with them. [...]
TT [EN] after *gApp*	[...] It **especially pisses me off** that people enter without complying with those rules, so you know: to read them and comply with them. [...]
TT [ZH] before *gApp*	[...] 人们在不遵守这些规则的情况下进入的球尤其让我感动, 所以你知道: 阅读它们并遵守它们。[...]
TT [ZH] after *gApp*	[...] 人们在不遵守这些规则的情况下进入, 这让我特别生气, 所以以你知道: 阅读它们并遵守它们。[...]

As for the case of *tocar los huevos*, there was a visible difference between these two language directionalities: whereas for the ES>EN scenario the conversion into the continuous form ameliorated Google Translate's performance by 2% (1-case difference), in the case of the ES>ZH directionality there was a 2% worsening.

Concerning the MWE *tocar las narices*, the continuous forms resulted in a 4% worsening (2-case difference) in the ES>EN directionality and no amelioration in the ES>ZH scenario. Finally, with regard to *tocar las pelotas*, gApp ameliorated Google Translate's performance by 6% (3-case difference) in ES>EN directionality and by 2% (1-case divergence) in ES>ZH directionality.

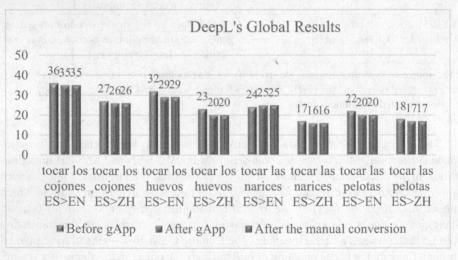

Fig. 2. DeepL's results for the MWEs under study

Regarding DeepL's performance before and after *gApp*, we can observe the results for the MWEs under study in Fig. 2. First of all, similarly to the case of Google Translate, equal results were also yielded here for both the automatic and the manual conversion. In absolute terms, compared to Google Translate, DeepL delivers a much better performance both for the discontinuous and continuous forms of these four somatisms in both ES>EN and ES>ZH directionalities. Nevertheless, the continuous forms in the ES>EN directionality only achieved positive results with *tocar las narices* with an improvement by 2% (1-case difference). In the case of the other three somatisms (*tocar los cojones, tocar los huevos* and *tocar las pelotas*), a slight worsening of the results can be observed: −2% (1-case difference), −6% (3-case difference) and −4% (2-case difference), respectively. Regarding the continuous forms in the ES>ZH directionality, all these somatisms resulted in a slight worsening: −2%, −6%, −2% and −2% respectively.

Once all the cases have been analysed and classified, the global results are displayed in Fig. 3. In the ES>EN directionality for Google Translate, the conversion into the continuous form led to an amelioration by 3.5% (7-case difference) both through *gApp* and through the manual conversion. In the ES>ZH scenario, both *gApp* and the manual conversion increased Google Translate's accuracy by 3% (6 cases). Regarding DeepL, the conversion into the continuous form obtains worse results by 2.5% (5-case difference) in the ES>EN directionality and by 3% (6 cases) in the ES>ZH directionality.

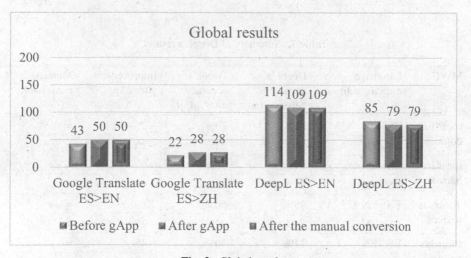

Fig. 3. Global results

Finally, a summary of all the results presented in this Section is illustrated in Tables 6 and 7.

Table 6. Summary of Google Translate's results

MWE	Language directio-nalities	Google Translate's accuracy before *gApp*	Google Translate's accuracy after *gApp*	Improvement after *gApp*	Manual conversion
tocar los cojones	ES>EN	22%	32%	10%	=
	ES>ZH	10%	22%	12%	=
tocar los huevos	ES>EN	14%	16%	2%	=
	ES>ZH	6%	4%	−2%	=
Tocar las narices	ES>EN	34%	30%	−4%	=
	ES>ZH	20%	20%	0%	=
tocar las pelotas	ES>EN	16%	22%	6%	=
	ES>ZH	8%	10%	2%	=
Global results	ES>EN	21.5%	25%	3.5%	=
	ES>ZH	11%	14%	3%	=
Final average	ES>EN/ZH	16.25%	19.5%	3.25%	=

Table 7. Summary of DeepL's results

MWE	Language directio-nalities	DeepL's accuracy before *gApp*	DeepL's accuracy after *gApp*	Improvement after *gApp*	Manual conversion
tocar los cojones	ES>EN	72%	70%	−2%	=
	ES>ZH	54%	52%	−2%	=
tocar los huevos	ES>EN	64%	58%	−6%	=
	ES>ZH	46%	40%	−6%	=
Tocar las narices	ES>EN	48%	50%	2%	=
	ES>ZH	34%	32%	−2%	=
tocar las pelotas	ES>EN	44%	40%	−4%	=
	ES>ZH	36%	34%	−2%	=
Global results	ES>EN	57%	54.5%	−2.5%	=
	ES>ZH	42.5%	39.5%	−3%	=
Final average	ES>EN/ZH	49.75%	47%	−2.75%	=

5   Analysis of Results

Global results have shown how *gApp*'s automatic conversion managed to achieve an analogous performance to the manual conversion. This is chiefly due to *gApp*'s refined detection system both in terms of final average precision (95.3%) and recall (99.5%), which means that only 4.7% of the irrelevant results could enter the system and exclusively 0.5% of the relevant results were not successfully detected. Those cases that were especially difficult to parse by *gApp* were mainly instances of verbs appearing in the gap in their infinitive, gerund and imperative forms with an enclitic pronoun as we can observe in Tables 8 and 9 (with a translation of the sequence in bold under each extract).

Table 8. Instance of an irrelevant result with the pattern "tocar [1–3 tokens] los cojones" converted by *gApp*

	KWIC extracts
Irrelevant result	Pero a mí lo que me gustan son las hembras, si **a veces me toca tocarle las pelotas a un fulano**, no quiere decir nada porque yo no miro ni siento nada, por que ¡yo soy todo un varón! ['**Sometimes I have to touch the balls to a guy**.']
Inappropriate conversion by *gApp*	Pero a mí lo que me gustan son las hembras, si **a veces me toca las pelotas tocarle a un fulano**, no quiere decir nada porque yo no miro ni siento ni siento nada, por que ¡yo soy todo un varón! ['**Sometimes it really bothers me to touch a guy**']

Table 9. Instance of an irrelevant result with the pattern "tocar [1–3 tokens] las narices" converted by *gApp*

	KWIC extracts
Irrelevant result	Se llaman pobres o excluidos, **ojalá nunca le toque romperle las pelotas a algún pelotudo** (valga la redundancia) como Ud ['**I hope he never gets to irritate an idiot**']
Inappropriate conversion by *gApp*	Se llaman pobres o excluidos, **ojalá nunca le toque las pelotas romperle a algún pelotudo** (valga la redundancia) como Ud ["**I hope it never bothers him to break an idiot**."]

Instances in Tables 8 and 9 contain concordances with the pattern "tocar [1–3 tokens] los cojones" and "tocar [1–3 tokens] las pelotas" which can be considered irrelevant results because they are not related to discontinuous forms of the MWEs *tocar los cojones* and *tocar las pelotas*, respectively. In both examples in Tables 8 and 9 we can detect the verb *tocar* with the meaning here of 'having to do something', directly followed by the MWEs *tocar las pelotas* and *romper las pelotas*, the latter being the diatopic variant of Argentinian Spanish for the idiom *tocar las pelotas*. In this context, the incorrect parsing of the infinitive verbs with an enclitic pronoun *tocarle* and *romperle* as "adverbs" has led *gApp* to identify them as modifiers splitting the MWEs *tocar los cojones* and *tocar las pelotas*, which has finally resulted in the inappropriate conversions with completely different meanings, as we could observe in Tables 8 and 9. These cases with inappropriate conversions caused by incorrect parsing emphasise the need for further optimisation of *gApp*'s POS tagger and syntactic parser in order to encompass inflection in all its forms (Derczynski et al. 2013; Neunerdt et al. 2013; Gui et al. 2017).

Global results also demonstrate that *gApp* was able to deliver a notable performance in terms of relative improvement (when contrasting the results between discontinuous and continuous forms) for Google Translate. Regarding the ES>EN directionality, Google Translate has shown a relative improvement by 3.5% between discontinuous and continuous forms after the conversion with *gApp* and the manual conversion. Concerning the ES>ZH directionality, the continuous forms enhanced Google Translate's accuracy by 3%. However, it can be observed that the conversion into the continuous form obtained worse results for DeepL by 2.5% in the ES>EN directionality and by 3% in the ES>ZH directionality.

In absolute terms, DeepL has shown a better performance both before and after the conversion with *gApp* compared to Google Translate. However, the NMT systems under analysis have proved to still necessitate further enhancements in order to deliver an optimal performance. In the case of the analysed MWEs, regarding the ES>EN directionality and in spite of the conversion with *gApp*, Google Translate could only reach an average accuracy percentage of 25%, while DeepL achieved 57%. In the ES>ZH directionality, Google Translate achieved 14% of adequate translations after the conversion, while DeepL could only attain a maximum final accuracy of 42.5%.

Table 10. Summary of *gApp*'s results for experiments 1–7

	Language directio-nalities	NMTs analysed	NMTs' accuracy before *gApp*	NMTs' accuracy after *gApp*	Improvement after *gApp*	Manual conversion
7	ES>EN	Google Translate	21.5%	25%	3.5%	=
		DeepL	57%	54.5%	−2.5%	=
	ES>ZH	Google Translate	11%	14%	3%	=
		DeepL	42.5%	39.5%	−3%	=
	Total		33%	33.25%	0.25%	=
Total (experiments 1–6)			58.3%	70.9%	12.5%	+0.6%
Total (experiments 1–7)			54.8%	65.6%	10.8%	+0.5%

As we can observe in Table 10, the outcomes with VNIC somatisms from experiment 7 are, on average, 25.3% lower than our six previous experiments regarding NMT accuracy before *gApp* (33% in experiment 7 vs. 58.3% in experiments 1–6) and 37.7% after *gApp* (33.25% vs. 70.9%), which might be due to the different typology of MWEs as well as the inclusion of a new language directionality (ES>ZH). In this regard, further experiments in this additional language combination are required in order to verify whether the conversion of discontinuous MWEs can also result in a considerable improvement in NMT performance into Chinese.

On the other hand, a sharp contrast can be observed when comparing the results in both language directionalities (ES>EN vs. ES>ZH). In ES>ZH, Google Translate's performance declined by 10.5% (21-case difference) in the discontinuous and by 11% (20-case divergence) in the continuous scenario, while DeepL resulted in a decrease of 14.5% (29-case difference) and 15% (30-case divergence) respectively. The main reason behind this decrease can be found in the fact that DeepL's ES>ZH translation pivots through English, as there are more training data available in the latter language. See, for instance, the different performance of DeepL when translating *tocar las narices* into English and into Chinese in Table 11.

Table 11. Instance of DeepL's mistranslation in English and Chinese for the *tocar las narices*

	KWIC extracts
ST [ES]	[…] tu actitud de llegar, acusarnos, intentar dejarnos por tontos, exigirnos que hay que hacer ciertas cosas, y poner la plantilla "discutido" … Pues la verdad, **toca las narices** bastante. […]
	DeepL's outcomes
TT [EN]	[…] your attitude of arriving, accusing us, trying to make fools of us, demanding that we have to do certain things, and putting the template "discussed"… Well, the truth is, it's quite **touching**. […]
TT [ZH]	[…] 你的态度是到了, 指责我们, 试图愚弄我们, 要求我们必须做某些事情, 并把模板 "讨论"……嗯, 事实是, 这很令人感动。[…]

Table 11 shows that, in the ES>ZH directionality, *tocar las narices* has been translated as 令人感动 *lìng rén gǎndòng* ('moving' o 'touching'). A possible explanation for this mistranslation can be found in the English target text for the ST somatism in the ES>EN directionality: *touching*. In this regard, the Chinese phrase 令人感动 *lìng rén gǎndòng* does not have any type of relation (be it lexical or semantic) with the source-text Spanish idiom *tocar las narices*, so the only way to understand the final translation into Chinese is with the following pivoting through English:

toca las narices bastante > *it's quite* touching [lexically related to *tocar* in Spanish] > 这很令人感动 ['causing a strong feeling or emotion', therefore semantically related to *touching* in English].

These errors caused by pivoting through English emphasise the need of the NMT systems under analysis for more training data in language combinations different from English, in order to avoid English-centred NMT outcomes (Hidalgo-Ternero and Corpas Pastor 2022c, Hidalgo-Ternero et al. 2022).

6   Conclusion

The findings of our study confirm our hypothesis: the system *gApp* can, on average, improve the quality of the neural machine translation of discontinuous MWEs by converting them into their continuous form. More specifically, *gApp* has proved to enhance NMT for the analysed MWEs with a final average amelioration by 0.25% in the ES>EN/ZH directionalities, attaining analogous results to the manual conversion.

However, as we have been able to observe in Table 10, the improvement in this study has been considerably lower than the one in our previous experiments 1–6, which allows us to perceive that MWE discontinuity does not always pose a challenge to Neural Machine Translation. In this regard, in the light of the specific worsenings that have been detected after the conversion of these MWEs for DeepL, a possible solution can be to adapt *gApp*'s lexicon to the final NMT system in question. In this way, besides choosing the source language (Spanish, French or Italian, in the case of *gApp*), final users will also have the option to select the NMT system that they will eventually employ (in our case, VIP, ModernMT, Google Translate or DeepL), so that the different MWEs conforming the lexicon will be enabled or disabled depending on their positive or negative performance with the specific NMT system, in order to progressively develop a customised NMT-adapted *gApp*.

Another important limitation has been detected in *gApp*'s detection lexicon as it has not been able to automatically filter out all irrelevant results due to improper detection in 4.7% of the cases. In this regard, it is essential to optimise *gApp*'s POS tagger and syntactic parser so that it can successfully deal with verb inflection in all its manifestations. These are, therefore, some of the challenges that still lie ahead of us in the relentless race to bridge the *gApp* between machine and human translation.

Acknowledgements. This research has been carried out within the framework of several research projects (ref. PID2020-112818GB-I00, UMA18-FEDERJA-067, P20-00109, E3/04/21, UMA-CEIATECH-04 and 03/2021-Embassy of France in Spain) at Universidad de Málaga (Spain).

References

Koike, K.: Relaciones paradigmáticas y sintagmáticas de las locuciones verbales en español. In: Cuartero Otal, J., Emsel, M. (eds.) Vernetzungen Bedeutung in Wort, Satz und Text. Festschrift für Gerd Wotjak zum 65. Geburtstag, pp. 263–275. Peter Lang, Frankfurt (2007)
Bargmann, S., Sailer, M.: The syntactic flexibility of semantically non-decomposable idioms. In: Sailer, M., Markantonatou, S. (eds.) Multiword Expressions: Insights from a Multi-Lingual Perspective, pp. 1–29. Language Science Press (2018)
Bentivogli, L., Bisazza, A., Cettolo, M., Federico, M.: Neural versus phrase-based machine translation quality: a case study. arXiv (2018)

Colson, J.-P.: Multi-word units in machine translation: why the tip of the iceberg remains problematic – and a tentative corpus-driven solution. In: MUMTT 2019 (2019)

Constant, M., et al.: Multiword expression processing: a survey. Comput. Linguist. **43**(4), 1–92 (2017)

Corpas Pastor, G.: Detección, descripción y contraste de las unidades fraseológicas mediante tecnologías lingüísticas. In: Olza, I., Manero, E. (eds.) Fraseopragmática. Colección Romanistik, pp. 335–373. Frank & Timme (2013)

Derczynski, L., Ritter, A., Clark, S., Bontcheva, K.: Twitter part-of-speech tagging for all: overcoming sparse and noisy data. In: Mitkov, R., Angelova, G., Bontcheva, K. (eds.) Proceedings of the International Conference on Recent Advances in Natural Language Processing, pp. 198–206. INCOMA Ltd. (2013)

Seco, M., Andrés, O., Ramos, G.: Diccionario fraseológico documentado del español actual, locuciones y modismos españoles, 2ª edición. Aguilar (2017)

ELIS – European Language Industry Survey: 2018 Language Industry Survey – Expectations and Concerns of the European Language Industry (2018)

ELIS – European Language Industry Survey: 2020 Language Industry Survey – 2020 before & after COVID-19 (2020)

ELIS – European Language Industry Survey: 2021 Language Industry Survey (2020)

Fazly, A., Cook, P., Stevenson, S.: Unsupervised type and token identification of idiomatic expressions. Comput. Linguist. **35**(1), 61–103 (2009)

Foufi, V., Nerima, L., Wehrli, E.: Multilingual parsing and MWE detection. In: Parmentier, Y., Waszczuk, J. (eds.) Representation and Parsing of Multiword Expressions: Current Trends, pp. 217–237. Language Science Press (2019)

Gui, T., Zhang, Q., Huang, H., Peng, M., Huang, X.: Part-of-speech tagging for Twitter with adversarial neural networks. In: Palmer, M., Hwa, R., Riedel, S. (eds.) Proceedings of the 2017 Conference on Empirical Methods in Natural Language Processing, pp. 2411–2420. Association for Computational Linguistics (2017)

Hidalgo-Ternero, C.M.: Google Translate vs. DeepL: analysing neural machine translation performance under the challenge of phraseological variation. In: Mogorrón Huerta, P. (ed.) Multidisciplinary Analysis of the Phenomenon of Phraseological Variation in Translation and Interpreting. MonTI Special Issue 6, pp. 154–177 (2020)

Hidalgo-Ternero, C.M.: El algoritmo ReGap para la mejora de la traducción automática neuronal de expresiones pluriverbales discontinuas (FR>EN/ES). In: Corpas Pastor, G., Bautista Zambrana, M.R., Hidalgo-Ternero, C.M. (eds.) Sistemas fraseológicos en contraste: enfoques computacionales y de corpus, pp. 253–270. Comares (2021)

Hidalgo-Ternero, C.M., Corpas Pastor, G.: Bridging the 'gApp': improving neural machine translation systems for multiword expression detection. Yearb. Phraseol. **11**, 61–80 (2020). https://doi.org/10.1515/phras-2020-0005

Hidalgo-Ternero, C.M., Corpas Pastor, G.: Qué se traerá gApp entre manos… O cómo mejorar la traducción automática neuronal de variantes somáticas (ES>EN/DE/FR/IT/PT). In: Seghiri, M., Pérez Carrasco, M. (eds.) Aproximación a la traducción especializada. Peter Lang (2022a, forthcoming)

Hidalgo-Ternero, C.M., Corpas Pastor, G.: A la cabeza de la traducción automática neuronal asistida por gApp: somatismos en VIP, DeepL y Google Translate. In: Corpas Pastor, G., Seghiri, M. (eds.) Aplicaciones didácticas de las tecnologías de la interpretación. Comares (2022b, forthcoming)

Hidalgo-Ternero, C.M., Corpas Pastor, G.: ReGap: a text preprocessing algorithm to enhance MWE-aware neural machine translation systems. In: Monti, J., Corpas Pastor, G., Mitkov, R. (eds.) Recent Advances in MWU in Machine Translation and Translation technology. John Benjamins Publishing Company (2022c, forthcoming)

Hidalgo-Ternero, C.M., Lista, F., Corpas Pastor, G.: gApp-assisted NMT: how to improve the neural machine translation of discontinuous multiword expressions (IT>EN/DE). Language Resources and Evaluation (2022, under review)

Junczys-Dowmunt, M., Dwojak, T., Hoang, H.: Is neural machine translation ready for deployment? A case study on 30 translation directions. arXiv (2016)

Kilgarriff, A., Rychly, P., Smrz, P., Tugwell, D.: The sketch engine. In: Proceedings of the 11th EURALEX International Congress, pp. 105–116 (2004)

Lohar, P., Popović, M., Alfi, H., Way, A.: A systematic comparison between SMT and NMT on translating user-generated content. In: 20th International Conference on Computational Linguistics and Intelligent Text Processing (CICLing 2019) (2019)

Mellado Blanco, C.: Fraseologismos somáticos del alemán. Peter Lang, Frankfurt (2004)

Monti, J., Seretan, V., Corpas Pastor, G., Mitkov, R.: Multiword units in machine translation and technology. In: Mitkov, R., Monti, J., Corpas Pastor, G., Seretan, V. (eds.) Multiword Units in Translation and Translation Technology, pp. 1–37. John Benjamins (2018)

Neunerdt, M., Trevisan, B., Reyer, M., Mathar, R.: Part-of-speech tagging for social media texts. In: Gurevych, I., Biemann, C., Zesch, T. (eds.) GSCL 2013. LNCS (LNAI), vol. 8105, pp. 139–150. Springer, Heidelberg (2013). https://doi.org/10.1007/978-3-642-40722-2_15

Parra Escartín, C., Nevado Llopis, A., Sánchez Martínez, E.: Spanish multiword expressions: looking for a taxonomy. In: Sailer, M., Markantonatou, S. (eds.) Multiword Expressions: Insights from a Multi-Lingual Perspective, pp. 271–323. Language Science Press (2018)

Ramisch, C.: Multiword Expressions Acquisition: A Generic and Open Framework. Theory and Applications of Natural Language Processing. Springer, Cham (2015). https://doi.org/10.1007/978-3-319-09207-2

Ramisch, C., Villavicencio, A.: Computational treatment of multiword expressions. In: Mitkov, R. (ed.) Oxford Handbook on Computational Linguistics, 2ª ed (2018)

Rohanian, O., Taslimipoor, S., Kouchaki, S., An Ha, L., Mitkov, R.: Bridging the gap: attending to discontinuity in identification of multiword expressions. In: Burstein, J., Doran, C., Solorio, T. (eds.) 2019 Conference of the North American Chapter of the Association for Computational Linguistics: Human Language Technologies, vol. 1, pp. 2692–2698 (2019)

Shterionov, D., Superbo, R., Nagle, P., Casanellas, L., O'Dowd, T., Way, A.: Human versus automatic quality evaluation of NMT and PBSMT. Mach. Transl. 32(3), 217–235 (2018). https://doi.org/10.1007/s10590-018-9220-z

Wang, H., Wu, H., He, Z., Huang, L., Church, K.W.: Progress in machine translation. Engineering (2022, forthcoming)

Wyrwoll, C.: User-generated content. In: Wyrwoll, C. (ed.) Social Media, pp. 11–45. Springer, Wiesbaden (2014). https://doi.org/10.1007/978-3-658-06984-1_2

Zaninello, A., Birch, A.: Multiword expression aware neural machine translation. In: Proceedings of the 12th Conference on Language Resources and Evaluation (LREC 2020), pp. 3816–3825 (2020)

Make + Adjective Combinations During the Years 1850–1999: A Corpus-Based Investigation

Ljubica Leone[(⊠)]

Lancaster University, Lancaster LA1 4YW, UK
l.leone1@lancaster.ac.uk

Abstract. The present study aims to describe the linguistic features of *make* + adjective combinations (e.g. *make clear, make sure*) and their transformation from the Late Modern English (LModE) period to Present Day English (PDE). Specifically, the objective is to examine the syntactic features and phraseological variation exhibited by these combinations from the year 1850 to 1999.

Studies with a synchronic orientation have examined verb + adjective combinations and described their linguistic status and peculiarities (Quirk et al. 1985; Biber et al. 1999). Other works have studied the diachronic development of these verbs from Old English (OE) to modern times (Claridge 2000; Mindt 2011) and they have often mentioned verbs formed with *make* which are considered prototypical examples of the whole category of verb + adjective combinations (Mindt 2011). However, to date, no studies have provided a detailed analysis of combinations formed with *make* and have examined their development from the LModE time to PDE.

The present study aims to fill this gap and to describe the linguistic features of combinations formed with *make* during the years 1850–1999. It is a corpus-based investigation undertaken on the multi-genre ARCHER corpus which covers the years 1600–1999.

The analysis reveals that *make* + adjective combinations are characterized by phraseological variability over time which intertwines with stable features: processes of renewal affected instances during the LModE time whereas more stable features are attested in the 1900s and 1950s.

Keywords: *Make* + adjective combinations · Phraseological variation · LModE · PDE · Corpus-based

1 Introduction

The English verb system includes verbs with a phraseological structure known as multi-word verbs (MWVs) (Quirk et al. 1985; Biber et al. 1999; Huddleston and Pullum 2002). MWVs include different kinds of verbs with a complex internal constituency and multi-layered structure that often render them semi-idiomatic or idiomatic instances. Specifically, there are phrasal verbs (e.g. *go on, set up*), prepositional verbs (e.g. *deal*

G. Corpas Pastor and R. Mitkov (Eds.): EUROPHRAS 2022, LNAI 13528, pp. 133–145, 2022.
https://doi.org/10.1007/978-3-031-15925-1_10

with, insist on), phrasal-prepositional verbs (e.g. *get on with, set up in*), verbo-nominal combinations (e.g. *have a look, do homework*), and verb-adjective combinations (e.g. *cut short, get clear*) (Quirk et al. 1985; Biber et al. 1999; Huddleston and Pullum 2002). Following the traditional approach to phraseology (Cowie 1998), all these verbs form phraseological units characterised by diverse degrees of fixedness, with meanings ranging from literal to idiomatic, which set them apart from all cases classified as collocations, that is, words that tend to co-occur together (Sinclair 1991), or multi-word-expressions that in computational linguistics refer to "linguistic forms spanning conventional word boundaries" that are often idiosyncratic (Constant et al. 2017: 1).

Research undertaken to date has extensively examined MWVs from a theoretical perspective (Bolinger 1971; Fraser 1974) or described their diachronic evolution since Old English (OE), when they were first established as new lexicalised forms (Denison 1981; Brinton 1988, 1996; Claridge 2000). However, despite wide knowledge, there are some areas open to investigation concerning the group of verb + adjective combinations that have to date received limited attention because they are "not very numerous" (Claridge 2000: 66), or maybe due to the unpredictability of the instances.

Verb + adjective combinations are verbs composed of a base verb (e.g. *to get, to cut*) that can combine with an *unlimited* number of adjectives (e.g. *clear, open*). The fact that verb + adjective combinations lack fixedness, which is one of the defining features of phraseological forms (Gries 2008; Svensson 2008), makes their linguistic analysis heavily dependent on the theoretical background adopted, and this has also affected the description of one of the most productive verbs in the English language, *make*, which occurs in many combinations.

Make + adjective combinations, indeed, have been treated as members of MWVs (Quirk et al. 1985; Biber et al. 1999; Claridge 2000; Mindt 2011), or as collocations due to the high degree of variability of the adjective following the base *make* (Quirk et al. 1985). Some works have also highlighted that the linguistic status of a combination is determined by the following adjective. For example, Huddleston and Pullum (2002) state that adjectives such as *short* work as particles and render the combination a fixed multi-word unit (MWU); others like *necessary* render the combination "syntactically exceptional" as they need to occur with extrapositional *it* as in *think it necessary* (Huddleston and Pullum 2002: 289).

Moreover, the analysis of *make* + adjective combinations is further complicated by the fact that they occur as continuous forms, that is, with the verb immediately followed the adjective, as in (1), or with an intervening direct object (DO) between the verb and the adjective, as in (2). The DO is sometimes filled with the impersonal *it*, as in (3):

(1)   ...to **make sure** that no hidden flaws exist...(1900s)
(2)   Rob, **make your mind easy** about this. (1850s)
(3)   ...to grasp the conditions which **make it necessary** for the Delimitation Commission...(1900s)

The syntactic variability that *make* + adjective combinations allow turns out to intertwine with the phraseological variability of the constituents and the unpredictability of the combinations. These aspects appear to weaken the cohesion between the base verb *to make* and the following adjective, which has also stimulated current debates around the phraseological status of these combinations.

Make + adjective combinations have a special role within all verb + adjective combinations, as they have been seen as a prototypical example of the whole group (Mindt 2011). They are very frequently used in both early periods and current times (Francis 1993; Claridge 2000; Mindt 2011). However, to date, there are no studies examining their use and development during the recent history of English.

These considerations have inspired the present research, which aims to fill this gap and to describe the linguistic features and processes of innovation affecting *make* + adjective combinations over the years 1850–1999.

This paper is organised as follows: Sect. 2 includes the theoretical background, and Sect. 3 introduces the research aims. Section 4 describes the corpus used, and Sect. 5 is devoted to the method. Section 6 discusses the results, while Sect. 7 reports the conclusions.

2 Theoretical Background

Many grammars such as those written by Quirk et al. (1985), Biber et al. (1999), and more recently by Huddleston and Pullum (2002), have included *make* + adjective combinations in the sections devoted to MWVs and examined them as lexemes that allow syntactic variability. On other occasions, verb + adjective combinations including those formed with *make* have been treated as prototypical examples of the link between lexis and grammar: they have been defined as "particular syntactic structures [which] tend to co-occur with particular lexical items, and – the other side of the coin – lexical items [which] seem to occur in a limited range of structures" (Francis 1993: 143).

Other works with a synchronic orientation include Mindt's (2011) study on the use of verb + adjective combinations in the 1990s. An examination of instances included in the British National Corpus (BNC), which is the corpus Mindt (2011) used in her research, has revealed that *make* is among the most frequent bases that co-occur in combination with adjectives: it is preceded by combinations formed with *to be* and immediately followed by combinations including other bases, such as *become, seem, feel, remain, find, look, appear, sound, get, believe*, and *render*.

Research on the diachronic aspects of *make* + adjective combinations, on the other hand, is very limited. First, Jespersen (1928) examines all combinations from a theoretical perspective and also mentions combinations such as *make merry* and *make bold*. He highlights that the origin of these combinations lies in the omission of a reflexive pronoun during earlier periods when the predicative was established as a bounded element, giving rise to a kind of *be*-relationship already observed in the copular verb *to be* (Fraser 1974). On the other hand, Visser (1993: 237) adopts a more descriptive approach to highlight the link *make* + adjective combinations have with copular verbs, which grants them the status of "quasi-copulas".

A focus on more recent times characterises Claridge's (2000) work, which examines *make* + adjective combinations as members of MWVs and describes their evolution across the Early Modern English (EModE) time (1640–1740). She proves that these combinations behave similarly to phrasal verbs but also preserve some peculiarities, such as the status of *make*, which often occurs as a "functional element" with the following adjective carrying most of the meaning (Claridge 2000: 120). Similar considerations apply to verb + adjective combinations of the Late Modern English (LModE) time as examined by Leone (forthcoming), who investigates the role performed by analogy and syntactic reanalysis in the development of verb + adjective combinations. During the LModE time, in particular, verb + adjective combinations, including those formed with *make*, are affected by analogical processes that favour the establishment of new combinations via direct formation or the obsolescence of other instances. At the same time, syntactic reanalysis, which is a process that significantly affects other MWVs of the time (Leone 2016), was not operative in the case of verb + adjective combinations (Leone forthcoming).

The absence of studies on verb + adjective combinations during the years 1850–1999 may be considered the point of departure for the present study, which aims to examine their recent history up to PDE. For this purpose, following an attested trend (Mindt 2011), the combinations formed with *make* were chosen as case studies to identify stable features and processes of innovation from 1850 to 1999.

3 Research Aims

The present study aims to describe the history of verb + adjective combinations formed with the base *make* during the years 1850–1999. Specifically, the aims are as follows:

- To describe the frequency of use and productivity of *make* + adjective combinations during the years 1850–1999.
- To identify processes of innovation, or conversely stable uses, characterising *make* + adjective combinations.
- To examine phraseological variability of *make* + adjective combinations over time.

4 Data: The ARCHER Corpus

The present study has been undertaken on the ARCHER (A Representative Corpus of Historical English Registers) corpus, which is a multi-genre corpus containing around 1.8 million words of British and American English (Biber et al. 1994; Yáñez-Bouza 2011). Specifically, it includes data belonging to many genres, such as advertising, drama, fiction, sermons, journals, legal, medicine, newspapers and periodicals, early prose, science, letters, and diaries.

The ARCHER corpus covers the years from 1650 to 1999, which are divided into eight sections of five decades each, i.e. 1600–1649, 1650–1699, 1700–1749, 1750–1799, 1800–1849, 1850–1899, 1900–1949, 1950–1999. Given that the present study aims to examine *make* + adjective combinations in the years 1850–1999, I only accessed the sections covering these years.

Following the approach adopted in previous studies on *make* + adjective combinations (Mindt 2011), I only selected the section of the ARCHER corpus devoted to British English, and I excluded those based on American English. The sections of the ARCHER corpus that focus on British English will be conventionally referred to as B-ARCHER throughout the present paper. This exclusion of American English from the analysis was considered a necessary step to avoid any interferences derived from external factors working differently in two diverse geographical areas that may have affected the results.

The architecture and size of the B-ARCHER corpus (1850–1999) are shown in Table 1.

Table 1. The B-ARCHER corpus

Time	Conventional name	No. of tokens
1850–1899	1850s	327,065
1900–1949	1900s	320,335
1950–1999	1950s	314,265
Total no. of tokens		961,665

As shown in Table 1, the B-ARCHER overall includes 961,665 tokens that are distributed across the various temporal windows. Given that the present research aims to describe the development of the verb-adjective combinations formed with *make* without accounting for register-based differences, the number of tokens included in each register has been excluded from Table 1. The B-ARCHER corpus has been accessed via the CQPweb server (Hardie 2012, 2018).

The fact that the B-ARCHER is a relatively small corpus, given that it does not reach one million words, does not impede a generalisation of the results. Generally, small corpora are not considered to be "robust enough for lexical studies (especially the frequency of words over time)" (Davies and Chapman 2016: 146); however, their representativeness could justify their use since this sometimes can even be "more important than the sheer size of the corpus" (Brezina 2018: 221).

5   Method

The present study is a corpus-based investigation aiming to examine the transformation of verb + adjective combinations formed with the base *make* over the years 1850–1999. It matches the principles of the Neo-Firthian tradition (Sinclair 1991; Stubbs 2002) with the traditional approach to the phraseology of the Soviet school (Cowie 1998). Specifically, three steps were followed in the analysis:

1. Identification of the unit of analysis

All instances of the verb *to make* were retrieved by querying the B-ARCHER corpus on the CQPweb (Hardie 2012). Given that the word *make* occurs only as a verb (OED), I did not use the annotated version of the B-ARCHER corpus. The analysis was undertaken with searches based on the wild card *make** and by typing all other word types.

2. Identification of adjectives used in combination with the base *make*

To identify all adjectives occurring with the base *make*, the data included in each of the temporal windows available on the B-ARCHER corpus were examined via concordances. All instances of *make* occurring in combination with an adjective, or followed by a DO and an adjective, were included in the analysis, whereas *make* + Noun combinations such as *make arrangements* were excluded.

Given that adjectives follow the base *make*, the concordances were sorted + 1 to the right and examined one by one, to identify cases of DO insertion between the base verb and the adjective.

3. Quantitative and qualitative treatment of the results

Once all instances were retrieved, they were examined quantitatively in terms of raw frequency (Rf), normalised frequency (Nf) standardised with the base of 10,000 words (hereafter Nf per 10K), and percentages, which allow comparative analysis within the various sections of the B-ARCHER corpus.

The level of productivity of the verb *to make* has been expressed with the Type/Token Ratio (TTR), which is a test that measures the degree of lexical variability (Brezina 2018) and the ability of an item to combine with other elements to form new lexemes.

To examine the processes of change, all selected instances were examined one by one. First, combinations with *to make* were categorised according to their syntactic features into four groups: (1) verb + adjective + *that* clause/DO; (2) verb + DO + adjective (+ *that* clause); (3) passive forms; (4) intransitive forms. Second, all instances were analysed using a concordancer, as qualitative analysis of the context of use can give information on phraseological variability and processes of change.

6   Results and Discussion

6.1   *Make* + Adjective Combinations During the Years 1850–1999

The examination of the instances included in the B-ARCHER corpus reveals that verb-adjective combinations formed with the base verb *to make* occur 238 times, which corresponds to 2.47 Nf per 10K. This means that they are rather rare in the data if considering that combinations formed with *to make* are the most frequent in the group of verb + adjective combinations in Claridge's (2000) and Mindt's (2011) works. Specifically, *make* + adjective combinations are ranked in the first position by Claridge (2000: 111) as they occur 530 times and are immediately followed by combinations formed with *to take* showing 491 matches; on the other hand, these combinations represent 88% of all verb + adjective combinations in PDE, as observed by Mindt (2011: 82).

To test the distribution of *make* + adjective combinations over the years, I calculated the Rf and Nf per 10K and set Fig. 1 and Table 2.

Observation of the rates exhibited by *make* + adjective combinations reveals that they are increasingly used in the 1900s and that they slightly decline in the 1950s. However, the calculation of the Diff % between the subcorpora of the B-ARCHER partly weakens the existence of variation within the decades: the Diff % between the 1850s and 1900s is

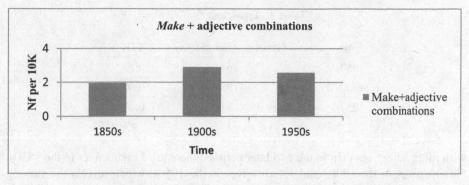

Fig. 1. Distribution of *make* + adjective combinations in 1850–1999

Table 2. Frequency of *make* + adjective combinations

Time	Raw frequency	Normalised frequency
1850s	64	1.95
1900s	93	2.90
1950s	81	2.52

+ 48.37, whereas the Diff % between the Sections 1900s and 1950s is −12.64. Overall, this entails that, while the increase in the 1900s is remarkable and is a sign of ongoing innovation, the decline attested in the 1950s should be interpreted as a reflex of stability in use. Figure 1 and the calculation of Diff % suggest that *make* + adjective combinations are affected by ongoing changes in the LModE period, while they are relatively stable verbs during modern times when, in all likelihood, they were affected by a process of consolidation and conventionalisation.

The examination of ongoing innovation can be tested further with the use of a measure of the lexical variability of *make* + adjective combinations, which can be expressed through the Type/Token Ratio (TTR). TTR is, indeed, a test that measures the degree of variability of selected instances, and in the case of *make* + adjective combinations, it also works as a measure that helps to quantify the phraseological variation of the verb *to make* over time. The existence of different variants is an important area of investigation into phraseological descriptions (Gill 2008). Indeed, variants may work as "the reaffirmation of the *open choice* principle" Gill 2008: 104, referring to Sinclair (1991), which can affect phraseological semi-fixed combinations (Gill 2008) such as the *make* + adjective combinations and determine linguistic innovation over time. The TTR of each subsection of the B-ARCHER is represented in Table 3.

The examination of the No. of types is an important point of departure to examine the transformation of *make* + adjectives over time. First, it provides data about how many different adjectives were used in the investigating structure in each subcorpora. Indeed, *make* + adjective combinations are less used in the 1850s, but have a higher level of productivity in this period, which means that in the 1850s *to make* is combined

Table 3. Types, tokens, TTR

Time	No. of types	No. of tokens	TTR
1850s	51	64	0.79
1900s	56	93	0.60
1950s	53	81	0.65

with more adjectives than in the two later periods: there are 51 adjectives in the 1850s, 56 adjectives in the 1900s and 53 adjectives in the 1950s, which reveals the varying tendency of *make* to combine with various adjectives and ideally create new forms. This introduces another aspect worthy of note, that is the fact that *make* is more prone to innovation in the 1850s than in the other periods, as in the 1850s it exhibits the highest rate in terms of productivity. Specifically, the examination of the TTR suggests that there is a rather stable level of productivity of the verb *to make* in the 1900s and 1950s, which are characterised by rates attested at 0.60 and 0.65, respectively, whereas a more marked difference is observable in the 1850s, characterised by TTR of 0.79.

These results need to be interpreted in light of the frequency of use exhibited in each temporal window: the 1850s is the section that exhibits a frequency that is more limited than those shown in the 1900s and 1950s, while being featured with the highest level of productivity. This means that *to make* can select other adjectives during the years 1850–1899 and may give rise to new phraseological verbs whose use may also become frequent in the following years.

6.2 Syntactic Features Over the Years 1850–1999

The coexistence of stable features that intertwine with signs of ongoing innovation is the point of departure when describing the syntactic behaviour of combinations over the years 1850–1999. Similar to other members of the group of verb + adjective combinations, combinations formed with *make* occur in the passive pattern, as in (4), and with transitive verbs allowing for two syntactic patterns: (1) verbs (V) followed by the adjective (Adj.) and the DO, as in (5); (2) verbs followed by the DO and an adjective, as in (6):

(4) … from the powers that were should their purpose **be made known**. (1850s)
(5) What else was it that **made old** Betsy bide in ditch for best of an hour… (1900s)
(6) …in the end, it was he who nearly **made her late** for the ceremony. (1950s)

To test the ongoing innovation of the patterns of use of *make* + adjective combinations, I calculated the Nf of each of the groups and set Fig. 2 and Table 4:

Examination of the rates of each of the patterns reported in Fig. 2 and Table 4 reveals that *make* + adjective combinations show a stable trend over the years which is characterised by the prominence of the V + DO + Adj. patterns in all subcorpora. Moreover, this pattern is followed by passive forms and V + Adj. + DO in all sections, meaning that, from a syntactic perspective, *make* + adjective combinations have acquired

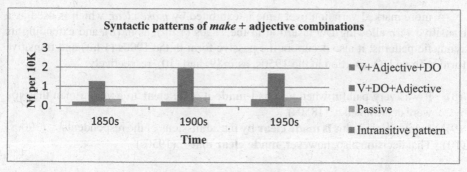

Fig. 2. Syntactic patterns over the years 1850–1999

Table 4. Frequencies of *make* + adjective combinations (syntactic patterns)

Time	V+Adj.+DO Rf and Nf		V+DO+Adj. Rf and Nf		Passive Rf and Nf		Intransitive pattern Rf and Nf	
1850s	7	0.21	42	1.28	12	0.36	3	0.09
1900s	11	0.34	63	1.96	15	0.46	4	0.12
1950s	11	0.38	54	1.71	15	0.47	0	0

a rather stable use since the 1850s, with limited variation afterwards. The intransitive forms are, instead, very rare in all sections and even go down to zero in the 1950s.

The distribution of these verb patterns within the various sections and examination of single instances reveal that *make* + adjective combinations are especially used in the transitive pattern and occur with the verb immediately followed by the DO and the adjective. At the same time, there are limited instances of passive forms, which suggests a tendency to occur in active patterns. This trend suggests that increasing stability characterises *make* + adjective combinations, which creates a line of continuity with previous times featured with stable features (Claridge 2000; Leone forthcoming); At the same time, it grants the year 1900 the status of dividing line between more variable uses and standardised uses that are attested in PDE.

There are combinations that, on the other hand, show variability over time and change their syntactic preferences, such as *make happy*, *make clear*.

The verb *make happy*, indeed, does not occur in the 1850s with the pattern V + DO + Adj., whereas it occurs 5 times with this pattern in the 1900s and 1950s, as in (7).

(7) What right had she to suppose that she could **make** Archie **happy** by marrying him? (1950s)

A more marked variation over time is exhibited by *make clear,* which is used as a transitive verb allowing DO insertion in the 1850s (1 hit), as in (8), and extending its syntactic patterns: it also occurs in the passive form in the 1900s (1 hit) and transitive form with no DO insertion in the 1950s, as in (9) and (10), respectively:

(8)   It was very painful when you had **made** it quite **clear** to a young man that you were determined ...(1850s)
(9)   In my opinion, this **is made clear** by the admissions of the respondents ...(1900s)
(10) That decision also, however, **made clear** that ...(1950s)

The rates are, in all cases, very limited but meaningful, because they show that the *make* + adjective combinations were also modifying their syntactic preferences in more recent times.

6.3 Phraseological Variation of *Make* + Adjective Combinations

Verb + adjective combinations formed with *make* have been classified as phraseological forms that have an unpredictable constituency since the causative/resultative *make* can select "an unknown number of adjectives" (Claridge 2000: 69). This entails that the description of the diachronic evolution of these combinations should also include consideration of the adjectives that frequently occur in combination with *to make* over the years 1850–1999. At the same time, it should focus on whether, and the extent to which, the lexical preferences exhibited by the base verb *to make* have changed over time.

To test the phraseological variability of *make* + adjective combinations and ongoing renewal over the years, I calculated the number of *hapax legomena* and noticed that they occur in each section, and they are typical features of 1850–1999. Indeed, there are 44 *hapaxes* in the 1850s, 41 in the 1900s and 38 in the 1950s, which suggests that while this is a typical tendency of the combinations in all cases, they are also declining. The fact that the 1950s shows 38 *hapaxes* may be interpreted as a sign of increasing stability in contemporary times, but also of ongoing renewal in the previous times: *hapaxes* tend to decline in use over time. Moreover, the examination of frequent verbs and their variability over the sections, as shown in Table 5, reveals that even when well-established, the various forms undergo variation over time. While some verbs such as *make easy/uneasy,* and *make sure* exhibit a declining trend in the 1950s, the others show the opposite trend.

Specifically, observation of Table 5 reveals that, for example, *make easy/uneasy* show a decreasing trend and move from an Nf 0.18 to 0.03, whereas *make clear* becomes more frequent in the 1950s, when its rate is attested at 0.28.

Overall, this means that combinations that are characterised by a similar constituency do not show the same frequency of use over time, which suggests the existence of ongoing processes of change. *Make* + adjective combinations reported in Table 5 prove that *make* changes in its preferences during the years 1850–1999, and that this happens especially after 1900. This supports the idea that the LModE time is characterised by changes that coexist with stable features, as extensively claimed in the literature (Hundt

Table 5. The most frequent *make* + adjective combinations (Rf and Nf per 10K)

Verb	1850s Rf – Nf		1900s Rf – Nf		1950s Rf – Nf	
make happy/unhappy	2	0.06	2	0.06	4	0.12
make clear	1	0.03	7	0.21	9	0.28
make easy/uneasy	6	0.18	4	0.12	1	0.03
make possible/impossible	-		4	0.12	6	0.19
make difficult	1	0.03	3	0.09	4	0.12
make sure	2	0.06	3	0.09	2	0.06

2014). Stability and change have emerged as the defining properties of *make* + adjective combinations in the recent history of English.

7 Concluding Remarks

The analysis reveals that *make* + adjective combinations exhibit stable features that intertwine with signs of ongoing innovation. Specifically, the major aspects are as follows:

- There has been increasing use of *make* + adjective combinations since 1850, whereas the rates attested in the 1900s and 1950s are rather stable. At the same time, the level of productivity of *make* + adjective combinations decreases from 1900 and becomes stable afterwards.
- *Make* + adjective combinations exhibit limited syntactic variation after the 1900s and especially occur in the pattern V + DO + Adj. Some verbs modified their syntactic preferences in more recent times.
- There is phraseological variability, which is relatively stable over the years. Some instances change their preferences after 1900.

Future research will include the examination of other verb + adjective combinations of the years 1850–1999 and an evaluation of register-based differences in the ARCHER corpus. Moreover, the analysis will include the examination of the most frequent combinations and their comparison within the various registers to evaluate the existence of register-specific preferences in lexical choice.

References

Biber, D., Finegan, E., Atkinson, D.: ARCHER and its challenges: compiling and exploring a representative corpus of historical English registers. In: Fries, U., Schneider, P., Tottie, G. (eds.) Creating and Using English Language Corpora. Papers from the 14th International Conference on English Language Research on Computerized Corpora, Zurich 1993, pp. 1–13. Rodopi, Amsterdam (1994)

Biber, D., Johansson, S., Leech, G., Conrad, S., Finegan, E.: Longman Grammar of Spoken and Written English. Pearson Education Limited, Harlow (1999)

Bolinger, D.: The Phrasal Verb in English. Harvard University Press, Cambridge, MA (1971)

Brezina, V.: Statistics in Corpus Linguistics. Cambridge University Press, Cambridge (2018)

Brinton, L.J.: The Development of English Aspectual System Aspectualizers and Post-verbal Particles. Cambridge University Press, Cambridge (1988)

Brinton, L.J.: Attitudes toward increasing segmentalization. Complex and phrasal verbs in English. J. English Linguist. **24**(3), 186–205 (1996)

Claridge, C.: Multi-word Verbs in Early Modern English. A Corpus-based Study. Rodopi, Amsterdam/Atlanta (2000)

Constant, M., Eryigit, G., Monti, J., van der Plas, L., Ramisch, C., Rosner, M., and Todirascu, A.:: Multiword expression processing: a survey. Assoc. Comput. Linguist. **43**(4), 837–892 (2017)

Cowie, A.P. (ed.): Phraseology: Theory, Analysis, and Applications. Oxford University Press, Oxford (1998)

Davies, M., Chapman, D.: The effect of representativeness and size in historical corpora: an empirical study of changes in lexical frequency. In: Chapman, D., Moore, C., Wilcox, M. (eds.) Studies in the History of the English Language VII: Generalizing vs. Particularizing Methodologies in Historical Linguistic Analysis, pp. 131–150. De Gruyter, Berlin/Boston (2016)

Denison, D.: Aspects of the History of English Group-Verbs, with Particular Attention to the Syntax of the ORMULUM. University of Oxford, Oxford, PhD diss. (1981)

Francis, G.: A corpus-driven approach to grammar. Principles, methods and examples. In: Baker, M., Francis, G., Tognini-Bonelli, E. (eds.) Text and Technology: in Honour of John Sinclair, pp. 137–156. John Benjamins Publishing Company, Amsterdam/Philadelphia (1993)

Fraser, B.: The Verb-Particle Combination in English. Taishukan Publishing Company, Tokyo (1974)

Gill, P.: Reassessing the canon. 'Fixed' phrases in general reference corpora. In: Granger, S., Meunier, F. (eds.) Phraseology. An Interdisciplinary Perspective, pp. 95–108. John Benjamins Publishing Company, Amsterdam/Philadelphia (2008)

Gries, S.T.: Phraseology and linguistic theory: a brief survey. In: Granger, S., Meunier, F. (eds.) Phraseology. An Interdisciplinary Perspective, pp. 3–25. John Benjamins Publishing Company, Amsterdam/Philadelphia (2008)

Hardie, A.: CQPweb—combining power, flexibility and usability in a corpus analysis tool. Int. J. Corpus Linguist. **173**, 380–409 (2012)

Hardie, A.: Using the spoken BNC2014 in CQPweb. In: Brezina, V., Love, R., Aijmer, K. (eds.) Corpus Approaches to Contemporary British Speech. Sociolinguistic Studies of the Spoken BNC2014, pp. 27–30. Routledge, New York/London (2018)

Huddleston, R., Pullum, G.K.: The Cambridge Grammar of the English Language. Cambridge University Press, Cambridge (2002)

Hundt, M. (ed.): Late Modern English Syntax. Cambridge University Press, Cambridge (2014)

Jespersen, O.: A Modern English Grammar. On Historical Principles. 7 Volumes. Ejnar Munksgaard/Allen, Copenhagen/London (1928)

Leone, L.: Syntactic reanalysis and analogical generalization in the Late Modern English period: verb-adjective combinations in focus. In: Lavidas, N., van Gelderen, E., Bergs, A., Sitaridou, I. (eds.) On Language Change. The Naxos Papers (forthcoming)

Leone, L.: Phrasal verbs and analogical generalization in Late Modern Spoken English. ICAME J. **40**, 39–62 (2016)

Mindt, I.: Adjective Complementation: An Empirical Analysis of Adjectives followed by That-Clauses. John Benjamins Publishing Company, Amsterdam/Philadelphia (2011)

Oxford English Dictionary (OED). http://oed.com

Quirk, R., Greenbaum, S., Leech, G., Svartvik, J.: A Comprehensive Grammar of the English Language. Longman, London (1985)

Sinclair, J.: Corpus, Concordance Collocation. Oxford University Press, Oxford (1991)

Stubbs, M.: Words and Phrases Corpus Studies of Lexical Semantics. Blackwell Publishing, Malden/Oxford (2002)

Svensson, M.H.: A very complex criterion of fixedness: non-compositionality. In: Granger, S., Meunier, F. (eds.) Phraseology. An Interdisciplinary Perspective, pp. 81–93. John Benjamins Publishing Company, Amsterdam/Philadelphia (2008)

The ARCHER Corpus. https://cqpweb.lancs.ac.uk/

Visser, F.T.: An Historical Syntax of the English Language. E.J. Brill, Leiden (1963)

Yáñez-Bouza, N.: ARCHER past and present (1990–2010). ICAME J. **35**, 205–236 (2011)

Metonymy in Spanish/L2 Teaching: A Cognitive Analysis of Color Idioms and Their Inclusion in the Córdoba Project Database

Beatriz Martín-Gascón(✉) 🆔

Universidad de Córdoba, Córdoba, Spain
z82magab@uco.es, beatricemartingascon@gmail.com

Abstract. This chapter examines the implementation of conceptual metonymy (Lakoff 1987; Littlemore 2009; Panther et al. 2009) in the design of didactic resources for the Spanish/L2 classroom. More specifically, the pedagogical potential of cognitive-informed techniques for teaching metonymic idioms with color is explored. Results from the cognitive analysis of the target idioms will be compiled at a metonymy database by the Córdoba Project (FFI2012-36523). The main objective is thus to reflect on the learning potential of raising Spanish/L2 learners' awareness of the ubiquity of metonymy-guided inferencing. We also aim to contribute to enlarging our metonymy database. To this end, conceptual metonymy is first explored from a Cognitive Linguistics perspective. Then, we briefly present evidence that attests its operation under and above the lexicon. To do so, we focus on the metonymic motivation of color idioms in Spanish. Based on our findings, we i) reflect upon the advantages of familiarizing learners with inferential reasoning using metonymy and considering CL-based principles and ii) contribute to developing the metonymy database.

Keywords: Conceptual metonymy · Teaching · Idioms · Metonymy database · Cognitive linguistics

1 Introduction

Metonymy is a pervasive component of everyday speech. It permeates language, as it is a fundamental mechanism of human conceptualization and a natural inferencing schema (Panther 2005). The interest for studying the role of metonymy in second language (L2) teaching and learning has grown in the last decade, especially within the field of Cognitive Linguistics (CL). A significant number of studies following this enterprise have focused on metaphorical extensions when learning vocabulary (Boers 2000a, b, 2001; Boers and Lindstromberg 2008; Kalyuga and Kalyuga 2008) and grammar (Littlemore, 2009; Tyler 2012; Tyler et al. 2010). These investigations have shown that tasks that require learners to associate metaphorical expressions with concrete meaning lead to higher vocabulary and grammar retention. However, empirical work applying metonymy in L2 pedagogy has been rather scarce. Studies focusing on this under-researched area have been almost exclusively carried out within the CL framework (Barcelona 2010; Castañeda-Castro and

G. Corpas Pastor and R. Mitkov (Eds.): EUROPHRAS 2022, LNAI 13528, pp. 146–159, 2022.
https://doi.org/10.1007/978-3-031-15925-1_11

Sánchez-Cuadrado 2021; Chen and Lai 2011, 2012, 2015; Littlemore 2009; Littlemore et al. 2016). In this chapter, the role of metonymy inferencing in concept-formation, e.g., the process of building an entrenched conceptualization of the different meanings of a word within a phraseological unit (PU) will be addressed. Furthermore, and based on results, we will contribute to the metonymy database created by the Córdoba Project.

In Sect. 2, we will look into the description of conceptual metonymy from a CL perspective. We will review research offering evidence that metonymy is an inferential schema operating under and above the lexicon (2.1.). Section 3 will present the corpus of metaphorical color idioms (with white, black, and red as source domains) which has served as a basis for the cognitive-based analysis. Section 4 will show results from the analysis of the target idioms. To do so, examples in Spanish and their English counterparts will be offered and explored. In Sect. 5, these will be addressed from a pedagogical perspective. We believe that boosting learners' awareness of metonymic processes in their native language and L2 can contribute to building a robust network of uses linked by metonymic extensions. It goes beyond the purpose of this research to present a full didactic sequence. We rather aim to give some recommendations and present some examples of tasks that foster metonymic thinking. Section 6 will describe the metonymy dataset that has served as a tool to collect metonymic phraseological units for this study.

2   Metonymy in Cognitive Linguistics

Metonymy is exemplified through phrases such as 'la Moncloa' or 'the White House' to refer to the Spanish and US governments, respectively. Scholars in the field of CL have argued that metonymy (as well as metaphor) is neither a device for language embellishment, as claimed by traditional rhetoric nor a contextual effect, as contended by relevance theorists (Papafragou 1996; Rebollar 2015). It is rather a reflection of our reason and imagination (Gibbs 2006). As such, metonymy becomes a fundamental component in our categorization of the world (Lakoff 1993), as well as a ubiquitous cognitive process (Barcelona 2002a, 2013). A consequence of this pervasiveness is that metonymy operates concurrently at different analytical levels (Barcelona 2002a, 2005, 2013). In CL, and more particularly within the Cognitive Model Theory (Ruiz de Mendoza and Peña Cervel 2008), it is viewed as a means of modelling our world knowledge on a par with propositional (or frame) structure (Fillmore 1985), and with image-schematic structure (Johnson 1987). According to Ruiz de Mendoza (2005), frames and image schemas are considered non-operational models and are the source of conceptual domains. A commonly accepted definition is offered by Barcelona (2010), who describes it as "a cognitive process whereby one concept is used to mentally activate (i.e., 'to make us think of') another concept with which it is closely related in experience" (p. 134). In more updated definitions, he refers to metonymy as an "asymmetric mapping" (2013, p. 15) (not systemic as in metaphor) "of a conceptual entity, the source, onto another conceptual entity, the target. Source and target are in the same frame and their roles are linked by a pragmatic function, so that the target is mentally activated" (2019, p. 356). Take, for instance, example (1) retrieved from Barcelona's metonymy database (FFI2012-36523 project), which compiles basic and higher-level conceptual metonymies in English and Spanish.

(1) He is a real *brain*! [*intelligent person*]
(2) La '*cerebrito*' española que triunfa en el mundo de la natación. 'The Spanish 'little brain' who triumphs in swimming.'

In (1), the lexeme 'brain' initiates a chain of metonymic extensions (BRAIN FOR MIND FOR INTELLIGENCE). 'Brain' metonymically refers to an intelligent person. There exists a functional link (PART FOR WHOLE) between 'brain' (the body organ that contains thoughts and is associated with rationality or as defined by the Cambridge Dictionary "the organ inside the head that controls thought, memory, feelings, and activity) and the person. More specifically, the brain (a body part) metonymically activates one's personality trait (intelligence). In Spanish the constructed meaning of a 'thinking person' can be interpreted as a 'smart person' as well, as in the newspaper headline in (2).

2.1 Metonymy: More Than a Lexical Phenomenon

An important aspect that has often been overlooked, even by cognitive linguists, is that metonymy operates lexically, but also under and above the lexicon. See Barcelona (2013) for a comprehensive review of the literature examining how metonymy operates in i) phonological categorization, ii) grammatical behavior of morphemes, iii) grammar recategorization, and iv) pragmatic inferencing. For space constraints, we will briefly report a few studies with examples that attest the claim that metonymy functions at more than one linguistic level.

Among research looking at the role that metonymy plays in the motivation of certain derivational morphemes, studies have focused on e.g., {ful}, as in 'armful' (Barcelona 2005, 2009; Radden 2005; Palmer et al. 2009). This morpheme derives nouns from nouns. Webster's and OED define it as "the quantity of A that fills or would fill B" (see other examples like *worldful* or *bottleful*). Barcelona (2002a), and Radden (2000) argue that the regular sense of this morpheme appears to be motivated by the DEGREE OF FILLING OF THE CONTAINER FOR QUANTITY OF THE CONTENT FILLING IT metonymy. This latter is at the same time a manifestation of VERTICALITY FOR QUANTITY. In Martín-Gascón and Barcelona (in press), the authors offer an example (3) of metonymy-induced pronominal anaphors (see also Langacker 1999, 2009; Ruiz de Mendoza and Pérez 2001; Ruiz de Mendoza and Otal-Campo 2002). In (3), the antecedent of 'there' is a metonymic target in the dominion of a referent point which is active in discourse: 'Mexican food'. The metonymy PART (FOOD) FOR WHOLE (COUNTRY) is here at work.

(3) She loves *Mexican food* even though she's s never been *there*.
(4) You're *sleeping on the couch* tonight.

In (4), adapted from Martín-Gascón and Barcelona's (in press) work, metonymy is acting at a discourse level. More context would be needed to infer meaning; yet our knowledge of the world tells us that when a speaker says that someone is 'sleeping on the couch tonight', he or she is not in good terms with the hearer. As a result, it is inferred that this latter will not sleep with the former in his or her bed, as usual. Other studies examining pragmatic inferencing include Barcelona (2002b, 2003, 2005, 2009) and Panther and Thornburg (2007), among others.

3   Corpus of Color Idioms

For this study, a list of PU, more specifically idioms where color contributes to the meaning, were targeted. From a CL perspective, idioms are the product of a conceptual system and are metonymically motivated. They are conventional expressions for which cultural models play a significant role (Köveces and Szabó 1996). The Spanish examples were retrieved and adapted from a blog entry on the LAE Madrid website (https://lae madrid.com/expresiones-en-espanol/?lang=es). We selected one idiom per color: *blanco* ('white'), *negro* ('black'), *rojo* ('red'), *verde* ('green'), *rosa* ('pink'), *azul* ('blue'), and *morado* ('purple'). In this study, due to space constraints, we only offer the analysis of three color idioms: *blanco, negro* and *rojo.*

4   Corpus Analysis and Results

4.1   *Blanco* ('White')

In Spanish we have the metonymic idiom '*quedarse en blanco*', which literally translates as 'remain in white'. To examine whether English also uses the color white to refer to not getting results from something, we examined the English Web 2020 Corpus in Sketch Engine and asked two American English native speakers for triangulation. Furthermore, we checked definitions in Collins Dictionary. Results from the English Web 2020 testing the frequency and usage of the English counterparts revealed a high frequency of the expression 'to draw a blank' (5,798 cases) (Table 1) and an even higher co-occurrence with *go,* as in 'to go blank' (9,190 cases) (Table 2). Examples 5 and 6 are some of the utterances found in the Corpus. *

(5)   There are also scars on her body that indicates some history of violence, but Charlie *draws a blank* as to what has happened.

(6)   I dial a number and the moment someone answers, I *go blank* I forget whom I want to speak with.

Table 1. Corpus results for 'to draw a blank'

Corpus size (tokens) expression	43,125,207,462 'Draw a blank'
Number of hits	5,798
Number of hits per million tokens	0.13
Percent of whole corpus	0.00001344%

Table 2. Corpus results for 'to go blank'

Corpus size (tokens) expression	43,125,207,462 Go blank'
Number of hits	9,190
Number of hits per million tokens	0.21
Percent of whole corpus	0.00002131%

In (7), we have the English translation for this idiom ('to draw a/to go blank') offered by the native speakers, who claimed it to be a commonly used PU. The word 'blank' comes from Old French *blanc* meaning "having empty spaces".

(7) El profesor me preguntó por la respuesta, pero me quedé en blanco. 'The professor asked me for the answer, butIdrew a blank/went blank.'

This idiom is defined in Collins Dictionary as an informal way to 'fail in an attempt; be unsuccessful', as in 'We've drawn a blank in the investigation' or as to 'fail to comprehend or be unable to recollect', as in 'She asked me for the address, and I drew a blank'. The meaning of this latter tightly corresponds to that in (5). The Spanish PU has a biological explanation and thus is physically motivated. When someone *se queda en blanco* (see Fig. 1), it is a sign that there is a crisis in our memory functioning. Our memories somehow *remain* inaccessible for a certain period of time as a result of a blockage in the route that normally is at work when we access information. This phenomenon happens especially under pressure (Sattizahn et al. 2016). The metonymy that seems to be at play is EFFECT FOR CAUSE. The color white is the synthesis of all colors, and it has been associated to light, purity, and goodness (Molina Plaza 2015, p. 42). Yet, in this case, a relationship is established between white and nothingness. In one of the English translations ('to draw a blank', Fig. 2), the experiencer of the memory blockage takes a more active role than in the Spanish counterpart.

Fig. 1. Quedarse en blanco.

Fig. 2. 'To draw a blank'

4.2 *Negro* ('Black')

Black input has been linked to negative affect (Mey 2005), evil, anger ('black looks', 'black words' (Molina Plaza 2015). When someone says in Spanish '*ver todo negro*' as in (8), he or she is evaluating a particular situation as being highly negative. In English the linguistic constructions related to this concept also invoke negative connotations (e.g., Vereza and Puente 2017, p. 3). From a CL perspective, associations like this one are believed to be conceptually motivated. Concrete domains such as darkness, in their metonymic link with the black color, confer a negative value in both languages. However, when assessing a situation as negative, the idiom under study does not translate in English using the metaphor BLACK IS BAD/DIFFICULT. English uses more literal expressions such as 'to feel hopeless' (example 9; 5,889 cases).

(8)   Por más que le intente convencer, María lo *ve todo negro*.
       'No matter how hard I try to convince her, María *sees everything in black*.'
(9)   If you wallow in that monotony, you'll quickly find yourself becoming unhappy and *feeling hopeless* about your work.

4.3 *Rojo* ('Red')

When being angry or embarrassed, the physiological response of redness in the face is explicitly shown. According to Kövecses (2010, p. 173), such a physical reaction is the result of both body heat and internal pressure. This latter –internal pressure– is, as he claims, present in many languages including English. Conceptualized physiology, that is, the conceptual metonymies, provides the motivation to conceptualize the embarrassed person metaphorically as a pressurized container. As can be seen in example 10, this also applies to Spanish. Furthermore, when someone 'turns red' (example 11; 27,019 cases) or '*se pone rojo*', that is, when he or she exhibits face reddening (EFFECT), the emotional CAUSE (embarrassment) is activated.

(10)   Se puso rojo cuando descubrí lo que escondía. 'He turned red when I found out what he was hiding.'
(11)   So now he's getting crazy, *turning red*.

5 Pedagogical Potential

CL tenets have been claimed to shed light into L2 teaching and learning (Langacker 2008; Pütz 2007; Tyler 2017). Achard (1997) called for the effectiveness of CL for research in L2 learning already two decades ago, "because of its explanatory power of the formal properties of linguistic forms and acquisition processes, and because it affords a satisfying conceptual integration of the structural and social aspects of L2 acquisition" (p. 159). Among the various concepts in CL which have been regarded as relevant for the L2 teaching-learning process, metonymy has been argued to be a key cognitive process in "extracting language knowledge from language use" (Littlemore et al. 2010, p. 2).

Yet, unlike metaphor research, empirical studies applying metonymy in L2 pedagogy have been scarce and almost exclusively carried out within the CL framework. Barcelona (2010) and Littlemore (2009) are among the few scholars highlighting the relevance of explicitly teaching metonymy in the classroom. They stress the importance of figurative language for a full communicative competence. Littlemore (2009) warns about the challenge of teaching and acquiring metonymy in the L2. Metonymy not only serves a wide variety of functions (from evaluative attitudes to humor and pragmatic inferencing, among others), its use also varies across languages. Furthermore, this author affirms that developing the conceptual motivation of language can be a beneficial departure from an approach that is exclusively communicative.

A list of general recommendations appears in Littlemore (2009) and is further complemented in Barcelona (2010) and Martín-Gascón and Barcelona (in press). These suggestions —which are summarized in Table 3 below— aim at raising L2 learners' awareness of the pervasiveness of metonymy-guided inferencing.

Table 3. Suggestions for metonymy application

Recommendations when applying metonymy in the L2 classroom
Include simple and clear explanations and illustrations
Avoid technical language
Begin with warm-up tasks in the native language that call for associative thinking e.g., 'Why do you think we refer to the US government as "the White House"?'
Ask about metonymy-based referring expressions learners might be familiar with
Offer simple examples of conventionalized pragmatic inferencing e.g., 'Could you sit next to X?' meaning: 'Could you go help X do exercise Y?'
Explain language- and culture-specific factors (i.e., cognitive models) that ease the use of a metonymy in the learners' native language and limit its use in the L2
Encourage metonymy-guided thinking through the exploitation of metonymic connections within one frame and across domains
Exploit the metonymic motivation of conceptual metaphors

With regard to exploiting the metonymic motivation of metaphors (last item in Table 3), learners can be presented with two images: one of a rose, erect, with long stems armed with thorns, swirling petals and a red vivid colour (Fig. 3); and one of a person 'able to withstand any life-raining storm' (Johnson 2013) in good shape and health (Fig. 4).

Fig. 3. Source entity   **Fig. 4.** Target entity

6   Inclusion in a Metonymy Database (the Córdoba Project)

The metonymy database belongs to an ongoing project at the Universidad de Córdoba financed by the Ministry of Science and Innovation. It is a useful reference tool that aims to provide with a comprehensive model for the description and interpretation of metonymies. The linguistic expressions present metonymy at different levels: morphemic, phrasal, clausal, etc. Among the objectives of this study was to contribute to enlarging this database by incorporating results from a metonymic analysis of color idioms. To do so, we followed a highly structured entry model illustrated in Barcelona, Blanco-Carrión, and Hernández-Gomariz chapters (2018). The entry model (Table 4) establishes a set of parameters and descriptive criteria applied to over 300 metonymies registered in the literature. Since it is an ongoing project, new entries, like the ones derived from this work, are regularly being added. We include the color idiom '*ponerse rojo*' ('to turn red') as in '*Se puso rojo* cuando descubrí lo que escondía' to serve as an example.

In this sentence, the subject (he) is an indirect experiencer. The face and neck area are the elements that suffer most directly the physical effect of reddening. We have thus grounds for implying that the WHOLE FOR PART metonymy is at work, which is an active zone metonymy. The most relevant metonymy, however, is the PART FOR PART metonymy. When stating that '*se puso rojo*' (EFFECT) i.e., he exhibited the physiological response of reddening, the emotional CAUSE (embarrassment) for that response is activated. In this particular example, there is someone who was first in an emotional state of rest; then, an external cause appears, i.e., another person realizing that he was hiding something. This external factor causes him to change that initial state, to temporarily go from one state of rest to another of embarrassment.

Table 4. Entry model. Retrieved from Barcelona (2018, pp. 29–31).

1. Category label (to be reproduced exactly from the source [book/article, paper, report, etc.] at the lowest level mentioned by the author): effect for cause, etc. ADDITIONAL REMARKS: WHOLE ENTITY FOR ACTIVE ZONE and PART FOR PART
2. Hierarchical level: Four major levels, with various degrees of generality: —Generic level: WHOLE FOR PART —**High level** (sublevels: Top high / High / Low High) **High:** WHOLE ENTITY FOR ACTIVE ZONE and PART FOR PART —**Basic level** (sublevels: Top basic / Basic / Low basic) **Basic:** Top basic: WHOLE PHYSICAL ENTITY FOR ACTIVE ZONE Basic: WHOLE PHYSICAL ENTITY FOR PHYSICAL ACTIVE ZONE —Low level (sublevels: Top low / Low / Lowest) ADDITIONAL REMARKS: **None**
3. Purely schematic, simply typical, prototypical (Barcelona 2011). **Prototypical** ADDITIONAL REMARKS: **None**
4. Examples of the metonymy offered by the author at any of the hierarchical levels discussed by her/him + Label each example to indicate the taxonomic domain (feelings, objects, geographical entities, actions, etc.) activated by the source and the target in these examples. *Se puso rojo* **cuando descubrí lo que escondía** **Taxonomic domain activated by the source: a whole experiencing entity: (he)** **Taxonomic domain activated by the target: a part of that experiencing entity: (the face and neck area)** ADDITIONAL REMARKS: **None**
5. Conventionality: **Conceptual conventionality only** (guiding reasoning, purely inferential/pragmatic purpose). Conceptual and linguistic conventionality (reflected in the motivation of conventional linguistic meaning or form, and / or in the guidance of inferencing to the morphosyntactic categorization of a construction; indicate which of these two areas the metonymy is involved in). ADDITIONAL REMARKS: **None**
6. Language: English / Spanish / The relevant sign language, including the national variety of the oral languages and the regional / national sign language. **Spanish** ADDITIONAL REMARKS: **None**
7. Linguistic domains / levels at which the metonymy is attested. 7.1 Grammatical rank: —**Phrase: change-of-state construction *ponerse rojo*** 7.2 Meaning: **(a) Constructional Meaning (motivational function):** (i) prototypical conventional meaning of a grammatical construction

(*continued*)

Table 4. (*continued*)

(ii) non-prototypical conventional meaning of a grammatical construction
(iii) implied (inferred), non-conventional meaning of a grammatical construction
+ Guiding morphosyntactic categorization? Yes / **No**
Involving compression? Yes / **No**
(b) Utterance and discourse meaning (general pragmatic inferences) Yes / No
7.3 Constructional form Yes / No
(i) Prototypical conventional form of a grammatical construction
(ii) Non-prototypical conventional form of a grammatical construction
+ Guiding morphosyntactic categorization? Yes / **No**
7.4 Grammatical process involved (if any) (e.g., the metonymy may motivate an instance of grammaticalization, of affixal derivation, of conversion, etc.) Yes / No
7.5 Main function
—Motivational
—Inferential
—Referential
ADDITIONAL REMARKS: **None**

---

8. Metonymic trigger(s): factors leading to or blocking the operation of the metonymy; use single / double underline for less /more important co-textual triggers.
(i) Co-textual: the construction *ponerse rojo*
(ii) Contextual other than co-textual:
— knowledge of grammatical structure
— frames / ICMs: embarrassment ICM
— cognitive-cultural context
— situational context
— communicative context (participants, time and place of utterance, etc.)
— communicative aim and rhetorical goals of the speaker / writer, genre, etc.
— other contextual / pragmatic factors
ADDITIONAL REMARKS: **None**

---

9. Metonymic chaining (as in Barcelona 2005)? Yes / No
Indicate the metonymy/ies chained to the metonymy under analysis according to the author (in the diachronic or synchronic motivation of the form or the meaning of a construction; in the referential value of an NP; or in a metonymy-guided inferential chain). **NO**

---

10. Conceptual connections to other metonymic hierarchies. Can the metonymy be included in other hierarchies apart from those in Field 2?
ADDITIONAL REMARKS: **None**

---

11. Patterns of interaction with metaphor and with other metonymies: NO
11.1 In the conceptual motivation of metaphor or metonymy (introduction to Barcelona 2000, and Barcelona 2002):
(1) A metonymy motivates the existence of a metaphor (register only if the author mentions this point).
(2) A metaphor motivates the existence of a metonymy (register only if the author mentions this point).
11.2 In the conceptual motivation of the conventional form or meaning of a construction (register only if one or more authors studying the metonymy and cited in the entry have mentioned this point).

(*continued*)

Table 4. (*continued*)

11.3 In discourse understanding: Indicate any combination observed between the metonymy under analysis and one or more metaphors or metonymies in the example(s) analyzed by the author, whether or not the author states this. ADDITIONAL REMARKS: **None**
12. (Reference to) Relevant contextualized authentic corpus examples for parameters 1, 6, 7, 8, 9, and 11. **This entry field is applicable at the corpus analysis stage.**
13. Reference to the books/ articles, papers, reports, etc. that have studied the metonymy. **Koskela, A. (2011): "Metonymy, category broadening and narrowing, and vertical polysemy". In R. Benczes, A. Barcelona y F. J. Ruiz de Mendoza Ibáñez. *Defining Metonymy in Cognitive Linguistics. Towards a consensus view* pp. 125-146). Amsterdam: John Benjamins.**
14. Entry first completed by: **Author** Date: **04/05/2022** Revised by* **Supervisor** Date: *(enter a new name and date line for each revision) ADDITIONAL REMARKS: **None.**

7   Conclusions and Further Research

This chapter has offered some examples and suggestions for boosting metonymic thinking in the L2 classroom. Particularly, frequent idioms with colors have been addressed as a means to make learners more aware of the pervasiveness of metonymy-guided inferencing and its operation at different analytical levels. Results from the metonymic-based analysis will be compiled in the Córdoba Project Database. The assembling of the database is however a work in progress. We believe that its culmination will grant scholars and language instructors who are interested in the synergy between theory and pedagogy linguistic instantiations to build a robust network of uses. Due to space constraints, we have only presented the preliminary results of our analysis and have illustrated how our entry model works through one example of many. In future studies we will try to overcome these limitations by providing readers with a didactic sequence based on findings from a comprehensive CL-informed examination of expressions with color in English and Spanish. Furthermore, results from new entries including color idioms will soon be available in the database.

Acknowledgments. The present study is part of the Project 'Researching conceptual metonymy in selected areas of grammar, discourse, and sign language with the aid of the University of Córdoba Metonymy Database (METGRADISL&BASE)'(PGC2018-101214-B-1I00), which is supported by the Ministry of Science and Innovation, from the 'Mind, language and brain' area.

References

Achard, M.: Cognitive grammar and SLA investigation. J. Intens. Engl. Stud. **11**, 157–176 (1997)

Barcelona, A.: Clarifying and applying the notions of metaphor and metonymy within cognitive linguistics: an update. In: Dirven, R., Pörings, R. (eds.) Metaphor and Metonymy in Comparison and Contrast, pp. 207–277. Mouton de Gruyter, Berlin (2002a)

Barcelona, A.: On the ubiquity and multiple-level operation of metonymy. In: Lewandowska-Tomaszczyk, B., Turewicz, K. (eds.) Cognitive Linguistics Today, pp. 207–224. Peter Lang, Frankfurt (2002b)

Barcelona, A.: The case for a metonymic basis of pragmatic inferencing: evidence from jokes and funny anecdotes. In: Panther, K.U. Thornburg, L.L. (eds.) Metonymy and Pragmatic Inferencing, pp. 81–102. John Benjamins, Amsterdam/Philadelphia (2003)

Barcelona, A.: The multilevel operation of metonymy in grammar and discourse with particular attention to metonymic chains. In: Ruiz de Mendoza Ibáñez, F., Peña Cervel, S. (eds.) Cognitive Linguistics: Internal Dynamics and Interdisciplinary Interaction. Cognitive Linguistics Research, pp. 313–352. Mouton de Gruyter, Berlin (2005)

Barcelona, A.: Motivation of Construction Meaning and Form: The roles of metonymy and inference. In: Panther, K.U., Thornburg, L., Barcelona, A. (eds.) Metonymy and Metaphor in Grammar, pp. 363–401. John Benjamins, Amsterdam/Philadelphia (2009)

Barcelona, A. Metonymy in conceptualization, communication, language and truth. In: Burkhardt, A., Nerlich, B. (eds.) Tropical Truth (s). The Epistemology of Metaphor and other Tropes, pp. 271–295. de Gruyter, Berlin/New York(2010)

Barcelona, A.: Metonymy is not just a lexical phenomenon. On the operation of metonymy in grammar and discourse. In: Niels-Lennart, J., Minugh, D.C. (eds.) Selected Papers from the Stockholm Metaphor Festival, pp. 13–46. Acta Universitatis Stockholmiensis, Stockholm (2013)

Barcelona, A.: General description of the metonymy database in the Córdoba project, with particular attention to the issues of hierarchy, prototypicality, and taxonomic domains. In: Blanco-Carrión, O., Barcelona, A., Pannain, R. (eds.) Conceptual Metonymy: Methodological, Theoretical, and Descriptive Issues, pp. 26–5. John Benjamins Publishing Company (2018)

Barcelona, A.: Metonymy. In: Dąbrowska, E., Divjak, D. (eds.) Cognitive Linguistics-Foundations of Language, pp. 353–385. De Gruyter Mouton, Berlin (2019)

Blanco-Carrión, O.: Conventionality and linguistic domain (s) involved in the characterization of metonymies (for the creation of a detailed typology of metonymy). In: Blanco-Carrión, O., Barcelona, A., Pannain, R. (eds.) Conceptual Metonymy: Methodological, Theoretical, and Descriptive Issues, pp. 55–75. John Benjamins Publishing Company (2018)

Boers, F.: Enhancing metaphoric awareness in specialised reading. Engl. Specif. Purp. **19**(2), 137–147 (2000a)

Boers, F.: Metaphor awareness and vocabulary retention. Appl. Linguis. **21**(4), 553–571 (2000b)

Boers, F.: Remembering figurative idioms by hypothesizing about their origin. Prospect **16**(3), 34–43 (2001)

Boers, F., Lindstromberg, S.: Closing chapter: from empirical findings to pedagogical practice. In: Boers, F., Lindstromberg, S.: (eds.) Cognitive linguistic approaches to teaching vocabulary and phraseology, pp. 375–393. De Gruyter, Berlin, New York (2008)

Castañeda Castro, A., Sánchez Cuadrado, A.: El papel de la metonimia en la enseñanza del sistema verbal del español a aprendientes de español L2/LE. Círculo de Lingüística Aplicada a la Comunicación **87**, 71–95 (2021)

Chen, Y.C., Lai, H.L.: The effects of EFL learners' awareness and retention in learning metaphoric and metonymic expressions. In: Proceedings of the 25th Pacific Asia Conference on Language, Information and Computation, pp. 541–548 (2011)

Chen, Y.C., Lai, H.L.: EFL learners' awareness of metonymy-metaphor continuum in figurative expressions. Lang. Aware. **21**(3), 235–248 (2012)

Chen, Y.C., Lai, H.L.: Developing EFL learners' metaphoric competence through cognitive-oriented methods. Int. Rev. Appl. Linguis. Lang. Teach. **53**(4), 415–438 (2015)

Fillmore, C.J.: Frames and the Semantics of Understanding. Quad-erni di semantica **6**, 222–254 (1985)

Gibbs, R.W., Jr.: Metaphor interpretation as embodied simulation. Mind Lang. **21**(3), 434–458 (2006)

Hernández-Gomariz, I.: Analysis of metonymic triggers, metonymic chaining, and patterns of interaction with metaphor and with other metonymies as part of the metonymy database in the Córdoba project. In: Blanco-Carrión, O., Barcelona, A., Pannain, R. (eds.) Conceptual Metonymy: Methodological, Theoretical, and Descriptive issues, pp. 75–94. John Benjamins Publishing Company. (2018)

Johnson, M.: The Body in the Mind: The Bodily Basis of Meaning, Imagination, and Reason. University of Chicago Press, Chicago (1987)

Johnson, N.: Poemhunter. https://www.poemhunter.com/poem/a-woman-is-like-a-rose/. Accessed 4 May 2020 (2012)

Kalyuga, M., Kalyuga, S.: Metaphor awareness in teaching vocabulary. Lang. Learn. J. **36**(2), 249–257 (2008)

Kövecses, Z.: Metaphor: A Practical Introduction. Oxford University Press, Oxford (2010)

Kövecses, Z., Szabó, P.: Idioms: a view from cognitive semantics. Appl. Linguis. **17**(3), 326–355 (1996)

Lakoff, G.: Women, Fire, and Dangerous Things: What Categories Reveal About the Mind. The University of Chicago Press, Chicago (1987)

Lakoff, G.: The Contemporary Theory of Metaphor. Metaphor and Thought. Cambridge University Press (1993)

Langacker, R.W.: Assessing the cognitive linguistic enterprise. In: Janssen, T., Redeker, G. (eds.) Cognitive linguistics: Foundations, Scope, and Methodology. pp. 13–59. Mouton de Gruyter, Berlin and New York (1999)

Langacker, R.W.: Cognitive grammar as a basis for language instruction. In: Robinson, P., Ellis, N.C. (eds.) Handbook of Cognitive Linguistics and Second Language Acquisition, pp. 66–88. Routledge, New York and London (2008)

Langacker, R.W.: Investigations in Cognitive Grammar. In investigations in Cognitive Grammar. De Gruyter Mouton (2009)

Littlemore, J.: Applying Cognitive Linguistics to Second Language Learning and Teaching. Palgrave Macmillan, Hampshire (2009)

Littlemore, J., Juchem-Grundmann, C.: (ed): Applied cognitive linguistics in second language learning and teaching. AILA Rev. **23**(1). (2010)

Littlemore, J., Arizono, S., May, A.: The interpretation of metonymy by Japanese learners of English. Rev. Cogn. Linguis. **14**(1), 51–72 (2016). Published under the auspices of the Spanish Cognitive Linguistics Association

Martín-Gascón, B., Barcelona, A.: Transfer of reference: metaphor and metonymy. In: The Routledge Handbook of Second Language Acquisition, Morphosyntax and Semantics. Routledge (In Press)

Mey, J.L.: Horace and Colors: A World in Black and White. Haptačahaptaitiš: Festschrift for Fridrik Thordarson on the Occasion of his 77th Birthday, pp. 163–176. (2005)

Molina Plaza, S.: Black and White Metaphors and Metonymies in English and Spanish: A Cross-cultural and Corpus Comparison, pp. 39–63. Yearbook of Corpus Linguistics and Pragmatics (2015)

Palmer, G., Rader, R.S., Clarito, A.D.: The metonymic basis of a 'semantic partial': Tagalog lexical constructions with ka. In: Panther, K.U., Thornburg, I. Barcelona, A. (eds.) Metonymy and Metaphor in Grammar, pp. 111–144. John Benjamins, Amsterdam (2009)

Panther, K U.: The role of conceptual metonymy in meaning construction. In: Ruiz de Mendoza Ibáñez, F.J., Peña Cervel, S. (eds.) Cognitive Linguistics: Internal Dynamics and Interdisciplinary Interaction, pp. 353–386. Mouton de Gruyter, Berlin/New York (2005)

Panther, K.U., Thornburg, L.: Metonymy. In: Geeraerts, D., Cuyckens, H. (eds.) Handbook of Cognitive Linguistics, pp. 236–263. Oxford University Press, Oxford (2007)

Panther, K.U., Thornburg, L.L., Barcelona, A. (eds.): Metonymy and Metaphor in Grammar, vol. 25. John Benjamins Publishing, Amsterdam (2009)

Papafragou, A.: On metonymy. Lingua **99**(4), 169–195 (1996)

Plaza, S.M.: Black and White Metaphors and Metonymies in English and Spanish: A Cross-cultural and Corpus Comparison. Yearbook of Corpus Linguistics and Pragmatics, pp. 39–63 (2015)

Pütz, M.: Cognitive linguistics and applied linguistics. In: Geeraerts, D., Cuyckens, H. (eds.) The Oxford Handbook of Cognitive Linguistics, pp. 1139–1159. Oxford University Press, Oxford (2007)

Radden, G.: The ubiquity of metonymy. In: Otal Campo, J.L., Navarro, I., Ferrando, I., Bellés Fortuño, B. (eds.) Cognitive and Discourse Approaches to Metaphor and Metonymy, pp. 11–28. Universitat Jaume I, Castelló (2005)

Rebollar, B.E.: A relevance-theoretic perspective on metonymy. Procedia Soc. Behav. Sci. **173**, 191–198 (2015)

Ruiz de Mendoza Ibáñez, F.J., Otal Campo, J.L.: Metonymy, Grammar and Communication. Comares, Albolot (2002)

Ruiz de Mendoza, F., Pérez, L.: Metonymy and the grammar: motivation, constraints and interaction. Lang. Commun. **21**(4), 321–357 (2001)

Ruiz de Mendoza, F.J.: Construing meaning through conceptual mappings. In: Fuertes, P. (ed.), Lengua y sociedad: aportaciones recientes en Lingüística Cognitiva, Lingüística del Corpus, Lenguajes de Especialidad y Lenguas en Contacto, pp. 19–38. Universidad de Valladolid, Valladolid (2005)

Ruiz de Mendoza, F.J., Peña Cervel, S.: Grammatical metonymy within the action frame in English and Spanish. In: González Álvarez, E.M., Mackenzie, J.L., Gómez González, M.Á. (eds.) Current Trends in Contrastive Linguistics: Functional and Cognitive Perspectives, pp. 251–280. John Benjamins Publishing. Amsterdam (2008)

Sattizahn, J.R., Moser, J.S., Beilock, S.L.: A closer look at who "chokes under pressure." J. Appl. Res. Mem. Cogn. **5**(4), 470–477 (2016)

Tyler, A.: Cognitive Linguistics and Second Language Learning: Theoretical Basics and Experimental Evidence. Routledge, New York (2012)

Tyler, A.: Second language acquisition. In: Dancygier, B. (ed.) The Cambridge Handbook of Cognitive Linguistics, pp. 73–90. Cambridge University Press, Cambridge (2017)

Tyler, A., Mueller, C.M., Ho, V.: Applying cognitive linguistics to instructed L2 learning: the English modals. AILA Rev. **23**(1), 30–49 (2010)

Vereza, S.C., Puente, R.L.: Embodied cognition in "black metaphors": the BAD IS DARK metaphor in biblical texts. Signo **42**(75), 02–14 (2017)

Bootstrapping a Lexicon of Multiword Adverbs for Brazilian Portuguese

Izabela Müller[1]([✉])(iD), Nuno Mamede[2,3](iD), and Jorge Baptista[1,3](iD)

[1] Universidade do Algarve - FCHS, Campus de Gambelas, 8005-139 Faro, Portugal
{a74074,jbaptis}@ualg.pt
[2] Universidade de Lisboa - IST, Av. Rovisco Pais, 1049-001 Lisbon, Portugal
Nuno.Mamede@tecnico.ulisboa.pt
[3] INESC-ID Lisboa - Human Language Technology Lab, Lisbon, Portugal
https://www.hlt.inesc-id.pt/

Abstract. This paper presents the process for bootstrapping a computational lexicon of multiword adverbs for Brazilian Portuguese (PT-BR) from an already existing lexicon built for the European variety of the language (PT-PT). This ongoing work aims to identify, collect, and provide a syntactical description of multiword adverbs in PT-BR, in order to produce a comprehensive lexicon of multiword adverbs in Portuguese. First, existing resources for this part-of-speech are presented, followed by the methods adopted for building this novel resource. Up to the present moment, approximately 700 new PT-BR multiword adverbs entered the lexicon, totaling, nearly 2,300 entries. We assessed this new lexical resource against a sample of 1,000 sentences, taken from a publicly available corpus collected from Brazilian Portuguese journalistic texts. Results are promising, although there is still room for improvement, given that the F-measure only reached a suboptimal 0.66 mark. We estimate that another 2,100 PT-BR adverbs will enter the lexicon, totaling +4,000 multiword adverbs in Portuguese.

Keywords: Multiword adverbs · Computational lexicon · Portuguese

1 Introduction

This paper presents an ongoing effort aimed at building a large-scale, highly granular lexicon of *compound adverbs* – or adverbial multiword expressions (MWE) – of Portuguese. We start with data derived from a previous study on compound adverbs in European Portuguese [25]. The main motivation for this study is to expand this already existing lexicon of adverbial expressions in European Portuguese (PT-PT), with multiword adverbs in Brazilian Portuguese (PT-BR) and provide a formal classification of their syntactic properties.

In order to properly frame this work, some clarification of concepts and terminology is required. In Portuguese traditional grammar and dictionaries, the term to designate compound (or multiword) adverbs is *adverbial locutions*,

G. Corpas Pastor and R. Mitkov (Eds.): EUROPHRAS 2022, LNAI 13528, pp. 160–174, 2022.
https://doi.org/10.1007/978-3-031-15925-1_12

a term we will not use in this paper. Compound (or multiword) adverbs [12,13] are multiword expressions (MWE) whose word combination is *frozen*, i.e., highly constrained, and their meaning is often *idiomatic*, i.e., non-compositional; as one can see, for example, in (1):

(1)   [*O Pedro riu-se*] *às bandeiras despregadas*
'Pedro laugh heartily/his head off (lit: to the flags unfurled)'.

In this compound adverb, the preposition *a* 'to', the determiner *as* 'the_fem.pl', the noun *bandeiras* 'flags', and the adjective *despregadas* 'unfurled' are frozen together. (In the examples, the adverb detaches from the base sentence, shown between square brackets. A tentative translation is provided, eventually accompanied by a literal, word-by-word equivalent). These expressions combine a sequence of words that often do not allow for any variations (substitution, insertion, deletion, transposition). At the same time, the overall meaning and syntactic properties can not be derived from the individual meaning that its elements (the noun or the adjective) indicate when used separately.

Their syntactic properties, namely, the syntactic relation they hold, either with the entire clause, or with some element within the clause, are often unrelated to their formal structure; hence those properties can be encoded as lexical features in the same way as for simple words. For this purpose, we adopted the syntactic classification by [22]. In the example above, the adverb is a *sentence-internal modifier* (M) since it cannot occur at the beginning of a sentence when in its negative form (negation), as shown in (2):

(2)   ***Às bandeiras despregadas, o Pedro não se riu.*
'At the flags unfurled, Pedro did_not laugh';

while it can be detached from the base-sentence with a clefting structure (3):

(3)   *Foi às bandeiras despregadas que o Pedro se riu.*
'It was at the flags unfurled that Pedro laughed'.

Furthermore, the adverb directly operates on the verb *rir* 'laugh' of the base sentence and has a double semantic value, functioning both as a MANNER adjunct (MV) – and thus is an adequate answer to the interrogative with *Como?* 'how', as shown in (4),

(4)   **Q:** Como *se riu o Pedro?* **A:** [*Ele riu-se*] *às bandeiras despregadas*
'How did Pedro laugh?/[He laughed heartily/his head off';

and, secondarily, as an quantifier-intensifier (MQi) equivalent to *muito* 'a lot/very much'.

Additionally, on another dimension of the interplay between the adverb and the predicate it operates on, there is a solid distributional constraint on the adverb selection, since it can only operate on the verb *rir* 'laugh'. Still, the adverb is just an adjunct of the verb, being zeroable, and without changing the overall syntactic and semantic properties of *rir*, e.g., the distributional constraints on the subject (a human noun), the intransitive structure, without complements, and the free alternation between pronominal/non-pronominal construction: *rir/rir-se* 'laugh/laugh himself'. Thus, we distinguish these expressions from verbal idioms [10], where the adverb and the verb are frozen together (5), and the verb shows significantly different properties when used separately (6):

(5)   *O Pedro fala pelos cotovelos*
       'Pedro talks a lot (lit.:by/through his elbows)'

(6)   *O Pedro fala com o João/desse assunto (*pelos cotovelos)*
       'Pedro talks with João/about this topic by/through his elbows'.

In a computational lexicon, compound adverbs can be organized based on their internal structure, that is, the sequence of categories (or part-of-speech, *PoS*), as proposed by [12,13]. This formal, taxonomical approach helps group together MWEs with similar formal properties. For example, the adverb above, *às bandeiras despregadas*, belongs to the formal class PCA, defined by the internal structure *Prep*[osition]-*N*[oun]-*Adj*[ective]. Some elements of this class may allow either the fronting (7)–(8); constraints on the distribution of determiners can also be observed:

(7)   [*O Pedro conseguiu o emprego*] *por(_ o) mérito próprio.*
       'Pedro got the job on his own merit';

(8)   [*O Pedro conseguiu o emprego*] *por(_ o) próprio mérito.*
       '*idem*'.

Compound adverbs appear quite often in texts and, like other types of MWE, they are an important challenge to natural language processing [8,30] (see [11] for some examples of issues with parsing MWE in Portuguese texts).

This paper aims to combine these two aspects of the description, the formal, taxonomical formalization of multiword adverbs and the in-depth description of their syntactic-semantic properties. We bootstrap an extension of the existing computational lexicon of Portuguese compound adverbs, integrating many new Brazilian Portuguese, variety-specific, lexical entries not previously considered, in a way similar to the method proposed by M. Gross [14]. In the course of this lexicographic effort, we established a clear distinction, whenever adequate, between those MWE that are exclusive of only one of the language's varieties (PT-PT and PT-BR). This type of linguistic resource could be valuable, for example, in a language variety identification task [17,35]. To assess the scope of this enhancement, we used a sub-corpus of sentences from a publicly available corpus distributed by the PARSEME project.[1] We focused on the partition of the corpus that has already undergone parsing under the Universal Dependencies framework [27],[2] so any results we obtain may be later compared with that

---

[1] https://gitlab.com/parseme/parseme_corpus_pt (July 29, 2022). All the URL in this paper were verified on this date).

[2] https://gitlab.com/parseme/parseme_corpus_pt/-/raw/master/pt_gsd-ud-train. cupt.

approach outputs. The corpus consists of journalistic texts taken from online editions. This corpus is publicly available and has been annotated for part-of-speech and syntactic dependencies. We considered only the raw text of the corpus for this paper. We were not interested in comparing any annotation in the corpus with our own at an earlier stage of our linguistic/lexicographic work.

A random sample of 1,000 sentences was manually and independently annotated by two experts, following a set of guidelines. We compared annotations and discussed our findings until reaching a consensus. Then, the original and the improved lexicon were applied, and the results compared.

This paper is organized as follows: In this first section, we have presented the central topic, concepts based on theoretical fundamentals, and the motivations of our study. In Sect. 2, we present extant Portuguese lexical resources, both computational lexicons and paper dictionaries, and briefly describe their contents concerning adverbial MWEs and their usefulness for the current work. Section 3, presents some related work regarding the compilation of adverbial MWEs and their syntactical properties in various languages. Section 4 explains the methodological framework. In Sect. 5, we present the corpus selection and the criteria employed for annotation. In Sect. 6, we provide the results obtained from the annotations. Finally, Sect. 7, draws future expected outcomes from this work.

2   Lexical Resources for Portuguese Multiword Adverbs

An existing European Portuguese computational lexicon (henceforward, **DICT1**) containing 2,800 adverbs, both simple and compound (= multiword), developed for the STRING [20], was the starting point for bootstrapping a more comprehensive resource for the language. These include the Portuguese compound adverbs from [7] (see Table 1), originally described by [25].

Table 1. Breakdown of (European) Portuguese adverbial MWE, from [7]. The conventional code of the class partially captures the internal structure of the adverbial MWE, defined by its constituents: *Prep*: preposition, *Det*: determiner, *Adj*: adjective and *Conj*: conjunction and *C* the frozen elements, usually a noun.

Class	Structure	Example	Count
PC	*Prep C*	*a pares* 'in pairs'	430
PDETC	*Pred Det C*	*pelo menos* 'at least'	430
PAC	*Prep Adj C*	*com o devido respeito* 'with all due respect'	130
PCA	*Prep C Adj*	*por marioria absoluta* 'by absolute majority'	240
PCDC	*Prep C_1 de C_2*	*por conta da casa* 'on the house'	130
PCPC	*Prep C_1 Prep C_2*	*nada mais nada menos* 'nothing more nothing less'	150
PCONJ	*Prep C_1 Conj C_2*	*mais cedo ou mais tarde* 'sooner or later'	90
PCDN	*Prep C de N*	*à custa de* 'at the expense of'	150
PCPN	*Prep C de N*	*em virtude de* 'by virtue of'	50
		Total	1,800

This lexicon consists of: (i) approximately 1,000 simple, derived, adverbs ending in *-mente* '-ly' (*Adv-mente*), along with the adjectival base from which they derive. This information is necessary to deal with coordination phenomena as in *lenta e atentamente* 'slow[ly] and attentively' [4]; (ii) approximately 1,800 multiword (compound) adverbs [7,25], also with their respective syntactic-semantic classification, as well as their formal classification, based on the internal structure of the compound word, using the typology developed by [12]. They also include their syntactic-semantic classification [9], based on [22]. Another 6,000 simple *Adv-mente* are also part of the lexicon, with information on the base adjective, but without the syntactic classification.

This syntactic-semantic classification distinguishes 9 main types of adverbial constructions: 3 types of adverbs modifying the whole sentence/clause (e.g. *Felizmente, ele fez isso* 'Fortunately, he did that'), and 6 sentence/clause-internal modifiers (e.g. *Futuramente, ele fará isso* 'In the future, he will do that');
The available resources for adverbial constructions, whether in paper dictionaries or electronic dictionaries in Brazilian Portuguese are scarce; thus, the need for a comprehensive study focused on, first, their recognition as MWE adverbs, and, moreover, a detailed syntactic and semantic description of these expressions.

In order to complete and extend the lexical resources above with Brazilian Portuguese entries, the [19] dictionary has been systematically examined. (Other relevant dictionaries could include [1,24,29,31,32,34]. This task is still ongoing. The dictionary [19] contains approximately 5,000 multiword adverbial constructions in Brazilian Portuguese, with their definitions. For some expressions, the author also provides the etymology. These expressions are not syntactically classified, and the dictionary mingles adverbs with many other types of multiword expressions. Therefore, a manual, careful, and one-by-one consultation is required. Though there is no indication of which variety these expressions belong, a large percentage coincides with those of the European Portuguese, already included in the initial computational lexicon.

In the next section, we provide a brief review of related work.

3   Related Work

The parsing system PALAVRAS, developed by [5], for the Portuguese language (with some coverage on PT-BR), includes several adverbial MWE (linked by '=' in his notation), and some description of their syntactic properties, including, for example, the conjunction adverbs (e.g. *por=conseqüência* 'consequently'), some quantifiers (um=pouco and *um=tanto* 'a little'), some temporal expressions (*até=então*, 'so far', *muitas=vezes*, 'many times'), manner adverbs (*em=troca*, 'in exchange'), and focalizers (*nem=mesmo*, 'not even'), among others. We did not find a quantification of the compound/MWE adverbial expressions in this system.

We found comparable work for other languages. For example, an electronic dictionary containing 6,800 multiword adverbs with their syntactic and semantic descriptions is available in French [18]. In Japanese, the *Dictionary of*

Multi-Word Expressions (JDMWE) [33] catalogs 6,000 adverbial expressions, registering their syntactic functions, structure, and mobility within sentences. In Czech, [36] studied 407 compound adverbs, adding 103 units to an existing morphological MWE dictionary. For Spanish, [6] developed an adverbial frozen expressions dictionary, which contains about 6,000 entries formalized and classified into 11 classes following [12] syntactic criteria; also, in Spanish, SENTI-TEXT [23], a lexicon specifically built for Sentiment Analysis, includes 2,255 MWE adverbs.

In recent years, there has been a renewal of interest in the study and processing of multiword expressions, namely under the scope of the PARSEME COST/EU project.[3] Within this project dedicated to the investigation of verbal MWEs, particularly in view of Natural Language Processing (NLP), limited, if any, resources regarding adverbial MWE are reported or have been made available, and none for the Portuguese language, especially the PT-BR variety.

There is reason to support that more comprehensive coverage of adverbial MWE in existing Portuguese corpora is necessary. In fact, [11] has shown that such expressions are often not captured by existing NLP systems, which manage them as strings of simple words.

4 Building the Lexicon

From the initial lexicon of 1,800 compound adverbs in PT-PT (originally built by [25]), a new lexicon, including novel PT-BR expressions, is being built (henceforward, **DICT2**). This section presents the steps we followed to collect the PT-BR compound adverbs and adverbial expressions and complete, in this way, the existing lexicon of STRING [20], **DICT1**. As this is a work in progress, the data presented here is only an initial part of the large-coverage lexical resource.

For this purpose, we determined clear-cut criteria to either include or dismiss entries appearing in the source dictionaries (collected primarily from [19,29]); that is, we endeavoured to produce a clear definition of adverbial MWEs. Some of these criteria have already been sketched in Sect. 1. Besides, we were particularly interested in relatively well-known and commonly used adverbs, whose usage could be verified in texts on the internet or by consulting open-access *corpora*. For example, *a par e passo* 'at the same time' (from Lat: *pari passu* id.') is relatively common in Brazilian texts, and, even if somewhat literary, it is still considered a common expression, so we included it in the lexicon. By contrast, the old expression *de consum* 'together', attested since the 14th century, seems to have fallen out of use, in spite of the fact that it still appears in some dictionaries (e.g. *Priberam* online[4], or Houaiss[5]).

Some MWE form productive strings and are, for the most part, compositional in their meaning. It is the case of temporal expressions [2,3,15,16]. For example, temporal expressions such as *de noite* 'at night', *na próxima semana* 'next

---

[3] https://typo.uni-konstanz.de/parseme/index.php/the-action/about-cost.

[4] https://dicionario.priberam.org.

[5] https://houaiss.uol.com.br/.

week', allow for a broad range of formal and lexical variation (the time-related nouns: *noite* 'night', *dia* 'day', *manhã* 'morning', *tarde* 'afternoon', *madrugada* 'dawn'; *semana* 'week', *mês* 'month', *ano* 'year'; and the modifiers: *próxima* 'next', *seguinte* 'following', *passada* 'past'). On the other hand, several MWEs, even if they also denote time, e.g. *de agora em diante* 'from now on', show much more internal fixedness, matching our criteria to enter the lexicon.

We have been particularly attentive to collecting *idioms*, especially non-compositional, adverbial MWE, such as *no tempo da carochinha* 'in the time of the old wives' tale' (lit: in the time of the little roach), whose meaning derives from a traditional fable/tale; or, likewise, *no tempo dos Afonsinos* 'in the time of the Aphonsines' (=the first Portuguese kings), meaning 'in the distant past'; or, more colorfully, *no dia de São Nunca (à tarde)* lit.: 'on Saint Never's day (in the afternoon)', meaning 'never'.

Comparative compound adverbs, previously studied by [28], such as [*comer, morrer*] *como um passarinho* 'eat/die like a little bird', as modifiers on verbs; and [*surdo*] *como uma porta* 'deaf as a door', as modifiers on adjectives; pose interesting challenges to parsing and have already been integrated into the STRING's lexicon and grammar [20]. Though only (exclusively) Brazilian expressions have been noted, they were not included in this study and will be presented in another paper.

The formal classification is the same used in [7], following [12]. Some classes have been added to the previous lexicon, namely: **PF** *Prep* <finite-tensed clause>: *até onde a vista alcança* 'as far as the eye can see'; **PJC** - *Conj Prep C*: *como de costume* 'as usual'; **PV** *Prep* <infinitive clause>: *com as mãos a abanar^{PT-PT}/abanando^{PT-BR}* (lit.: with the hands wagging/waving') 'empty handed'-(superscript indices $^{PT-PT}$ and $^{PT-BR}$ indicate the language variety of the MWE.) Table 2 shows the content of the former (**Dict1**) and the current (**Dict2**) adverbial MWE lexicon.

So far, 671 new compound adverbs have been added to the lexicon, totaling 2,236 MWE adverbs (+40.3%). As seen in Table 2, though the relative proportion of the classes did not undergo significant change, some classes reported a substantial boost: there was a significant increase in the PC (44%) and PDETC (41%), which were also the largest classes in the initial lexicon. The expressions belonging to the classes PCDN and PCPN, marked with '*', and originally considered by [7,25], were moved to categories of prepositions or conjunctions within the STRING system. Therefore we do not consider them further in this paper.

Table 3 shows the current breakdown of the MWE adverbs per syntactic-semantic class. Notice that the number of entries in DICT2 is smaller since some expressions have multiple meanings and can belong to more than one syntactic-semantic class. So far, the syntactic-semantic classification of the new adverbs is mostly on-going (and marked as *WIP* = work in progress). We can briefly mention that the manner class (MV) constitutes almost half of the entries (45%), followed by temporal adverbs (MT; 11%), disjunctive adverbs (PA; 10%), and conjunctive adverbs (PC; 5%).

Table 2. Evolution of the adverbial MWE lexicon: **DICT1** refers to the initial number of entries in [25] and reported in [7], and updated for this paper; **DICT2** indicates the current content of the adverbial MWE lexicon; '%'indicates the relative proportion of classes.

Class	Dict1	%	Dict2	%
PC	473	0.25	682	0.29
PDETC	438	0.23	617	0.26
PAC	123	0.07	151	0.06
PCA	189	0.10	259	0.11
PCDC	138	0.07	174	0.07
PCDN*	150	0.08	–	0.00
PCPC	210	0.11	281	0.12
PCPN*	50	0.03	–	0.00
PCONJ	60	0.03	98	0.04
PF	24	0.01	43	0.02
PJC	10	0.01	14	0.01
PV	–	0.00	17	0.01
Total	**1,865**		**2,236**	

Table 3. MWE adverbs per syntactic-semantic classes, (mostly) following the classification scheme of [22]

ClassSemSynt	Count	%
MV	1,130	0,45
MS	71	0,03
MQ	71	0,03
MP	2	<0.01
MT	269	0,11
ML	40	0,02
MF	10	<0.01
PC	118	0,05
PS	27	0,01
PA	241	0,10
WIP	547	0,22
Total	**2,526**	

Concerning the distribution of the dictionary entries per language variety, we observed that 1,539 MW adverbs correspond only to European Portuguese (PT-PT), and 427 were exclusive of the Brazilian variety (PT-BR); 335 MW adverbs occur in both varieties; 35 new adverbs have not yet been classified. Notice that several PT-PT adverbs may eventually occur in PT-BR corpora; as this is a work in progress, and given the sources that we are currently exploring, the number of adverbs exclusive of PT-BR is likely to increase.

As expected, the number of exclusively PT-PT expressions (e.g., *nem à lei da bala* lit.: 'not even at the law of the bullet', 'not even if under the utmost coercion') is still more prominent than the set of exclusively PT-BR (e.g., *onde o vento faz a curva* lit.: 'where the wind makes the turn' 'very far away').

Since the collection of PT-BR expressions is still underway, the figures reported above refer only to the entries already collected and encoded in the lexicon. We collected adverb MWEs from the source dictionary in the alphabetic order until the entry *de resto* 'besides', which corresponds to approximately 33% of the dictionary entries. It is apparent that the previously unbalanced number of exclusively PT-PT expressions is now much more even. Based on the size of the lexicon covered so far, we estimate collecting 2,100 additional new entries in this campaign.

One cannot help but notice that 15% of the MWE entries are common to both varieties: *à paisana* 'plainclothed', *em flagrante* 'in the act'. A corpus-based study will ensue, and this figure will likely increase, mainly because adverbs currently marked as PT-PT only may appear in PT-BR corpora.

It is worth noting that sometimes the distinction between variants may be very subtle. In the PT-PT CETEMPúblico corpus,[6] the adverb *em flagrante.* 'in the act' frequency is $3.68 * 10^{-6}$, while in the PT-BR NILC/São Carlos corpus,[7] it is only $1,47 * 10^{-6}$. However, the combination *em flagrante delito* ' in flagrante delicto' (from Lat. 'id.') seems to be much more common (264 instances in 700) in PT-PT than in PT-BR (only 12 instances in 500). In that case, whenever a MWE appears in the corpus, eventually above a given threshold (yet to be decided), it will be deemed to belong to that variety's lexicon. In the absence of any evidence in the corpora consulted, the relative frequency of exact match in the web, in a query limited to the top domains .pt and .br, will be used as a guiding criterion.

In other cases, a common expression exists in both varieties, e.g., *por um triz* 'just barely', and it has other equivalent forms, but they are mutually exclusive, that is, they only occur in one of the language varieties: *por uma unha negra* lit.:'by a black fingernail' 'idem' in PT-PT and *por um fio de cabelo* lit: 'by a string of hair' 'idem' in PT-BR.

The lexicon was formatted so it could be processed by the UNITEX [26],[8] cross-platform corpus processing suite, though the data is independent of the format and can be exported to other systems, namely to STRING [20]. Figure 1. 4 shows some entries of the MWE adverbs' lexicon. The codes after the string corresponding to the adverb indicate: the part-of-speech (ADV=adverb), the formal class (PCPC, PC), and the syntactic-semantic class (MV = manner adverb, MTf = time (frequency) adverb), and the language varieties (PT/BR). In the next section, we describe the corpus collection and annotation for a preliminary assessment of this novel language resource.

---

[6] https://www.linguateca.pt/cetempublico.

[7] https://www.linguateca.pt/acesso/corpus.php?corpus=SAOCARLOS.

[8] https://unitexgramlab.org/.

```
de pé em pé,.ADV+PCPC+MV+BR+EN="slowly"
de ponta a ponta,.ADV+PCPC+MV+PT+BR+EN="end-to-end"
de porta em porta,.ADV+PCPC+MV+PT+BR+EN="door to door"
de quando em quando,.ADV+PCPC+MTf+PT+BR+EN="from time to time"
de quando em vez,.ADV+PCPC+MTf+PT+BR+EN="from time to time"
de relance,.ADV+PC+MV+PT+BR+EN="at a glance"
```

Fig. 1. Some entries of the lexicon of MWE adverbs.

5   Corpus Collection and Annotation

In order to run this experiment, we collected a sample of 1,000 sentences with 20,725 words from the Brazilian Portuguese PARSEME Shared task corpus,[9] and manually examined the texts, in order to identify adverbial MWEs.

The selection of this corpus considered two critical criteria. Firstly, it is publicly available so any annotation we produce is comparable with its own annotation. This, however, is not the goal of this paper, and we only used the textual material to verify the adopted values of the new extended lexicon against the original version. The second reason for choosing this corpus is because it is a relatively recent text. The corpus consists mainly of journalistic texts taken from online editions, and is public and accessible. One of the striking characteristics of this corpus is the number of sentences related to soccer. Among the expressions used in soccer, many are adverbial, especially those of manner.

The corpus was then independently annotated by two linguists, using the same set of guidelines. The two annotators are native speakers of each variety of Portuguese, so a collaborative effort was necessary to assure consistency. Regarding the criteria, they are roughly the same as those adopted for selecting MWE adverbs from the dictionaries, namely, discarding productive temporal expressions, comparative frozen adverbs, and prepositional or conjunctional adverbial MWE. Adverbial phrases regularly derived from support verb constructions with predicate nouns and the support *estar Prep*, 'to be + preposition' or its variants have also been discarded [21]. After comparing the two annotations, and some discussion, the annotators agreed on a final set of 155 tags. Because of the small sample and the reduced number of annotations, we did not calculate the inter-annotator agreement. Most of the mismatches were due to annotators' distractions or some fluctuation in the consistency of the annotation process. This annotated corpus constitutes the reference (or golden standard) against which we will compare the result of the lexicon (DICT1 and DICT2). Here are some examples of tagged sentences:

E, {pois bem.ADV}, *quem era Jack Riley?.*
'And, well, who was Jack Riley?'
Vamos querer tirar uma foto, {com certeza.ADV}*!*
'We will want to take a picture for sure!'

---

[9] https://gitlab.com/parseme/parseme_corpus_pt.

{Ao todo.ADV}, *são 29 em Santa Catarina.*
'Altogether, there are 29 in Santa Catarina.'

6   Evaluation

The raw corpus was processed with UNITEX [26], in a simple pattern-matching mode. Notice that this system does not disambiguate part-of-speech tags (PoS), as other NLP systems often do (namely STRING). It simply checks whether a string found in the text is in the lexicon or not and produces a list of the candidate MWEs found in the corpus. With that list, automatic annotation consisted of bracketing the matched strings and adding the corresponding PoS, in the exact same way as the manual annotation of the reference corpus.

Each version of the lexicon was applied in turn: the older version DICT1 and the new one, DICT2. We ignored the remaining lexical resources, distributed within the system. Then, we compared the annotated corpus with the manually defined reference (golden standard). Table 4 shows the results from this evaluation.

Table 4. Evaluation results using Dict1 and Dict2 on the same corpus. **TP** are true-positive cases (the result from applying the lexicon to the corpus is the same as in the reference), FP are false-positive cases (the system produced a tag absent from the reference), and FN are false-negative (a tag in the reference had been missed). Results are provided with the usual metrics of Precision (P), Recall (R) and F-measure (F). Precision is defined as $TP/(TP + FP)$, Recall is given by $TP/(TP + FN)$, and F is the harmonic mean of the two previous metrics, $(2 * P * R)/(P + R)$.

Results	DICT1	DICT2
TP	90	96
FP	29	50
FN	52	48
Total	171	194
P	0.76	0.66
R	0.63	0.67
F	0.69	0.66

Though the sample is small, this is the first formal evaluation of this lexical resource. In general, while results are promising, they show that there is still much room for improvement, since F is relatively low (0.66-0.69). Ambiguity played a significant role in this lower mark, since Unitex performs no disambiguation on PoS-tagging, and any string matching an adverbial MWE gets tagged. The increase in the size of the lexicon is responsible for the more significant number of FP cases (from 29 to 50).

Looking into the MWE adverbs present in the corpus, a significant percentage (39 instances, 25.2%) constitute quantifiers: *mais de* 'more than' (15), *cerca de* 'about/around' (11), *pelo menos* 'at least' (3), *menos de* 'less than' (2), *a mais* 'some few more/extra' (2), *a menos* 'some few less'(2), *ao todo* 'overall/in total' (2), *para lá de*$^{PT-BR}$ 'very' (1), *um tanto* 'a bit/somewhat' (1).

Another important subset consists of temporal expressions such as *em horário de pico*$^{PT-BR}$ 'at peak hour/during rush hour', *em breve* 'soon'; and the large family of expressions built around the noun *vez* 'turn/time' (20), often denoting FREQUENCY or functioning as conjunctive adverbs (some of these constitute productive strings, not aimed at by the annotation process): *cada vez mais* 'more and more', *pela primeira/segunda/... /última vez* 'for the first/second/... /last time', *muitas vezes* 'often/many times', *duas vezes* 'twice', *outra vez* '(once) again', *mais uma vez* 'one more time/once again/more', *por vezes* 'sometimes', *às vezes* 'sometimes', *por sua vez* 'in turn', *dessa vez* 'this time', *em vez disso* 'instead of that', *em [apenas] oito vezes* 'just eight times'.

Also considerable is the number of *conjunctive* adverbs [22], which link the current sentence to previous (sentences in) discourse, *no entanto* 'however' (6), *em seguida* 'next'; these also include *appositive* adverbs, like *ou seja* 'that is' and (*como*) *por exemplo* 'for example'. Finally, a relatively high number of expressions *é que* (7), often involved in (emphatic) clefting processes, are dealt with as adverbs: *Elas* é que.ADV *têm um caráter hercúleo* 'It is they_fem.sg. who have a Herculean character'. In some cases, the original word spacing (here indicated by '_' had been changed in the corpus, preventing the system from capturing the compound adverb: *tão_-_ somente* 'only'.

An interesting finding of this exercise is the fact that very few exclusively Brazilian Portuguese adverbs occur in this sample. Besides those mentioned before, one can also add *de virada*$^{PT-BR}$, 'Turn around victory.' and *cabeça a cabeça*$^{PT-BR}$ 'Head to head.', e.g.

> *Estamos na disputa* cabeça a cabeça.ADV *com o Brasil.*
> 'We are in head-to-head competition with Brazil.'
> *A vitória* de virada.ADV *por 4 a 3 sobre o Joinville* ... (football)
> 'The come-from-behind/turn around 4-3 victory over Joinville ...'

Indeed, a larger sample would have made it possible to spot a larger number of Brazilian idiomatic adverbs.

7 Conclusion and Future Work

In this paper, we presented a method for bootstrapping the construction of a computational lexicon of multiword adverbs of Brazilian Portuguese, taking as a starting point an already existing lexicon of the same type of expressions, previously built for the European variety, and implemented in STRING [20]. About 700 new adverbs were collected from several sources, particularly from [19], and integrated into the lexicon. The task of collecting, classifying, and syntactically describing these new expressions is still underway. We estimate that another

2,100 new MWE adverbs will enter the lexicon at the end of this campaign, totaling more than 4,000 entries. These numbers are approximate and exclude productive, often compositional, adverbial MWEs, such as temporal expressions, which constitute a large set of lexical adverbial structures in the language. In fact, many of these families of adverbs [2,3] have already been encoded in STRING as local grammars [20], and they can capture many thousand different expressions adequately.

The experiment of applying the newly built lexicon to a sample of 1,000 sentences yields promising results, but there is still much room for improvement, as F-measure only reached a suboptimal 0.66 mark. As usual, ambiguity is a pervasive phenomenon, and we expect that implementing this new resource in STRING will allow us to precisely assess the impact of MWE in several NLP tasks, namely PoS tagging. This study may also contribute to several NLP applications, such as the automatic detection of language varieties [17], enabling automatic detection of Portuguese varieties (PT-PT and PT-BR) [35].

In the near future, we expect to conclude the task of systematically collecting the adverbs from the current lexicographic sources and complete the formalization of the lexicon. The following step consists in providing the syntactic description of the entries, aiming at an in-depth characterization of the grammar of these adverbs. Finally, we expect to compare the current results (and those we will obtain with a more extensive lexicon) with the PoS-tagging and parsing results taken from the UD-processed partition of the PARSEME corpus.

Acknowledgements. Research for this paper was partially supported by national funds through FCT, Fundação para a Ciência e a Tecnologia, under project UIDB/50021/2020.

References

1. Almeida, J.J.: Dicionário de Calão e Expressões Idiomáticas. Editora Guerra & Paz (2019)
2. Baptista, J.: Manhã, tarde, noite. Analysis of temporal adverbs using local grammars. Seminários de Linguística (3), 1–27 (1999)
3. Baptista, J., Guitart, D.C.: Compound temporal adverbs in Portuguese and in Spanish. In: Ranchhod, E., Mamede, N.J. (eds.) PorTAL 2002. LNCS (LNAI), vol. 2389, pp. 133–136. Springer, Heidelberg (2002). https://doi.org/10.1007/3-540-45433-0_20
4. Baptista, J., Vieira, L.N., Diniz, C., Mamede, N.: Coordination of -mente ending adverbs in Portuguese: an integrated solution. In: Caseli, H., Villavicencio, A., Teixeira, A., Perdigão, F. (eds.) PROPOR 2012. LNCS (LNAI), vol. 7243, pp. 24–34. Springer, Heidelberg (2012). https://doi.org/10.1007/978-3-642-28885-2_3
5. Bick, E.: The Parsing System Palavras: automatic grammatical analysis of Portuguese in a constraint grammar famework. Aarhus Universitetsforlag (2000)
6. Català, D.: Les adverbs composés: approches contrastives en linguistique appliquée. Ph.D. thesis, Universitat Autònoma de Barcelona, Barcelona (2003)
7. Català, D., Baptista, J., Palma, C.: Problèmes formels concernant la traduction des adverbes composés (espagnol/portugais). Langue(s) Parole 5, 67–82 (2020)

8. Constant, M., Eryigit, G., Monti, J., van·der Plas, L., Ramisch, C., Rosner, M., Todirascu, A.: Multiword expression processing: a survey. Comput. Linguis. **43**(4), 837–892 (2017)

9. Fernandes, G.: Automatic disambiguation of -mente ending Adverbs in Brazilian Portuguese. Master's thesis, Universidade do Algarve and Universitat Autònoma de Barcelona, Faculdade de Ciências Humanas e Sociais, Faro, Portugal (2011)

10. Galvão, A., Baptista, J., Mamede, N.: New developments on processing European Portuguese verbal idioms. In: Prolo, C.A., de Oliveira, L.H.M. (eds.) 12th Symposium in Information and Human Language Technology, pp. 229–238. Salvador, BA (Brazil), 15–18 October 2019

11. Gonçalves, M., Coheur, L., Baptista, J., Mineiro, A.: Avaliação de recursos computacionais para o português. Linguamática **12**(2), 51–68 (2020)

12. Gross, M.: Grammaire transformationnelle du français: 3 - Syntaxe de l'adverbe. ASSTRIL, Paris (1986)

13. Gross, M.: Lexicon-grammar. In: Brown, K., Miller, J. (eds.) Concise Encyclopedia of Syntactic Theories, pp. 244–259. Pergamon, Cambridge (1996)

14. Gross, M.: A bootstrap method for constructing local grammars. In: Proceedings of the Symposium on Contemporary Mathematics, pp. 229–250. University of Belgrad (1999)

15. Hagège, C., Baptista, J., Mamede, N.: Portuguese temporal expressions recognition: from te characterization to an effective ter module implementation. In: STIL'2009. 7th Brazilian Symposium in Information and Human Language Technology. NILC-CMSC/USP, São Carlos, Brasil (2009)

16. Hagège, C., Baptista, J., Mamede, N.: Caracterização e processamento de expressões temporais em Português. Linguamática **2**(1), 63–76 (2010)

17. Jauhiainen, T., Lui, M., Zampieri, M., Baldwin, T., Lindén, K.: Automatic language identification in texts: A survey. J. Artif. Intell. Res. **65**, 675–782 (2019)

18. Laporte, E., Voyatzi, S.: An electronic dictionary of French multiword adverbs. In: Language Resources and Evaluation conference. Workshop Towards a Shared task for Multiword Expressions, pp. 31–34 (2008)

19. de Macedo Rocha, C.A., Rocha, C.E.P.d.M.: Dicionário de locuções e expressões da língua portuguesa. LEXIKON Editora (2011)

20. Mamede, N., Baptista, J., Diniz, C., Cabarrão, V.: String - a hybrid statistical and rule-based natural language processing chain for Portuguese. In: Computational Processing of the Portuguese Language (PROPOR 2012), vol. Demo Session, p. s/p. PROPOR, PROPOR, Coimbra, Portugal, 17–20 April 2012

21. Marques Ranchod, E.: Analyse d'adverbes par verbes supports: exemples du portugais. Linx **34**(1), 211–218 (1996)

22. Molinier, C., Levrier, F.: Grammaire des adverbes: description des formes en -ment. Droz, Genève (2000)

23. Moreno-Ortiz, A., Pérez-Hernández, C., Del-Olmo, M.: Managing multiword expressions in a lexicon-based sentiment analysis system for Spanish. In: Proceedings of the 9th Workshop on Multiword Expressions, pp. 1–10 (2013)

24. Neves, O.: Dicionário de Expressões Correntes. Coleção "Outros Dicionários", 2nd edn., augmented edition Editorial Notícias, Lisboa, Portugal (2000)

25. Palma, C.: Estudo Contrastivo Português-Espanhol de Expressões Fixas Adverbiais. Master's thesis, Universidade do Algarve, Faculdade de Ciências Humanas e Sociais, Faro, Portugal (2009)

26. Paumier, S., et al.: Unitex 3.2 - User Manual. Université de Paris-Est/Marne-la-Vallée - Institut Gaspard Monge, Noisy-Champs 9 September 2021

27. Rademaker, A., Chalub, F., Real, L., Freitas, C., Bick, E., de Paiva, V.: Universal dependencies for Portuguese. In: Proceedings of the Fourth International Conference on Dependency Linguistics (Depling), pp. 197–206. Pisa, Italy September 2017. http://aclweb.org/anthology/W17-6523
28. Ranchhod, E.M.: Frozen adverbs - Comparative forms 'Como C' in Portuguese. Linguisticae Investigationes **XV**(1), 141–170 (1991)
29. Riva, H.C.: Dicionário onomasiológico de expressões idiomáticas usuais na língua portuguesa no Brasil. Universidade Estadual Paulista (UNESP) (2009)
30. Sag, I.A., Baldwin, T., Bond, F., Copestake, A., Flickinger, D.: Multiword expressions: a pain in the neck for NLP. In: Gelbukh, A. (ed.) CICLing 2002. LNCS, vol. 2276, pp. 1–15. Springer, Heidelberg (2002). https://doi.org/10.1007/3-540-45715-1_1
31. Santos, A.N.: Novos Dicionários de Expressões Idiomáticas. Edições João Sá da Costa, Lisboa (1990)
32. Schwab, A.: Locuções Adverbiais. Fundação da Universidade Federal do Paraná, second edition edn. (1985)
33. Shudo, K., Kurahone, A., Tanabe, T.: A comprehensive dictionary of multiword expressions. In: Proceedings of the 49th Annual Meeting of the Association for Computational Linguistics: Human Language Technologies, pp. 161–170 (2011)
34. Simões, G.A.: Dicionário de Expressões Populares Portuguesas. Publicações D. Quixote, Lisboa, Portugal (1993)
35. Zampieri, M., Gebre, B.G.: Automatic identification of language varieties: the case of Portuguese. In: KONVENS2012-The 11th Conference on Natural Language Processing, pp. 233–237. Österreichischen Gesellschaft für Artificial Intelligende (ÖGAI) (2012)
36. Žižková, H.: Improving compound adverb tagging. In: RASLAN 2018 Recent Advances in Slavonic Natural Language Processing, p. 103 (2018)

Figurative Expressions with Verbs of Ingesting in Croatian

Jelena Parizoska[1]([⊠]) [iD] and Jelena Tušek[2] [iD]

[1] Faculty of Teacher Education, University of Zagreb, Zagreb, Croatia
jelena.parizoska@ufzg.hr
[2] Faculty of Humanities and Social Sciences, University of Zagreb, Zagreb, Croatia
jtusek@ffzg.hr

Abstract. This paper explores figurative expressions in Croatian which contain verbs of ingesting, more specifically *eat* verbs and *gobble* (manner of eating) verbs. The aim is to determine which aspects of the source domain serve as the basis for metaphorization and whether there is any difference between the two types of verbs with regard to their figurative potential. We conducted a study of seven verbs of ingesting in the Croatian web corpus hrWaC. The results show that metaphorical expressions with *eat* verbs profile ingestion with all its phases, e.g. *pojesti živce* komu (lit. eat up someone's nerves) 'drive someone up the wall'. In contrast, figurative uses of *gobble* verbs focus on drawing something down the throat (usually hastily), e.g. *gutati samoglasnike* 'swallow syllables', *žderati resurse* 'devour resources'. The results also show that *eat* verbs are predominantly used literally, whereas the uses of *gobble* verbs are mostly figurative. Furthermore, figurative meanings of *gobble verbs* are associated with specific lexico-grammatical patterns. On a more general level, this study shows that metaphoricity is dependent on local factors such as lexical features of words from the source domain as well as grammatical constructions.

Keywords: Verbs of ingesting · Figurative expressions · Metaphorization · Lexico-grammatical patterns · Croatian

1 Introduction

In conceptual metaphor theory, food is shown to be one of the most common source domains [1, pp. 18–23]. As eating and drinking are basic human experiences, they provide a rich source of metaphorical conceptualizations in many languages [2, 3]. Croatian is no exception in that regard, and this can be seen in expressions such as *hrana za dušu* (lit. food for the soul) 'spiritual sustenance' and *lako/teško probavljiv* (lit. easy/difficult to digest) 'easy/difficult to accept'. Among source-domain terms used to express these concepts, verbs relating to the intake of food and beverages seem to be particularly productive in figurative usage. Here are some examples of figurative expressions containing verbs of ingesting from the Croatian web corpus hrWaC:

(1) Taj bolid *jede* gume.

© The Author(s), under exclusive license to Springer Nature Switzerland AG 2022
G. Corpas Pastor and R. Mitkov (Eds.): EUROPHRAS 2022, LNAI 13528, pp. 175–189, 2022.
https://doi.org/10.1007/978-3-031-15925-1_13

'That race car eats tires.'

(2) S onu stranu kanala vatra *guta* ostatke nečijeg doma.

'On the other side of the canal the fire is devouring (lit. swallowing) the remnants of someone's home.'

(3) Te priče *ne piju vodu*.

'Those stories do not hold water (lit. drink water).'

In (1) tire wear is conceptualized as a vehicle eating a physical object, in (2) *gutati* 'swallow' relates to the destruction of an object by fire, and in (3) the idiomatic expression *ne pije vodu* 'not hold water' refers to an argument that does not seem to be true.

Metaphorical uses of ingesting verbs in Croatian have not yet been explored. Existing studies of those verbs in other languages primarily deal with global factors such as semantic relations between source and target domains, while the impact of the syntagmatic environment on the figurativeness of verbs has largely remained out of focus.[1] Most studies typically examine *eat* verbs (i.e. 'eat' and 'drink') whereas *gobble* (manner of eating) verbs have been somewhat neglected. However, corpus data and dictionary entries show that the latter also commonly occur in metaphorical expressions.[2] Moreover, dictionaries of Croatian record a larger number of figurative senses for *gobble* verbs than for *eat* verbs. For example, the Comprehensive Dictionary of Standard Croatian [7] lists one figurative sense for *jesti* 'eat' ('cause continual worry' as in *problemi me jedu* lit. problems are eating me 'I'm plagued by problems'), four senses for *žderati* 'devour' and nine for *gutati* 'swallow'.

In this study we will explore figurative expressions with verbs of ingesting in Croatian by taking into consideration local factors: verb type (*eat* verbs vs. *gobble* verbs) and the characteristics of grammatical constructions in which they occur. The aim is to determine which aspects of the source domain serve as the basis for metaphorization, and whether there is any difference between the two types of verbs with regard to their figurative potential. Using data from the Croatian web corpus hrWaC, we will look into the relationship between figurative uses and collocational patterns.

The paper is organized as follows. Section 2 gives a brief overview of the theory, viz. of metaphorization of source-domain terms, the relationship between metaphoricity and grammar, and the figurative potential of verbs. Sections 3 describes the methodology used to examine constructions with verbs of ingesting in the hrWaC corpus. Section 4 presents the results and Sect. 5 contains the discussion and conclusion.

---

[1] Some studies of verbs of ingesting in English explore the relationship between figurative uses and grammatical constructions [4, 5].

[2] The terms *eat* verbs and *gobble* verbs have been adopted from Levin [6].

2 Theoretical Background

Words from the source domain of food are used metaphorically to describe a variety of concepts. For instance, a number of figurative uses of verbs of ingesting in English are manifestations of the IDEAS ARE FOOD conceptual metaphor [8, pp. 46–47], as in *swallow a story* ('believe completely'), *devour a book* ('read quickly and with great enthusiasm') and *digest information* ('understand'). It has also been established that metaphorical extensions of verbs of eating and drinking are widespread cross-linguistically and a number of those constructions are fixed expressions and idioms [3]. Given that one of the central issues in figurative language research is the link between language and thought, cognitive linguistic studies typically explore structural similarities between source and target domains, e.g. swallowing food and accepting ideas, digesting food and understanding information [1, pp. 83–84]. Corpus-based research of metaphor focuses on words which regularly co-occur and collocations are used to establish figurative uses of words [9, 10, 11]. One of the key findings of those studies is that there are grammatical differences between literal and figurative uses. It has also been found that figurative constructions display lexico-grammatical fixedness.

Studies of figurative uses of source-domain terms in Croatian are relatively scarce and primarily deal with expressions related to body parts [12, 13]. These studies have found a connection between metaphoricity and grammatical constructions. For example, in the expression *u čijim očima* (lit. in someone's eyes) 'in someone's opinion' the preposition *u* 'in' and the locative case of the noun signal a container conceptualization. Cognitive linguistic studies of Croatian have also shown that metaphors largely appear in relational expressions, such as those containing a verb and one or more arguments, e.g. *navući bijes* 'draw ire', *nacija može cvasti* 'the nation can blossom' [14]. With regard to metaphorical uses of verbs in general, it has been found that a verb's figurative potential – the possibility of conveying ideas that go beyond its literal meaning – is activated in the syntagmatic environment [15]. Thus, concrete verbs become carriers of figurative meaning when they occur with non-default arguments. A case in point is the Croatian verb *hraniti* 'feed' whose figurativeness is activated in SVO constructions with abstract objects, as in *hraniti znatiželju* (lit. feed curiosity) 'stimulate curiosity' [16]. This can be tied in with Hanks' [17] notion of meaning potential: a word's actual meanings are only activated in use, by other words with which it regularly occurs. Furthermore, corpus analyses of collocational patterns show that a word's meanings are associated with a set of collocates and syntactic constructions. Thus, some patterns of figurative uses of verbs of ingesting in English include: an activity eats (up) money, time or other resource; humans drink in information; one institution swallows up another; idiomatically, a person swallows a bitter pill [17, pp. 286–287][3].

Verbs of ingesting in Croatian have not been dealt with from the cognitive linguistic perspective, but it may be assumed that they provide a rich source of metaphorical conceptualizations which give rise to figurative expressions. As Croatian differentiates between simple verbs of ingesting ('eat' and 'drink') and those specifying the manner of ingesting, lexical features of individual items could play a role in the selection of

---

[3] Cf. also the entries for *eat*, *drink* and *swallow* in the Pattern Dictionary of English Verbs (https://pdev.org.uk/).

elements from the source domain which are mapped onto target domains. The aim is to establish which aspects of the source domain serve as the basis for metaphorization of verbs of ingesting. We will also determine the figurative potential of those verbs by examining collocational patterns. Verbs of ingesting which commonly occur with non-default arguments are expected to have a high figurative potential.

3   Methods

We performed a study of seven verbs of ingesting in the Croatian web corpus hrWaC (1.2 billion words) using the Sketch Engine [18]. The following items were selected from the Croatian Verb Valence Lexicon [19, pp. 77–79]: *jesti* 'eat', *piti* 'drink', *pojesti* 'eat up', *popiti* 'drink up' (*eat* verbs); *gutati* 'swallow', *progutati* 'swallow up' and *žderati* 'devour' (*gobble* verbs). The main criterion for the selection of verbs was that they should be rated above 3.5 for concreteness (1 – abstract, 5 – concrete) in the Croatian Psycholinguistic Database [20][4]. Constructions containing highly concrete verbs and non-default or abstract complements were expected to convey figurative meanings. The verb *gutati* 'swallow' is the only item not included in the database and the other six verbs are rated for concreteness as follows: *jesti* 4.56, *piti* 4.63, *pojesti* 4.51, *popiti* 4.46, *progutati* 4.11, *žderati* 4.33.[5] Another factor that was considered in the selection of verbs is their syntactic environment. According to word sketches in the hrWaC corpus, all seven verbs most typically occur in the SVO construction with accusative nouns.

We conducted three types of queries for each verb. First, we extracted a random sample of 200 concordances that includes all types of grammatical constructions in which a given verb appears (intransitive, transitive, reflexive). Next, we extracted a random sample of 200 concordances of the SVO construction. In both cases, examples which were incorrectly tagged were removed. Finally, using the Word Sketch option, we examined accusative nouns that typically occur as objects. We performed a qualitative and quantitative analysis of corpus data: we looked into the meanings of constructions (literal or figurative) and what kind of entities are referred to by the subject and object of the verb (e.g. a person, a physical object, an abstract entity). The findings are presented in the following section.

4   Results

Two groups of results were obtained. Firstly, the uses of the four *eat* verbs are predominantly literal, i.e. they refer to ingesting food and beverages, as in *jesti meso* 'eat meat', *piti kavu* 'drink coffee', *pojesti sendvič* 'have a sandwich', *popiti pivo* 'have a beer'. By contrast, figurative uses account for a large proportion of examples of the three *gobble* verbs – *gutati* 'swallow', *progutati* 'swallow up' and *žderati* 'devour'. In fact, about two thirds of examples of *gutati* and *progutati* respectively are metaphorical, both in the random sample which includes various types of grammatical constructions and in the SVO sample. This is shown in Table 1.

---

[4] http://megahr.ffzg.unizg.hr/en/?page_id=609.

[5] The verb *gutati* was included in this study because its English counterpart *swallow* is rated as highly concrete (547 on a scale from 100 to 700) in the MRC Psycholinguistic Database (https://websites.psychology.uwa.edu.au/school/mrcdatabase/uwa_mrc.htm).

Table 1. Figurative uses of verbs of ingesting in the hrWaC corpus

Verb	Sample	Total number of examples	Examples of figurative use	% (Figurative uses)
jesti 'eat'	Random	164	3	2%
	SVO	186	6	3%
piti 'drink'	Random	180	10	6%
	SVO	195	15	8%
pojesti 'eat up'	Random	200	35	18%
	SVO	200	42	21%
popiti 'drink up'	Random	197	9	5%
	SVO	200	7	4%
gutati 'swallow'	Random	197	123	62%
	SVO	197	118	60%
progutati 'swallow up'	Random	198	134	67%
	SVO	197	131	66%
žderati 'devour'	Random	195	82	42%
	SVO	195	68	35%

Furthermore, there are statistically significant differences in the SVO sample between metaphorical and non-metaphorical senses of jesti 'eat' and *gutati* 'swallow' (χ^2 (1, N = 382) = 144.85, $p < .0001$, $\varphi_c = .62$; large effect size) as well as between *jesti* 'eat' and *žderati* 'devour' (χ^2 (1, N = 378) = 59.38, $p < .0001$, $\varphi_c = .40$; medium effect size). With regard to objects, *jesti* 'eat' predominantly occurs with nouns referring to types of food, e.g. *čokolada* 'chocolate', *kolači* 'cakes', *riba* 'fish', *voće* 'fruit'. In contrast, some of the most common collocates of *gutati* 'swallow' in the SVO sample are *kilometri* 'kilometers', *knjige* 'books' and *struja* 'electric power', while *žderati* 'devour' typically occurs with *gume* 'tires', *resursi* 'resources' and *baterija* 'battery'.

The results also show that figurative uses of the three *gobble* verbs are associated with specific lexico-grammatical patterns, many of which are relatively fixed expressions and idioms. Some examples include *gutati suze* (lit. swallow tears) 'try hard not to cry', *progutati ponos* 'swallow your pride', *mrak je progutao* koga (lit. darkness swallowed someone) 'disappear without a trace', *žderati živce* komu (lit. devour someone's nerves) 'drive someone up the wall'. In the following subsections the semantic and syntactic characteristics of the figurative constructions with verbs of ingesting will be presented in detail.

4.1 *Eat* Verbs

Figurative uses of two basic verbs of ingesting – *jesti* 'eat' and *piti* 'drink' – are rare. For example, among nouns which are the most typical collocates of *jesti*, only two occur in constructions with figurative meanings: the quote *revolucija jede svoju djecu* ('the revolution devours its children') and *jesti govna* (lit. eat crap). The latter is used with two meanings illustrated by (4) and (5), respectively:

(4) Ako šuti, nema mu druge nego *jesti govna*.

'If he stays silent, he has no choice but to endure humiliation (lit. eat crap).'

(5) Vas trojica nešto dogovarate o čemu mi nemamo pojma. Ma *jedite govna*.

'You three guys are making arrangements about something that we know nothing about. Why don't you sod off (lit. eat crap).'

In (4) *jesti govna* refers to putting up with demeaning treatment, while in (5) *jedite govna* is an expression of contempt. In the latter case, the verb is always used in the imperative form.

Figurative uses of *piti* 'drink' occur in two idiomatic expressions – *piti krv na slamku komu* (lit. drink someone's blood with a straw) 'get under someone's skin' and *ne pije vodu što* (lit. something does not drink water) 'not hold water':

(6) I sad mi moj 20 mjesečni dječak lagano *pije krv na slamku*.

'And now my 20-month-old boy is beginning to get under my skin (lit. drink my blood with a straw).'

(7) Bilo kako bilo, unaprijed znaš da ti ova teorija *ne pije vodu*.

'In any case, you already know that this theory doesn't hold water (lit. drink water).'

Piti krv na slamku komu 'get under someone's skin' typically occurs with a human subject, which indicates that annoyance is usually caused by another person. On the other hand, nouns which occur as the subject of *ne pije vodu* 'not hold water' refer to abstract entities, e.g. *teorija* 'theory', *priča* 'story', *argument* 'claim'.

The remaining two items in this group, *pojesti* 'eat up' and *popiti* 'drink up', are perfective verbs which profile the ingestion of food or liquids from the beginning to its completion, e.g. *pojesti jabuku/sendvič/ručak* 'have an apple/a sandwich/lunch'; *popiti kavu/čaj/piće* 'have coffee/tea/a drink'[6]. In addition to ingesting liquids, *popiti* 'drink up' may also refer to ingesting solids such as medicine, as in *popiti tabletu* 'take a pill'. In such cases, the verb signifies absorbing an item, that is, swallowing it whole without chewing.

When used figuratively, both *pojesti* and *popiti* occur in relatively fixed constructions. For example, the most frequent metaphorical uses of *pojesti* 'eat up' are the idiomatic expressions *pojeo vuk magare* (lit. the wolf ate the donkey) 'as if nothing had ever happened' and *mrak je pojeo* koga (lit. darkness ate someone) 'disappear without a trace', as in (8) and (9):

---

[6] *Pojesti* and *popiti* may be classified as what Janda [21] terms Natural Perfectives. Those are verbs which describe the completion of the corresponding imperfective activity, in this case *jesti* 'eat' and *piti* 'drink'.

(8) Na kraju od pobune, kako biste i očekivali, nije bilo ništa. **Pojeo vuk magare**.

'Eventually, as one might have expected, the revolt came to nothing. It's as if
nothing had ever happened (lit. the wolf ate the donkey).'

(9) Postavio je uvjet da njegov odvjetnik i novinar moraju svjedočiti uhićenju jer je
strahovao kako **će ga pojesti mrak**.

'He demanded his lawyer and the journalist be present at the arrest because he
feared that he would disappear without a trace (lit. that darkness would eat him
up).'

  Pojesti also occurs in two fixed expressions which describe annoyance (10) and the
negative effects of alcohol and drugs on one's cognitive abilities (11):

(10)   Motor i mjenjač su OK, ali ostale sitnice ti mogu **pojesti živce**.

'The engine and the gear box are fine, but other little things can drive you up the
wall (lit. eat up your nerves).'

(11)   Ponekad mi se čini da ne zna složit rečenicu. Ili su mu **alkohol i droga pojeli
mozak**.

'Sometimes it seems to me he can't put two sentences together. Or it's that alcohol
and drugs killed his brain (lit. ate up his brain).'

  Popiti 'drink up' is used with a wider range of objects in figurative expressions than
pojesti 'eat up'. The most frequent metaphorical uses of *popiti* in the hrWaC corpus
include:

(12) a. *popiti svu pamet svijeta* (lit. drink all the smartness in the world) 'be a smart
aleck'
b. *popiti krv* komu (lit. drink up someone's blood) 'drive someone crazy'
c. *popiti živce* komu (lit. drink up someone's nerves) 'drive someone up the wall'
d. *popiti batine* (lit. drink up a beating) 'get a thrashing' (slang)
e. *popiti gol* (lit. drink up a goal) 'receive a goal (in soccer)' (slang)
f. *popiti ban* (lit. drink up a ban) 'get banned from an internet forum' (slang)
g. *popiti metak* (lit. drink up a bullet) 'get shot' (slang)

h. *vrane su popile mozak* komu (lit. crows have drunk someone's brain) 'be out of one's mind'

In literal uses *pojesti* 'eat up' focuses solely on completion, while *popiti* 'drink up' incorporates an additional element of meaning, which is to absorb an item completely. This is based on the fact that a person may put something in their mouth that is not water or a beverage and swallow it whole (e.g. a pill). This is the basis for metaphorical uses of *popiti* in expressions such as *popiti batine* 'get a thrashing' and *popiti gol* 'receive a goal'.

Overall, data from the hrWaC corpus shows that the four *eat* verbs examined in this study are predominantly used literally. Thus, the basic sense of *jesti* 'eat' and *piti* 'drink' – putting something through the mouth into the stomach by swallowing it – serves as the basis for metaphorical extensions. Furthermore, by virtue of the fact that *jesti* and *piti* refer specifically to the ingestion of food and drinks, figurative uses such as *jesti govna* (lit. eat crap) 'endure humiliation' and *piti krv na slamku* komu (lit. drink someone's blood with a straw) 'get under someone's skin' describe unpleasant experiences and therefore express negative evaluation. The basis for figurative uses of the perfective verbs *pojesti* 'eat up' and *popiti* 'drink up' is complete absorption (as in *popiti tabletu* 'take a pill'). This can be seen in expressions in which the two verbs are interchangeable, e.g. *droga je pojela/popila mozak* komu (lit. drugs ate up/drank up someone's brain) 'drugs killed someone's brain' and *pojesti/popiti živce* komu (lit. eat up/drink up someone's nerves) 'drive someone up the wall'.

In contrast to *eat* verbs, the uses of *gobble* (manner of eating) verbs are predominantly figurative. The features of figurative expressions with *gobble* verbs are described in the following subsection.

4.2 *Gobble* Verbs

Three manner of eating verbs were examined in hrWaC: *gutati* 'swallow', *progutati* 'swallow up' and *žderati* 'devour'. The literal meaning which serves as the basis for figurative uses is passing something (not necessarily food) down the throat quickly and, in the case of the imperfective verbs *gutati* and *žderati*, in large amounts. Some examples include *gutati tablete* 'pop pills', *progutati slinu* 'gulp down saliva', *žderati janjetinu* 'gorge on lamb'.

Figurative uses of all three verbs commonly appear in lexico-grammatical patterns. The largest number of patterns were found for the verb *gutati* 'swallow' and the majority of those are SVO constructions with fillable slots. The SVO constructions form two groups based on whether the subject refers to a human being or an inanimate entity. In each group, nouns that typically collocate with *gutati* form clusters, each of which is associated with a specific metaphorical meaning. The figurative uses of *gutati* are described and exemplified in Table 2.

Table 2. Figurative uses of *gutati* 'swallow' in the hrWaC corpus

Typical collocates in word sketch	Meaning	Example
propaganda 'propaganda', *laži* 'lies', *bajke* 'fairy tales'	believe without question	*gutati* laži iz medija 'believe lies in the media'
stripovi 'comic books', *romani* 'novels', *knjige* 'books', *krimići* 'murder mysteries'	read eagerly	Kao klinac sam *gutao* stripove i knjige. 'When I was a kid, I devoured comics and books.'
samoglasnici 'vowels', *slogovi* 'syllables', *riječi* 'words'	pronounce indistinctly	Ima loš izgovor, *guta* samoglasnike. '[She] has a bad pronunciation, she swallows vowels.'
gorčina 'bitterness', *ljutnja* 'anger', *ponos* 'pride'	refrain from expressing a feeling	Da bi pomogla osobi koju voli, ona *guta* svoju ljutnju. 'In order to help her loved one, she is suppressing her anger.'
(idiom) *gutati svaku riječ* lit. swallow someone's every word	listen avidly to someone	Mala je buljila u njega i *gutala svaku* njegovu *riječ*. 'The girl stared at him, drinking in his every word.'
(idiom) *gutati knedle* lit. swallow lumps in your throat	be nervous or upset; eat humble pie	Pola gledališta je suzdržavalo suze i *gutalo knedle*. 'Half the audience were fighting back tears and had lumps in their throats.'
(idiom) *gutati suze* lit. swallow tears	try hard not to cry	*Gutam suze*, ali ne odustajem. 'I'm on the verge of tears, but I won't give up.'
(idiom) *gutati govna* lit. swallow crap	endure humiliation	Svi smo jednom *gutali govna* zbog ljubavi. 'All of us have at some point put up with humiliation for love's sake.'
(idiom) *gutati čiju prašinu* lit. swallow someone's dust	not be as successful as another person or organization	AMD je uvijek *gutao* Intelovu *prašinu*. 'AMD has always lagged behind Intel.'
kilometri 'kilometers', *zavoji* 'bends (in the road)', *cesta* 'road'	travel (a distance) quickly	automobil *guta* kilometre kao od šale 'the car eats up miles with ease'

(continued)

When the subject of *gutati* in figurative constructions is a human being, what they "swallow" may be something from the outside (e.g. lies, propaganda, books) or something that comes from within them (e.g. syllables, anger). In the first case, a person

Table 2. (*continued*)

Typical collocates in word sketch	Meaning	Example
baterija 'battery', *benzin* 'gas', *resursi* 'resources', *struja* 'electric power', *memorija* 'computer memory', *novac* 'money'	use large amounts of resources	besplatne aplikacije *gutaju* bateriju 'free apps eat up the battery'
vatra 'fire', *plamen* 'flames'	destroy	plamen *guta* kuću 'the house is swallowed up by flames'
tama 'darkness', *noć* 'night'	cause to disappear from view	Hladna noć *je gutala* ulicu. 'The house disappeared into the cold night.'

absorbs something eagerly, as if they had not chewed it properly before swallowing it. For instance, in *gutati propagandu* 'swallow propaganda' the target domain has a potentially negative influence on a person, i.e. they have not carefully considered it. In the latter case, the meanings of figurative expressions are based on the conceptualization of the human body as a container. For example, in *gutati ljutnju* (lit. swallow anger) a person suppresses the feeling as if by not letting it come up their throat; therefore, anger remains inside the body and other people are unaware of how the person feels. When inanimate nouns are the subject of *gutati*, the entities which they designate are conceptualized as living beings that ingest something by swallowing it. Thus, mobile phone applications swallow the battery, cars swallow gas, flames swallow forests, buildings and vehicles, darkness swallows the daylight. In all such constructions the focus is on one entity absorbing another so that it eventually disappears.

The second manner of eating verb that was examined in the corpus is *progutati* 'swallow up', which is the perfective counterpart of *gutati*. Figurative uses of *progutati* focus on the completion of a given event. The most frequent figurative constructions with *progutati* are:

(13) a. *vatra je progutala* što (lit. fire swallowed something up) 'fire destroyed something'
b. *mrak je progutao* koga (lit. darkness swallowed someone up) 'disappear without a trace'
c. *progutati knedlu* (lit. swallow a lump in your throat) 'be nervous or frightened'
d. *progutati ponos* 'swallow your pride'
e. *progutati gorku pilulu* 'swallow a bitter pill'
f. *progutati udicu* (lit. swallow a hook) 'fall for something hook, line, and sinker'
g. *progutati priču* (lit. swallow a story) 'believe something that is unlikely to be true'

The subject of *progutati* in figurative constructions may be a human being or an inanimate entity. When a person swallows something up metaphorically, it is typically a physical object which has an unpleasant taste or something that humans are not meant to consume.

Hence the negative evaluation of expressions such as *progutati gorku pilulu* 'swallow a bitter pill' and *progutati udicu* 'fall for something hook, line, and sinker'. Constructions in which the subject is an inanimate noun describe situations in which one entity envelops another as if by swallowing it whole. Thus, when a fire swallows up a house or a forest, it destroys it completely; when darkness swallows up people, they disappear without a trace. The data also shows that *progutati* and its imperfective counterpart *gutati* share several collocates when used with figurative meanings. In such cases, *progutati* denotes the completion of the activity expressed by *gutati*. Some examples include *plamen je gutao/progutao* što 'the flames devoured something', *gutati/progutati laži* 'believe lies', *gutati/progutati suze* 'fight back tears', *gutati/progutati uvrede* 'put up with insults'.

Finally, the verb *žderati* 'devour' was also examined. The literal basis for metaphorical extensions is eating something greedily and to excess (e.g. *žderati janjetinu/hamburgere/kokice* 'gorge on lamb/hamburgers/popcorn'). The most frequent figurative meaning is using large amounts of resources, usually wastefully. In this usage, *žderati* collocates with nouns such as *resursi* 'resources', *baterija* 'battery', *gume* 'tires', *memorija* 'computer memory', *novac* 'money' and *struja* 'electric power'.

Another frequent figurative use of *žderati* relates to people experiencing distress. The literal image is that of an entity gradually destroying a person by devouring them. In this usage, *žderati* occurs in SVO constructions in which the subject refers to the cause of distress and the object to the person experiencing it:

(14) Budući da je ambiciozan, on i dalje sudjeluje u utrkama ali ne uspijeva biti prvi i *to ga ždere*.
'Being ambitious, he still participates in races but does not manage to win and he is really eaten up by it (lit. it is devouring him).'

Žderati is also used metaphorically in the expression *žderati živce* komu (lit. devour someone's nerves), which refers to annoyance:

(15) I ta spoznaja *mi ždere živce*.
'And this realization is driving me up the wall (lit. devouring my nerves).'
(16) Ovakve osobe poput našeg Alana *mi žderu živce* sa njihovim neznanjem i arogancijom.
'The kind of people like our Alan drive me up the wall (lit. devour my nerves) with their ignorance and arrogance.'

In this figurative expression, the subject of *žderati* designates the cause of annoyance, which may be an abstract entity (15) or a person (16).

Žderati may also be used reflexively (*žderati se* lit. devour oneself), in which case it is figurative, referring to a person feeling anxious or concerned about something. *Žderati se* frequently occurs with the adverbs *iznutra* 'inside' and *zbog* 'because of':

(17) Ovako *se ždereš iznutra* dok izvana glumiš da ti je to svejedno.
'This way you're tormented on the inside (lit. you're devouring yourself on the inside), while on the outside you're pretending that you don't care.'

(18) Ako ti se javljaju sumnje *ne žderi se zbog* toga, to je normalno.
  'If you're having doubts, don't fret about it (lit. don't devour yourself over it), that's normal.'

Constructions with *iznutra* 'inside' indicate that the person experiencing distress is not showing it to other people, while those with *zbog* 'because of' specify the cause of anxiety.

Corpus data shows that people's experiences relating to distress and anxiety may also be expressed metaphorically by the verb *jesti* 'eat'. Moreover, in this usage *jesti* occurs in the same types of lexico-grammatical patterns as *žderati* 'devour', e.g. *to me jede* (lit. it is eating me) 'it is bugging me', *jesti* koga *iznutra* (lit. eat someone on the inside) 'cause continual worry', *jesti se zbog* čega (lit. eat yourself over something) 'be anxious about something'. However, constructions with *jesti* describe being anxious or concerned in a neutral way, whereas those with *žderati* refer to a more intense experience and express negative evaluation.[7]

5   Discussion and Conclusion

The findings of this study show that different aspects of the source domain are used in the metaphorization of verbs of ingesting, depending on their type. Thus, metaphorical uses of *eat* verbs profile ingestion with all its phases, whereas *gobble* verbs focus on a specific aspect of that process. As *eat* verbs refer to the ingestion of items that provide nourishment, when used metaphorically, they occur with nouns which refer to things that humans are not meant to consume, e.g. *jesti govna* (lit. eat crap) 'endure humiliation', *pojesti živce* komu (lit. eat up someone's nerves) 'drive someone up the wall', *popiti metak* (lit. drink up a bullet) 'get shot'. On the other hand, *gobble* verbs profile passing something down the throat quickly and usually in large amounts, as in *gutati samoglasnike* 'swallow vowels', *gutati/žderati novac* (lit. swallow/devour money) 'cost a lot of money'. The reason for this difference in metaphorization between the two types of verbs may not only be that *gobble* verbs describe manner of eating and thus have more specific meanings, but it may also be related to the fact that *gobble* verbs need not refer to the intake of food and drinks. For instance, *gutati* 'swallow' and *progutati* 'swallow up' commonly occur with non-default objects when used literally (e.g. *gutati tablete* 'pop pills', *gutati prašinu* 'inhale dust', *progutati slinu* 'swallow up saliva'), which is not the case with *eat* verbs.

Gobble verbs have been found to occur with a wider set of collocates than *eat* verbs and to have a larger number of metaphorical meanings. For example, in the SVO construction, *eat* verbs predominantly occur with nouns referring to types of food or drink and the literal meaning is the most frequent one. In contrast, among the most frequent objects of *gobble* verbs are nouns which do not refer to food, and the uses of those verbs are mostly figurative, e.g. *gutati knjige/kilometre* (lit. swallow books/kilometers), *progutati ponos/udicu* (lit. swallow up your pride/a hook), *žderati resurse/gume* (lit.

---

[7] This may be due to the fact that *žderati* originally referred to animal behavior, as noted in the Dictionary of Croatian [22, p. 17]. Furthermore, in its literal uses *žderati* is similar to *gutati* 'swallow' in that it refers to eating greedily and in large amounts.

devour resources/tires). In some figurative uses, *eat* and *gobble* verbs share collocates, for example *jesti/žderati živce* komu (lit. eat/devour someone's nerves) 'drive someone up the wall', *mrak je pojeo/progutao* koga (lit. darkness ate someone up/swallowed someone up) 'disappear without a trace'. Such expressions profile events in which the focus is on the result rather than the manner of eating. For instance, the expression *mrak je pojeo/progutao* koga (lit. darkness ate someone up/swallowed someone up) focuses on the fact that an entity has been ingested (metaphorically, a person has disappeared), whereas the manner of ingesting (manner of disappearance) is not important. However, such cases are fairly rare, which may be due to the fact that *gobble* verbs have developed specialized meanings in the target domain.

With regard to the semantic and syntactic features of figurative expressions with all seven verbs examined in this study, corpus data shows that their figurative uses usually appear in relatively fixed constructions, a number of which are idioms, e.g. *ne pije vodu* što (lit. something does not drink water) 'not hold water', *progutati gorku pilulu* 'swallow a bitter pill'. Furthermore, figurative uses of *gobble* verbs are associated with lexico-grammatical patterns which have fillable slots, such as: a person swallows a proposition ('believe unquestioningly'); a person swallows (up) a feeling ('refrain from expressing'); a machine swallows/devours resources ('use a lot of something wastefully'); a fire swallows up an object ('destroy completely'). Overall, this confirms the results of previous corpus studies of metaphorical uses of words from various source domains, which show that figurative meanings tend to be expressed by a restricted range of grammatical patterns [9, 23, 24].

On a more general level, this study has shown that metaphorization of verbs of ingesting does not only depend on global factors such as the existence of conceptual metaphors (e.g. IDEAS ARE FOOD), but also on the lexical features of source-domain terms and grammatical constructions. Even though the seven verbs of ingesting examined in this study belong to the same source domain, the literal meanings of *eat* verbs are schematic and those of *gobble* (manner of eating) verbs are more specific. Lexical specificity seems to play a role in metaphorical conceptualizations, i.e. in the ways in which the source domain is utilized. Manner of eating verbs lend themselves more easily to being used figuratively (that is, they have a higher figurative potential) and their metaphorical uses are associated with specific lexico-grammatical patterns. This is in line with approaches to metaphoricity as a local phenomenon [25]: figurative uses of words are highly dependent on local factors such as the lexical features of words and the conceptual characteristics of grammatical constructions in which they appear.

One issue that remains to be studied is the role of local and global factors from a comparative linguistic point of view. On the one hand, finding a predominance of cross-linguistically common metaphors such as IDEAS ARE FOOD would tip the balance towards more global factors. On the other hand, establishing a dominant role of language-specific patterns would suggest that local factors prevail. Where this balance lies remains to be seen in future research.

References

1. Kövecses, Z.: Metaphor: A Practical Introduction, 2nd edn. Oxford University Press, Oxford/New York (2010)

2. Newman, J.: Eating and drinking as sources of metaphor in English. Cuadernos de Filología Inglesa **6**(2), 213–231 (1997). https://doi.org/10.7939/R37940W85
3. Newman, J. (ed.): The Linguistics of Eating and Drinking. John Benjamins, Amsterdam/Philadelphia (2009). https://doi.org/10.1075/tsl.84
4. Newman, J., Rice, S.: Transitivity schemas of English EAT and DRINK in the BNC. In: Gries, S.T., Stefanowitsch, A. (eds.) Corpora in Cognitive Linguistics: Corpus-Based Approaches to Syntax and Lexis, pp. 225–260. Mouton de Gruyter, Berlin/New York (2007). https://doi.org/10.1515/9783110197709.225
5. Croft, W.A.: Connecting frames and constructions: a case study of 'eat' and 'feed.' Constr. Frames **1**(1), 7–28 (2009). https://doi.org/10.1075/cf.1.1.02cro
6. Levin, B.: English Verb Classes and Alternations: A Preliminary Investigation. The University of Chicago Press, Chicago (1993)
7. Veliki rječnik hrvatskoga standardnog jezika [Comprehensive Dictionary of Standard Croatian]. Školska knjiga, Zagreb (2015)
8. Lakoff, G., Johnson, M.: Metaphors We Live By. The University of Chicago Press, Chicago (1980)
9. Deignan, A.: Metaphor and Corpus Linguistics. John Benjamins, Amsterdam/Philadelphia (2005). https://doi.org/10.1075/celcr.6
10. Deignan, A.: The grammar of linguistic metaphors. In: Stefanowitsch, A., Gries, S.T. (eds.) Corpus-Based Approaches to Metaphor and Metonymy, pp. 106–122. Walter de Gruyter, Berlin (2006). https://doi.org/10.1515/9783110199895.106
11. Deignan, A.: Corpus Linguistics and Metaphor. In: Gibbs, R.W. (ed.) The Cambridge Handbook of Metaphor and Thought, pp. 280–294. Cambridge University Press, Cambridge (2012). https://doi.org/10.1017/CBO9780511816802.018
12. Stanojević, M.-M., Parizoska, J., Banović, L.: Schematic idioms and cultural models. In: Brdar, M., Omazić, M., Pavičić Takač, V. (eds.) Cognitive Approaches to English: Fundamental Interdisciplinary and Applied Aspects, pp. 321–344. Cambridge Scholars Publishing, Newcastle upon Tyne (2009)
13. Stanojević, M.-M.: Hladne glave i vruća srca o tijelu i emocijama u hrvatskom [A cool-headed and warm-hearted view of the body and emotions in Croatian]. In: Brković, I., Pišković, T. (eds.) Tijelo u hrvatskome jeziku, književnosti i kulturi. Zbornik radova 45. seminara Zagrebačke slavističke škole, pp. 175–198. FF press/Zagrebačka slavistička škola, Zagreb (2017)
14. Stanojević, M.-M.: Metaphorical and non-metaphorical dimensions of the term *nacija* in Croatian online discourse. In: Šarić, Lj., Stanojević, M.-M. (eds.) Metaphor, Nation and Discourse, pp. 259–286. John Benjamins, Amsterdam/Philadelphia (2019). https://doi.org/10.1075/dapsac.82.11sta
15. Tsvetkov, Y., Boytsov, L., Gershman, A., Nyberg, E., Dyer, C.: Metaphor detection with cross-lingual model transfer. In: Toutanova, K., Wu, H. (eds.) Proceedings of the 52nd Annual Meeting of the Association for Computational Linguistics, pp. 248–258. Association for Computational Linguistics, Baltimore, Maryland (2014). https://doi.org/10.3115/v1/P14-1024
16. Tušek, J., Peti-Stantić, A., Vasung, A.: Figurative potential of concrete verbs in South Slavic languages. In MEGACRO Project Final Conference The building blocks of information transfer in language processing, Faculty of Humanities and Social Sciences, University of Zagreb, Zagreb, Croatia, 7–8 October 2021. https://drive.google.com/file/d/1qLRKfgteiqCnC57Ay sgwL85trpbK2r1x/view. Accessed 18 May 2022
17. Hanks, P.: Lexical Analysis: Norms and Exploitations. MIT Press, Cambridge, MA (2013). https://doi.org/10.7551/mitpress/9780262018579.001.0001
18. Croatian Web (hrWaC 2.2, ReLDI). https://www.sketchengine.eu/. Accessed 18 May 2022

19. Mikelić Preradović, N.: CROVALLEX: Valencijski leksikon glagola hrvatskoga jezika [CROVALLEX: Croatian Verb Valence Lexicon]. FF Press, Zagreb (2019). https://doi.org/10.17234/9789531756105

20. Peti-Stantić, A., et al.: The Croatian psycholinguistic database: estimates for 6000 nouns, verbs, adjectives and adverbs. Behav. Res. Methods 53(4), 1799–1816 (2021). https://doi.org/10.3758/s13428-020-01533-x

21. Janda, L.: Aspectual clusters of Russian verbs. Stud. Lang. 31(3), 607–648 (2007). https://doi.org/10.1075/sl.31.3.04jan

22. Rječnik hrvatskoga ili srpskoga jezika: Dio XXIII [Dictionary of the Croatian/Serbian language: Part 23]. Yugoslav Academy of Sciences, Zagreb (1975–1976). https://dizbi.hazu.hr/a/?pr=i&id=196759. Accessed 18 May 2022

23. Stanojević, M.-M.: Konceptualna metafora i gramatika [Conceptual metaphor and grammar]. In: Stanojević, M.-M. (ed.) Metafore koje istražujemo: suvremeni uvidi u konceptualnu metaforu, pp. 91–115. Srednja Europa, Zagreb (2014)

24. Stanojević, M.-M., Tralić, I., Ljubičić, M.: Grammatical information and conceptual metaphors: the case of anger. In: Peti-Stantić, A., Stanojević, M.-M. (eds.) Language as Information: Proceedings from the CALS Conference 2012, pp. 131–154. Peter Lang, Frankfurt am Main (2014)

25. Stanojević, M.-M.: Metafora na razmeđu koncepata, jezika i diskursa [Metaphor at the intersection of concepts, language and discourse]. Jezikoslovlje 21(2), 149–178 (2020). https://doi.org/10.29162/jez.2020.6

Some Insights on a Typology of French Interactional Prefabricated Formulas in Spoken Corpora

Marie-Sophie Pausé[ID] and Agnès Tutin[✉][ID]

LIDILEM, U. Grenoble Alpes, 621 avenue Centrale, 38400 Saint-Martin-d'Hères, France
{marie-sophie.pause,agnes.tutin}@univ-grenoble-alpes.fr

Abstract. This study deals with interactional prefabricated formulas (IPFs) in French, these usual formulas used in spoken or written interactions, such as *how shall I put it ?*; *you bet !*; *see you later*; *you're welcome*; *nice to see you*; *that's fine*. These expressions, often called "routine formulae" have not been much listed and studied, unlike other types of expressions, although they are very common. We propose a broad typology of these formulas from meta-enunciative IPFs (*on va dire* 'let's say') to direct interactional expressions (*c'est bon* 'it's OK') or ritual formulas (*bonne journée* 'have a nice day'). An annotation scheme has been developed to account for the different aspects of these elements including main types, semantic labels, clause types and lemmatization. A first annotation of the main types carried out on diverse extracts of oral corpora shows a contrasted distribution according to the genres. This prompts us to recall that spoken corpora do not constitute a uniform genre with respect to these phraseological phenomena.

Keywords: Pragmatic phraseology · Routine formulae · Spoken corpora · Annotation

1 Introduction

Although work on interaction has been developed considerably in recent years, particularly in the areas of syntax and interactional pragmatics, few studies have been devoted to the lexicon or phraseology of interaction. There is, however, a set of recurrent expressions, specific to oral and written interactions, which deserve to be identified and studied within the framework of phraseology, such as (for English) *how shall I put it ?*; *you bet !*; *see you later*; *you're welcome*; *nice to see you*; *that's fine*. These expressions have often been described as "conversational routines" (Coulmas 1979) or "routine formulae" (Cowie 2001). Several studies have been devoted recently to this topic in French (Blanco & Mejri 2018, Kauffer 2013; 2019; Krzyżanowska et al. 2021). However, a large inventory and classification of these expressions remains to be done, in particular for French. To better explore this field, we have undertaken an empirical work of annotation on spoken corpora, in a combined corpus-based and corpus-driven approach, in order to identify interactional phraseological units and to classify them.

G. Corpas Pastor and R. Mitkov (Eds.): EUROPHRAS 2022, LNAI 13528, pp. 190–205, 2022.
https://doi.org/10.1007/978-3-031-15925-1_14

We will first propose a definition of Interactional Prefabricated Formulas with a brief state of the art. We will then present the annotation scheme, including several parameters. Some results from the annotated corpus will be presented in a last section.

2   Interactional (Prefabricated) Formulas

2.1   Definition

This study deals with interactional prefabricated formulas (hereafter IPFs), these usual formulas used in spoken or written dialogues, more than in monologal discourses, such as *how shall I put it ?*; *you bet !*; *see you later*; *you're welcome*; *nice to see you*; *that's fine*. Common dialogues are full of these prefabricated formulas, as we can observe on the transcript of an interview of Alice Munro, 2013 laureate for the Nobel prize of literature (1) (IPFs are underlined).

(1) [AM] ...]. <u>I just wanted to thank you, very much</u>. This is quite a wonderful thing for me. It's a wonderful thing for the short story.

[AS] It is indeed, and may we congratulate you in turn. It's a wonderful day.

[AM] Thank you very, very much.

[AS] How did you hear the news?

[AM] Um, let me see, I was wandering around this morning, early. [...]

http://www.nobelprize.org/prizes/literature/2013/munro/interview/   (accessed 05/20/2022)

Contrary to idioms and collocations, which are lexical pieces within sentences, these phraseological elements, like proverbs, have the particularity of being complete clauses, with an illocutionary value, which can be used by themselves. These formulas have been explored under various names, from the Bally's "phraséologie exclamative" (1921 [1951]), to the "conversational routines" of Coulmas (1979; 1985), Corpas Pastor (1996) or Lüger (2007), through the "énoncés liés" of Fónagy (1982) and Martins-Baltar (1995), with a slightly variable extension from one author to another.

In this study, we define interactional prefabricated formulas, with the following properties:

a)   They are complete clauses, with an illocutionary value, even if they can be embedded as subordinate clauses or parenthetical clauses, as *how shall I say it* in example (2) hereafter.

b)   They are recurrent in interactions. Most of them are frequent in dialogues.

c)   They are ready-made formulas, used in specific situations. Many of them are strongly determined by the context. To reply politely to a *thank you*, a French speaker can pick a formula from the following list: *de rien*, *il n'y a pas de quoi* [you're welcome] or *tout le plaisir est pour moi* [it's my pleasure].

d)   Most of them cannot be interpreted literally and are not semantically compositional. For this reason, a direct translation would be ineffective, as observed in the previous examples.

(2) Mr. Russ Powers: From that standpoint, and certainly from the biographies that you provided us, you are all very qualified contributors to do this, so I just wanted to — how shall I say it — be assured that you had the time to do the job properly. (Chambre des communes, Canada, 2 novembre 2005)

This broad definition allows us to embrace a wide range of formulas, as we will see later.

2.2 Typology of Formulas

Classifications in Phraseology and Interactional Studies. IPFs have been studied in the framework of different approaches, both in phraseology and in interactional analysis.

Several phraseological typologies have already been developed to account for these "ready-made sentences"; even if, to our knowledge, no exhaustive corpus-based description has yet been undertaken, especially for French. This issue has been addressed by several authors in French. For example, Fónagy (1982) distinguishes "meta-sentences" from "énoncés liés", specific to certain situations (greetings or congratulations), from more generic formulas, for example linked to the expression of a feeling. Cowie (2001), shows the difference between "routine formulae", which are very constrained from the situational point of view (and close to the "pragmatemes" of Mel'čuk (2015) and Blanco and Mejri (2018)) and "speech formulae", which apply to broader situations. However, as far as we know, it is in Spanish and German phraseology that we find the most advanced typologies.

In Spanish phraseology, Zuluaga (1980) identifies a subset of functionally marked "phraseological statements": " 'dichos' and ready-made phrases" whose interpretation is made in context, dialogue clichés, formulas specific to narrative texts and pragmatic fixed formulas, which refer to stereotypical social situations, comparable to Mel'čuk's and Blanco and Mejri's (2018) pragmatemes. Another type concerns interjective phraseological utterances, with an essentially expressive purpose. Like Zuluaga, Corpas Pastor (1996) distinguishes several types of routine formulas, but it is López-Simó (2016) who proposes — to the best of our knowledge — the finest typology, with 4 main types of utterances, subdivided into several subtypes: interpersonal phrases, related to social interactions, personal phrases, which often have an affective function, impersonal formulas, not directly related to the participants of the dialogue, and metacommunicative formulas.

In German phraseology, we also find detailed typologies such as that of Lüger (2007) who proposes two main groups of expressions: a) expressions with a broad social function (contact, identity,…) and b) expressions with a discursive function (evaluative, communicative functions,…).

In interactional analysis, these formulas have been theorized as "conversational routines" (Coulmas 1979; 1985). The typologies that have been developed are often based on speech act theory (cf. "actes de langage stéréotypés" Kauffer (2019); see also Ronan (2015)). There are various studies on specific contexts of language use, such as commercial interactions (Kerbrat and Traverso 2008). There are also several studies on discourse modalisers (Perrin 2012). To date, few studies propose general typologies based on corpora.

For our part, the typology we chose is close to that of López-Simó, but we will see that many formulas belong simultaneously to several types.

Our Typology. Classifying IPFs in a clear-cut manner is an ambitious undertaking given that many formulas are polysemous and that the same formula can have several functions.

We have therefore opted for non-exclusive classes. Although some are incompatible, most of the categories we have identified can be combined. We use the main classes identified by Tutin (2019):

a) meta-enunciative formulas: deal with the context of enunciation and comment what is said and how it is said
    1. most of them are parenthetical clauses
    2. they are optional and often moveable
b) reactive formulas: express a reaction — opinion, evaluation or emotion — to the interaction or to a situation. They tend to be clausal, but there are also parenthetical uses (Pausé et al. 2022).
c) situational sentences: statement only interpretable regarding the context
d) ritual formulas (pragmatemes): associated with specific and constrained social or communicative situations.

Each class contains types described in Table 1. As we will see, the basic element of our annotation scheme is the type.

Table 1. Types of IPFs' classes.

Classes	Types	Description
Meta-enunciatve	Metalinguistic (MMet)	Comment on the referential content of the message: reformulation, approximation, correction, etc. Example: You could put it that way
	Meta-conative (MCon)	Calling the interlocutor's attention to the referential content of the message. Example: You see
	Meta-negociative (MNeg)	Indication of an internal negotiation by the speaker on his or her adherence to the referential content of the message. Example: I think
Reactive	Expressive (RExp)	Expression of an emotion of the speaker regarding an object or a situation. Example: Not half!
	Interative (RInt)	Speaker's reaction to what he or she or someone else says, or to an event or situation. Example: I agree

(*continued*)

Table 1. (*continued*)

Classes	Types	Description
Situational	Evaluative (SEval)	Speaker's appreciation of an object or situation. Example: Not bad!
	Non evaluative (SNEval)	Statement only interpretable regarding the situation of enunciation. Example: Sounds familiar
Ritual (pragmatemes)	Greetings (PrG)	Ritual formula specific to the opening and closing greetings of an interaction. Example: How are you?
	Politeness (PrP)	Ritual formula specific to the marks of politeness. Example: Take your time
	Other (PrO)	Other ritual formula. Example: What can I get you?

As previously mentioned, an IPF can have several types and categorization is strongly dependent on the context of enunciation. In the example (3) *bien sûr* 'of course' is used to specify the speaker's agreement to the addressee's request. In the example (4), the speaker indicates a concession regarding the evidence of a fact.[1]

(3) [In a cheesemonger's shop, a client is ordering]

C10des fromages blancs faisselle de six [cottage cheese strainer]

VE2oui [yes]

VE2<PPI type="RInt">bien sûr</PPI> [certainly]

[cheesemonger's]

 (4) VE2vous avez essayé de nouveaux établissements ou pas lyon [did you try new places in Lyon ?]

C17euh oui on a fait le le celsius [yes we went to "le celsius"]

VE2ah <PPI type="SitNEval">ça me dit quelque chose</PPI> celsius [celsius sounds familiar]

C17c' était le nouveau là confluence [it's the new one, in confluence]

VE2ah oui [oh yes]

VE2<PPI type="MNeg">bien sûr</PPI> [of course]

VE2dans l' ancien local de le bec [in the former area of "le bec"]

C17oui oui [yes yes]

[cheesemonger's]

Table 2 shows examples of formulas associated with functional types.

---

[1] Corpus is introduced in Sect. 3.2.

Table 2. Example of type attribution to IPFs.

IPF	MMet	MCon	MNeg	RInt	SEval	RExp	Sit	PRG	PRP	PRO
Qu'est-ce que je vous sers ? [What can I get you ?]										+
Bien sûr ![1] [Certainly !]					+					
Bien sûr[2] [Obviously]			+							
C'est pas grave [That's ok]					+				(+)	
Tu te rends pas compte [You don't realize]		+								
Vas-y [Go on]		+							(+)	
On peut le dire comme ça [You could put it that way]	+									
Comme vous disiez [As you were saying]	+	+								
La honte ! [Shame !]					+	+				
Bonne idée [Good idea]				+	+					

3 Annotation of Formulas

3.1 State of the Art

Pragmatic annotation is booming and several projects have emerged over the last few years. For English, we can mention Dialogue *Annotation and Research Tool* and *SPICE-Ireland Corpus* projects (Weisser 2019, Ronan 2015). Archer et al. (2008) also present some work based on dialogue act schemes. A recent French study called *Théorie de la langue en acte*, is based on C-ORAL-ROM (Cresti et al. 2011). These works are not focused on formulas: fixed and free elements are annotated indistinctly regarding speech act categories, unlike Eshkol-Taravella and Grabar (2017), who were interested in the typology of reformulation markers with annotation in ESLO and in a corpus constructed from the *Doctissimo* forum. Nevertheless, this study only concerns a subpart of prefabricated formulas. To our knowledge, no previous work has been undertaken on pragmatic multiword expressions on a large scale.

3.2 CEFC-Orfeo Corpus

The CEFC corpus (*Corpus d'Étude pour le Français Contemporain*) was developed within the framework of the ANR ORFÉO project (*Outils et Recherche sur le Français Écrit et Oral*) (Benzitoun and Debaisieux 2020). It includes a representative subset of freely available written and spoken textual data. The spoken part constitutes the largest and most diversified corpus of this type, including numerous samples of spoken French: conversations, interviews, various meetings and public speeches, for a total of 3,088,443 words. The Orfeo tree corpus — the oral part of the corpus — includes syntactic annotations in dependencies (Kahane and Gerdes 2020, Deulofeu and Valli 2020, Nasr et al. 2020). The corpus can be downloaded from Ortolang platform.[2]

For this exploratory annotation work, we selected samples belonging to different interaction genres: informal conversation, interviews, interaction in a store and work meeting. All participants are native French speakers (Table 3).

Table 3. Composition of the corpus

Subcorpora	Context	Speakers	Number of words	Corpora source
repas_francais [french_lunch]	Lunch shared by two friends. They talk about their studies and homework	2 women, students (22 years old)	8883	Clapi
commerce_fromagerie [cheesemonger's]	Commercial interactions in a cheesemonger's shop	3 vendors: 1 woman and 2 men (20–50 years old), several clients	23670	Clapi
reunion_conception_mosaic_architecture [work_meeting]	Working meeting of architects	1 woman interior designer (30–40 years old) and 2 men interior designer and architect (30–40, 40–50 years old)	15229	Clapi
Isabelle_Legrand_F_32_Anne-Lies_Simo-Groen_F_30_RO [interview]	Sociolinguistic interview on neighborhood life	3 women, 2 (about 30 years old) and 1 (about 60 years old)	16966	CFPP

3.3 Main Elements of Annotation Scheme

In the IPF annotation process, the identification of formulas was performed semi-automatically using a dictionary and a grammar applied onto the corpus, with the help of the Nooj tool (Silberztein 2016).[3] Then, we made a first selection and delimited the

---

[2] https://www.ortolang.fr/market/corpora/cefc-orfeo (accessed 05/20/2022).

[3] We use an incremental procedure by enriching the IPF lists integrated gradually into NooJ.

selected formulas with tags < PPI > < /PPI > (French acronym for *Phrases Préfabriquées des Interactions* corresponding to IPF). We then manually went through the whole corpus with the help of the audio versions to tag other formulas. We had to make decisions regarding various issues such as the annotation of discontinuous items, delimitation of the formulas (should we include depending syntactic elements?) and lexical variants.

- Delimitation of IPFs and Variants

Formulas are annotated with the < PPI > element and the attribute "type" with one or several types presented in Table 2. The variants are not discriminated for the moment but will be addressed with lemmatization (cf. section 3.4). Modifiers (underlined in the following examples) are integrated in the IPF when they are inserted in the formula (example (5)) and not at the periphery (example (6)).

(5) < PPI type = "RExp_SEval" > c'est assez chouette < /PPI > [it's pretty good] [cheesemonger's]

(6) oui < PPI type = "RInt" > je vois < /PPI > très bien [I can see fine] [interview]

- Discontinuous elements

Due to segmentation rules (Nasr et al. 2020), some turns are split into several segments, as for example (7). We use *next* and *prev* to indicate the link between parts of the same formula, according to the French Treebank model (Abeillé et al. 2019).

(7) MAR < PPI_next type = "SEval" > il y a pas de < /PPI > [*No problems*]
MAR<PPI_prev>problèmes</PPI> [french_lunch]

- Optional arguments

Some IPFs have an optional argument, as for example (8) in which the argument of "ça n'a rien à voir" [it was never about [that]] is not always expressed. We introduced < VAL > < /VAL > to tag the marker of active valency.

(8) a. c'est sûr que ça < PPI type = "SEval" > ça n'a rien à voir < /PPI > [It sure doesn't have anything to do with that] [interview]

b. <PPI type="SEval">ça n'a rien à voir</PPI> <VAL>avec</VAL> le lieu d'habitation [It has nothing to do with dwelling] [interview]

This tag is also used to delimit valency markers of epistemic modality verbs (cf. *fr. rection faible*; Blanche-Benveniste & Willems 2007, Apothéloz 2003), as for example (9).

(9) [...] < PPI type = "MNeg" > je pense < /PPI > < VAL > que < /VAL > après si tu si tu te donnes des délais il y a un moment où forcément tu vas te dire merde il faut que je me bouge [I think that if you give yourself deadlines there is a moment when you will inevitably say to yourself shit I must move] [repas_francais]

- IPFs and syntactic constructions

Besides the formulas, we identify some constructions (Fillmore 2008; Croft and Cruse 2004; Lakoff 1987) specific to the oral language during the annotation process. We tag them with <CONSTR> </CONSTR> for further studies. These are combinations partially lexicalized and specific turns semantically compositional. <VAR> tag is used to delimit variables that are part of the active valency of a formula or construction, as for example (10).

(10) <CONSTR> c'est quoi </CONSTR> <VAR>une Bagnolétaise<VAR> alors

This first step of the annotation scheme allows us to identify and characterize the formulas at a macro level. The second step currently implemented offers a more precise semantic description.

3.4 Secondary Elements of Annotation Scheme

- Semantic labels

The distinction made according to the classes and types introduced in Table 1. is not sufficient for didactic or linguistic applications. In order to offer a database of formulas and annotated examples usable for pedagogical purposes, it is necessary to add functional and semantic information as proposed by Bidaud (2002) in her dictionary of *Structures figées de la conversation*.

We are thus currently establishing pragmatico-semantic labels closely related to functional types, such as:

- 'reformulation' (meta-enunciative > metalinguistic): *on peut le dire autrement* [to put it another way], *je veux dire* [I mean]
- 'agreement' (reactive > interactive): *c'est bon pour moi* [that's fine by me], *c'est noté* [noted], *on fait comme ça* [do it that way]
- 'interaction opening' (pragmateme > opening): *vous allez bien* [are you alright], *ça fait longtemps* [it's been a long time], *mes respects* [My respects]
- 'expression of surprise' (reactive > expressive): *la vache* [my gosh], *c'est dingue* [it's crazy]

Unlike functional types, labels cannot be combined. When an IPF belongs to several types, each type must have a corresponding label. In the examples (10) and (11), IPFs that express difficulty are employed. We see that *c'est chaud* [it's crazy hard"] is both evaluative and expressive. The formula contains an emotional side with the expression of contrariety. IPFs *c'est chaud* and *c'est pas évident* share a label "difficulty_appreciation" but the first is also labeled with "contrariety".

(11) VE2 < PPI type = "SEval_RExp" label = "difficulty_appreciation_contrariety" > c' est chaud < /PPI > parce qu' on est en train dese dire qu'on a pas le temps [It's crazy hard because we are telling ourselves thatwe don't have time]
    [cheese_factory]

(12) JUD < PPI type = "SEval" label = "difficulty_appreciation" > c' est pas évident
< /PPI > [it's not easy] [repas_francais]

Note that the emotion expressed by an IPF is strongly dependent on the context of enunciation. This is one of the particularities of expressive formulas which are often linked to a paradigm of emotions. Thus, *c'est chaud* can express "contrariety", "tension" or "excitement".

This list of labels is still under development and is elaborated empirically, based in part on existing typologies (among others Bidaud 2002; Lopez-Simo 2016; Gharbi 2020).

- Grammatical mood

Our annotation scheme does not include speech act annotation, in line with Austin and Searle, contrary to Ronan (2015) and Weisser (2019). However, we find it important to annotate grammatical mood[4] in a simple way, to differentiate several kinds of formulas. It should also be remembered that our corpus does not include punctuation, in accordance with the usual practice of annotating spoken corpora, which does not allow us, for example, to identify interrogative formulas with the question mark.

For convenience, we use only three values, based mainly on morphological and lexical markers and prosody:

a) assertion: this includes declarative sentences, but also exclamative ones, as it appears practically impossible to distinguish the latter two types on the basis of formal cues.

b) interrogation: corresponds to question-like clauses, whether they include specific markers such as *qui* as in *c'est de la part de qui* [who's calling?] or not (e.g. *c'est pour aujourd'hui ou pour demain* 'Lit. is it for today or for tomorrow?' [what are you waiting for], where prosody must be exploited[5].

c) injunction: corresponds roughly to orders and commands, and is realized mainly by the imperative mode (e.g. *prends-en de la graine* 'Lit. take some grain' [watch and learn]) and some subjunctive forms (e.g. *que je ne t'y reprenne pas* [don't let me catch you again])

Syntactic modality is essential to distinguish several values of formulas. For example, the very frequent fomula *ça va* can have several values according to the syntactic modality:

- assertive modality: en. "its ok", situational formula
- assertive modality: en. "I'm fine", interactional reactive formula
- interrogative modality: en. "is it ok?", interactional reactive formula
- interrogative modality: en. "how are you?", ritual formula

---

[4] "Mood" refering here to historical grammatical conception, in opposition with semantic conception linked with "modality" that expresses the spearker's attitude regarding his statement (Gosselin et al. 2010, Nuyts et al. 2016).

[5] Remember that polar questions in spoken French generally have the same syntactic structure as the declarative clauses. Only the prosody distinguishes them.

- Lemmatization and Variant issues

Lemmatization of formulas is essential to account for the variability of these elements according to several parameters:

– grammatical number/person variation: *comment vas-tu* vs *comment allez-vous*? [how are you]
– tense variation: *ça fait un bail* vs *ça faisait un bail* [it has been a while]
– inclusion of modifiers, as mentioned in 3.3.
– omission of the negation marker *ne*: *ca ne fait rien* vs *ça fait rien* [it doesn't matter].

However, it should be remembered that this variation is not systematic for every parameter. For example, the formula *tu parles* is not attested in the second person plural (the *tu* has a generic value here).

It is necessary to choose a form as lemma among the variants. We have decided to choose the most common parameters for spoken French, selecting the present tense, favoring the second person singular and the negation without *ne*. Table 4 illustrates the annotation of formulas that are part of the semantic paradigm of difficulty assessment.

Table 4. Illustration of parameters of annotation

IPF	Lemma	Mood	Type	Label	Annotation format
c'est chaud	c'est chaud	declarative	SEval + RExp	difficulty assessment + contrariety	\<PPI lemma = "c' est chaud" mod = "declar" type = "SEval_RExp" label = "appr_ diff_contrar"> c' est chaud \</PPI >
c'est super chaud	c'est chaud	declarative	SEval + RExp	difficulty assessment + contrariety	< PPI lemma = "c' est chaud" mod = "declar" type = "SEval_RExp" label = "appr_ diff_contrar" > c' est super chaud < /PPI >
ça va être sport	ça va être sport	declarative	SEval + RExp	difficulty assessment + contrariety	< PPI lemma = "ça va être sport" mod = "declar" type = "SEval_RExp" label = "appr_ diff_contrar" > ça va être sport < /PPI >
c'est pas évident	c'est pas évident	declarative	SEval	difficulty assessment	< PPI lemma = "c'est pas évident" mod = "declar" type = "SEval_RExp" label = "appr_ diff" > c'est pas évident < /PPI >

4 Some Observations on the Annotated Corpus

At present, 4 samples of the spoken corpus have been annotated by 2 expert annotators (the authors of this article). A first evaluation on a sample of the corpus (15222 words) shows an inter-annotator agreement of 67% on the annotation of types in this first phase. Disagreements were discussed and decided upon in a concerted manner.

Some interesting observations could be made from the annotated corpora, although the results should be taken with caution given the small sample size.

4.1 Productivity of Formulas

First of all, we can observe interesting differences in the number and variety of formulas (see Fig. 1). They are almost twice as numerous in the informal conversation as in the work meeting. The spontaneity of interactions, which is greater in the casual context than in the professional context, seems to have an impact on the productivity of expressions. We also notice a lower productivity in the sociolinguistic interview context, which also corresponds to a partially supervised interaction. The remarkable frequency of the commercial context can be explained by the large number of speakers, by the importance of ritual formulas (greetings, thanks) and by the fact that regular customers have informal relationships with the vendors.

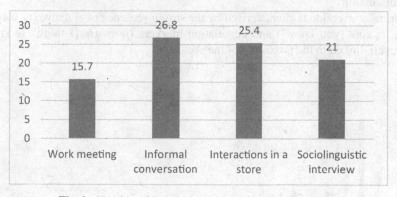

Fig. 1. Number of Interactional Formulas per 1000 words

If we now turn to the number of different expressions (ratio of the total number of formulas to the number of different formulas), we observe interestingly a much larger difference in friendly (2,9) and store interactions (2,9) than in professional interactions (3,6) and interviews (3,9). In the latter two types, the speakers' turns of speech are also longer and the speakers' statuses are more fixed. The expressions is the less spontaneous contexts are both less numerous and less varied.

4.2 Distribution of Types

The identification of the most frequent formulas in the 4 samples reveals that many expressions do not seem to be specific to a particular sub-genre. For example, *c'est vrai* [that's right] or *d'accord* ([it is true] and [agree]) appear in the 10 most frequent expressions in the 4 sub-genres. This is not very surprising, since these formulas refer to agreement and confirmation, which are present in all kinds of texts. There do seem to be cross-genre formulas, as observed in Tutin (2019), even if it should be remembered that most formulas are polyfunctional (and observation of functions beside formulas is necessary).

The observation of functional types shows interesting specificities (as can be seen on Fig. 2):

– the work meeting is punctuated by negotiation and interaction formulas aimed at reaching a collective decision by evaluating possible situations. Negotiation markers such as *c'est vrai* [it's true], *je trouve* [I find], *je pense* [I think] are especially numerous.
– conversations in shops are characterized by the unsurprisingly high presence of greetings (*au revoir* [goodbye], *bonne journée* [have a good day], *à bientôt* [see you soon]) and the strong presence of direct interaction marks related to purchasing transactions (*d'accord* [OK], *c'est bon* [it's OK], *bien sûr* [of course]).
– the sociolinguistic interview involves speakers in an asymmetric situation. The interviewee's speech is close to a monologue where the speaker looks for the most appropriate formulations, using metaenunciative markers (*on va dire* [let's say]) or trying to moderate his words (*je pense* [I think]). On the other side, the interviewer uses many backchannel markers such as *d'accord* [OK] to encourage the addresee to continue the discussion.
– informal conversion is characterized by the strong presence of conative (*tu vois* [you see], *tu sais* [you know]) and negotiation markers (*je pense* [I think], *je crois* [I believe]), linked to the proximity of the speakers

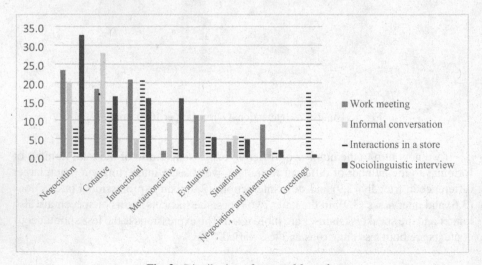

Fig. 2. Distribution of types of formulas

This first comparison of formulas in various discourse genres predictably highlights the great difference in usage, which encourages us to develop this annotation work on more samples.

5 Conclusion

Interactional prefabricated formulas are a central topic in phraseology which needs to take a more serious interest in oral genres. However, this issue is rather complex, as it requires skills not only in semantics and syntax, but also in pragmatics and interactions. Observation and annotation work also need a good knowledge of spoken corpora.

We have proposed here a typology of formulas based on classes and types and validated in corpus with a systematic annotation. Semantic labels are being developed in parallel with grammatical mood and lemmatization. To our knowledge, no such work has been done to date. First observations show a great diversity of formulas linked to a) genres of interactions b) proximity of speakers c) their status in interaction. This finding is not surprising given the diversity of interactions. These parameters will have to be taken into account for larger scale observations.

References

Corpus

CLAPI: http://clapi.ish-lyon.cnrs.fr/. Accessed 01 June 2022

CFPP: http://cfpp2000.univ-paris3.fr/. Accessed 01 June 2022

Abeillé, A., Clément, L., Liégeois, L.: Un corpus arboré pour le français: le French Treebank. TAL **60**(2), 19–43 (2019)

Apothéloz, D.: La rection dite "faible": grammaticalisation ou différentiel de grammaticité ?. Verbum, La grammaticalisation en français. **25**(3), 241–262. Presses Universitaires de France, Nancy (2003)

Archer, D., Culpeper, J., Matthew D.: Pragmatic annotation. In: Kytö, M., Lüdeling, A. (eds.) Corpus Linguistics: An International Handbook, pp. 613–642. Mouton de Gruyter, Berlin (2008)

Bally, C.: Traité de stylistique française. Klincksieck, Paris (1921)

Benzitoun, C., Debaisieux, J. M.: Orféo: un corpus et une plateforme pour l'étude du français contemporain. Langages. **219**(3), 160p. (2020)

Bidaud, F.: Structures figées de la conversation. Analyse contrastive français-italien. Peter Lang, Bern/Berlin (2002)

Blanche-benveniste, C., Willems, D.: Un nouveau regard sur les verbes faibles. Bulletin de la Société de Linguistique de Paris **102**, 217–254 (2007)

Blanco, X., Mejri, S.: Les pragmatèmes. Champion, Paris (2018)

Corpas Pastor, G.: Manual de fraseología española. Gredos, Madrid (1996)

Coulmas, F.: On the sociolinguistic relevance of routine formulae. J. Pragmat. **3**(3–4), 239–266 (1979)

Coulmas, F.: Conversational Routine: Explorations in Standardized Communication Situations and Prepatterned Speech, vol. 96. Walter de Gruyter, Berlin (1985)

Cowie, A.P. (ed.): Phraseology. Theory, Analysis, and Applications. Oxford University Press, Oxford (2001)

Cresti, E., Massimo, M., Tucci, I.: Annotation de l'entretien d'Anita Musso selon la Théorie de la langue en acte. Lang. Fr. **170**(2), 95–110 (2011)

Croft, W., Cruse, A.: Cognitive Linguistics. Cambridge University Press, Cambridge (2004)

Deulofeu, J., et Valli, A.: « Lexique et classement en parties du discours dans ORFÉO ». Langages. **219**(3), 53–68 (2020)

Eshkol-Taravella, I., Grabar, N.: Taxinomie dans les reformulations du point de vue de la linguistique de corpus. Syntaxe et Sémantique **1**(18), 149–184 (2017)

Fillmore, Ch.: Frame Semantics Meets Construction Grammar. In Bernal, E., DeCesaris, J. (eds.) Proceedings of the XIII EURALEX International Congress, 49–69. Institut Universitari de Lingüística Aplicada, Barcelone (2008)

Fónagy, I.: Situation et signification. John Benjamins Publishing, Amsterdam (1982)

Gharbi, N.: Analyse sémantico-pragmatique et discursive: les formules expressives de la conversation. Université Grenoble Alpes-Université de Sfax, Thèse de doctorat (2020)

Gosselin, L.: Les modalités en français: la validation des représentations. Rodopi, Netherlands/New York (2010)

Kahane, S., Gerdes, K.: Annotation syntaxique du français parlé: Les choix d'ORFÉO. Langages **219**(3), 69–86 (2020)

Kerbrat-Orecchioni, C., Traverso, V. (eds): Les interactions en site commercial: invariants et variation. ENS éditions, Lyon (2008)

Kauffer, M.: Le figement des «actes de langage stéréotypés» en français et en allemand». Pratiques: théories, pratique, pédagogie, 159–160, 42–54 (2013)

Kauffer, M.: Les "actes de langage stéréotypés": essai de synthèse critique. Cah. Lexicol. **1**(114), 149–171 (2019)

Krzyżanowska, A., Grossmann, F., Kwapisz-Osadnik, K.: Les formules expressives de la conversation Analyse contrastive: français-polonais-italien. Episteme, Lublin (2021)

Lakoff, G.: Women, Fire, and Dangerous Things: What Categories Reveal about the Mind. Chicago University Press, Chicago (1987)

López-Simó, M.: Fórmulas de la conversación. Propuesta de definición y clasificación con vistas a su traducción español-francés, francés-español. Thèse de doctorat, Université d'Alicante (2016)

Lüger, H.: Pragmatische Phraseme: Routineforme. In: Burger, H. (eds) Phraseologie: ein internationales Handbuch der zeitgenössischen Forschung, pp. 444–459. Mouton de Gruyter, Berlin (2007)

Martins-Baltar, M.: Énoncés de motif usuels: figures de phrase et procès en déraison. Cahiers du français contemporain **2**, 87–118 (1995)

Mel'čuk, I.: Clichés, an understudied subclass of phrasemes. Yearbook of Phraseology. **6**(1), 55–86 (2015)

Nasr, A., Dary, F., Bechet, F., Fabre, B.: Annotation syntaxique automatique de la partie orale du ORFÉO. Langages **219**(3), 87–102 (2020)

Nuyts, J., Van der Auwera, J. (eds.): The Oxford Handbook of Modality and Mood. Oxford University Press, Oxford (2016)

Pausé, MS., Tutin, A., Kraif, O., Coavoux, M.: Extraction de Phrases Préfabriquées des Interactions à partir d'un corpus arboré du français parlé: une étude exploratoire. In: Neveu, F., Prévost, S., Steuckardt, A., Bergounioux, G., Hamma, B. (eds.) 8e Congrès Mondial de Linguistique Française (CMLF) 2022. SHS Web of Conferences, 138, Orléans (2022)

Perrin, L.: Modalisateurs, connecteurs, et autres formules énonciatives. Arts et Savoirs, 2 (2012). http://journals.openedition.org/aes/500. Accessed 14 April 2022

Ronan, P.: Categorizing expressive speech acts in the pragmatically annotated SPICE Ireland corpus. ICAME J. **39**, 25–45 (2015)

Silberztein, M.: Formalizing Natural Languages: the NooJ Approach. Max Silberztein. Wiley Editions, Hoboken (2016)

Tutin, A.: Phrases préfabriquées des interactions: quelques observations sur le corpus CLAPI. Cah. Lexicol. **114**, 63–91 (2019)

Weisser, M.: The DART annotation scheme: form, appliability & application. Stud. Neophilol. **91**(2), 131–153 (2019)

Zuluaga, A.: Introducción al estudio de las expresiones fijas. Peter Lang, Berne (1980)

Specialized Idioms: From LGP to LSP Phraseological Paradigm

José Luis Rojas Díaz[1]([✉]) [iD], Juan Manuel Pérez Sánchez[2] [iD],
and Alejandro Arroyave Tobón[2] [iD]

[1] Institución Universitaria Pascual Bravo, Calle 73 N° 73A – 226, Medellin, Colombia
`jose.rojasd@pascualbravo.edu.co`
[2] Universidad de Antioquia, Calle 67 # 53-108, Medellín, Colombia
`{jmanuel.perez,alejandro.arroyave}@udea.edu.co`

Abstract. In the last decades there has been an ever-increasing interest in the study of phraseology in language for specific purposes (LSP). Literature shows that the definitions offered by descriptive studies focus mainly on the alleged obligatory presence of terms (specialized lexical units) as components of specialized phraseological units. Recent studies have shown, however, that LSP phraseology has more features in common with phraseology in language for general purposes (LGP) than has been traditionally claimed by scholars in the fields of LSP and Terminology. This paper presents four specialized phraseological unit (SPU) instantiations per language in Spanish, English, and French. The units of analysis were extracted from two bilingual (Spanish-English and French-English) dictionaries related to Commerce and Economics. These specialized phraseological units were identified and classified by means of a revised definition of specialized phraseological unit and a taxonomy for their classification based on LGP studies. This taxonomy presents specialized phraseological units as a category containing three subcategories, namely (i) specialized idioms, (ii) specialized collocations, and (iii) specialized pragmatemes. The analysis carried out on the above-mentioned twelve specialized phraseological units, shows evidence of semantic, syntactic, and lexical idiomaticity, thus proving the existence of specialized idioms. This framework can be used as a tool to evaluate the feasibility of using the suggested taxonomy and definition for the identification and classification of specialized phraseological units in LSP domains other than Commerce and Economics.

Keywords: Specialized idioms · Specialized phraseology · Terminology · LSP

1 Introduction

The study of phraseology in languages for specific purposes (LSP) and its relationship with lexicographic resources has interested several scholars in the last decades (Bevilacqua 2004; Buendía Castro and Faber 2015; Leroyer 2006; Rojas Díaz in press; Tschichold 2008; Veisbergs 2020). Nevertheless, the description around the categories offered for the classification of specialized phraseological units (SPUs) either focuses on collocations, thus leaving out, in most cases, the description of SPUs that share characteristics

G. Corpas Pastor and R. Mitkov (Eds.): EUROPHRAS 2022, LNAI 13528, pp. 206–220, 2022.
https://doi.org/10.1007/978-3-031-15925-1_15

with idioms in language for general purposes (LGP) or uses the term collocation as a synonym of SPU, a category in which specialized idioms (SpIs) are often included.

According to Rojas Díaz (in press) SpIs are a subcategory of SPUs that, similarly to LGP idioms, are characterized by their idiomaticity. Therefore, this paper is intended to offer a characterization of SpIs based on the SPU taxonomy and SpI definition offered by Rojas Díaz (in press) with examples taken from two bilingual (Spanish-English and Spanish-French) specialized lexicographic resources of Commerce and Economics the *Diccionario de Comercio Internacional – Importación y Exportación, Inglés-Español/Spanish-English* (Alcaraz and Castro Calvín 2007) (henceforth DCI) and the *Vocabulaire de l'économie et des finances* (Commission générale de la terminologie et de néologie 2012) (henceforth VEF).

1.1 From LGP to LSP Phraseology

Undoubtedly, the origin of the denomination of phraseology and its units of study have been a matter of discussion among scholars. On the one hand, some authors suggest that the term was originally coined by western structuralist linguists (García-Page Sánchez 2008; Zuluaga 1980). On the other hand, others state that phraseology emerged (as a discipline) as part of Soviet linguistic studies during the 1940's (Carneado Moré and Tristá 1985; Cowie 1998). However, it is unquestionable that the term phraseology was coined to denominate an idiomatic linguistic phenomenon that has been studied and expanded by many authors from several other linguistic traditions (see Table 1).

Table 1. Denominations of phraseology by different authors according to Cowie (1998, p. 7)

Author	Denomination
Vinogradov (1947)	Phraseological unit (phraseological fusion, phraseological unity, phraseological combination)
Amosova (1963)	Phraseological unit (idiom, phraseme/phraseoloid)
Cowie (1981)	Composite (pure idiom, figurative idiom, restricted collocation)
Mel'čuk (1988)	Semantic phraseme (idiom, collocation)
Gläser (1986)	Nomination (idiom, restricted collocation)
Howarth (1996)	Composite unit (pure idiom, figurative idiom, restricted collocation)

Mel'čuk (1998, 2012, 2013, 2015) has played a leading role in the discipline by providing a comprehensive analysis of phraseological units including a detailed taxonomy for the classification of PUs in LGP. His initial definition of 'non-free phrases' sets the basis for the characterization of his taxonomies:

A phrase is non-free (=phraseologized) if at least one of its lexical components L_1 is selected by the speaker in a linguistically constrained way – that is, as a function of the lexical identity of other component(s) (Mel'čuk 2012, p. 33)

Mel'čuk's description and characterization of his subcategories were expanded in his subsequent works (1998, 2012, 2015). However, although his ground-breaking tax-onomies (See Fig. 1) offer an explanation for an extensive number of phraseological instantiations, his terminology is somehow difficult to use in an applied context such as the classification and indexation of PUs in lexicographic resources.

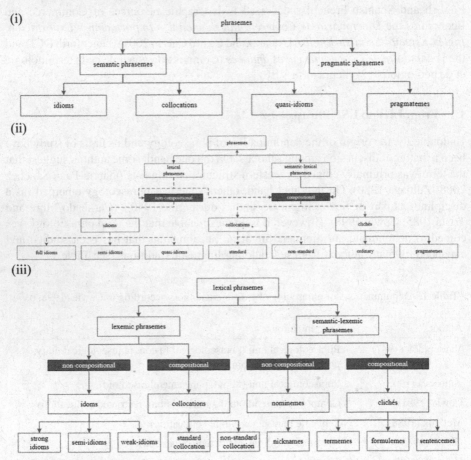

Fig. 1. Mel'čuk's phraseme[1] typologies: (i) (1998, p. 30), (ii) (2012, p. 42), and (iii) (2015, p. 68)

As seen in Fig. 1, the development of Mel'čuk's taxonomies maintains three main categories all along his works (1998, 2012, 2015), namely (i) idioms, (ii) collocations, and (iii) pragmatemes.

Although the denomination of the object of study of phraseology tends to differ among phraseology scholars, a set of common characteristics of PUs can be identified among the various definitions, specifically: (i) they are phrasal structures that follow syntax rules, (ii) they tend to be fixed in language by reiterative use, but not fully

---

[1] Phraseme is used in the works by Mel'čuk as a synonym of phraseological unit.

fixed (stereotypical), (iii) they permit the insertion and the variation of new elements, and (iv) their meanings are figurative (Corpas Pastor 1996, p. 6; Gries 2008; Mellado Blanco 2004, p. 17). The concept of figurative meaning has commonly been considered a synonym of the concepts of semantic idiomaticity and semantic opacity:

> [The] meaning of an idiom, arrived at through the operation of the semantic component on such a deep structure, is not some kind of amalgamation of the meanings of the parts of the structure. Rather, the meaning of an idiom is comparable to the meaning of a single lexical item. For example, the meaning of the idiom frequently used as example – 'kick the bucket' – is not made up of the meanings associated with 'kick', 'bucket', 'definite article', etc., but it is very much like the meaning of 'die' (Chafe 1968, p. 111).

Nevertheless, Chafe's awareness of the magnitude (in terms of both, importance, and conceptual extension) of idiomaticity is such, that he offers, from an early stage in the study of phraseology, signs of what he denominates the 'peculiarities' of idioms:

> These four peculiarities of idioms – their anomalous meaning, the transformational deficiencies, the ill-formedness of some of them, and the greater text frequency of well-formed idioms relative to their literal counterparts – must all be explained by a theory of language adequate to cope with idiomaticity (1968, pp. 111–112).

Chafe's 'peculiarities of idioms' related to idiomaticity are later described in detail in the work by Baldwin and Kim (2010). First, the authors make a distinction between the concepts of idiomaticity and compositionality. On the one hand, Baldwin and Kim (2010) define idiomaticity as the "markedness or deviation from the basic properties of the component lexemes." (Baldwin and Kim 2010, p. 269). On the other hand, compositionality is "the degree to which the features of the parts of a MWE[2] combine to predict the features of the whole" (Baldwin and Kim 2010, p. 269). Moreover, Baldwin and Kim (2010) assert that, in most cases, researchers have used the term 'compositionality' to refer only to 'semantic idiomaticity,' while 'idiomaticity' can occur at different linguistic levels, as seen in Table 2.

Table 2. Idiomaticity levels and their definitions according to Baldwin and Kim (2010, pp. 269–271)

Levels of idiomaticity	
Level	Definition
Lexical idiomaticity	Occurs when one or more components of an MWE are not part of the conventional English lexicon. For example, *ad hoc* is lexically marked in that neither of its components (ad and hoc) are standalone English words

(continued)

---

[2] The authors use 'multi-word expression' (MWE) "as a synonym of 'multiword unit,' 'multi-word lexical item,' 'phraseological unit,' and 'fixed expression;' there is also variation in the hyphenation of 'multiword,' with 'multi-word' in common use.

Table 2. (*continued*)

Levels of idiomaticity	
Level	Definition
Pragmatic idiomaticity	It is the condition of a MWE being associated with a fixed set of situations or a particular context [...] 'all aboard' [is an] example of a pragmatic MWE [...] [it] is a command associated with the specific situation of a train station or dock, and the imminent departure of a train or ship
Semantic idiomaticity	Semantic idiomaticity is the property of the meaning of a MWE not being explicitly derivable from its parts [...] for example, 'middle of the road' usually signifies "non-extremism, especially in political views,"
Statistical idiomaticity	Occurs when a particular combination of words occurs with markedly high frequency, relative to the component words or alternative phrasings of the same expression
Syntactic idiomaticity	Occurs when the syntax of the MWE is not derived directly from that of its components. [...] For example, 'by and large,' is syntactically idiomatic in that it is adverbial in nature but made up of the anomalous coordination of a preposition (by) and an adjective (large)

As presented earlier in this section (see Fig. 1), Mel'čuk's works (1998, 2012, 2013, 2015) have described thoroughly several, if not all, of the possible levels of idiomaticity by offering an answer to Chafe's petition for a linguistic explanation of the phraseological phenomenon.

1.2 LSP Phraseology: An Alternative Definition and Taxonomy

The above-mentioned issues related to idiomaticity, and compositionality have not been explored as in depth in LSP phraseology as they have been in LGP phraseology. LSP phraseology has even been considered by some scholars as a non-coherent research subject due to the lack of studies in that area (Kjær 2007, p. 507). Although Kjær's statement regarding the lack of studies in LSP phraseology can be easily counterargued by highlighting the studies done in the last two decades, it is true that idiomaticity has not been tackled directly in many of the reference definitions of SPU offered by several LSP and terminology scholars (e.g., Bevilacqua 2004, p. 28; Blais 1993, p. 52; Gouadec 1992, p. 550; L'Homme 1998, p. 515; Lorente Casafont 2002; Pavel 1993, p. 29; Picht 1987, p. 151).

In addition, LSP phraseology scholars (similarly to the case in LGP phraseology) have used a plethora of denominations when referring to the object of study of LSP phraseology (e.g., LSP phrase, phraseologism, LSP collocation, specialized lexical combinations, legal phraseological unit). On this regard, Rojas Díaz states that there is a rationale behind the use of these denominations:

[LSP phraseology authors] intend to distinguish it [the object of study of LSP phraseology] from the object of study of LGP phraseology (especially within lexicography). Therefore, the question arises whether LSP phraseology should be denominated as such or whether another denomination should be used instead to name the study of phraseological units specifically in the context of specialized languages. Rojas Díaz (in press, p. 6)

However, according to Rojas Díaz (in press), the main difficulty behind the definitions that have been offered by LSP and terminology scholars is their constant claim that a term must be among the unit's constituents:

[…] previous definitions in LSP phraseology tend to focus on the presence of a ter-minological unit in the phrase. Nevertheless, several SPUs (e.g., 'at arm's length', 'los cinco dragones' [the five dragons]) were metaphorical in nature, meaning that they entail a terminological *tenor*, […] by means of non-terminological *vehicles* […] (Rojas Díaz, in press, p. 25).

Rojas Diaz's finding (in press, p. 25) goes in line with Faber Benítez and López Rodríguez (2012) and L'Homme (2020) when they state that:

Trying to find a distinction between terms and words is no longer fruitful or even viable, and the best way to study specialized-knowledge units is by studying their behavior in texts (Faber Benítez and López Rodríguez 2012, p. 22).

Stating that a linguistic item is a term is considering its meaning from the per-spective of a special subject field. There is no such a thing as a term in essence; a linguistic unit becomes a term relative to their subject field in which it is consid-ered. […] This also means that even common linguistic items can become terms in specialized domains. […] Finally, a linguistic item can also be a relevant term in fields of knowledge (L'Homme 2020, p. 59).

The statements provided by Faber Benítez and López Rodríguez (2012, p. 22), and L'Homme (2020, p. 59), along with the descriptive conclusions offered in the paper by Rojas Díaz (in press, p. 25) offer enough evidence to provide an alternative defini-tion of SPU and a taxonomy for their classification in which SPU is the hypernym of three hyponyms: (i) specialized idiom (SpI), (ii) specialized collocations (SpC), and (iii) specialized pragmatemes (SpP) (see Fig. 2).

A combination of words (including, but not necessarily, monolexical terms) that evidences idiomaticity at least at one of the possible levels (lexical, pragmatic, semantic, statistical, or syntactic) and that, when used in a certain LSP domain, acquires a specialized meaning (Rojas Díaz, in press, p. 26).

Both the definition of SPU and the taxonomy for their classification offered by (Rojas Díaz, in press, p. 27) will be used in this paper as the basis for the description of SpIs.

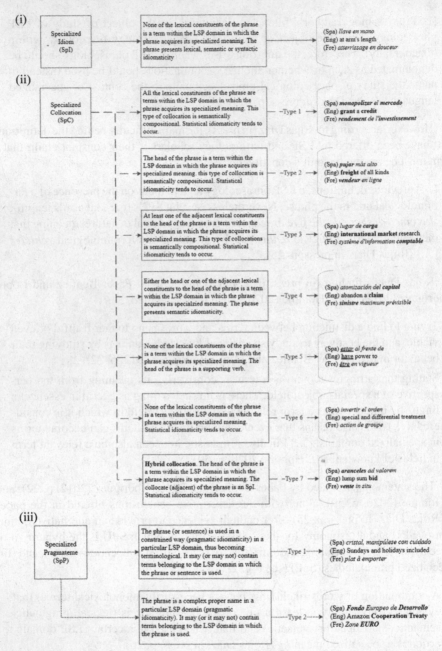

Fig. 2. SPU taxonomy (Rojas Díaz, in press, p. 27) based on the works by Mel'čuk (1998, pp. 6–8; 2012, pp. 37–40; 2013); (i) SpIs, (ii) SpCs, and (iii) SpPs

2 Specialized Idioms in the LSP Domain of Commerce and Economics

2.1 SpI Sample Characterization

In his taxonomy, Rojas Díaz (in press, p. 27) characterizes SpIs as phrases that lack a monolexical term within their word forms (in this case, related to Commerce and Economics) that undergo a certain level of idiomaticity (semantic, syntactic, or lexical). In this article, twelve SpIs in three different languages, namely (i) Spanish, (ii) English, and (iii) French were selected as a means to characterize SpIs:

- Spanish (from the DCI – Spanish/English):

  - *Los Cinco Tigres*
  - *de igual a igual*
  - *de conformidad con*
  - standby

- English (from the DCI – English/Spanish):

  - at short notice
  - door-to-door
  - in good order and condition
  - *del credere*

- French (from the VEF – French/English):

  - *atterrissage en douceur*
  - *d'époque*
  - *faire-savoir*
  - *in situ*

The selected SpIs were looked up in terminological databases (IATE[3] and TER-MIUM plus[4]), LGP dictionaries, and query portals (*Diccionario de la lengua española*[5], *Fundéu RAE*[6], Merriam-Webster[7], *Centre National de Ressources Textuelles et Lexicales*[8]) in order to retrieve their corresponding meanings in both LSP and LGP. Some of the findings and the analysis done to these SpIs are presented in the following section.

---

[3] https://iate.europa.eu/home.
[4] https://www.btb.termiumplus.gc.ca/tpv2alpha/alpha-eng.html?lang=eng.
[5] https://dle.rae.es/.
[6] https://www.fundeu.es/.
[7] https://www.merriam-webster.com/.
[8] https://www.cnrtl.fr/.

2.2 Data and Analysis: Idiomaticity and Specialized Idioms

As indicated in Sect. 1.2, one of the key features of SPUs is their figurative meaning. It is evident that a considerable number of PUs have originated by means of either metaphorical or metonymic processes, or both. Tables 3 and 4 offer three examples each one of the PUs that present semantic idiomaticity by means of metaphorical (Table 3) and metonymic (Table 4) processes.

Table 3. Examples of SPUs with semantic idiomaticity through metaphorical processes

Semantic idiomaticity (metaphors)		
Los Cinco Tigres (Spanish)		
Terminological DB (TERMIUM plus)	DCI (Spanish-English)	LGP (RAE)
Collective name used colloquially for Hong Kong, Singapore, South Korea, Taiwan (Formosa) and Thailand, the common denominator being their high economic growth rates and their geographical proximity	ECON Five Dragons or Five Tigers; it refers to Hong Kong, Taiwan, Singapore, South Korea, and Thailand	Not found
at short notice (English)		
Terminological DB (IATE)	DCI (English-Spanish)	LGP (Merriam-Webster)
Not found	FIN *con breve plazo de aviso o notificación*; V. at call	Immediately after one has been told about something
atterrissage en douceur (French)		
Terminological DB (IATE)	VEF (French-English)	LGP (CNRTL)
Approach adopted by the Commission and embodied in the adoption of a range of measures to ease the transition when the EU's milk quotas are abolished	*Récession maîtrisée et progressive*	Not found

Table 3 shows three units found in our study where metaphor can be identified as the semantic mechanism underlying their figurative meanings. In the first place, the Spanish SPU *"Los Cinco Tigres"* [the Five Tigers] is used as a collective noun phrase to refer to the five powerful economies of Hong Kong, Taiwan, Singapore, South Korea, and Thailand. In this case, the grounds for the metaphorical use of the word 'tigers' is the power associated to both the literal and the figurative referents.

In the case of English, in the unit "at short notice," having the meaning "immediately after one has been told about something" time is conceived as a physical entity that can be measured in terms of size.

Finally, the use of the French unit *"atterrissage en douceur"* [soft landing] with the meaning "controlled and progressive recession" is based on a comparison between the non-traumatic experience of a soft landing and the equivalent ease of the controlled transition from a prosperous economic situation to a recession. In this case the *tertium comparationis* or grounds for the metaphorical relationship would be the concept of "smoothness."

Table 4. Examples of SPUs with semantic idiomaticity through metonymical processes

Semantic idiomaticity (metonymies)		
de igual a igual (Spanish)		
Terminological DB (IATE)	DCI (Spanish-English)	LGP (RAE)
(The communication) directly between devices that operate on the same communications level on a network, without the intervention of any intermediary devices such as a host or server	Exp: *igual a igual, de* (GEN at arm's length; S. Without granting any favors, with total independence, under conditions of full equality of opportunity.)	loc. Adv. *Como a una persona de la misma categoría o clase social. Se tratan, hablan de igual a igual*
door-to-door (English)		
Terminological DB (IATE)	DCI (English-Spanish)	LGP (Merriam-Webster)
Form of direct selling where goods are sold to a consumer on his/her doorstep	*fr:* LOGÍST *puerta a puerta*; *equivale a* gate-to-gate, warehouse-to-warehouse	Going or made by going to each house in a neighborhood
d'époque (French)		
Terminological DB (IATE)	VEF (French-English)	LGP (CNRTL)
Expression found attached to another one. No definition is offered	*Se dit d'un objet, autrefois en usage, qui revient au goût du jour*	*Réalisé dans le style d'une époque donnée, qui reflète ses caractéristiques*

Table 4 contains three PUs whose figurative meanings are the result of metonymic processes. Kövecses and Radden (1998) identified more than 30 types of metonymic relationships between the vehicle entity—i.e., "the word or phrase that is being used metonymically" (Knowles and Moon 2006, p. 54)—and the target entity—i.e. "the intended meaning or referent" (Knowles and Moon 2006, p. 54)—. Here, we follow Kövecses and Radden's (1998) classification to analyze the three metonymical PUs chosen for the present study.

In the first unit, i.e., *"de igual a igual"* [from equal to equal], the metonymic relationship identified is defining PROPERTY FOR CATEGORY, since the characteristic 'equal' is used as the vehicle to gain access to the target entity (CATEGORY), which is the person involved in the negotiation or transaction.

As for the English unit, the expression "door to door" is used metonymically to refer to the action of transporting goods from a facility of origin to a destination facility. In this case, the metonymic relationship is PART OF A THING FOR THE WHOLE THING since the word door is used as the vehicle to refer to the whole facility.

Finally, the PU *"d'époque"* [of epoch/vintage] is used in French to refer to "an object, formerly in use, which returns to the taste of the day." Here, the word *époque* is used as a general term to refer to the specific period during which the object in question was popular. Thus, the metonymic relationship identified in this unit is a CATEGORY FOR A MEMBER OF THE CATEGORY, where the category is the general concept of epoch, while the member of that category is the period in which the object in question was in vogue.

However, as described in Fig. 2, SpIs could undergo other types of idiomaticity (see Tables 5 and 6).

Table 5. Examples of SPUs with syntactic idiomaticity

Syntactic idiomaticity		
de conformidad con (Spanish)		
Terminological DB (IATE)	DCI (Spanish-English)	LGP (RAE)
[*lo dispuesto/previsto/establecido en*]: following (a specified rule or provision.)	LAW under; S. *a tenor de lo dispuesto en, en virtud de, al amparo de, comprendido en, contemplado en*	locs. Prepos. **Conforme a**: *Con arreglo a, a tenor de, en proporción o correspondencia a, de la misma suerte o manera que. Conforme a derecho, a lo prescrito, a lo que anoche determinamos. Se te pagará conforme a lo que trabajes*
in good order and condition (English)		
Terminological DB (TERMIUM plus)	DCI (English-Spanish)	LGP (Merriam-Webster)
A recital in a bill of lading respecting the condition of the subject of the bill	DER/LOGIST/*en buen estado y condiciones*; V. goods in bad order	Working properly

(continued)

Table 5. (*continued*)

faire-savoir (French)		
Terminological DB (IATE)	VEF (French-English)	LGP (CNRTL)
Effective dissemination of information about the performance and achievements of an entity or industry for the purpose of promotion, outreach, or awareness	*Diffusion efficace d'informations sur les performances et les réalisations d'une entité ou d'un secteur d'activité dans un but de promotion, de vulgarisation ou de notoriété*	*subst. Masc. Inv. Le/faire-savoir/qui présidait à la communication devenait un faire persuasif ayant, à l'autre bout de la chaîne, un faire interprétatif correspondant et opposé. Le changement de perspective ainsi obtenu se résumait en ceci que persuader, s'il reste encore en partie un faire-savoir, est surtout, et en premier lieu, un faire-croire*

The three expressions analyzed in Table 5 clearly show syntactic idiomaticity since their structures do not coincide with the syntax of a free sentence. Moreover, their components belong to certain parts of speech that do not give any clues as to their actual function, e.g., "*de conformidad con*" [in accordance with] (Prep N Prep) and "in good order and condition" (Prep N Conj N) do not include any adverb in their morphosyntactic patterns but they have an adverbial function. An interesting finding can be observed in the French expression *faire-savoir* consisting of two infinitive verbs linked by a hyphen (V - V) that fulfill the function of an invariable masculine noun referring to the effective dissemination of information.

Finally, Table 6 shows three expressions found in our study that evidence lexical idiomaticity, in each of the three languages studied. These SpIs consist of lexical components that do not belong to the lexicon of the language in which they are used. For example, in English we have an SpI of Italian origin (*del credere*), while in French the expression found is of Latin origin (*in situ*). On the one hand, "*del credere*" is used to refer to an added premium to cover the risk of non-payment. In French, on the other hand, we have the expression *in situ*, an idiom of Latin origin that means 'in the place', 'on site', and is used to refer to something that is observed, found, or executed in the very place where it currently is or where it has originated.

Table 6. Examples of SPUs with lexical idiomaticity

Lexical idiomaticity		
standby/stand-by (in Spanish from English)		
Terminological DB (IATE)	DCI (Spanish-English)	LGP (Fundéu)
Something that can be relied on in an emergency; short-term standby credits	**standby**1 *v:* GRAL *estar a la expectativa, quedar a la espera de órdenes, estar en lista de espera.* [Exp. **Standby**2 (DER *cumplir; mantener, reafirmar*), **stand-by**1 (DER *reserva, recurso*), **stand-by**2 (DER *suplente, de reserva, de repuesto, en lista de espera*)	*Modo de espera o en reposo, en referencia al que adoptan determinados aparatos cuando no están completamente encendidos, y estar a la expectativa de algo o estar a la espera de algo, en contextos más generales, son alternativas preferibles en español a* stand-by
del credere (in English from Italian)		
Terminological DB (IATE)	DCI (English-Spanish)	LGP (Merriam-Webster)
The remuneration which a commission agent receives from his principal in respect of his del credere	n: FIN "del credere", *riesgo de impago; prima añadida para cubrir el riesgo de impago*	Relating to or guaranteeing performance or payment by third persons to a principal in connection with transactions entered into by an agent for the principal usually in return for higher commissions
in situ (in French from Latin)		
Terminological DB (IATE)	VEF (French-English)	LGP (CNRTL)
In the natural or original position or place	***vente in situ***: *Vente publique de biens mobiliers sur les lieux mêmes où résident les propriétaires*	*Dans son cadre naturel, à sa place normale, habituelle*

3   Conclusions

LGP studies have provided theoretical and descriptive input to create a novel taxonomy for the classification of specialized idioms, specialized collocations, and specialized pragmatemes.

Our study shows that SPUs that do not contain any term occur in the LSP domain of Commerce and Economics. This type of SPUs evidence semantic, syntactic, and lexical idiomaticity, which confirms that they are specialized idioms and that they share more linguistic features with their LGP counterparts than has been traditionally claimed by canonical literature on LSP phraseology.

Semantic idiomaticity was found in the sample mainly through the occurrence of metaphors and metonymies. Syntactic idiomaticity, in turn, occurs in structures that do not coincide with the syntax of free sentences; while lexical idiomaticity has been identified in units containing lexical components borrowed from a foreign language.

A cross-linguistic and cross-disciplinary study must be carried out in order to prove the accuracy of the taxonomy proposed by Rojas Díaz (in press, p. 27) for the identification of SpIs, SpCs, and SpPs, in other LSP domains.

References

Alcaraz, V.E., Castro Calvín, J.: Diccionario de Comercio Internacional – Importación y Exportación, Inglés-Español/Spanish-English. Ariel (2007)

Amosova, N.N.: Osnovy Anglijskoj Frazeologii. University Press (1963)

Baldwin, T., Kim, S.N.: Multiword expressions. In: Indurkhya, N., Damerau, F.J. (eds.) Handbook of Natural Language Processing, 2nd edn., pp. 267–292. CRC Press (2010)

Bevilacqua, C.: Unidades fraseológicas especializadas eventiva: descripción y reglas de formación en el ámbito de la energía solar. Ph.D. thesis, Universitat Pompeu Fabra, Barcelona (2004)

Blais, E.: Le phraséologisme. Une hypothèse de travail. Terminologies nouvelles. Terminologie et diversité culturelle 10, 50–56 (1993)

Buendía Castro, M., Faber, P.: Phraseological units in English-Spanish legal dictionaries: a comparative study. Fachsprache (3–4), 161–175 (2015)

Carneado Moré, Z., Tristá, A.M.: Estudios de fraseología. Academia de Ciencias de Cuba - Instituto de Literatura y Lingüística (1985)

Chafe, W.: Idiomaticity as an anomaly in the Chomskyan paradigm. Found. Lang. 4, 109–127 (1968)

Commission générale de la terminologie et de néologie. Vocabulaire de l'economieet des finances (2012). https://www.academie-francaise.fr/sites/academie-francaise.fr/files/eco nomie_finances_2012.pdf

Corpas Pastor, G.: Manual de fraseología española. Gredos (1996)

Cowie, A.P.: The treatment of collocations and idioms in learners' dictionaries. Appl. Linguis. 2(3), 223–235 (1981)

Cowie, A.P.: Introduction. In: Cowie, A.P. (ed.) Phraseology: Theory, Analysis, and Applications, pp. 1–20. Oxford University Press (1998)

Faber Benítez, P., López Rodríguez, C.I.: Terminology and specialized language. In: Faber Benítez, P. (ed.) A Cognitive Linguistics View of Terminology and Specialized Language, pp. 9–31. De Gruyter Mouton (2012)

García-Page Sánchez, M.: Introducción a la fraseología española: estudio de las locuciones, vol. 6. Anthropos (2008)

Gläser, R.: The grading of idiomaticity as a presupposition for a taxonomy of idioms. In: Schulze, R., Hüllen Llen, W. (eds.) Understanding the Lexicon: Meaning, Sense and World Knowledge in Lexical Semantics, pp. 264–279. Max Niemeyer (1986)

Gouadec, D.: Terminologie & terminotique: outils, modèles & méthodes. In: Gouadec, D. (ed.) Actes de la première Université d'automne en Terminologie Rennes 2–21 au 26 septembre 1992. La Maison du Dictionnaire (1993)

Gries, S.T.: Phraseology and linguistic theory: a brief survey. In: Granger, S., Meunier, F. (eds.) Phraseology: An Interdisciplinary Perspective, pp. 6, 3–25. John Benjamins Publishing Company, Amsterdam (2008)

Howarth, P.: Phraseology in English Academic Writing: Some Implications for Language Learning and Dictionary Making. Max Niemeyer (1996)

Kjær, A.-L.: Phrasemes in legal texts. In: Burger, H., Dobrovol'skij, D., Kühn, P., Norrick, N. (eds.) Phraseology, vol. I, pp. 506–516. Walter de Gruyter (2007)

Knowles, M., Moon, R.: Introducing Metaphor. Routledge, London (2006)

Kövecses, Z., Radden, G.: Metonymy: Developing A Cognitive Linguistic View. Cogn. Linguist. **9**, 37–77 (1998). https://doi.org/10.1515/cogl.1998.9.1.37

L'Homme, M.-C.: Caractérisation des combinaisons lexicales spécialisées par rapport aux collocations de langue générale. In: Fontenelle, T., Hiligsmann, P., Michiels, A. (eds.) EURALEX 1998 Proceedings, VIII International Congress of the European Association for Lexicography, vol. II, pp. 513–522. Éd. Université de Liège (1998)

L'Homme, M.-C.: Lexical Semantics for Terminology: An Introduction. John Benjamins Publishing Company (2020)

Leroyer, P.: Dealing with phraseology in business dictionaries: focus on dictionary functions - not phrases. Linguistik Online **27**(2), 183–194 (2006)

Lorente Casafont, M.: Terminología y fraseología especializada: del léxico a la sintaxis. In: Pérez Lagos, M.F., Guerrero Ramos, G. (eds.) Panorama actual de la terminología, pp. 159–180. Comares (2002)

Mel'čuk, I.: Semantic description of lexical units in an explanatory combinatorial dictionary: basic principles and heuristic criteria. Int. J. Lexicography **1**(3), 165–188 (1988)

Mel'čuk, I.: Collocations and lexical functions. In: Cowie, A.P. (ed.) Phraseology: Theory, Analysis and Applications, pp. 23–53. Oxford University Press (1998)

Mel'čuk, I.: Phraseology in the language, in the dictionary, and in the computer. In: Kuiper, K. (ed.) Yearbook of Phraseology, vol. 3, pp. 31–56. De Gruyter Mouton (2012)

Mel'čuk, I.: Tout ce que nous voulions savoir sur les phrasèmes, mais... Cahiers de lexicologie **102**, 129–149 (2013). https://doi.org/10.15122/isbn.978-2-8124-1259-2.p.0129

Mel'čuk, I.: Clichés, an understudied subclass of phrasemes. Yearb. Phraseology **6**(1), 55–86 (2015). https://doi.org/10.1515/phras-2015-000

Mellado Blanco, C.: Fraseologismos somáticos del alemán: un estudio léxico-semántico. Peter Lang (2004)

Pavel, S.: Neology and phraseology as terminology-in-the-making. In: Sonneveld, H., Loening, K. (eds.) Terminology: Applications in Interdisciplinary Communication, pp. 21–34. John Benjamins (1993)

Picht, H.: Terms and their LSP environment - LSP phraseology. Meta J. des Traducteurs **32**(2), 149–155 (1987). https://doi.org/10.7202/003836ar

Rojas Díaz, J.L.: 'Arm's length' phraseology? Building bridges from general language to specialized language phraseology – a study based on a specialized dictionary of International Commerce and Economics in Spanish and English. Terminology (in press)

Tschichold, C.: A computational lexicography approach to phraseologisms. In: Granger, S., Meunier, F. (eds.) Phraseology: An Interdisciplinary Perspective, pp. 361–376. John Bejamins Publishing Company (2008)

Veisbergs, A.: Phraseology in general bilingual dictionaries: idioms as equivalents of single words. In: Cotta Ramusino, P., Mollica, F. (eds.) Contrastive Phraseology: Languages and Culture in Comparison, pp. 331–343. Cambridge Scholars Publishing (2020)

Vinogradov, V.V.: Ob osnovnuikh tipakh frazeologicheskikh edinits v russkom yazuike. In: Shakhmatov, A.A. (ed.) 1864–1920 Sbornik statey i materialov, pp. 339–364. Nauka (1947)

Zuluaga, A.: Introducción al estudio de las expresiones fijas. Peter Lang (1980)

Author Gender Identification for Urdu Articles

Raheem Sarwar[✉] [iD]

Research Group in Computational Linguistics, RIILP, University of Wolverhampton,
Wolverhampton, UK
R.Sarwar4@wlv.ac.uk

Abstract. In recent years, author gender identification has gained considerable attention in the fields of computational linguistics and artificial intelligence. This task has been extensively investigated for resource-rich languages such as English and Spanish. However, researchers have not paid enough attention to perform this task for Urdu articles. Firstly, I created a new Urdu corpus to perform the author gender identification task. I then extracted two types of features from each article including the most frequent 600 multi-word expressions and the most frequent 300 words. After I completed the corpus creation and features extraction processes, I performed the features concatenation process. As a result each article was represented in a 900D feature space. Finally, I applied 10 different well-known classifiers to these features to perform the author gender identification task and compared their performances against state-of-the-art pre-trained multilingual language models, such as mBERT, DistilBERT, XLM-RoBERTa and multilingual DeBERTa, as well as Convolutional Neural Networks (CNN). I conducted extensive experimental studies which show that (i) using the most frequent 600 multi-word expressions as features and concatenating them with the most frequent 300 words as features improves the accuracy of the author gender identification task, and (ii) support vector machine outperforms other classifiers, as well as fine-tuned pre-trained language models and CNN. The code base and the corpus can be found at: https://github.com/raheem23/Gender_Identification_Urdu.

Keywords: Multiword expressions · Author profiling · Author gender identification

1 Background and Introduction

The Internet's rapid growth has given rise to a plethora of new ways to transmit information across time and geography. Online social networking platforms (such as Twitter, Myspace, and Facebook), e-commerce websites (such as eBay, Craiglist), and usenet newsgroups are all gaining popularity. However, this growth enables a variety of Internet abuses. Online communities are prone to deception, incorrect information, and other threats. The Internet Crime Complaint Center

G. Corpas Pastor and R. Mitkov (Eds.): EUROPHRAS 2022, LNAI 13528, pp. 221–235, 2022.
https://doi.org/10.1007/978-3-031-15925-1_16

(IC3) has received an average of 552,000 complaints every year over the last five years. These complaints include a wide range of Internet frauds that affect people all over the world. To date, IC3 has received 2,760,044 complaints, with a total loss of \$18.7 billion reported. Homeland security and law enforcement organisations have initiated programmes to avoid fraudulent attacks and trace the identity of offenders in order to safeguard against terrorism, predators, and other threats [6].

Anonymity is an important feature of online communities. In cyberspace, people may not need to reveal their genuine identities, such as their name, age, gender, or address [14, 15, 26, 36, 37, 39–44]. In many cases of Internet crime, the criminals seek to conceal their real identities. Therefore, developing an efficient and effective method for identity tracking in Internet forensics becomes critical. In this paper, I am primarily focused on the *author gender identification* task, which can be defined as follows: given an article (a text), identify whether the article is written by male or female. The author gender identification task has been extensively investigated for resource-rich Western languages such as English [18], and Spanish [32]. However, researchers have not paid enough attention to perform this task for Urdu articles. After a thorough search of Urdu literature, I found two relevant studies on texts written in the Roman Urdu (i.e., Urdu texts written in the Latin alphabet) [3, 10]. I note that this paper focuses on Urdu articles written in Urdu alphabet. The author gender identification task can be considered as a binary classification problem [11, 28]. To determine the gender of the articles authors', several types of features are suggested such as the most frequent function words, most frequent character n-grams, most frequent word n-grams, most frequent part-of-speech (POS) categories and their sequences, as well as other stylistic markers such as percentage of capital letters or punctuations, mean sentence length, etc. [1, 2, 5, 18, 20, 25, 32, 46]. Different machine learning classifiers such as Decision Trees, Logistic Regression, K Nearest Neighbours, Support Vector Machine, and Random Forest have been suggested to determine the target category [2, 4, 18, 25, 32]. This investigation explores the effectiveness of multi-word expressions (MWEs), word-based features and character-based features to perform the author gender identification task for the Urdu articles using machine learning classifiers. I compared the performance of the machine learning classifiers against the state-of-the-art fine-tuned pre-trained language models such as DistilBERT [33], mBERT [9], multilingual DeBERTa [16], and XLM-RoBERTa [7] as well as Convolutional Neural Networks (CNN).

Urdu is an Indo-Aryan language that borrowed a large percentage of its vocabulary from other languages such as Arabic and Persian [24]. The Ethnologue, a well-known reference source that publishes statistics on living languages, has ranked Urdu as the 11th most spoken language in the world in 2020. It is also widely acknowledged as a major South Asian language, with 490 million native speakers worldwide [23]. It is the official language of five Indian states, including Bhiar, Uttar Pradesh, and Jharkhand. It is the national language of Pakistan, which has a population of about 220 million people. According to the 2011 census of linguistic statistics conducted by the Indian government, India had 50,772,631 Urdu speakers. Urdu speakers can also be found in the United

Kingdom, the United States, Canada, Australia, the Middle East, and Europe. Urdu is often regarded as a low-resource language due to the lack of or inadequacy of various critical resources, such as gold standard datasets and fundamental natural language processing (NLP) toolkits, such as reliable tokenizers and stemmers [8]. My discussion, however, is focused on the limitations of Urdu in the context of the author gender identification task. Some key limitations are as follows.

- **Lack of attention.** Like other NLP tasks such as part-of-speech (POS) tagging, text categorisation, named entity recognition (NER) [12–14, 21, 22, 27, 34, 38, 45], the author gender identification task has also been extensively investigated for resource-rich languages such as English [18], and Spanish [32]. However, this is the first study on the author gender identification task for the Urdu articles.
- **Unavailability of resources.** Author gender identification is an important NLP task. However, as mentioned earlier, this task has never been performed on the Urdu articles and there is no existing corpus available to perform this task. Therefore in this paper I introduced a new corpus to perform this task on the Urdu articles which can be accessed at: https://github.com/raheem23/ Gender_Identification_Urdu.
- **Inapplicable features.** As mentioned earlier, a comprehensive set of features have been used to perform the author gender identification task on resource-rich Western languages. Many of these features, however, are not applicable to the Urdu language. The number of capital alphabets, the number of sentences that begin with capital alphabets, and the number of sentences that begin with a lowercase alphabet are among these features. Moreover, some of these features are difficult to extract from articles written in Urdu due to limited availability of the reliable NLP toolkits. The frequency of POS tags, the presence of sentiment, and the type of emotion are a few to mention. The intricacy and morphological richness of the Urdu language account for the hard nature of these aspects.
- **Missing application of deep learning.** Fine tuning pre-trained language models have achieved state-of-the-art results for various NLP tasks for resource-rich languages [29, 30, 47]. However, despite the existence of compelling evidence from the literature, no study has evaluated the performance of these models to perform the author gender identification task for low-resource languages such as Urdu.

The main purpose of this paper was to introduce a new corpus that can be used to investigate the author gender identification task for Urdu articles and formulate a solution that outperforms the state-of-the-art methods. In addition to this, I aimed at answering the following research questions.

- **RQ 1:** What are the best features to perform the author gender identification task for Urdu articles?
- **RQ 2:** Can the performance of the author gender identification task be improved by concatenating the most frequent MWEs with the most frequent words?

- **RQ 3:** Can classical machine learning classifiers outperform state-of-the-art pre-trained language models to perform the author gender identification task for Urdu articles?

Summary of Contributions. My main contributions are as follows.

- I created the first corpus to perform the author gender identification task on Urdu articles.
- I explored, for the first time, the effectiveness of MWEs for the author gender identification task in Urdu.
- I evaluated the effectiveness of the state-of-the-art pre-trained language models for the gender identification task and compared its performance against the machine learning classifiers and CNN. The experimental findings add new insights to existing knowledge.

The rest of the paper is organised as follows. Section 2 presents methodology. Section 3 describes the experimental studies and the findings. Section 4 contains the concluding remarks and future research directions.

2   Methodology

Overview. As can be seen in Fig. 1, my methodology consists of three main processes. Firstly, I created a data scraper to retrieve the articles from a newspaper website. These articles are published by male and female columnists. I then extracted features from each article and applied different well-known machine learning classifiers to these features to perform the author gender identification task. Each process is described in the following subsections.

2.1   Data Collection

I created a data scraper using the BeautifulSoup[1] and Newspaper[2] libraries in Python. These libraries are highly effective for extracting and curating articles from newspaper websites. I then used this scraper to collect the articles from the Dunya News Website. These articles were written by both male and female columnists. The summary of the dataset is given in Table 1. The dataset consists of 844 articles and there are equal number of articles from male and female authors. Moreover, the size of each article is fixed to only 250 tokens, which makes this task more challenging to perform.

2.2   Features Extraction and Concatenation

Before I explain the features extraction process, I briefly define the multi-word expressions as follows.

---

[1] https://beautiful-soup-4.readthedocs.io/en/latest/.
[2] https://newspaper.readthedocs.io/en/latest/.

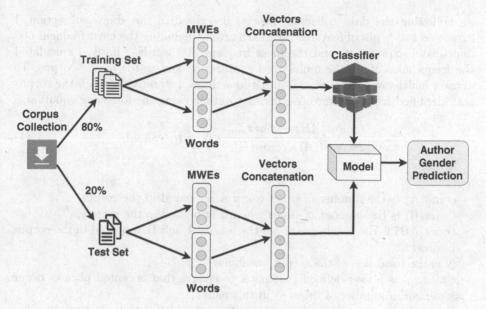

Fig. 1. An overview of the proposed author gender identification system for the Urdu articles.

Table 1. A summary of the dataset for the author gender identification task for Urdu articles

Gender	Number of articles	Number of words	Number of characters	Text length
Male	422	110,500	518,628	250
Female	422	110,500	515,810	250
Total	844	221,000	103,443,8	250

Multi-word expressions (MWEs) (sometime also known as word bigrams) are lexical entities made up of a number of orthographic words. Multi-word expressions make up a large component of any natural language's lexicon. They are a varied group of structures with a wide range of properties, all of which are differentiated by their distinctive behaviour. In terms of morphology, some multi-word expressions enable some constituents to freely inflect while restricting the inflection of others. Multi-word expressions may allow constituents to go through non-standard morphological inflections that they would not go through in isolation in some instances. Some multi-word expressions behave like words, while others behave like phrases; some appear in a set pattern and order, while others allow for numerous syntactic changes. The semantic opacity of multi-word expressions is their most distinguishing feature, yet compositionality in multi-word expressions is incremental, ranging from entirely compositional to wholly idiomatic [31].

Following the data collection process described in the above subsection, I extracted two types of features from each article including the most frequent 600 multi-word expressions and the most frequent 300 words. Firstly, I calculated the frequencies of all the multi-word expressions and words in the corpus. To extract multi-word expression from Urdu articles, I iterated through the corpus and identified frequent words occurring together using the following equation,

$$\frac{count(AB) - count_{min}}{count(A) * count(B)} * N > threshold \tag{1}$$

where:

- count(A) is the number of times token A appeared in the corpus;
- count(B) is the number of times token B appeared in the corpus;
- count(AB) is the number of times the tokens A and B appeared in the corpus in order;
- N is the total size of the corpus vocabulary
- $count_{min}$ is a user-defined parameter to ensure that accepted phrases occur a minimum number of times (5 in this paper)
- threshold is a user-defined parameter to control how strong is a relationship between two tokens (10 in this paper)

After I extracted all the multi-word expressions, I selected the most frequent 600 multi-word expressions from the corpus and used them as features for the author gender identification task. I also extracted the most frequent 300 words from the dataset and used them as features for the author gender identification task. After the features extraction process, each article was represented with two features vectors. I proposed to concatenate the 600 most frequent multi-word expressions and the 300 most frequent words vectors to obtain better performance in the author gender identification task, as shown in Fig. 1.

2.3   Machine Learning Classifiers and Deep Learning Models

After the features extraction and concatenation processes, I applied 10 well-known classifiers on these feature vectors to perform the author gender identification task with default parameter settings. These classifiers include Light Gradient Boosted Machine Classifier [19], Cat Boosted Classifier[3], Extreme Gradient Boosted Classifier, Gradient Boosting Classifier, Random Forest Classifier, Extra Trees Classifier, Ada Boost Classifier, K Nearest Neighbours Classifier [35], Decision Tree Classifier, and Support Vector Machine Classifier [17]. I used Scikit-Learn[4] library in Python for the implementation of these machine learning classifiers.

I also fine-tuned the state-of-the-art pre-trained language models such as DistilBERT [33], mBERT [9], multilingual DeBERTa [16], and XLM-RoBERTa [7]

---

[3] https://catboost.ai/en/docs/.

[4] https://scikit-learn.org.

to perform the author gender identification task for Urdu articles and compared their performance against the machine learning classifiers and Convolutional Neural Networks (CNN). The fine-tuning processes can be defined as training a pre-trained language model such as multilingual BERT on the author gender identification task corpus. The fine-tuning was performed using Hugging library with Pytorch deep learning framework. The parameters values used to fine-tune the multilingual pre-trained language models are given in Table 2. All models are base models, with 12 layers (with the exception of DistilBERT, which has 6 layers), a hidden size 768, and 12 attention heads. A summary of the CNN model is given in Table 3.

2.4   Evaluation Strategy and Evaluation Measure

I used accuracy as an evaluation measure where the train-test ratio was set to 80:20.

Table 2. Parameter settings for the fine-tuned pre-trained language models including mBERT, DistilBERT, XLM-RoBERTa and multilingual DeBERTa

Pre-trained language models	
Epochs	5
Batch size	8
Maximum length	250
Optimiser	Adam
Learning rate	2^{-5}
Validation split	0.2
Loss	Binary crossentropy
load_best_model_at_end	True
Seed	42

3   Experimental Studies

To achieve the objectives of this investigation and answer the research questions listed in Sect. 1, I conducted two main experimental studies. In the first study I evaluated the effectiveness of using multi-word expressions as features for the author gender identification task. I also evaluated the effectiveness of concatenating the 600 most frequent multi-word expressions (MWEs) with the 300 most frequent words and used them as features for the author gender identification task. In the second experimental study I compared the performance of the machine learning classifiers against the fine-tuned pre-trained language models and CNN.

Table 3. Summary of the CNN model for the author gender identification task for Urdu articles

Layer (type)	Output shape	Param #
embedding_6 (Embedding)	(None, 250, 900)	16206300
conv1d_18 (Conv1D)	(None, 250, 128)	460928
max_pooling1d_18 (MaxPooling1D)	(None, 125, 128)	0
conv1d_19 (Conv1D)	(None, 125, 64)	32832
max_pooling1d_19 (MaxPooling1D)	(None, 62, 64)	0
conv1d_20 (Conv1D)	(None, 62, 32)	8224
max_pooling1d_20 (MaxPooling1D)	(None, 31, 32)	0
flatten_6 (Flatten)	(None, 992)	0
dense_12 (Dense)	(None, 256)	254208
dense_13 (Dense)	(None, 1)	257

3.1 Effect of Most Frequent MWEs, Most Frequent Words and Their Concatenation on the Author Gender Identification Task

In this study I evaluated the effectiveness of: (i) the 600 most frequent multi-word expressions (MWEs) as features for the author gender identification task, (ii) the 300 most frequent words as features for the author gender identification task, and (iii) concatenating MWEs and words into one feature vector for the author gender identification task. As can be seen from Table 4, concatenating the 600 most frequent MWEs and the 300 most frequent words together reports the highest accuracy for the author gender identification task. It also implies that the information contained in these feature vectors is complementary and orthogonal. I also note that I have tried all combinations of the features vectors concatenation and "MWEs+Words" resulted in the best accuracy. In interest of brevity, the experimental results for the other features vectors concatenations are not given in Table 4

3.2 Performance Comparison Among Machine Learning Classifiers, CNN and Fine-Tuned Pre-trained Language Models

As mentioned earlier, fine-tuning the pre-trained language models such as BERT has reported state-of-the art results for many natural language processing tasks for resource-rich languages. However, the performance of fine-tuned pre-trained language models has never been evaluated on the author gender identification task for the Urdu articles. Therefore, it would be interesting to compare the performance of the fine-tuned pre-trained multilingual language models against the performance of the machine learning classifiers for the author gender identification task for Urdu articles. The experimental results are given in Table 5. The experimental results for the machine learning classifiers are obtained using the most frequent the 600 multi-word expressions (MWEs) and the 300 most frequent words as features using default parameters values. As can be seen from Table 5, the support vector machine classifier outperformed the rest of the machine learning classifiers, CNN and fine-tuned pre-trained language models.

Table 4. Effect of the feature vector concatenation process where the 600 most frequent multi-word expressions (MWEs) and the 300 most frequent words are used as the features for the author gender identification task.

Classifier	MWEs+Words	MWEs	Words
Light Gradient Boosted Machine Classifier	0.8814	0.7966	0.8531
Cat Boosted Classifier	0.8644	0.8701	0.8644
Extreme Gradient Boosted Classifier	0.8701	0.7910	0.8644
Gradient Boosting Classifier	0.8305	0.8475	0.8870
Random Forest Classifier	0.8983	0.8531	0.8531
Extra Trees Classifier	0.8418	0.8362	0.8701
Ada Boost Classifier	0.8249	0.7514	0.7853
K Nearest Neighbours Classifier	0.7571	0.6045	0.7119
Decision Tree Classifier	0.7288	0.7627	0.6949
Support Vector Machine Classifier	**0.9379**	0.8305	0.9209

Table 5. Performance comparison among the machine learning classifiers, fine-tuned pre-trained language models and CNN: the experimental results for the machine learning classifiers are obtained using the most frequent the 600 multi-word expressions (MWEs) and the 300 most frequent words as features using default parameters.

Machine learning classifiers and deep learning models	Accuracy
Light Gradient Boosted Machine Classifier	0.8814
Cat Boosted Classifier	0.8644
Extreme Gradient Boosted Classifier	0.8701
Gradient Boosting Classifier	0.8305
Random Forest Classifier	0.8983
Extra Trees Classifier	0.8418
Ada Boost Classifier	0.8249
K Nearest Neighbours Classifier	0.7571
Decision Tree Classifier	0.7288
Support Vector Machine Classifier	**0.9379**
CNN	0.8983
Multilingual BERT	0.8757
DistilBERT	0.5593
XML-RoBERTa	0.8531
Multilingual DeBERTa	0.9265

3.3   Effectiveness of Different Types and the Number of Features on the Accuracy

In addition, I conducted five studies to investigate impact of varying the number of (i) the most frequent MWEs, (ii) the most frequent words, (iii) the most frequent variable length word n-grams, (iv) the most frequent characters, and (v) the most frequent variable length character n-grams.

Effect of Varying the Number of MWEs as Features. As was already noted, one of the main goals of this investigation was to determine how well the author gender identification task might be performed utilising multi-word expressions (MWEs) as the features. Therefore, it would be intriguing to look into how changing the amount of MWEs affects the accuracy of the author gender identification task is performed. I specifically changed the number of most frequent MWEs from 100 to 8795 and then used machine learning classifiers to assess how well they performed. Table 6 shows that the maximum accuracy level was achieved when 600 MWEs were utilised as features, demonstrating their usefulness in the author gender identification task.

Effect of Varying the Number of the Most Frequent Words as Features. For the author gender identification task for Urdu articles, I modified the amount of the most frequent words used as features in this study to compare the performance of various classifiers. As shown in Table 7, the Support Vector Machine classifier achieved an accuracy of 93.22% when using the 600 most frequent words as features. However, I discovered that the best accuracy came from concatenating the 300 most frequent terms with the 600 most frequent MWEs (see Table 4 for more details).

Effect of Varying the Number of the Most Frequent Variable Length Words n-Grams as Features. The most frequent variable-length word n-grams, were used as features in this study to compare the effectiveness of various classifiers. The values of n ranged from 2 to 10. As shown in Table 8, the Support Vector Machine classifier achieved an accuracy of 87.57% when using the 600 most frequent variable length word n-grams as features.

Effect of Varying the Number of the Most Frequent Characters as Features. In this study, I looked at how well various classifiers performed at identifying the author's gender in Urdu by altering the amount of the most frequent characters used as features. As shown in Table 9, the accuracy is unaffected by changing the number of the most frequent characters used as features from 100 to 900, and the Cat Boosted Classifier reported an accuracy level of 82.49%.

Effect of Varying the Number of the Most Frequent Variable Length Character n-Grams as Features. In this study, I looked at how well various classifiers performed by altering the amount of the most frequent n-grams of variable length that are used as features, where n is between 2 and 10. Table 10 shows that the accuracy was 92.66% when the 300 most frequent variable length word n-grams were used as characteristics.

Table 6. Accuracy of the author gender identification task for Urdu articles using only most frequent MWEs as features.

Classifier	100	300	600	879
Light Gradient Boosted Machine Classifier	0.7910	0.7966	0.7966	0.7966
Cat Boosted Classifier	0.8249	0.8305	**0.8701**	0.8362
Extreme Gradient Boosted Classifier	0.7797	0.8023	0.7910	0.8079
Gradient Boosting Classifier	0.8192	0.8249	0.8475	0.8305
Random Forest Classifier	0.7910	0.8249	0.8531	0.8079
Extra Trees Classifier	0.8192	0.8023	0.8362	0.8136
Ada Boost Classifier	0.7853	0.7458	0.7514	0.7514
K Nearest Neighbours Classifier	0.6723	0.5932	0.6045	0.5763
Decision Tree Classifier	0.7175	0.7514	0.7627	0.7458
Support Vector Machine Classifier	0.8192	0.8305	0.8305	0.8192

Table 7. Accuracy of the author gender identification task using the most frequent words only as features.

Classifier	100	300	600	900
Light Gradient Boosted Machine Classifier	0.8475	0.8531	0.8870	0.9096
Cat Boosted Classifier	0.8701	0.8644	0.8927	0.8814
Extreme Gradient Boosted Classifier	0.8305	0.8644	0.8814	0.8870
Gradient Boosting Classifier	0.8305	0.8870	0.8644	0.8588
Random Forest Classifier	0.8192	0.8531	0.8983	0.8983
Extra Trees Classifier	0.8588	0.8701	0.8757	0.9040
Ada Boost Classifier	0.8475	0.7853	0.8814	0.8475
K Nearest Neighbours Classifier	0.6610	0.7119	0.7345	0.7345
Decision Tree Classifier	0.7232	0.6949	0.7119	0.6610
Support Vector Machine Classifier	0.8701	0.9209	**0.9322**	0.9266

Table 8. Accuracy of the author gender identification task for Urdu articles using the most frequent variable length words n-grams only as features where the values of the n are between 2 and 10.

Classifier	100	300	600	900
Light Gradient Boosted Machine Classifier	0.8305	0.8362	0.8418	0.8475
Cat Boosted Classifier	0.8475	0.8475	0.8588	0.8475
Extreme Gradient Boosted Classifier	0.8362	0.8192	0.8588	0.8531
Gradient Boosting Classifier	0.8418	0.8192	0.7910	0.8079
Random Forest Classifier	0.8475	0.8475	0.8079	0.8475
Extra Trees Classifier	0.8644	0.8305	0.8305	0.8249
Ada Boost Classifier	0.8249	0.7627	0.7458	0.8079
K Nearest Neighbours Classifier	0.7119	0.6271	0.6554	0.6045
Decision Tree Classifier	0.7232	0.7119	0.7458	0.7345
Support Vector Machine Classifier	0.8701	0.8079	**0.8757**	0.8701

Table 9. Accuracy of the author gender identification task using the most frequent characters as features.

Classifier	100	300	600	900
Light Gradient Boosted Machine Classifier	0.7853	0.7853	0.7853	0.7853
Cat Boosted Classifier	**0.8249**	0.8249	0.8249	0.8249
Extreme Gradient Boosted Classifier	0.8079	0.8079	0.8079	0.8079
Gradient Boosting Classifier	0.7627	0.7627	0.7627	0.7627
Random Forest Classifier	0.8192	0.8192	0.8192	0.8192
Extra Trees Classifier	0.8023	0.8023	0.8023	0.8023
Ada Boost Classifier	0.7910	0.7910	0.7910	0.7910
K Nearest Neighbours Classifier	0.6158	0.6158	0.6158	0.6158
Decision Tree Classifier	0.7119	0.7119	0.7119	0.7119
Support Vector Machine Classifier	0.6610	0.6610	0.6610	0.6610

Table 10. Accuracy of the author gender identification task for Urdu articles using the most frequent variable length characters n-grams as features.

Classifier	100	300	600	900
Light Gradient Boosted Machine Classifier	0.8531	0.8757	0.8644	0.8757
Cat Boosted Classifier	0.8475	0.8983	0.9209	0.9040
Extreme Gradient Boosted Classifier	0.8870	0.8983	0.8814	0.8927
Gradient Boosting Classifier	0.8192	0.8588	0.8814	0.8757
Random Forest Classifier	0.7966	0.8927	0.8588	0.8983
Extra Trees Classifier	0.8531	0.8701	0.8588	0.8588
Ada Boost Classifier	0.8023	0.8475	0.8079	0.8362
K Nearest Neighbours Classifier	0.7571	0.7797	0.8192	0.8362
Decision Tree Classifier	0.6893	0.7401	0.7514	0.7458
Support Vector Machine Classifier	0.8870	**0.9266**	0.9209	0.9266

4   Conclusions and Future Works

Author gender identification is an important natural language processing task. This task has been extensively investigated for resource-rich languages. However, the applications of this task are not limited to resource-rich languages only. Therefore, I presented the first investigation on the author gender identification task for Urdu articles. I also explored, effectiveness of the multi-word expressions for the author gender identification task. I propose to use the multi-word expressions as the features for the author gender identification task by concatenating them with most frequent words. The experimental findings revealed that, despite the popularity of the pre-trained language models for the natural language processing tasks, they are unable to outperform the classical machine learning classifiers in gender prediction for low-resource languages. In future, I plan to investigate the effect of article size and the number of articles per class on the accuracy of the author gender identification task.

References

1. Al-Ghadir, A.R.I., Azmi, A.M.: A study of Arabic social media users - posting behavior and author's gender prediction. Cogn. Comput. **11**(1), 71–86 (2019)
2. Alsmearat, K., Al-Ayyoub, M., Al-Shalabi, R., Kanaan, G.: Author gender identification from Arabic text. J. Inf. Secur. Appl. **35**, 85–95 (2017)
3. Baseer, F., Jaafar, J., Habib, A.: Gender and age identification through Romanized Urdu dataset. In: 2019 1st International Conference on Artificial Intelligence and Data Sciences (AiDAS), pp. 164–169. IEEE (2019)
4. Bassem, B., Zrigui, M.: Gender identification: a comparative study of deep learning architectures. In: Abraham, A., Cherukuri, A.K., Melin, P., Gandhi, N. (eds.) ISDA 2018 2018. AISC, vol. 941, pp. 792–800. Springer, Cham (2020). https://doi.org/10.1007/978-3-030-16660-1_77
5. Baxevanakis, S., Gavras, S., Mouratidis, D., Kermanidis, K.L.: A machine learning approach for gender identification of Greek tweet authors. In: Makedon, F. (ed.) PETRA 2020: The 13th PErvasive Technologies Related to Assistive Environments Conference, Corfu, Greece, June 30–July 3, 2020. pp. 57:1–57:4. ACM (2020)
6. Cheng, N., Chandramouli, R., Subbalakshmi, K.: Author gender identification from text. Digit. Invest. **8**(1), 78–88 (2011)
7. Conneau, A., et al.: Unsupervised cross-lingual representation learning at scale. CoRR abs/1911.02116. http://arxiv.org/abs/1911.02116 (2019)
8. Daud, A., Khan, W., Che, D.: Urdu language processing: a survey. Artif. Intell. Rev. **47**(3), 279–311 (2016). https://doi.org/10.1007/s10462-016-9482-x
9. Devlin, J., Chang, M., Lee, K., Toutanova, K.: BERT: pre-training of deep bidirectional transformers for language understanding. CoRR abs/1810.04805. http://arxiv.org/abs/1810.04805 (2018)
10. Fatima, M., Hasan, K., Anwar, S., Nawab, R.M.A.: Multilingual author profiling on Facebook. Inf. Process. Manag. **53**(4), 886–904 (2017)
11. HaCohen-Kerner, Y.: Survey on profiling age and gender of text authors. Expert Syst. Appl. **199**, 117–140 (2022)
12. Hassan, S.U., et al.: Predicting literature's early impact with sentiment analysis in twitter. Knowl. Based Syst. **192** (2020)
13. Hassan, S.U., Aljohani, N.R., Shabbir, M., Ali, U., Iqbal, S., Sarwar, R., Martínez-Cámara, E., Ventura, S., Herrera, F.: Tweet coupling: a social media methodology for clustering scientific publications. Scientometrics **124**(2), 973–991 (2020)
14. Hassan, S.U., et al.: Exploiting tweet sentiments in altmetrics large-scale data. arXiv preprint arXiv:2008.13023 (2020)
15. Hassan, S.U., Sarwar, R., Muazzam, A.: Tapping into intra-and international collaborations of the organization of Islamic cooperation states across science and technology disciplines. Sci. Public Policy **43**(5), 690–701 (2016)
16. He, P., Gao, J., Chen, W.: Debertav 3: improving deberta using electra-style pre-training with gradient-disentangled embedding sharing. ArXiv (2021)
17. Hearst, M.A., Dumais, S.T., Osuna, E., Platt, J., Scholkopf, B.: Support vector machines. IEEE Intell. Syst. Their Appl. **13**(4), 18–28 (1998)

18. Ikae, C., Savoy, J.: Gender identification on twitter. J. Assoc. Inf. Sci. Technol. **73**(1), 58–69 (2022)
19. Ke, G., et al.: LightGBM: a highly efficient gradient boosting decision tree. In: Advances in Neural Information Processing Systems, vol. 30 (2017)
20. Kucukyilmaz, T., Deniz, A., Kiziloz, H.E.: Boosting gender identification using author preference. Pattern Recognit. Lett. **140**, 245–251 (2020)
21. Limkonchotiwat, P., Phatthiyaphaibun, W., Sarwar, R., Chuangsuwanich, E., Nutanong, S.: Domain adaptation of Thai word segmentation models using stacked ensemble. In: Proceedings of the 2020 Conference on Empirical Methods in Natural Language Processing, EMNLP 2020, 16–20 November 2020. Association for Computational Linguistics (2020)
22. Limkonchotiwat, P., Phatthiyaphaibun, W., Sarwar, R., Chuangsuwanich, E., Nutanong, S.: Handling cross and out-of-domain samples in Thai word segmentation. In: Findings of the Association for Computational Linguistics: ACL/IJCNLP 2021, Online Event, 1–6 August 2021. Association for Computational Linguistics (2021)
23. Malik, M.K.: Urdu named entity recognition and classification system using artificial neural network. ACM Trans. Asian Low-Resour. Lang. Inf. Process. **17**(1), 1–13 (2017)
24. Mohamed, E., Sarwar, R.: Linguistic features evaluation for hadith authenticity through automatic machine learning. Digit. Schol. Hum. (2021)
25. Mukherjee, A., Liu, B.: Improving gender classification of blog authors. In: Proceedings of the 2010 conference on Empirical Methods in natural Language Processing, pp. 207–217 (2010)
26. Nutanong, S., Yu, C., Sarwar, R., Xu, P., Chow, D.: A scalable framework for stylometric analysis query processing. In: 2016 IEEE 16th International Conference on Data Mining (ICDM), pp. 1125–1130. IEEE (2016)
27. Sabah, F., Hassan, S.U., Muazzam, A., Iqbal, S., Soroya, S.H., Sarwar, R.: Scientific collaboration networks in Pakistan and their impact on institutional research performance: a case study based on Scopus publications. Library Hi Tech (2018)
28. Safara, F., et al.: An author gender detection method using whale optimization algorithm and artificial neural network. IEEE Access **8**, 48428–48437 (2020)
29. Safder, I., et al.: Parsing AUC result-figures in machine learning specific scholarly documents for semantically-enriched summarization. Appl. Artif. Intell. **36**(1), 2004347 (2022)
30. Safder, I., et al.: Sentiment analysis for urdu online reviews using deep learning models. Exp. Syst. **38**, e12751 (2021)
31. Sag, I.A., Baldwin, T., Bond, F., Copestake, A., Flickinger, D.: Multiword expressions: a pain in the neck for NLP. In: Gelbukh, A. (ed.) CICLing 2002. LNCS, vol. 2276, pp. 1–15. Springer, Heidelberg (2002). https://doi.org/10.1007/3-540-45715-1_1
32. Sanchez-Perez, M.A., Markov, I., Gómez-Adorno, H., Sidorov, G.: Comparison of character n-grams and lexical features on author, gender, and language variety identification on the same Spanish news corpus. In: Jones, J.F., et al. (eds.) CLEF 2017. LNCS, vol. 10456, pp. 145–151. Springer, Cham (2017). https://doi.org/10.1007/978-3-319-65813-1_15
33. Sanh, V., Debut, L., Chaumond, J., Wolf, T.: Distilbert, a distilled version of BERT: smaller, faster, cheaper and lighter. ArXiv abs/1910.01108 (2019)
34. Sarwar, R., Hassan, S.U.: A bibliometric assessment of scientific productivity and international collaboration of the Islamic world in science and technology (s&t) areas. Scientometrics **105**(2), 1059–1077 (2015)

35. Sarwar, R., Hassan, S.U.: Urduai: Writeprints for Urdu authorship identification. Trans. Asian Low-Resour. Lang. Inf. Process. **21**(2), 1–18 (2021)
36. Sarwar, R., Li, Q., Rakthanmanon, T., Nutanong, S.: A scalable framework for cross-lingual authorship identification. Inf. Sci. **465**, 323–339 (2018)
37. Sarwar, R., Li, Q., Rakthanmanon, T., Nutanong, S.: A scalable framework for cross-lingual authorship identification. Inf. Sci. **465**, 323–339 (2018)
38. Sarwar, R., Mohamed, E.: Author verification of nahj al-balagha. Digit. Schol. Hum. (2022)
39. Sarwar, R., Nutanong, S.: The key factors and their influence in authorship attribution. Res. Comput. Sci. **110**, 139–150 (2016)
40. Sarwar, R., Porthaveepong, T., Rutherford, A., Rakthanmanon, T., Nutanong, S.: Stylothai: a scalable framework for stylometric authorship identification of Thai documents. ACM Trans. Asian Low-Resour. Lang. Inf. Process. **19**(3), 1–15 (2020)
41. Sarwar, R., Rutherford, A.T., Hassan, S.U., Rakthanmanon, T., Nutanong, S.: Native language identification of fluent and advanced non-native writers. ACM Trans. Asian Low-Resour. Lang. Inf. Process. **19**(4), 1–19 (2020)
42. Sarwar, R., Soroya, S.H., Muazzam, A., Sabah, F., Iqbal, S., Hassan, S.U.: A bibliometric perspective on technology-driven innovation in the gulf cooperation council (GCC) countries in relation to its transformative impact on international business. In: Technology-Driven Innovation in Gulf Cooperation Council (GCC) Countries: Emerging Research and Opportunities, pp. 49–66. IGI Global (2019)
43. Sarwar, R., et al.: *cag*: Stylometric authorship attribution of multi-author documents using a co-authorship graph. IEEE Access **8**, 18374–18393 (2020)
44. Sarwar, R., Yu, C., Nutanong, S., Urailertprasert, N., Vannaboot, N., Rakthanmanon, T.: A scalable framework for stylometric analysis of multi-author documents. In: Pei, J., Manolopoulos, Y., Sadiq, S., Li, J. (eds.) DASFAA 2018. LNCS, vol. 10827, pp. 813–829. Springer, Cham (2018). https://doi.org/10.1007/978-3-319-91452-7_52
45. Sarwar, R., Zia, A., Nawaz, R., Fayoumi, A., Aljohani, N.R., Hassan, S.-U.: Webometrics: evolution of social media presence of universities. Scientometrics **126**(2), 951–967 (2021). https://doi.org/10.1007/s11192-020-03804-y
46. Simaki, V., Aravantinou, C., Mporas, I., Kondyli, M., Megalooikonomou, V.: Sociolinguistic features for author gender identification: From qualitative evidence to quantitative analysis. J. Quant. Linguis. **24**(1), 65–84 (2017)
47. Trijakwanich, N., Limkonchotiwat, P., Sarwar, R., Phatthiyaphaibun, W., Chuangsuwanich, E., Nutanong, S.: Robust fragment-based framework for cross-lingual sentence retrieval. In: Findings of the Association for Computational Linguistics: EMNLP 2021, Virtual Event/Punta Cana, Dominican Republic, 16–20 November 2021. Association for Computational Linguistics (2021)

Author Index

Printed in the United States
by Baker & Taylor Publisher Services